ALISON WEIR

Britain's Royal Families

The Complete Genealogy

VINTAGE BOOKS

London

To Rankin, John and Kate

Published by Vintage 2008

4 6 8 10 9 7 5

Copyright © Alison Weir

Alison Weir has asserted her right under the Copyright, Designs
and Patents Act 1988 to be identified as the author of this work

First published in Great Britain by The Bodley Head 1989
First Pimlico edition 1996
New Pimlico edition 2002

Vintage
Random House, 20 Vauxhall Bridge Road,
London SW1V 2SA

www.vintage-books.co.uk

Addresses for companies within The Random House Group Limited
can be found at: www.randomhouse.co.uk/offices.htm

The Random House Group Limited Reg. No. 954009

A CIP catalogue record for this book
is available from the British Library

ISBN 9780099539735

The Random House Group Limited supports The Forest
Stewardship Council (FSC), the leading international forest
certification organisation. All our titles that are printed on
Greenpeace approved FSC certified paper carry the FSC logo.
Our paper procurement policy can be found at:
www.rbooks.co.uk/environment

Printed and bound in Great Britain by
CPI Bookmarque, Croydon, CR0 4TD

BRITAIN'S ROYAL FAMILIES

Alison Weir lives and works in Surrey. Her books include *Elizabeth the Queen, Mary, Queen of Scots, Eleanor of Aquitaine, Henry VIII: King and Court* and most recently, *Katherine Swynford.*

Author's Note

The reader may find it helpful to note the following points:

1. *Britain's Royal Families* covers the period from A.D. 800 to the present day. The monarchs belonging to each royal house appear in chronological order. Every member of the various royal dynasties of England, Scotland and Great Britain is included, even children who died in infancy. Since the succession has usually been invested in the male line, the descendants of female members of the royal families beyond the first generation have not been included, except where relevant to the succession. Likewise, the descendants of the illegitimate children of monarchs have not been included.

2. All names in the book have been Anglicised or Latinised for the sake of clarity. Where a person is known by more than one name, all the alternatives are given.

3. Where any fact or date is in dispute, this is indicated in the text, and all the possibilities are listed.

4. Many dates are either not known or disputed, and the following examples serve to illustrate how they appear in the text:

   Example 1 c.848 means around the year or date specified.
   Example 2 848/9 means during the period or years specified.
   Example 3 848? means the date has been estimated using circumstantial evidence and guesswork, and is purely conjectural.

5. The following rule applies to the listing of subjects by name:

   Example 1 Name followed by a question mark (?) means there is doubt that the person actually existed.
   Example 2 Name preceded by a question mark (?) means there is doubt that the name is correct.

6. County boundaries given are those relevant to the period in question.

Foreword

In 1965, when I was fourteen, I read for the first time an adult historical novel. It was about Katherine of Aragon, and was entirely forgettable, except for the fact that it left me with a thirst to find out more about its subject. Subsequently, I read many more novels, and then many history books, and my interest expanded from the Tudor period to encompass the whole sweep of British, indeed, European, history. But from the first, my chief fascination was with the British monarchy, and it became my ambition to produce a book that would provide the reader with a complete genealogical record of all the royal families of England, Scotland and Great Britain.

It has taken me more than 22 years to research this book. Throughout this time I have consulted countless books and articles in various libraries, visited sites of interest, and revised the manuscript at least eight times. It may seem strange, but despite the fact that there are numerous and detailed books on the British monarchy, and even on royal genealogy, there is not one that gives a complete record of all the members of the various royal houses and families. To obtain such a record, I have had to research each person individually, cross-checking the facts where possible from alternative sources, and re-checking against new works as they were published. I have used original, contemporary sources for verification wherever possible.

The result is *Britain's Royal Families*, which I am convinced will prove an invaluable aid to the student of royal history, and will provide much of interest for even the most casual of royalty watchers.

Alison Weir
London, 1989

Contents

CHAPTER ONE

The Saxon and Danish Kings of England

There have been kings in England for more than 2,000 years, and yet this realm has been a monarchy for little more than half that time. Up until the Dark Ages, kingship was basically tribal, invested in chieftains of Celtic or Romano-British stock. Then, in the middle of the 5th century, England began to feel the impact of the Barbarian invasions that were changing the face of Europe. Angles, Saxons and Jutes came to these shores, settled, and then colonised the land. There then evolved 7 kingdoms, known to historians as the Heptarchy. The earliest kingdom was established in Kent by Hengist, son of a Germanic chieftain, in around A.D. 455. The other kingdoms were Essex (the East Saxons), Sussex (the South Saxons), East Anglia (the East Angles), Lindsey, Bernicia, Deira, Mercia and Wessex (the West Saxons). Lindsey was centred around Lincoln; the names of its kings are not known to us, and it was very soon swallowed up by neighbouring kingdoms. Bernicia and Deira combined later on to form the kingdom of Northumbria, the first of the biggest three kingdoms to establish supremacy over the rest.

Christianity came to Kent in the late 6th century, and soon spread to the rest of the Heptarchy, although there were pagan influences still prevalent until the late middle ages. Not so welcome were the raids of the Vikings from Scandinavia, which were the scourge of England (and other countries also) from the 8th to the 11th centuries, and which attained their ultimate achievement in the Norman Conquest of 1066.

Northumbria was the first kingdom to achieve supremacy, and during the 7th century it was a centre for the arts and religion. Unfortunately, the light of learning was extinguished during the

1

following century because of the Viking raids. At that time, Mercia was in the ascendant. This kingdom comprised the Midlands and some of the southern counties. At its peak of supremacy, Mercia was governed by King Offa (*d.*796), who established firm government and overseas alliances. However, after his death, the kingdom declined because of ineffective leadership, leaving Wessex in the ascendant.

The kingdom of Wessex had been founded in A.D. 519 by a chieftain called Cerdic, who came to Britain from Germany in 494/5. His descendants, proud to bear his name, called themselves 'Cerdingas'. H.M. Queen Elizabeth II is a direct descendant of Cerdic. Later Saxon chroniclers would boastfully trace Cerdic's descent from Adam and Eve, via a mythical son born to Noah in the Ark, but of course this is pure fiction, for Cerdic's ancestors were in fact obscure tribal chieftains and elders.

Anglo-Saxon kingship was a blend of the mystical and the practical. The function of the king was to protect his people, by making war if necessary, and by giving them laws to obey. He was also sanctified by holy rites, which evolved into the coronation as we know it, the modern form of which dates from the crowning of King Edgar in 973. Anglo-Saxon kings of the House of Wessex had from time immemorial been crowned upon the ancient coronation stone at Kingston-upon-Thames, in a simple ritual which was not as complicated as the European ceremony adapted for Edgar by Archbishop Dunstan. Hence, the king, set apart by his anointing and crowning, and thereby invested with priestly attributes, was a champion of the Christian Church, who was deemed to hold his office from God.

The king was also expected to father sons for posterity, to ensure the succession and the stability of the kingdom. His wife was rarely accorded the title of 'Queen' in Wessex, but was usually styled 'Lady'. Succession was by primogeniture, supporting the right of the eldest son, although on several occasions the right of conquest prevailed over this.

As late as the 11th century, the Danes were still attempting to invade and conquer a by then united England, and they were ultimately successful, which is why our line of Anglo-Saxon monarchs is broken by four Danish interlopers. As a result of this, the succession in the 11th century was an ongoing problem, which was not finally resolved until 1066. In 1100, when Henry I married a princess of

Saxon descent, the old and the new royal houses at last joined in blood.

This handbook is about the monarchy, and it begins with the first ruler who properly may be accorded the title of monarch, Egbert of Wessex. Egbert was acknowledged in his time as an outstanding sovereign, who, by the end of his reign, was recognised by other, lesser, kings as overlord of most of England. For this reason, we must begin with Egbert. Unfortunately, his supremacy did not long survive his death, and the authority of his immediate descendants, the great Alfred included, was more or less confined to Wessex. It was not until more than a century after Egbert's death that the monarchy was properly established in England under King Athelstan.

King Egbert

FATHER: *Ealhmund, King of Kent.*

He was the son of Eafa of Wessex by a Kentish princess, whose identity is unknown. Ealhmund is known to have been reigning in Kent in 784 or 786. He died in 786 (?).

MOTHER: *Unknown.*

SIBLINGS: *St Alburga.*

She was either the daughter of Ealhmund by his unknown wife, or the daughter of that wife by another husband. She is called the half-sister of Egbert.

Alburga married Wulfstan, who was perhaps Ealdorman of Wiltshire. Upon her widowhood, she entered her husband's religious foundation at Wilton, which she is said to have converted into a nunnery. She died and was buried there in *c.*800 or *c.*810.

Egbert did not have any brothers.

EGBERT

He was born around 769/80. He became 'Subregulus' of Kent in 790/96, and succeeded Beorhtric as King of Wessex in 802. There is no record of his coronation. From 825 onwards, he had established his supremacy over all other rulers in England, and was effective overlord of all the south-eastern kingdoms. In 829, he succeeded Wiglaf as King of Mercia, although he was expelled the following year.

Egbert married (although no record exists of the date or the place):

Redburga

She is said to have been the sister of the King of the Franks (who, at that time, was Charlemagne), but her identity is uncertain, and hardly anything is known about her.

Issue of marriage:

1 *King Ethelwulf* (◊ page 5).

2 *Athelstan*

He became 'Subregulus' of Kent, Essex, Sussex and Surrey in 839, and also reigned as King of East Anglia. He died in *c.*851.

Athelstan married a lady about whom no information exists, and had issue:

(i) Ethelweard
He was 'Subregulus' of Kent. He died, probably unmarried, in 850.

3 *Edith*
She became a nun at Polesworth Abbey, Co. Warwick, where she later became Abbess. She died and was buried there, but the year is not recorded.

EGBERT

He died on 4 February (or after *c.*June), 839, and was buried in Winchester Cathedral. His bones are now in one of the mortuary chests there.

He was succeeded by his son Ethelwulf.

King Ethelwulf

FATHER: *Egbert, King of Wessex* (◊ page 4).
MOTHER: *Redburga* (◊ page 4).
SIBLINGS: (◊ page 4).

ETHELWULF

He was born around 795/810. He became 'Subregulus' of Kent, Essex, Sussex and Surrey in 825 or 828, and succeeded his father as King of Wessex on 4 February, 839. He was crowned, probably that same year, at Kingston-upon-Thames, Surrey. In 855/6, he resigned Wessex to his son Ethelbald, and confined his own authority to Kent, Sussex and Essex as 'Subregulus'.

Ethelwulf married firstly, in *c.*830 (although no record exists as to where):

Osburga

She was the daughter of Oslac of Hampshire or the Isle of Wight. She died in 846 or 852/5. (Osburga has sometimes been confused by historians with St Osburga, foundress of Coventry Abbey, who died c.1018).

Issue of marriage:

1 *Athelstan* (?)

Although some sources cite Athelstan as Ethelwulf's eldest son, he has almost certainly been confused with Athelstan, son of King Egbert, as the details of his life are identical. It is therefore improbable that Ethelwulf actually had a son called Athelstan.

2 *King Ethelbald* (◊ page 7).

3 *King Ethelbert* (◊ page 8).

4 *King Ethelred I* (◊ page 8).

5 *King Alfred* (◊ page 9).

6 *Ethelswitha*

She married, after 2 April, 853 (or 854/5), Burgred, King of Mercia (d.874) at the Palace of Chippenham, Wiltshire. Shortly after her widowhood in 874, she became a nun. She went on a pilgrimage to Rome in 888/9, but died in Paris on the way there. She was buried at either Pavia or Ticino in Italy.

Ethelwulf married secondly, on 1 or 15 October, 856, at Verberie sur Oise, France:

Judith

She was the daughter of Charles II, King of the Franks, by Ermentrude, daughter of Odo, Count of Orléans. She was born in c.843/4, and was crowned Queen of Wessex on her wedding day.

In 860, she married secondly her stepson, King Ethelbald (◊ page 7), at Chester, but the marriage was annulled that same year on grounds of consanguinity. She had no issue from either of these marriages.

In c.863, she married thirdly Baldwin I, Count of Flanders (d.c.879), at Auxerre, France, and had issue:

1 Charles (died young).

2 Baldwin II, Count of Flanders (d.918), who married Elfrida of Wessex (◊ page 10, under King Alfred), and had issue. One of their descendants was Matilda, wife of William I.

3 Rudolf, Count and Abbot of Cambrai.

4 Gunhilda, who married Wilfred I, Count of Barcelona (d.897).

Judith died in *c.*870.

ETHELWULF
He died on 13 January (or late in the year), 858, and was buried in Winchester Cathedral.

He was succeeded by his son Ethelbald.

King Ethelbald

FATHER: *Ethelwulf, King of Wessex* (◊ page 5).
MOTHER: *Osburga* (◊ page 5, under *King Ethelwulf*).
SIBLINGS: (◊ page 6, under *King Ethelwulf*).

ETHELBALD
He was born in *c.*834. He succeeded his father as King of Wessex on 13 January (or late in the year), 858, and was crowned soon afterwards at Kingston-upon-Thames, Surrey.

Ethelbald married, in 860 (although no record exists as to where):
Judith

She was his father's widow, and the marriage was frowned upon. It was annulled that same year. There was no issue from it. (Judith's details are given on pages 6 to 7, under King Ethelwulf).

ETHELBALD
He died on 20 December, 860, and was buried in Sherborne Abbey, Dorset.

He was succeeded by his brother Ethelbert.

King Ethelbert

FATHER: *Ethelwulf, King of Wessex* (◊ page 5).
MOTHER: *Osburga* (◊ page 5, under *King Ethelwulf*).
SIBLINGS: (◊ page 6, under *King Ethelwulf*).

ETHELBERT
He was born in *c.*836. He became 'Subregulus' of Kent in 853 or 855, and succeeded his brother Ethelbald as King of Wessex on 20 December, 860. He was crowned soon afterwards at Kingston-upon-Thames, Surrey.

He died, unmarried and childless, in 865/6, and was buried in Sherborne Abbey, Dorset.

He was succeeded by his brother Ethelred.

Ethelred I

FATHER: *Ethelwulf, King of Wessex* (◊ page 5).
MOTHER: *Osburga* (◊ page 5, under *King Ethelwulf*).
SIBLINGS: (◊ page 6, under *King Ethelwulf*).

ETHELRED I
He was born in *c.*840. He succeeded his brother Ethelbert as King of Wessex in 865/6, and was crowned shortly afterwards at Kingston-upon-Thames, Surrey.
Ethelred I married, in *c.*868 (although no record exists as to where): *(?)Wulfrida*
Nothing is known of her origin or dates.

Issue of marriage:

1 *Ethelwald*

He was born in *c*.868, and set himself up as King of York and Pretender to the throne of Wessex in 901, after the death of his uncle, King Alfred. He was killed defending his claims in 902/5 at the Battle of the Holm.

Ethelwald married a professed nun from Wimborne Minster, Dorset; her name is unknown.

2 *Ethelhelm*

He is perhaps to be identified with:

(a) an Ealdorman of Wiltshire, or

(b) an Archbishop of Canterbury who was consecrated in 919 and who died on 8 January, 923.

There is, unfortunately, no conclusive evidence to support either theory. It is possible that Ethelhelm died in 898.

ETHELRED I

He was killed on 23 April (after Easter), 871, at the Battle of Merton, and was buried at Wimborne Minster, Dorset, although some less reliable sources give his place of burial as Sherborne Abbey, Dorset. After his death, he was popularly reputed a saint.

He was succeeded by his brother Alfred.

King Alfred

FATHER: *Ethelwulf, King of Wessex* (⬦ page 5).
MOTHER: *Osburga* (⬦ page 5, under *King Ethelwulf*).
SIBLINGS: (⬦ page 6, under *King Ethelwulf*).

ALFRED

Known as 'the Great', he was born in 846/9 at Wantage, Dorset. He succeeded his brother Ethelred I as King of Wessex and Danish Mercia on 23 April, 871, and was perhaps crowned at Kingston-upon-

Thames, Surrey, although this is mere supposition, as there is no evidence for it.

Alfred married, in 868/9, at Winchester:

Ethelswitha

She was the daughter of Ethelred Mucel, Ealdorman of the Gainas (to be identified with Gainsborough, Lincolnshire?), by Edburga, a Princess of the Royal House of Mercia, perhaps the daughter of Coenwulf, King of Mercia, by his wife Elfrida.

After the death of King Alfred, Ethelswitha turned to religion, and became a nun at St Mary's Abbey, Winchester, in *c.*901. She died in Winchester on 5 or 8 December, 905, and was buried there in St Mary's Abbey; her remains were later removed to Winchester Cathedral. After her death, she was popularly reputed a saint.

Issue of marriage:

1 *Ethelfleda*

Born *c.*869, she married Ethelred, Ealdorman of Mercia (*d.*911), in 886/7 (certainly by the end of 889), and had issue:

1 Elfwynn (904?–after 919).

Ethelfleda was recognised as Lady of the Mercians in 911, after the death of her husband. She died on 12 June, 918, at Tamworth, Staffordshire, and was buried in Gloucester Cathedral.

2 *Edmund*

No dates are recorded, but he was possibly the eldest son, born around 870, as he was crowned in the lifetime of his father, following a European precedent set by Charlemagne. Asser, King Alfred's biographer, says Edmund died in infancy.

3 *King Edward the Elder* (◊ page 12).

4 *Elfrida*

She married Baldwin II, Count of Flanders (*d.*918), between 893 and 899, and had issue:

1 Arnulf, Count of Flanders (*d.*964), who married Adela of Vermandois, and had issue. One of their descendants was Matilda of Flanders, wife of William I.

2 Adelulf, Count of Boulogne (*d.*933).

3 Daughter.

4 Daughter.

Elfrida died on 7 June, 929 (?), in Flanders, and was buried in St Peter's Abbey, Ghent.

5 *Ethelgiva*

She became a nun at Shaftesbury Abbey, Dorset, where she was elected the first Abbess in *c*.888. She died and was buried in Shaftesbury Abbey in *c*.896.

6 *Ethelweard*

Born *c*.880. Very little is known of his life. He died on 16 (?) or 26 October, 920/22.

Ethelweard married a lady about whom no information exists, and had issue:

(i) *Elfwine*

He was killed at the Battle of Brunanburgh in 937, and was buried in Malmesbury Abbey, Wilts.

(ii) *Ethelwine*

He was killed at the Battle of Brunanburgh in 937, and was buried in Malmesbury Abbey, Wilts.

(iii) *Thurcytel*

Born *c*.907, he became a monk at his own foundation at Croyland Abbey, Lincs., in *c*.946, and was later elected Abbot there. He died on 12 July, 975, at Croyland Abbey, and was buried there.

KING ALFRED

He died on 25, 26 or 28 October, 899, and was buried in Newminster Abbey, Winchester. His remains were later removed to Hyde Abbey, Winchester, which was destroyed during the Reformation. The present site of his grave is unknown. His bones may possibly lie in one of the mortuary chests in Winchester Cathedral.

He was succeeded by his son Edward.

King Edward the Elder

FATHER: *King Alfred* (◊ page 9).
MOTHER: *Ethelswitha* (◊ page 10, under *King Alfred*).
SIBLINGS: (◊ page 10, under *King Alfred*).

KING EDWARD
Known as 'the Elder', he was born in *c.*871/2. He succeeded his father as King of Wessex on 25, 26 or 28 October, 899, and was crowned on 31 May or 8 June, 900, at Kingston-upon-Thames, Surrey.
Edward married firstly (although no record exists of the date or the place):
Egwina
She is described as 'a noblewoman', although her origins are unknown. William of Malmesbury, writing in the 12th century, states that her children were illegitimate, thereby suggesting that her marriage to Edward was uncanonical, but this is unlikely in view of the fact that her son succeeded Edward as undisputed king. She died in *c.*901/2.
Issue of marriage:
1 *King Athelstan* (◊ page 16).
2 *Alfred*
No dates are recorded, and very little is known about him. He may have died young.
3 *St Edith*
She married Sihtric Caoch, King of Northumbria (*d.*927), on 30 January, 925/6, at Tamworth, Staffordshire. After her widowhood, she became a nun at Polesworth Abbey, Warwickshire, in 927. That same year, she was transferred to Tamworth Abbey, Gloucestershire, where she was immediately elected Abbess. She died in *c.*927. After her death, she was canonised, and her Feast Day is 15 July.
Edward married secondly, in *c.*901/2 (although no record exists as to where):

Elfleda

She was the daughter of Ealdorman Ethelhelm by his wife Elswitha. She died in 920, and was buried in Winchester Cathedral.

Issue of marriage:

1 *Edwin*

He was perhaps 'Subregulus' of Kent. In 933, he drowned in the English Channel, perhaps murdered on the orders of his half-brother, King Athelstan. He was buried in St Bertin's Abbey, Flanders.

2 *Elfweard*

Information about Elfweard is conflicting. One source states he married and had children, but gives no details. Another source, less trustworthy, states he was a hermit at Bridgenorth, Salop. What is certain is that he died on 1 August, 924, at Oxford, and was buried in Winchester Cathedral.

3 *Edfleda*

No dates are recorded. She was a nun, but her community is not named: it was perhaps Winchester. She was buried in Wilton Abbey, Wiltshire.

4 *Edgiva* (or *Ogive*)

She married Charles III, King of France (*d*.929), between 916 and 919, and had issue:

1 Louis IV, King of France (921?–954), who married Gerberga (*d*.984), daughter of Henry the Fowler of Saxony, Holy Roman Emperor, and had issue.

Edgiva married secondly, Heribert III, Count of Vermandois, Meaux, and Troyes (*d*.995), in *c*.951 at St Quentin, France, and had issue:

2 Stephen I, Count of Vermandois (*b*.952?–1021).

3 Agnes (*b*.953).

Edgiva died in *c*.953, perhaps in childbirth. Some sources state she died in 948, in which case her second marriage took place earlier than is generally supposed.

5 *Edhilda*

She married Hugh Capet, Count of Paris and Duke of the French (*d*.956), in 926/7, and had issue:

1 Hugh, King of France (938?–996), who married Adelaide (*d*.1004/5), daughter of William, Duke of Aquitaine, and had issue.

Edhilda died on 26 January, 947. (Some sources state she died in c.938, or even earlier, but this is improbable.)

6 *Edith*

She married Otto I, Duke of Saxony and German Emperor (*d.*973), in c.925/30, and had issue:

1 Liudolf, Duke of Swabia (*d.*957), who married Ida, daughter of Hermann, Duke of Almayne, Swabia, and had issue.

2 Liutgarde, married Conrad, Duke of Lorraine.

Edith died on 26 January, c.946/7, in Germany, and was buried in the Cathedral of St Maurice, Magdeburg.

7 *Elfleda*

She became a nun at Winchester, where she died in c.963. She was buried in Wilton Abbey, Wilts.

8 *Elgiva*

No dates are recorded. She married 'a Prince near the Alps'. He has recently been identified, with near certainty, as Boleslaw II, Duke of Bohemia (*d.*999). Other, less probable, identifications have been made with Conrad III, King of Burgundy (*d.*993); Alberic, son of Majolus, Count of Narbonne; and Charles Constantine, King of Arles, son of either the Emperor Louis the Blind or Louis II, King of Arles.

9 *Ethelfleda*

No dates are recorded. She was perhaps a nun at Romsey Abbey, Hampshire, and may have been elected Abbess of Romsey, where she was later buried.

10 *Ethelhilda*

No dates are recorded. She was a lay sister or recluse at Romsey Abbey, Hampshire. She was buried in Wilton Abbey, Wiltshire.

Edward married thirdly, in 920 (?) (although no record exists of the date or the place):

Edgiva

She was the daughter of Sigehelm, Ealdorman of Kent, and she was born before c.905. She died on 25 August, 968, and was buried in Canterbury Cathedral.

Issue of marriage:

1 *Edmund I* (◊ page 16).

2 *St Edburga*

She became a nun at Nunnaminster Abbey, Winchester; she was

possibly elected Abbess, but this is unlikely. She died on 15 June, 960, and was buried in Nunnaminster Abbey. After her canonisation, her remains were translated to Pershore Abbey, Worcs.

3 *Edgiva*

She was married in infancy to 'Louis of Aquitaine, King of Arles', before 923. Her husband has not been successfully identified. He may have been Louis II, King of Arles, in which case the issue of the marriage may have been:

1 Charles Constantine, King of Arles (whose parentage is uncertain).

Louis may also be identified, with less credibility, with Louis the Blind, King of Lower Burgundy and Holy Roman Emperor (*d.*928). Some authorities cite Ebehard, Count of Nordgau (*d.c.*960), as the husband of Edgiva.

4 *King Edred* (◊ page 18).

5 *Thyra*

She is said to have been a daughter of Edward by Edgiva, but there is some doubt about this. No dates are recorded. She married Gorm the Old, king in North Jutland, and had issue:

1 Harold I, King of Denmark (*d.*986), who also married and had issue.

Edward is also reputed to have had the following **illegitimate issue**, although this is in dispute:

1 Gregory, Abbot of Einsiedlen in Germany.

KING EDWARD THE ELDER

He died on 17 July, 924/5, at Farndon-on-Dee, and was buried in Winchester Cathedral.

He was succeeded by his son Athelstan.

King Athelstan

FATHER: *King Edward the Elder* (◊ page 12).
MOTHER: *Egwina* (◊ page 12, under *King Edward the Elder*).
SIBLINGS: (◊ page 12, under *King Edward the Elder*).

ATHELSTAN
He was born in *c.*895. He succeeded his father as the first King of a united England on 17 July, 924/5, and was crowned on 4 September, 924/5, at Kingston-upon-Thames, Surrey. The monarchy in England may be said to have been properly established under King Athelstan. Athelstan never married, and had no issue. He died on 27 October, 939, at Gloucester, and was buried in Malmesbury Abbey, Wiltshire (his tomb dates only from the fifteenth century).

He was succeeded by his half-brother Edmund.

Edmund I

FATHER: *King Edward the Elder* (◊ page 12).
MOTHER: *Edgiva of Kent* (◊ page 14, under *King Edward the Elder*).
SIBLINGS: (◊ page 14, under *King Edward the Elder*).

EDMUND I
Known as 'the Magnificent', he was born in *c.*920/22. He succeeded his half-brother King Athelstan as King of England on 27 October, 939, and was crowned on 29 November, 939, at Kingston-upon-Thames, Surrey. From 944 onwards, he was the effective ruler of the whole of England until his death.

Edmund I married firstly, in *c.*940 (although no record exists as to where):

St Elgiva

Her origins are unknown. She died in *c.*944 or 946 at Shaftesbury Abbey, Dorset, where she was probably buried (or, less probably, at Shipton Abbey). She has sometimes, erroneously, been described as Abbess of Wilton. After her death, she was popularly reputed a saint.

Issue of marriage:

1 *King Edwy* (↷ page 19).
2 *King Edgar* (↷ page 20).
3 *Daughter* (*name not known*), who married Baldwin, Count of Hesdin.

Edmund I married secondly, in *c.*946:

Ethelfleda

She was the daughter of Alfgar, Ealdorman of the Wilsaetas (Wiltshire?), and was perhaps born at Damerham, Wiltshire. After Edmund's death, she perhaps married secondly Athelstan, an Ealdorman. She later became a nun at Shaftesbury Abbey, Dorset, where she died after 975, when her Will was dated. She was buried in Shaftesbury Abbey.

EDMUND I

He was murdered on 26 May, 946, at Pucklechurch, Dorset, when an outlaw named Liofa stabbed him whilst he was dining in his hall. He was buried in Glastonbury Abbey, Somerset.

He was succeeded by his brother Edred.

King Edred

FATHER: *King Edward the Elder* (↻ page 12).
MOTHER: *Edgiva of Kent* (↻ page 14, under *King Edward the Elder*).
SIBLINGS: (↻ page 14, under *King Edward the Elder*).

KING EDRED

He was born in *c*.923/5, and succeeded his brother Edmund I as King of England on 26 May, 946. He was crowned on 16 August, 946, at Kingston-upon-Thames, Surrey. He expelled the Danes from England in 954, thereupon establishing his authority throughout England.

One authority states that Edred had issue, but gives no details. I have found no other evidence to support this. There is no record of his having been married.

KING EDRED

He died on 23 November, 955, at Frome, Somerset, and was buried in Winchester Cathedral. His bones are now in one of the mortuary chests there.

He was succeeded by his nephew Edwy.

King Edwy

FATHER: *Edmund I* (◊ page 16).
MOTHER: *St Elgiva* (◊ page 17, under *Edmund I*).
SIBLINGS: (◊ page 17, under *Edmund I*).

KING EDWY
Known as 'the Fair', he was born in *c.*941/3 (certainly before 943). He succeeded his uncle King Edred as King of England on 23 November, 955, and was crowned at Kingston-upon-Thames *c.*26 January, 956. He was a weak king, and his authority was confined to Wessex from 958, his younger brother Edgar taking over the government of Northumbria and Mercia.
Edwy married, during the winter of 955/6 (although no record exists as to where):
Elgiva
 Her father is unknown; her mother, Ethelgiva, of unknown origin, is said by some sources to have been Edwy's mistress. The marriage was certainly frowned upon by the Church. Late sources state that it was annulled around 958, and that Elgiva was banished from court, possibly to Ireland, but these sources may be too late to be reliable. Elgiva died around September, 959, at Gloucester.

KING EDWY
He died on 1 October, 959, at Gloucester, and was buried in Winchester Cathedral.
 He was succeeded by his brother Edgar.

King Edgar

FATHER: *Edmund I* (◊ page 16).
MOTHER: *St Elgiva* (◊ page 17, under *Edmund I*).
SIBLINGS: (◊ page 17, under *Edmund I*).

KING EDGAR
Known as 'the Peaceable', he was born in 942/4. He took over the government of Northumbria and Mercia from his brother King Edwy in 958, and was styled King of those realms from that date. He succeeded Edwy on 1 October, 959, but was not crowned until 11 May, 973, as St Dunstan, the Archbishop of Canterbury, would not agree to crown Edgar until he amended his way of life. The coronation, which took place in Bath Abbey, followed the new form of service devised by St Dunstan and based on European models. This is the form of Coronation Rite used, with modifications, in the 20th century.

Edgar married firstly, in *c.*961/2 (although no record exists as to where):
Ethelfleda
Known as 'the Fair', she was the daughter of Ealdorman Ordmaer by his wife Ealda. Later sources allege that she was divorced by Edgar in *c.*964, so that he could marry his second wife, but this is probably a fabrication, and it is likely that Ethelfleda died in *c.*962/4, probably by 965 (although one unreliable source gives the date of her death as 972/3). She was buried in Wilton Abbey, Wiltshire, where she is said to have retired after her alleged divorce.

Issue of marriage:
1 *King Edward the Martyr* (◊ page 22).

Edgar married secondly, in *c.*964/5 (perhaps earlier) (although no record exists as to where):
Elfrida
Alternatively known as Alstrita or Elstrudis, she was the daughter of Ordgar, Ealdorman of Devon. She was born in *c.*945 at Lydford

Castle, Devon. She married firstly, in *c.*962/3, Ethelwald, Ealdorman of East Anglia (*d.*963), and had issue:

1 Edgar.
2 (?) Ethelfleda (963?–1016?), Abbess of Romsey. She may have been Ethelwald's daughter by his first wife, although one account says she was his posthumous child.

Elfrida is said to have had an adulterous affair with King Edgar whilst still married to Ethelwald, and some sources allege that Ethelwald was murdered on Edgar's orders. Elfrida was crowned with her husband on 11 May, 973, at Bath Abbey: this was the first instance of the coronation of a Queen of England. She became a nun in *c.*986 at Wherwell Abbey, Hampshire, where she died, possibly on 17 November, 1002 (?); she was alive in 999, but had died before the end of 1002. She was probably buried in Wherwell Abbey.

Issue of marriage:

1 *Edmund*

   He was born in *c.*965, and died in 970/72. He was buried in Romsey Abbey, Hampshire.

2 *Ethelred II* (◊ page 22).

King Edgar also had the following illegitimate issue:

By St Wulfrida (*c.*945–1000), Abbess of Wilton,

1 St Edith (962?–984), Abbess of Barking and Nunnaminster.

KING EDGAR

He died on 8 July, 975, at Winchester, and was buried in Glastonbury Abbey, Somerset.

He was succeeded by his son Edward.

King Edward the Martyr

FATHER: *King Edgar* (◊ page 20).
MOTHER: *Ethelfleda* (◊ page 20, under *King Edgar*).
SIBLINGS: *Edward did not have any full brothers or sisters.*

KING EDWARD
Known as 'the Martyr', he was born in *c*.962/3. He succeeded his father as King of England on 8 July, 975, and was crowned at Kingston-upon-Thames that same year (the date is unspecified). He was murdered on 18 March, 978 (not 979, as is sometimes stated), at Corfe Castle, Dorset, probably on the orders of his stepmother, Elfrida of Devon. He was buried in Wareham Abbey, Dorset; later on, his remains were moved to Shaftesbury Abbey, Dorset.

He was succeeded by his half-brother Ethelred.

Ethelred II

FATHER: *King Edgar* (◊ page 20).
MOTHER: *Elfrida of Devon* (◊ page 20, under *King Edgar*).
SIBLINGS: (◊ page 21, under *King Edgar*).

ETHELRED II
Known as 'the Unraed' or 'the Redeless' (both of which mean 'without counsel'), he was born in *c*.966/9. He succeeded his half-brother Edward as King of England on 18 March, 978, and was crowned on 4 April, 978 (or 4 May, 979), at Kingston-upon-Thames, Surrey. He abdicated in favour of King Sweyn in the autumn of 1013, and fled to

Normandy, but was restored to the throne after Sweyn's death on 3 February, 1014.

Ethelred II married firstly, in *c.*980/85 (although no record exists as to where):

Elgiva

Alternatively known as Elfleda, she was the daughter either of Ealdorman Ethelbert, or of Thored, Ealdorman of York, by his wife Hilda. She was born in *c.*963, and died in February, 1002, at Winchester.

Issue of marriage:

1 *Athelstan*

He was born in *c.*986, and was killed in battle, fighting the Danes, in *c.*1012/15. One writer, Thietmar of Merseberg, states that Athelstan was alive late in 1016, but he is an unreliable source, and it is thought that Athelstan was almost certainly dead by the end of 1015.

2 *Edmund II* (◊ page 28).

3 *Edgar*

He died in 1012/15 (or, less probably, in *c.*1008).

4 *Edred*

He died in 1012/15.

5 *Edric* (?)

He has perhaps been confused with his brother Edred, and may not have existed. No dates are recorded.

6 *Edward* (?)

He is said to have died by *c.*1004. The evidence for his existence is very slender; charters said to have been attested by him have been proved spurious.

7 *Edwy*

He was murdered in 1017 on the orders of King Canute, and was buried in Tavistock Abbey, Devon.

8 *Egbert*

He died in *c.*1005.

9 *Edith*

She married Edric Streona, Ealdorman of Mercia (who was executed in 1017), in *c.*1007/9, and had issue:

1 Son; name not known (born before 1009).

Edith perhaps married secondly Thurcytel Thorgils Havi, a Danish Earl in England (who was killed in 1039), and perhaps had issue:

2 Harold, who married Gunhilda of Wendland, a granddaughter of King Sweyn. Harold died in 1042.

10 *Elgiva*

She married Uhtred, Earl of Northumbria (who was killed in 1016 or 1018), and had issue:

1 Edith (◊ page 179, under Malcolm II, King of Scotland). She married Maldred of Scotland, Lord of Allerdale, and had issue.

11 *Wulfhilda*

She married Ulfcytel Snylling, Ealdorman of East Anglia (who was killed in 1016).

12 *Daughter*

Her name is not known. She married one Athelstan (who was killed in 1010).

13 *Daughter*

Her name is not known. She became Abbess of Wherwell, and died after 1051.

Ethelred II married secondly, on 5 April, 1002, at Winchester Cathedral:

Emma

She was the daughter of Richard I, Duke of Normandy, by his wife Gunnora, and she was born in *c*.985/7 in Normandy. In 1017, after the death of Ethelred II, she married secondly King Canute, and had issue (◊ page 30, under King Canute). She died on 14 March, 1052, probably at Winchester, and was buried in Winchester Cathedral. Her bones now lie in one of the mortuary chests there.

Issue of marriage:

1 *King Edward the Confessor* (◊ page 33).

2 *Alfred*

Born before 1012, he was styled 'Atheling'. He was brutally murdered on 5 February, 1037 (or, less probably, 1036), at Ely, Cambridgeshire, probably on the orders of Earl Godwine (◊ page 34, under Harold II). He was buried in Ely Cathedral.

3 *Goda*

Alternatively known as Godgifu, she was born between 1004 and 1014. She married firstly Drogo (or Dreux), Count of Mantes and the Vexin (*d*.1035), and had issue:

1 Ralph, Earl of Hereford (*d*.1057), who married Gytha, perhaps the daughter of Osgood Clapa, and had issue.

2 Walter III, Count of Mantes and the Vexin (*d.* after 1063), who married Biota, daughter of Herbert, Count of Maine.

3 Fulk, Bishop of Amiens (1030–1058).

Goda married secondly Eustace II, Count of Boulogne (*d.*1093), in *c.*1036. It is possible that there was a child of this union, probably a daughter who married and had issue. The only evidence pointing to this is the fact that Eustace of Boulogne had a grandson who was given as hostage to William I in 1067.

Goda was dead by 1049.

ETHELRED II

He died on 23 April, 1016, in London, and was buried in Old St Paul's Cathedral, London. His tomb was lost in the Great Fire of 1666.

He was succeeded by his son Edmund.

King Sweyn

FATHER: *Harold Bluetooth, King of Denmark.*
MOTHER: *Gunhilda, first wife of Harold, or Cyrid, his second wife, or Aesa, his concubine.*
SIBLINGS:
Thyra
She married Thorgils Sprakalegg, and had issue:
1 Gytha, mother of Harold II (↺ page 34).

KING SWEYN

Known as 'Forkbeard', he was born in *c.*960 in Denmark. He succeeded his father as King of Denmark on 1 November, 986. He is said by some sources to have been deposed in 987 and restored in 1000. He usurped the throne of England in the autumn of 1013, having defeated and deposed Ethelred II; he claimed the throne by right of conquest, but had no dynastic claim to it. He was never crowned.

Sweyn married firstly, in *c.*990 (although no record exists as to

where):
Gunhilda

She was probably the daughter of Mjeczislas I, Duke of Poland, by Dubrawka, daughter of Boleslaw I, Duke of Bohemia, or, less probably, the daughter of Boleslaw, King of Wendland. Sweyn later divorced her, probably before 1000. She died in *c.*1015. One source gives the date of her death as 992, but this must be wrong.

Issue of marriage:

1 *Harold*

He was born in *c.*994 in Denmark. He succeeded his father as King of Denmark on 3 February, 1014, and died in 1018/19.

2 *King Canute* (◊ page 30).

The following were possibly the children of Gunhilda, although they may have been the issue of Sweyn by his second wife (◊ below):

3 *Gytha*

She married Erik Hakonson, a Danish Earl in England, and Earl of Hlathir in Norway in 1013, and had issue:

1   Haakon, Earl of Worcester (*d.*1029/30), who married Gunhilda, daughter of Wytgeorn, King of Wendland (◊ below).

4 *Santslaue*

Alternatively called Svantoslava, she was born and died in Denmark. No dates are recorded.

5 *Thyra*

She is said to have been born in *c.*993 in Denmark – probably the eldest child of Sweyn and Gunhilda, although this is open to doubt. She married Godwine, later Earl of Wessex (◊ page 34, under Harold II), and had issue, but no details of them are recorded. She died in 1018.

6 *Daughter*

Her name is not known. She married Wytgeorn, King of Wendland, and had issue:

1   Gunhilda; she married firstly Haakon, Earl of Worcester (*d.*1029/30) (◊ above), and secondly, Harold (*d.*1042), son of Edith, the daughter of Ethelred II.

Sweyn married secondly, probably before 1000 (although no record exists as to where):

Sigrid

Alternatively known as Sigrith or Syritha, and called 'the Haughty', she was the daughter of Skogul Toste of Sweden, and was born in Sweden. She married firstly Eric VI, King of Sweden (*d*.995), and had issue:

1 Olaf Svenski, King of Sweden (*d*.1022), who married a lady called Astrid, and had issue.

One source gives the date of Sigrid's death as 995, but this is impossible. It is likely that she died before 1013, as she has never been referred to as Queen of England.

Issue of marriage:

1 *Astrid*

Alternatively called Estrith, or Margaret. She married either Richard II, Duke of Normandy (*d*.1027), or Robert II, Duke of Normandy (◊ page 40, under William I), between 1017 and 1027. If her husband was Robert, then he repudiated her shortly after the marriage took place. She married secondly Ulf Thorgilson, a Danish Earl in England (*d*.1035; he was the brother of Gytha, mother of Harold II), and had issue:

1 Sweyn Estrithson, King of Denmark (*d*.1074/6), who married a lady called Gunhilda. He left illegitimate issue only.

2 Beorn, Earl of Danish Mercia. He was murdered in 1049.

3 Osbeorn (*d*.1086?).

Sigrid may also have been the mother of Sweyn's four other daughters (◊ above).

KING SWEYN

He died on 3 February, 1014, at Gainsborough, Lincs., and was buried in England (location unknown). His remains were later moved to Roeskild Cathedral, Denmark.

He was succeeded by Ethelred II (◊ preceding chapter), who was in turn succeeded by Edmund, the son of Ethelred.

Edmund II

FATHER: *Ethelred II* (◊ page 22).
MOTHER: *Elgiva* (◊ page 23, under *Ethelred II*).
SIBLINGS: (◊ page 23, under *Ethelred II*).

EDMUND II
Known as 'Ironside', he was born between *c*.988 and 993. He succeeded his father as King of England on 23 April, 1016, and was crowned during the same month at Old St Paul's Cathedral in London.
Edmund II married, in late summer (August?), 1015, at Malmesbury, Wiltshire:
Edith
Her origins are unknown. She married firstly Sigeferth (son of Earngrim), a Thane in East Anglia (he was murdered in 1015). The date of her death is not known.
Issue of marriage (who may have been twins):
1 *Edward*
He was born in 1016: he was aged 41 at his death. He was styled 'Atheling', but spent the greater part of his youth in exile in Hungary. He died in 1057, in London, where he was buried in Old St Paul's Cathedral.
     Edward married (no record exists of the date), in Hungary:
Agatha
She was probably the daughter of Bruno, Bishop of Augsburg, and brother of Henry III, Emperor of Germany. With less probability, she was the daughter of Stephen, King of Hungary, by Gisela, daughter of Conrad II, Emperor of Germany, and sister of the Emperor Henry III. She is described as 'a kinswoman' of the Emperor Henry III. Upon reaching old age, she became a nun at Newcastle-upon-Tyne, probably after the death of her daughter, Queen Margaret of Scotland, in 1093.

Issue of marriage:

(i) *Edgar*

He was born in *c.*1053 (certainly by 1058) in Hungary, and was styled 'Atheling'. In October, 1066, the Witan in London elected him King of England upon hearing of the death of Harold II at Hastings. He was not crowned, and by December, 1066, he had submitted to William I and abandoned all claims to the throne. He died after 1125, perhaps in 1130 (?).

(ii) *Margaret*

(⇔ page 185, under Malcolm III, King of Scotland).

(iii) *Christina*

Born in Hungary, she became a nun, firstly – according to some authorities – at Wilton Abbey, Wiltshire, and then, in *c.*1086, at Romsey Abbey in Hampshire. She is sometimes called Abbess of Romsey, but only on very slender evidence. She died before 1102 (?).

2 *Edmund*

He was born either in 1016, or in 1017. He was taken to Hungary by his family in childhood, where he later died. Some sources state that he died young, but he must have lived at least into his teens.

Edmund married (no record exists of the date) in Hungary:

Hedwig

She was either the daughter of Stephen I, King of Hungary, by Gisela, daughter of Conrad II, Emperor of Germany, or the daughter of Henry II, Duke of Bavaria.

After Edmund's death, she married secondly Eppo, Count of Nellenburg.

EDMUND II

He died on 30 November, 1016, in Oxford or in London, and was buried in Glastonbury Abbey, Somerset.

He was succeeded by Canute, son of King Sweyn, who claimed the throne by right of conquest.

King Canute

FATHER: *King Sweyn* (◊ page 25).
MOTHER: *Gunhilda of Poland* (◊ page 26, under *King Sweyn*).
SIBLINGS: (◊ page 26, under *King Sweyn*).

KING CANUTE
Alternatively called Cnut or Knud, and known as 'the Great', he was
born in *c*.995 in Denmark. He succeeded Edmund II as King of
England on 30 November, 1016, claiming the throne by right of
conquest, and is said to have been crowned on 6 January (?), 1017, at
Old St Paul's Cathedral in London, although there is no contemporary evidence for this. He succeeded his brother Harold as King
of Denmark in 1018/19, and became King of Norway by right of
conquest in 1028.

Canute married, on 2 July, 1017 (although no record exists as to
where):

Emma
    She was the widow of Ethelred II (◊ page 22, under Ethelred II).
Issue of marriage:
1 *King Harthacanute* (◊ page 31).
2 *Gunhilda*
    Alternatively called Ethelfrida, she adopted the name Kunigunde
upon her marriage. Born in *c*.1020, she married Henry III, Emperor
of Germany (*d*.1056), on 10 June, 1036, at Nimeguen, Germany,
and had issue:
    1 Beatrice (*b*.1037), Abbess of Quedlinburg.
    Gunhilda died on 16 or 18 July, 1038, on the Adriatic coast.
3 *Daughter*
    Her name is not known; neither are her dates. She died aged about
8, and was buried in Bosham Church, Sussex.
Canute also had the following **illegitimate issue:**
    By Elgiva (996?–1044?), daughter of Alfhelm, Ealdorman of

Northampton, by his wife Wulfrun; some sources state that Elgiva was Canute's 'handfast' wife, according to Danish custom; others state that she was his repudiated wife; at all events, their union was uncanonical. They had issue:

1 Sweyn, King of Norway (1015?–1036/7).
2 Harold I (◊ page 32).

There were contemporary doubts in certain court circles that Canute was the father of Elgiva's two sons.

KING CANUTE

He died on 12 November, 1035, at Shaftesbury, Dorset, and was buried in Winchester Cathedral. His bones now lie in one of the mortuary chests there.

He was succeeded by his son Harthacanute.

King Harthacanute

FATHER: *King Canute* (◊ page 30).
MOTHER: *Emma of Normandy* (◊ page 30, under *King Canute*).
SIBLINGS: (◊ page 30, under *King Canute*).

KING HARTHACANUTE

Alternatively called Hardicanute, he was born in *c.*1018, and was designated titular King of Denmark in 1028. He succeeded his father as King of Denmark on 12 November, 1035, and as King of England on the same day, in his absence from that country. He remained in Denmark, and his authority in England was usurped by his half-brother Harold I in 1037. He was restored to the English throne on 17 March, 1040, upon the death of Harold I. He is said to have been crowned in June, 1040, at Canterbury Cathedral, Kent, but no contemporary evidence exists to show that he was consecrated at all.

KING HARTHACANUTE

He died unmarried (and childless), on 8 June, 1042, at Lambeth in London, and was buried in Winchester Cathedral.

He was succeeded by his half-brother Edward, the son of Ethelred II.

Harold I

FATHER: *King Canute* (?) (◊ page 30).
MOTHER: *Elgiva of Northampton, Canute's concubine or handfast wife.*
SIBLINGS: (◊ page 31, under *King Canute*).

HAROLD I

He was born in *c.*1016/17, perhaps at Northampton. He was probably illegitimate, but contemporary doubts as to his paternity were probably mere political propaganda. In 1037, when King Harthacanute was still in Denmark, Harold usurped the throne of England and was recognised as King, being crowned that same year at Oxford.

Harold I married (although no record exists of the date or the place):
Elgiva

Her origins are unknown, as are her dates.

Issue of marriage:

1 *Elfwine*

He was born in London, but no dates are recorded for his life. Some sources infer he was illegitimate, but they are unreliable. He became a monk at Sainte-Foi Abbey, Conques, Aquitaine, his own foundation.

HAROLD I

He died on 17 March, 1040, at Oxford, and was buried, according to a faint tradition, in the old Abbey Church of St Peter at Westminster. It is less probable that he was buried in Winchester Cathedral, as is sometimes stated. His body, after a dishonourable exhumation, was reburied, probably in St Clement Danes Church, Strand, London (less probably, in St Olave's Church, Southwark, London). He was succeeded by his half-brother Harthacanute, whom he had once deposed (◊ previous chapter), who, in turn, was succeeded by Edward, son of Ethelred II.

King Edward the Confessor

FATHER: *Ethelred II* (◊ page 22).
MOTHER: *Emma of Normandy* (◊ page 24, under *Ethelred II*).
SIBLINGS: (◊ page 24, under *Ethelred II*).

KING EDWARD
Known as 'the Confessor', he was born around *c.*1003/4 (by 1005) at Islip, Oxon. When he succeeded his half-brother King Harthacanute, on 8 June, 1042, the crown of England reverted from the usurping Danish dynasty to the line of Cerdic once more, and for the last time. Edward was crowned on 3 April, 1043, at Winchester Cathedral.
King Edward married, on 23 January, 1045 (although no record
   exists as to where):
Edith
   She was the daughter of Godwine, Earl of Wessex, by his wife Gytha (◊ page 34, under *Harold II*), and she was born in *c.*1020. Edith was perhaps anointed and crowned on her wedding day, but details of the ceremony have not been recorded. Her marriage to Edward was purely platonic, the King being unwilling, for religious reasons, to consummate it, hence there were no children. Edith died on 18 December, 1075, either at the Palace of Westminster or at Winchester, and was buried in Westminster Abbey.

KING EDWARD
He died on 4/5 January, 1066, at the Palace of Westminster, and was

buried in the new Westminster Abbey, built by his command and only recently consecrated.

He was succeeded by Harold, Earl of Wessex, his brother-in-law, to whom he left his throne, with the support of the Witan, there being no adult claimant to the crown of the line of Cerdic.

On 7 February, 1161, Edward the Confessor was canonised, thus becoming the only King of England to be made a saint.

Harold II

FATHER: *Godwine*

He was the son of Wulfnoth, Cyld of Sussex, and was born in *c*.987. He married firstly Thyra, daughter of King Sweyn, and secondly, in *c*.1019/20, Gytha (◊ below). He was first created Earl in 1018, but his earldom is unknown. He was created Earl of Wessex and Kent in 1020. He died on 15 April, 1053, at Winchester Castle, of apoplexy, and was buried in Winchester Cathedral.

MOTHER: *Gytha*

She was the daughter of Thorgils Sprakalegg by Thyra, daughter of Harold Bluetooth, King of Denmark (and sister of King Sweyn); some authorities state that Thorgils was the son of Thyra, not her husband. Gytha was born in Denmark. She married Earl Godwine in *c*.1019/20. She died in exile, perhaps in Flanders, after June, 1069.

SIBLINGS:

1 *Edith*

(◊ page 33, under King Edward the Confessor).

2 *Sweyn*

He was born in *c*.1023, and was created Earl of Mercia in 1043. He died on 29 September, 1052, in exile, at Lycia, near Constantinople, in Byzantium.

Sweyn had the following illegitimate issue:

By Edgiva, Abbess of Leominster, a nun whom he abducted and with whom he contracted an uncanonical marriage:

34

1 Haakon (*b*.1046/7).

2 Tostig.

3 *Tostig*

He was born in *c*.1026, and was created Earl of Northumbria in
c.1055. In that year, or later, he was also created Earl of
Northampton and Nottingham. He was deprived of his earldoms
on 3 October, 1065. He was killed on 25 September, 1066, at the
Battle of Stamford Bridge in Northumberland, fighting his brother
Harold II in alliance with Harold Hardraada, King of Norway.
Tostig was buried in York Minster.

Tostig married, in October, 1051 (although no record exists as
to where):

Judith

Alternatively known as Fausta, she was the daughter of Baldwin
IV, Count of Flanders, by Eleanor, daughter of Richard II, Duke
of Normandy. After Tostig's death, she married secondly Welf IV,
Duke of Bavaria.

Issue of marriage:

(i) *Skule*

He grew up, married, and had issue. No further details are
recorded.

(ii) *Ketel*

He grew up, married and had issue. No further details are
recorded.

4 *Gyrth*

He was created Earl of East Anglia in 1057, and was killed on 14
October, 1066, at the Battle of Hastings, Sussex.

5 *Leofwine*

He was created Earl of Kent, Surrey, Middlesex, Hertfordshire and
Buckinghamshire in *c*.1057, and was killed on 14 October, 1066,
at the Battle of Hastings, Sussex.

6 *Wulfnoth*

He died after 1087, either in Normandy, or at Salisbury, Wiltshire.

7 *Alfgar*

He is said to have been a monk at Rheims in France.

8 *Edgiva*

Nothing is known of her beyond her name.

9 *Elgiva*

She died in c.1066.

10 *Gunhilda*

She is said to have become a nun, either at St Omer in France, or at Bruges in Flanders. She died on 24 August, 1087, at Bruges, and was buried in Bruges Cathedral.

HAROLD II

Surnamed Godwineson, he was born in c.1020/22. He was created Earl of East Anglia in c.1045, and succeeded his father as Earl of Wessex on 15 April, 1053. He was created Earl of Hereford in 1058, and styled 'Duke of the English' from 1064. He succeeded Edward the Confessor as King of England on 6 January, 1066, having been chosen by the King as his successor with the support of the Witan. Harold II was crowned on 6 January, 1066, probably at St Paul's Cathedral in London (some authorities state he was crowned at Westminster Abbey, but there is no evidence for this).

Harold II married, either in c.1064 or in March (?), 1066, at York:
Edith

She was the daughter of Alfgar, Earl of Mercia, by Edgiva or Elgiva Malet, or by Elfleda, daughter of Ealdred, Earl of Northumbria. She was born in c.1042. She married firstly Gruffydd ap Llywelyn, King of Wales (killed in 1063), either in c.1050 or in c.1056/7, and had issue:

1 Meredith (*d.*1070).
2 Idwal (*d.*1070).
3 Nesta, who married Osbern FitzRichard, Lord of Richard's Castle and Byton, and had issue.

After the death of Harold, Edith went into exile on the Continent where she died after 1070.

Issue of marriage, who may have been twins:

1 *Harold*

He was born in December, 1066, in Chester. He grew up in exile on the Continent, and died after 1098.

2 *Ulf*

He was perhaps born in December, 1066, in Chester, although some authorities have stated that he was an illegitimate son of Harold by his mistress Edith Swanneshals (⋄ below). Ulf is said by some chroniclers to have drowned at sea before 1070, but he is recorded as being alive in 1087 in Normandy, after which he disappears from the records.

Harold II also had the following **illegitimate issue**:

Probably by Edith Swanneshals ('Swan Neck'):

1 Godwine.
2 Edmund.
3 Magnus.
4 Gunhilda; she became a nun at Wilton Abbey, Wiltshire.
5 Gytha; she married Vladimir II, Prince of Novgorod and Kiev (*d.*1125), and had issue. One of her descendants was Philippa, wife of Edward III.
6 Ulf (◊ above). He may have been Harold's legitimate son by his wife.

HAROLD II

He was killed on 14 October, 1066, at the Battle of Senlac (now known as the Battle of Hastings, although it took place eleven miles away at Battle in Sussex). Harold may have been felled by an arrow between his eyes, although this theory may be based upon a misinterpretation of the Bayeux Tapestry, in which case he was probably struck down by a sword stroke dealt by a mounted Norman knight. Harold was buried either on the battlefield or, less probably, on the seashore at Hastings. Later on, his remains were removed to Waltham Abbey, Essex.

He was succeeded by William, Duke of Normandy, the victor of Hastings.

CHAPTER TWO

The Norman Kings
of England

Harold II was the last of the Saxon Kings of England. His successor, William I, based his claim to the English throne upon a promise made to him more than a decade before 1066 by Edward the Confessor, who is said to have told William that he, Edward, would make him his successor.

In 1064, Earl Harold was shipwrecked upon the coast of Normandy. William kept him in honourable captivity until he had sworn upon holy relics to do all in his power to enforce William's claim to the English throne. William knew very well that at that time it seemed that Harold, the most powerful man in England next to the king, would be designated Edward's successor, which was what in fact happened. When, in the autumn of 1065, Edward was seen to be dying, the Witan considered all the claimants and decided that Harold, as the only man with the strength and maturity that befitted him to rule England, was the natural choice. Edward, on his deathbed, accordingly left his crown to Harold, who seized power in defiance of his oath to William.

William thereupon gathered an army, sailed to England, and defeated Harold on 14 October, 1066, at the Battle of Hastings.

At that time, there was only one living male representative of the ancient line of the Kings of Wessex, and that was the child Edgar the Atheling, the grandson of Edmund II. The Witan in London set him up as king as soon as they received the news of William's victory at Hastings, but it quickly became obvious that Edgar's impeccable claim to the throne would be no match for William's determination to wear the crown of England. Edgar submitted to William within 6 weeks, and William was crowned King of England in Westminster

Abbey on Christmas Day, 1066.

A new royal dynasty had been founded; the joining of England with Normandy brought England very much into the forefront of European affairs. William's followers received lands and honours, and thus founded aristocratic dynasties of their own in their new realm. A new order prevailed: England was feudalised and its Church and legal system were overhauled, and all things Saxon were disdained by the conquering Normans.

William's claim to the English throne had very little basis in dynastic terms. His great-aunt Emma had been wife to both Ethelred II and Canute, and William's wife Matilda was a descendant of King Alfred. Those were his only links to the English royal line. William's own ancestor, Rollo, who founded the duchy of Normandy in the 10th century, had been a Viking pirate. It was left to William's son, Henry I, to ally himself in blood to the ancient line of Cerdic: in 1100, he married Edith, the niece of Edgar the Atheling, much to the disgust of his Norman barons, who sneeringly referred to the royal couple as 'Godric and Godgifu', old Saxon names now fallen into disrepute. Yet the marriage was popular with the common people, who were, after all, Saxon, and later Kings would acknowledge that it was fitting that the blood of Cerdic flowed in their veins.

William I

FATHER: *Robert*

Known as 'the Devil' or 'the Magnificent', he was the son of Richard II, Duke of Normandy, by Judith of Brittany, and was born in *c*.1008 in Normandy. He perhaps married Astrid, daughter of King Sweyn, in *c*.1027, but repudiated her almost at once. He succeeded his brother Richard III as Duke of Normandy on 6 August, 1028, and died on 2 or 22 July, 1035, on pilgrimage at Nicea in Bithynia. William I was his illegitimate son.

MOTHER: *Herleva*

Alternatively called Arlette, she was the daughter of Fulbert, a tanner of Falaise in Normandy, by his wife Duxia. She was born in *c*.1012. She is said to have been noticed by Duke Robert as she sat washing clothes in a river. Their liaison produced two children (◊ below). Herleva married Herluin, Viscount of Conteville, between *c*.1029 and 1035, and had four (or perhaps as many as six) further children (◊ below). She died in *c*.1050, and was buried in the Abbey of St Grestain in France.

SIBLINGS:

Adeliza

She was born perhaps in 1029, before her mother's marriage to a Norman nobleman. She married firstly Enguerrand III, Count of Ponthieu (*d*.1053), and had issue:

1 Adelaide (alive in 1096).

Adeliza married secondly Lambert of Boulogne, Count of Lens in Artois (who was killed in battle in 1054), in *c*.1053, and had issue:

2 Judith (1054/5–after 1086); she married Waltheof, Earl of Northumbria and Huntingdon (who was executed in 1076), and had issue, including Matilda, wife of David I, King of Scotland.

Adeliza married thirdly Odo II, Count of Champagne (disinherited in 1071), and had issue:

3 Stephen, Count of Aumale (before 1070–1121/30), who married

Hawise, daughter of Ralph de Mortimer of Wigmore, and had issue.

Adeliza was styled Countess of Aumale in her own right from 1082. She died between 1087 and 1090.

William did not have any full brothers.

HALF-SIBLINGS (the children of his mother's marriage):

1 *Robert*

He was born in 1030/1, and was created Count of Mortain in *c.*1049 or *c.*1056. He was probably created Earl of Cornwall in *c.*1066/7. He died on 8 December, 1090/1, and was buried in the Abbey of St Grestain, France.

Robert married, before 1066:

Matilda

She was the daughter of Roger of Montgomery, Earl of Shrewsbury, by Mabel, daughter of William, Seigneur of Alençon-Bellême. The date of her death is not known; she was buried in the Abbey of St Grestain in France.

Issue of marriage:

(i) *William*

He was born before 1084. He succeeded his father as Count of Mortain on 8 December, 1090/1, and married a lady called Adelaide, of whom nothing more is known. He died after 1140.

(ii) *Emma*

She married William IV, Count of Toulouse (*d.*1094), and had issue.

Robert married secondly:

Almodis

She was perhaps a sister of Boson, Count of La Marche. After Robert's death, she perhaps married Roger of Montgomery.

2 *Odo*

He was born between *c.*1031 and 1035. He entered the Church and was consecrated Bishop of Bayeux in Normandy around 1049 and before 23 April 1050. He was created Earl of Kent in 1066/7; he was deprived of this earldom, which was not forfeited, in 1082, but restored in 1087. He was again deprived of the earldom of Kent in 1088, and this time it was declared forfeit, Odo being banished from England. He died in February, 1097, at Palermo, Sicily, and was buried in Palermo Cathedral.

Odo had the following illegitimate issue:

1 John.

3 *Emma* (?)

Historians now think she was probably fictitious. She is said to have married Richard of Goz, Viscount of Avranches (*d.c.*1082), and had issue:

1 Hugh, Viscount of Avranches, Earl of Chester (*c.*1047–1101), who married Ermentrude, daughter of Hugh, Count of Clermont, and had issue. Hugh died a monk.

4 *Muriel*

She married either William, Count of La Ferté-Macé, or, more probably, Eudo de Capello, Viscount of the Côtentin (it is possible that she had an unnamed sister who married William, Count of La Ferté-Macé – ◊ below). Muriel perhaps had issue by Eudo:

1 Muriel; she is said to have married Robert de la Haia (although there is no firm evidence for this).

Muriel's date of death is not known; she was buried in the Abbey of Bury St Edmunds, Suffolk.

5 *Sister* (?)

Her existence is uncertain and her name unknown. She was possibly the sister who married William, Count of La Ferté-Macé.

6 *Isabella*

She married Henry, Count of Séez, and had issue:

1 St Osmund, Bishop of Salisbury (*d.*1099).

WILLIAM I

Known as 'the Bastard', and later as 'the Conqueror', he was born in *c.*1027/8 at Falaise Castle in Normandy. He succeeded his father as Duke of Normandy on 22 July, 1035, despite his bastardy, as Duke Robert had no legitimate son. William became Count of Maine by right of conquest in 1063. He defeated Harold II at the Battle of Hastings on 14 October, 1066, and claimed the crown of England by right of inheritance (according to William, Edward the Confessor had promised to make him his successor) and by right of conquest. William I formally acceded to the throne of England on 25 December,

1066, and was crowned on that same day in Westminster Abbey, his being the first coronation to take place in the Abbey, which set a precedent for almost all future coronations.

William I married, in *c.*1050/52 at the Cathedral of Notre Dame d'Eu in Normandy:

Matilda

She was the daughter of Baldwin V, Count of Flanders, by Adela, daughter of Robert II, King of France. She was born in *c.*1032, and was crowned Queen Consort on 11 May, 1068, either at Westminster Abbey or in Winchester Cathedral. Matilda died on 2 November, 1083, at Caen in Normandy, and was buried in the Abbey of the Holy Trinity, her own foundation known as the Abbaye aux Dames, Caen, Normandy.

Issue of marriage:

1 *Robert*

Known as 'Curthose', he was born in *c.*1052/4 in Normandy. He succeeded his father as Duke of Normandy on 9 September, 1087, but was deprived of the dukedom by his brother Henry I on 28 September, 1106, after losing the Battle of Tinchebrai in Normandy. Robert was henceforth a prisoner in England for the rest of his life. He died on 3, 10 or 15 February, 1134/5, still in captivity, at Cardiff Castle, and was buried in Gloucester Cathedral.

Robert married, in 1100, at Apulia, Sicily:

Sybilla

She was the daughter of Geoffrey, Count of Conversano. She died around February or March, 1103, at Rouen in Normandy, probably in childbed, although one chronicler states she was poisoned by a rival for her husband's affections. She was either buried at Caen in Normandy, or in Rouen Cathedral, Normandy.

Issue of marriage:

(i) *William*

Known as 'Clito', he was born in 1101 at Rouen in Normandy. In the Spring of 1127, he was created Count of Flanders by right of inheritance through his grandmother Matilda of Flanders. He died on 27 July, 1128, at the Abbey of St Bertin, St Omer, France, of wounds received at the Battle of Alost, and was buried in the Abbey of St Bertin, St Omer, France.

William married firstly, in 1123 (although no record exists

as to where):
Sybilla
She was the daughter of Fulk V, Count of Anjou, by Aremburga, daughter of Hélias I, Count of Maine. She was born between 1112 and 1116. Her marriage to William Clito was annulled in 1124. She married secondly, Thierry of Alsace, Count of Flanders (*d.*1168), in 1134, and had issue, including:
1 Matthew I, Count of Flanders and Boulogne (*d.*1173), who married Mary, daughter of King Stephen, and had issue.
Sybilla retired in middle age to the Abbey of St Lazarus in Bethlethem, where she became a nun. She died and was buried there in 1165.

William married secondly, in January, 1128 (although no record exists as to where):
Joan (or Giovanna)
She was the daughter of Ranieri, Marquess of Montferrat, by Gisla, daughter of William I, Count of Burgundy. No dates are recorded.

(ii) *Henry*
He was born in 1102. He was killed whilst hunting in the New Forest in Hampshire; the year is not known.

Robert also had the following illegitimate issue:
By a priest's wife or mistress:
1 Richard (killed in the New Forest in 1100).
2 William (killed *c.*1110 at the Battle of Jerusalem, fighting the Infidel). He was Lord of Tortosa.
By an unknown woman:
3 Daughter (name not known); she married Hélias of Saint-Saëns, Count of Arques.

2 *Richard*
He was born before 1054 (or 1056?) in Normandy, and is said to have been created Duke of Bernay in Normandy. He was gored to death by a stag in 1075 or 1081, whilst hunting in the New Forest, Hampshire, and was buried in Winchester Cathedral.

3 *Cecilia*
She was born in *c.*1054/5 in Normandy, and entered the novitiate at the Abbey of the Holy Trinity, Caen, her mother's foundation, on 18 June, 1066. She was professed there as a nun on 5 April, 1075,

and was elected Abbess of Caen in 1112. She died on 3 July, 1126, at Caen, where she was buried in the Abbey of the Holy Trinity.

4 Adeliza

She was possibly born in 1055. Ordericus Vitalis states that she took religious vows early in life. Robert of Torigny states that she was at one time betrothed to Harold II when he was Earl of Wessex. She was probably dead by 5 January, 1066.

5 William II (◊ page 46).

6 Constance

She was born in c.1057 or c.1061 in Normandy. She married Alan IV Fergant, Duke of Brittany (d.1119), at Caen, Normandy, in c.1086. She died on 13 August, 1090, perhaps poisoned by her servants, and was buried in the Church of St Melans, near Rhedon, Brittany. Sandford, writing in the 17th century, perpetrated the myth that she was married 25 years and was buried in the Abbey of Bury St Edmunds, Suffolk.

7 Adela (◊ page 51, under *King Stephen*).

8 Henry I (◊ page 47).

9 Agatha

Alternatively called Elgiva, or Margaret, she may have been born in 1064. She was married by proxy to Alfonso VI (d.1109), King of Galicia and Léon, at the Abbey of the Holy Trinity, Caen, Normandy, but died before 1074, before the marriage could be consummated. She was buried in Bayeux Cathedral, Normandy.

10 Matilda

Very little is known of her. She died unmarried before 1112.

Note: There is no evidence that either William or Matilda were the parents of Gundrada, Countess of Surrey. Charters attesting this have been proved spurious.

WILLIAM I

He died on 9 September, 1087, at the Priory of St Gervais, Rouen, Normandy, of wounds received at the siege of Mantes. He was buried in St Stephen's Abbey, Caen, Normandy, his own foundation.

He was succeeded in England by his son William (and in Normandy by his son Robert).

William II

FATHER: *William I* (◊ page 40).
MOTHER: *Matilda of Flanders* (◊ page 43, under *William I*).
SIBLINGS: (◊ page 43, under *William I*).

WILLIAM II

Known as 'Rufus', he was born between *c.*1056 and 1060 in Normandy. He succeeded his father as King of England on 9 September, 1087, and was crowned on 26 September, 1087, in Westminster Abbey. He never married.

William is said by an unreliable 18th-century source to have had the following **illegitimate issue**:

1 Berstrand.

WILLIAM II

He was killed, perhaps murdered on the orders of his brother Henry, by an arrow in his back on 2 August, 1100, in the New Forest, Hampshire. He was buried in Winchester Cathedral.

He was succeeded by his brother Henry.

Henry I

FATHER: *William I* (◊ page 40).
MOTHER: *Matilda of Flanders* (◊ page 43, under *William I*)
SIBLINGS: (◊ page 43, under *William I*).

HENRY I

Known as 'Beauclerk' or 'the Lion of Justice', he was born in September, 1068, at Selby, Yorkshire. He became Lord of Domfront in 1092, and Count of Coutances and Bayeux in 1096. He succeeded his brother William II as King of England on 3 August, 1100, and was crowned on 5/6 August, 1100, at Westminster Abbey. He usurped the duchy of Normandy on 28 September, 1106, after defeating his brother Robert, its lawful Duke, at the Battle of Tinchebrai.

Henry I married firstly, on 11 November 1100, at Westminster Abbey:

Matilda

She was christened Edith, but adopted the name Matilda upon her marriage as it was thought the Norman barons might not respect a queen with a Saxon name. She was the daughter of Malcolm III, King of Scotland, by St Margaret, a great-granddaughter of Ethelred II, and her marriage to Henry I represented the union of Norman and Saxon royal lines. Matilda was born probably in the autumn of 1080, and was crowned Queen Consort on 11 or 14 November, 1100, at Westminster Abbey. She died on 1 May, 1118, at the Palace of Westminster, and was buried in Westminster Abbey.

Issue of marriage:

1 *Euphemia*

She was perhaps the child born in late July or early August, 1101, at Winchester, who died young.

2 *Adelaide*

She adopted the name Matilda upon her marriage. (◊ page 59, under Henry II).

3 *William*

He was born before 5 August, 1103, at Winchester. Styled 'Atheling', he was designated Duke of Normandy in 1120. He drowned on 25 November, 1120, when the White Ship sank off Barfleur in Normandy.

William married, in June, 1119, at Lisieux in Normandy:

Matilda

She was christened Alice, but adopted the name Matilda upon her marriage, although she is sometimes called Isabella. She was the daughter of Fulk V, Count of Anjou, by Aremburga, daughter of Hélias I, Count of Maine, and sister to Sybilla, wife of William Clito, grandson of William I. She was born between *c.*1107 and 1111 in Anjou. After her husband drowned, she became in *c.*1121 a nun at Fontevrault Abbey in France, where she was elected Abbess in 1148. She died at Fontevrault Abbey in 1154, and was perhaps buried there. There was no issue of her marriage to William.

4 *Richard*

He drowned with his brother William on 25 November, 1120, when the White Ship sank off Barfleur in Normandy. Some sources state that the Richard who drowned in the White Ship was Henry I's natural son, and that his legitimate son Richard died in infancy. However, both Robert of Gloucester and the Saxon Chronicle state that Queen Matilda's son Richard drowned in the White Ship.

Henry I married secondly, on 29 January (or, less probably, 2 February), 1121, at the Chapel Royal in Windsor Castle:

Adeliza

Alternatively known as Adelicia, Adela, Adelaide, Adeline or Alice, she was the daughter of Geoffrey VII, Count of Louvain, Duke of Lower Brabant and Lower Lorraine, by Ida, daughter of Albert III, Count of Namur and Countess of Namur in her own right. There are no records of Adeliza's date of birth, but she was described as 'nubile' in 1120, thus she was perhaps born between *c.*1103 and *c.*1106. She was crowned Queen Consort on 30 January (or, less probably, 3 February), 1121, at Westminster Abbey. After the death of Henry I, she married secondly William d'Albini, Earl of Arundel (*d.*1176), after 1136 and before September, 1139, and had issue:

1 William, 2nd Earl of Arundel (before 1150–1193); he married Matilda, daughter of James de St Hilary du Harcourt, and had issue.

2 Reyner.

3 Henry.

4 Geoffrey.

5 Alice (d.1188); she married firstly John, Count of Eu, Lord of Hastings (d.1170), and had issue. She married secondly Alvred de St Martin (d. after 1189).

6 Olivia. She died young, and was buried in Boxgrove Priory, Sussex.

7 Agatha. She died young, and was buried in Boxgrove Priory, Sussex.

Adeliza became a nun at Affligem Abbey, near Alost in South Brabant, in c.1149/50. She died on 23/24 March (or 23 April), 1151 at Affligem Abbey, and was buried there.

Henry I also had the following **illegitimate issue**:

By Sybilla (also known as Adela or Lucy), daughter of Sir Robert Corbet of Alcester, Co. Warwick, and afterwards wife of Herbert FitzHerbert (d. by 1165):

1 Robert Fitzroy of Caen, Earl of Gloucester (1090/95–1147); he married Mabel (d.1157), daughter of Robert FitzHamon, Earl of Gloucester, and had issue. There is no certain evidence to show that Sybilla really was Robert's mother, who may have been an unknown woman of Caen.

2 Reginald or Rainald of Dunstanville, Earl of Cornwall (by 1110?–1175); he married Beatrice, daughter of William FitzRichard, and had issue.

3 William (by 1105–after 1187); he married a lady called Alice, of whom nothing more is known.

4 Sybilla (⟡ page 192, under Alexander I, King of Scotland).

5 Gundrada (alive in 1130).

6 Rohese (d. after 1176); she married Henry de la Pomerai (d.c.1167), and had issue.

By Ansfrida, widow of Anskill, a knight and tenant of Abingdon Abbey:

7 Richard of Lincoln (drowned in the White Ship, 1120).

8 Fulk (b. before 1100); he either died young, or grew up and became a monk at Abingdon Abbey.

9 Juliana (1090?–after 1136); she married Eustace of Breteuil, Lord of Pacy (d.1136), and had issue. In widowhood, she became a nun at Fontevrault Abbey. There is some doubt that Ansfrida was her

mother, but circumstantial evidence makes this likely.

By Nesta, Princess of Deheubarth (*d.c.*1114), daughter of Rhys ap Tewdwr, Prince of Deheubarth, by Gladys of Powys, and wife of Gerald de Windsor (*d.* by 1136):

10 Henry FitzHenry (1103? or 1105?; by 1109–killed 1157); he married an unknown lady and had issue.

By Edith, daughter of Forn Sigulfson, Lord of Greystoke, Cumberland (*d.*1173); afterwards wife of Robert d'Oilli:

11 Robert FitzEdith, Baron of Okenhampton (*d.*1172); he married Matilda, Dame du Sap, daughter of Robert d'Avranches, and had issue.

By Isabella of Meulan (*b.c.*1102/7), daughter of Robert de Beaumont, Earl of Leicester, and afterwards Countess of Pembroke:

12 Isabella or Elizabeth (*b.*1120?). Died unmarried.

By Edith, of unknown origin (*d.* after 1130):

13 Matilda or Mary (1090?–1120: drowned in the White Ship); she married Rotrou II, Count of Perche (*d.*1144), and had issue.

By unknown mothers:

14 William de Tracy (*d.*1136? or 1140?); he married an unknown lady and had issue.

15 Gilbert (1130?–1142).

16 Matilda; she married Conan III, Duke of Brittany (*d.*1148), and had issue.

17 Constance or Matilda; she married Richard or Roscelin, Viscount of Beaumont-le-Maine, and had issue including Ermengarde, wife of William the Lyon, King of Scotland.

18 Eustacia; she married William Gouet III, Lord of Montmirail.

19 Alice or Aline; she married Matthew de Montmorenci, Constable of France, and had issue.

20 Matilda, Abbess of Montvilliers.

21 Daughter (name not known), who was betrothed at one time (*c.*1109) to William de Warenne.

22 Joan or Elizabeth; she married Fergus of Galloway, and had issue.

23 Emma; she married Guy de Laval.

24 Daughter (name not known), to be betrothed to Hugh FitzGervais in *c.*1110.

25 Sybilla of Falaise; she married Baldwin de Boullers.

HENRY I

He died on 1/2 December, 1135, at St Denis le Fermont in the Forest of Angers, near Rouen, Normandy, of food poisoning. He was buried in Reading Abbey, Berkshire, his own foundation. His tomb was destroyed during the Reformation.

He was succeeded by his nephew Stephen of Blois, although he had made his barons swear allegiance to his daughter Matilda as his successor.

King Stephen

FATHER: *Stephen Henry*

He was the son of Theobald III, Count of Blois; he married Adela of Normandy (♭ below) in 1080 at Breteuil in France, and again in 1081 at Chartres Cathedral, France. He succeeded his father as Count Palatine of Blois, Brie, Chartres and Meaux before 1090. He was killed on 19 May, 1102, during the siege of Ramula in the Holy Land, being slain by the Saracens after the battle of Ascalon.

Stephen had the following illegitimate issue:

1 Emma; she married Herbert II, Count of Maine, and had issue.

MOTHER: *Adela*

She was the daughter of William I by Matilda of Flanders, and she was born in c.1062 in Normandy. During her widowhood, she became a nun at the Cluniac Priory of Marigney-sur-Loire in the Diocese of Autun in France in c.1122. She died in 1137 or 1138 at Marigney, and was buried in the Abbey of the Holy Trinity, Caen, Normandy.

SIBLINGS:

1 Humbert, Count of Virtus (*d.* young).

2 William, Count of Chartres, Lord of Sulli (*d.* after 1104); he married Agnes (*d.* after 1104), daughter of Giles, Lord of Sulli, and had issue. William is described in the chronicles as an idiot, and was disinherited in favour of his younger brother Theobald in the

succession to Blois.

3 Theobald IV, Count of Blois (1085/91?–1152); he also became Count of Champagne, and married Matilda, daughter of Ingelbert II, Duke of Carinthia, and had issue.

4 Henry; he was born in c.1099 at Winchester, and became a monk at the Priory of Cluny in France during his childhood. He later transferred to Bermondsey Abbey, Surrey, where he became Abbot. He was elected Abbot of Glastonbury in Somerset in 1126. He was nominated Bishop of Winchester on 4 October, 1129, and consecrated on 17 November, 1129. He died on 6 August, 1171, at Winchester, and was buried in Winchester Cathedral.

5 Philip, Bishop of Châlons (d.1100).

6 Odo; he has perhaps been confused with Henry, who is referred to as Eudes in one charter.

7 Matilda or Lucy; she married Richard d'Avranches, 2nd Earl of Chester. Both were drowned in 1120 when the White Ship sank off Barfleur in Normandy.

8 Agnes; she married Hugh III de Puiset, and had issue.

9 Adela or Lithuise; she married Miles de Brai, Viscount of Troyes and Lord of Montlheri. The marriage was later annulled.

10 Eleanor (d.1147); she married Raoul, Count of Vermandois.

11 Alice; she married Reginald III, Count of Joigni.

KING STEPHEN

He was born in c.1096/7 (before 1100) at Blois, France. He was created Count of Mortain before 1115, and became Count of Boulogne in right of his wife before 1125. On 22 December, 1135, he usurped the throne of England upon the death of Henry I, who had left it to his daughter Matilda, to whom the barons had sworn allegiance. However, this had been given unwillingly, and it was generally felt that women were unfit to rule, hence Stephen met with little opposition, and was crowned on 26 December, 1135, at Westminster Abbey. By 1141, his weak government saw many of his nobles disillusioned and turning to Matilda, who invaded England that year. Stephen was deposed between 7 and 10 April, 1141, and imprisoned, while Matilda attempted to consolidate her claim to rule England. She failed in this, due to her haughtiness and high-handed approach to government, which alienated her supporters. Stephen was eventually released, and restored to the throne on 1 November, 1141; he was again crowned, on 25 December, 1141, at Canterbury Cathedral in Kent, and once again, in 1146, at Lincoln Cathedral.

King Stephen married, before 1125:

Matilda

She was the daughter of Eustace III, Count of Boulogne, by Mary, daughter of Malcolm III, King of Scotland, and sister to Matilda, wife of Henry I. Matilda was born around 1103/5, and became Countess of Boulogne in her own right on the death of her father. She was crowned Queen Consort on 22 March, 1136, at Westminster Abbey. She died on 2/3 May, 1152, at Hedingham Castle, Essex, and was buried in Faversham Abbey, Kent. Her tomb was destroyed during the Reformation.

Issue of marriage:

1 *Baldwin*

He was born in *c.*1126, and died perhaps before 2 December (?), 1135 (certainly before 1137), in the Tower of London. He was buried in the Priory of the Holy Trinity, Aldgate Without, London.

2 *Eustace*

He was born between *c.*1127/31, or perhaps in December, 1135. He was created Count of Boulogne at Christmas, 1146/7, and is said to have also been created Earl of Huntingdon, but this is unlikely. Eustace was crowned King of England in 1152, during his father's lifetime, but he never lived to succeed him, dying on 10 or 16 August, 1153, at Bury St Edmund's, Suffolk. He was buried in Faversham Abbey, Kent.

Eustace married, in February, 1140, in Paris:

Constance

She was the daughter of Louis VI, King of France, by Adelaide, daughter of Umberto II, Count of Savoy and Maurienne, and she was born in *c.*1128. After Eustace's death, she married secondly Raymond V (*d.* 1194), Count of Toulouse, in 1154, and had issue:

1 Raymond VI, Count of Toulouse (1156–1222); he married firstly Ermensinda de Pelet (*d.*1176); he married secondly Beatrice of Beziers, whom he repudiated; he married thirdly, and bigamously, Bourguigne de Lusignan, Princess of Cyprus, whom

he also repudiated; he married fourthly Joan, daughter of Henry
II, and had issue.
2 William (or Alberic, or Alfonso), surnamed Taillefer (d.1183/4).
3 Baldwin (d.1212).
4 Alesia (d.1183); she married Roger, Viscount of Beziers.
5 Laura; she married Odo, Count of Comminger.
Constance died on 16 August, 1176, at Rheims in France.

3 *William*

He was born between c.1132 and 1137. He became Earl of Surrey in
right of his wife before 1148/9. He succeeded his mother as Count
of Boulogne on 17 August, 1153, and succeeded his father as Count
of Mortain on 25 October, 1154. He was killed on 11 October,
1159, at the siege of Toulouse in France, and was buried in the
Hospital of Montmorillon, Poitou, France.

William married, before 1148/9, although no evidence exists as
to where:

Isabella

She was the daughter of William de Warenne, 3rd Earl of Surrey, by
Adela, daughter of William Talvas, Count of Ponthieu, and she was
born in c.1136/7. After the death of William, she married secondly
Hamelin of Anjou, Earl of Surrey (1129?–1202), a bastard brother
of Henry II. Hamelin adopted her surname 'de Warenne' when the
couple were married in April, 1164. They had issue:
1 William, 5th Earl of Surrey (d.1240); he married Matilda, who
was perhaps a member of the Albini family. He married secondly
Matilda (d.1248), daughter of William Marshal, 4th Earl of
Pembroke, and had issue. He also had illegitimate issue.
2 Matilda (d.c.1212); she married firstly Henry, Count of Eu and
Baron Hastings (d.1183), and had issue, and secondly Henry
d'Estouteville of Eckington, Co. Derby (d. after 1231).
3 Isabella; she married firstly Robert de Lascy, and secondly
Gilbert de l'Aigle, Lord of Pevensey, Sussex.
4 Ela; she married firstly Robert de Newburn, and secondly
William FitzWilliam of Sprotborough.
5 Mary, Margaret or Matilda (d. after 1208); it may have been she,
and not her sister Isabella, who married Gilbert de l'Aigle.
Isabella died on 13 July, 1199 or 1203, and was buried in the
Chapter House, Lewes Priory, Sussex.

4 Matilda

She was born in c.1133/4, and was married in infancy at c.Easter, 1136, to Waleran de Beaumont, Count of Meulan (1104–1166). She died either before 1137 or in 1141 in the Tower of London, and was buried in the Priory of the Holy Trinity, Aldgate Without, London.

5 Mary

She was born in c.1136; she was dedicated to religion in her infancy and entered as a novice at Lillechurch Priory, Kent. She transferred to Romsey Abbey, Hampshire, where she was professed a nun between c.1148 and 1155. She was elected Abbess of Romsey after 1155. She succeeded her brother William as Countess of Boulogne on 5 October, 1159. She was abducted from her convent in 1160 by Matthew I, Count of Flanders and Boulogne (d.1173), who made her his wife in defiance of her religious vows around the same time. They had issue:

1 Ida, Countess of Boulogne (1161?–1216); she married firstly Gerard III, Count of Gueldres (d.1183), and secondly Berthold IV, Duke of Zehringen (d.1186); and thirdly Reginald de Tree, Count of Dammartin, and had issue.

2 Matilda (1162?.–c.1211); she married Henry I, Duke of Louvain and Brabant (c.1158–1235), and had issue.

Mary's marriage was annulled in c.1169, and she re-entered the religious life at the Benedictine nunnery of St Austrebert, near Montreuil, France, where she died and was buried in 1182.

King Stephen also had the following **illegitimate issue**:

By Dameta, a gentlewoman of Normandy:

1 Gervaise, Abbot of Westminster (c.1115/20–1160).

2 Almaric; he is called a brother of Gervaise in charters.

3 Ralph; he is called a brother of Gervaise in charters.

By unknown mothers:

4 William; he is mentioned only in 17th- and 19th-century genealogies.

5 Sybilla (d.c.1141); she married Hervey le Breton of Léon, Earl of Wiltshire (d.1168).

KING STEPHEN

He died on 25 October, 1154, in a monastery at Dover, Kent, and was buried in Faversham Abbey, Kent. His tomb was destroyed during the Reformation.

He was succeeded by his second cousin Henry, son of the Empress Matilda.

CHAPTER THREE

The Angevin or Plantagenet
Kings of England

When, in 1120, the *White Ship* sank off Barfleur in Normandy, Henry I lost to the sea, not only four of his children, but also both his legitimate heirs. His second marriage in 1121 produced no issue, and when he died in 1135, his only surviving child was a girl, the Empress Matilda, then wedded to her second husband, Geoffrey, Count of Anjou. Matilda was in Anjou when her father died, and the crown of England was seized by Stephen of Blois, her cousin, in defiance of the oath of allegiance that he and other magnates had taken to Matilda as Henry's successor. Matilda triumphed only briefly over Stephen, in 1141, when the crown came tantalisingly within her reach, but she alienated by her hauteur and overbearing manner many of her supporters, and eventually had to retire from the conflict. Yet she continued to promote the cause of her son Henry as heir to England, and in 1153, when faced by an invading army led by that young, determined and very capable man, Stephen had to bow to public opinion and name him his successor. Thus came about the Treaty of Wallingford, which passed over the claims of Eustace and William, Stephen's sons, and recognised that of Henry of Anjou, who succeeded without hindrance to the throne of England the following year, Eustace having died some months previously, which most thought was very fortunate.

Thus was established the Angevin or Plantagenet dynasty. The name 'Plantagenet' comes from the sprig of broom flower (Latin: *planta genista*) that Henry's father Geoffrey was accustomed to wearing in his hat. That name, however, was not formally adopted by the dynasty until the 15th century, when Richard, Duke of York, was the first to use it as a surname to emphasise his claim to the throne during the Wars of the Roses.

The Plantagenets were a dynamic race, one of the most energetic and brilliant families of rulers the world has known. Reputedly descended from a witch, Melusine, who married an early Count of Anjou then vanished in a puff of smoke when he forced her to attend Mass – a tale the Angevin Kings were fond of relating – they ruled England for over 300 years, and for more than 200 of those years the crown passed, usually peacefully, from father to son. What occurred to break this pattern will be related in the next chapter.

Henry II

FATHER: *Geoffrey*

Surnamed Plantagenet after the broom flower he wore in his hat, he was the son of Fulk V, Count of Anjou, by Aremburga, daughter of Hélias I, Count of Maine; his sisters were married to a grandson of William I and the son of Henry I. Geoffrey was born on 24 August, 1113, and married the Empress Matilda on 3 April, 22 May or 17 June, 1128, at Le Mans Cathedral, Anjou. He succeeded his father as Count of Anjou in 1129, and was proclaimed Duke of Normandy on 19 January, 1144, after conquering the duchy. He died on 7 September, 1151, at Château du Loire, France, and was buried in Le Mans Cathedral, Anjou.

Geoffrey had the following illegitimate issue:

By Adelaide of Angers:

1 Hamelin, who adopted the surname 'de Warenne' upon marriage, Earl of Surrey (1129?–1202); he married Isabella de Warenne, daughter-in-law of King Stephen, and had issue.

By unknown mothers:

2 Mary, Abbess of Shaftesbury, Dorset (*d.c.*1216).

3 Emma (*d.* before 1214?); she married firstly Guy, Sire de Laval (*d.*1170/73), and secondly David ap Owen, Prince of East Gwynnedd (*d.*1204), and had issue.

MOTHER: *Matilda*

Christened Adelaide, she adopted the name Matilda on her first marriage. She was the daughter of Henry I by Matilda of Scotland, and she was born in *c.*February (by August), 1102, either at Winchester or in London. She married firstly Henry V, Emperor of Germany (*d.*1125), on 7 January, 1114, at Mainz in Germany, and was crowned there the same day. She was crowned again, with her husband, in 1117, in St Peter's Basilica, Rome, by the Pope. On 7 April, 1141, having deposed and imprisoned King Stephen in pursuance of her claim to the English throne (she was her father's rightful heir and Stephen a usurper), she assumed the title 'Lady of the English', never officially being styled Queen of England. She was deposed in favour of Stephen on 1 November, 1141, having failed to consolidate her position. Matilda died on 10 September, 1167, at the Abbey of Notre Dame des Prés, near Rouen, Normandy, and was buried firstly in the Convent of Bonnes at Nouvelles; soon afterwards, her remains were moved to Bec Abbey, Normandy, and later to Rouen Cathedral.

SIBLINGS:

1 *Geoffrey*

He was born on 1 June, 1134, at Rouen or at Argentan, Normandy, and was created Count of Nantes in *c.*1150. He died unmarried on 26 July, 1158, at Nantes, Brittany, where he was buried.

2 *William*

He was born on 21 July, or in August, 1136, at Argentan in Normandy or at Angers, France, and was called Count of Poitou. He died unmarried on 30 January, 1164, at Rouen, Normandy, and was buried in Rouen Cathedral.

Henry II did not have any sisters.

HENRY II

Known as 'FitzEmpress' or 'Curtmantle', he was born on 5 March, 1133, at Le Mans, Anjou. He became Count of Touraine and Maine in 1151, and succeeded his father as Duke of Normandy and Count of Anjou on 7 September, 1151. He became Duke of Aquitaine in right of his wife on 18 May, 1152. He succeeded his second cousin Stephen as King of England on 19 December, 1154, and was crowned on that day in Westminster Abbey.

Henry II married, on 18 May, 1152, at Poitiers Cathedral, Poitou:

Eleanor

She was the daughter of William X, Duke of Aquitaine, by Aenor, daughter of Aimery I de Rochefoucauld, Viscount of Châtellérhault, and she was born around 1120/22, either at the ducal palace in Poitiers, or the Ombriere Palace, Bordeaux, or, according to local tradition, at Belin Castle, Guienne. She succeeded her father as Duchess of Aquitaine and Countess of Poitou on 9 April, 1137. She married firstly Louis VII, King of France (*c.*1120/21–1180), on 25 July, 1137, at Bordeaux Cathedral, and had issue:

1 Marie (1145–1198); she married Henry I, Count of Champagne (1127–1181), and had issue.
2 Alice (1150–1197/8); she married Theobald V, Count of Blois (d.1191), and had issue.

Louis divorced Eleanor on grounds of consanguinity on 18 March, 1152. She was crowned Queen Consort with her second husband Henry II on 19 December, 1154, at Westminster Abbey. Eleanor died on 1 April, 1204, at Fontevrault Abbey, France, where she was buried.

Issue of marriage:

1 *William*

He was born on 17 August, 1153, at Poitiers, Poitou, and was styled Count of Poitiers. He died in c.April or June, 1156, at Wallingford Castle, Berkshire, and was buried in Reading Abbey, Berkshire.

2 *Henry*

He was born on 28 February, 1155, at Bermondsey Palace, Surrey. He was crowned King of England on 14 June, 1170, at Westminster Abbey, during the lifetime of his father, being styled King of England, Duke of Normandy, and Count of Anjou. Thereafter he was known as 'the Young King'. He was again crowned on 27 August, 1172, at Winchester Cathedral. He died on 11 June, 1183, at the house of a burgher, Etienne Fabri, at Martel in Quercy, France, and was buried in Le Mans Cathedral, Anjou; his remains were later removed to Rouen Cathedral in Normandy.

Henry married, on 2 November, 1160, at Rouen Cathedral, Normandy:

Margaret

She was the daughter of Louis VII, King of France, by Constance, daughter of Alfonso VII, King of Castile, and she was born early in 1158. She was crowned Queen Consort with her husband on 27 August, 1172, at Winchester Cathedral. After the death of the Young King, she married secondly Bela III, King of Hungary (1148–1196), in 1185/6. She died in 1197 at Acre on a pilgrimage to the Holy Land.

Issue of marriage:

(i) *William*

He was born on 19 June, 1177, in Paris, and died there on 22 June, 1177.

3 *Matilda*

She was born in June, 1156, either in London or, less probably, at Windsor Castle. She married Henry V 'the Lion', Duke of Saxony and Bavaria (1129–1195), on 1 February, 1168, at Brunswick Cathedral, Germany, and had issue:

1 Richenza (1172–1210); she married firstly Geoffrey III, Count of Perche (*d.*1202), and had issue, and secondly Enguerrand III, Lord of Coucy.
2 Henry, Duke of Saxony and Bavaria (1175–1227); he married Agnes (*d.*1204), daughter of Conrad of Hohenstaufen, Count Palatine of the Rhine, and had issue.
3 Lothaire (1181–1191).
4 Son (name not known) (*b.&d.* 1182?).
5 Otto IV, Holy Roman Emperor, Earl of York and Count of Ponthieu (1183?–1218); he married firstly Beatrice of Swabia, daughter of Philip, Emperor of Germany, and secondly Mary, daughter of Henry I, Duke of Brabant.
6 William, Duke of Lüneberg and Brunswick (1184–1213); he married Helen, daughter of Waldemar I, King of Denmark.
7 Matilda.
8 Eleanor (?).
9 Gertrude (*d.*1197); she married Canute VI, King of Denmark (1163–1202).
10 Ingibiorg (?); she is said to have married Waldemar II, King of Denmark (1170–1241).

Matilda died on 28 June, 1189, at Brunswick in Germany, and was buried in Brunswick Cathedral.

4 *Richard* I (↺ page 66).

5 *Geoffrey*

He was born on 23 September, 1158, in England, and was styled Earl of Richmond and Duke of Brittany in right of his wife shortly after 6 September, 1181. He was either trampled to death during a tournament, or died of a fever, on 18 or 19 August, 1186, in Paris, and was buried in the Cathedral of Nôtre Dame, Paris.

Geoffrey married, in July, 1181 (although no record exists as to where):

Constance

She was the daughter of Conan IV, Duke of Brittany and Earl of

Richmond, by Margaret of Huntingdon, granddaughter of David I, King of Scotland. Constance was born around 1160/62 in Brittany. After the death of Geoffrey, she married secondly Ranulf de Blundeville, 4th Earl of Chester (1172?–1232), on 3 February, 1188. This marriage was dissolved in 1199 after Constance deserted her husband. She married thirdly Guy of Thouars (d.1213) in 1199 at Angers in Anjou, and had issue:

1 Alice, Duchess of Brittany and Countess of Richmond (1201–1221); she married Peter of Dreux, Duke of Brittany (1187?–1250), and had issue.

2 Katherine (b.1201); she married Andrew de Vitre of Brittany.

Constance died on 3, 4 or 5 September, 1201, at Nantes, Brittany, in childbirth, although some sources say she died of leprosy. She was buried in Villeneuve Abbey, Nantes, Brittany.

Issue of marriage:

(i) *Eleanor*

She was born in 1184, and was styled Countess of Richmond from 27 May, 1208. She spent most of her life in honourable confinement, King John realising that her claim to the throne was superior to his own. She died, perhaps murdered or starved to death, on 10 August, 1241, at Bristol Castle (or, less probably, at Corfe Castle, Dorset), and was buried in St James's Church, Bristol. Her remains were later removed to Amesbury Abbey, Wiltshire.

(ii) *Matilda*

She was born in 1185, and died young.

(iii) *Arthur*

He was born on 29 March, 1187 at Nantes, Brittany, and – as his father's posthumous son – was styled Duke of Brittany from birth. He was styled Earl of Richmond from 18 April, 1199. He is said, with good probability, to have been murdered by order of King John because of his (Arthur's) superior claim to the throne of England, probably on 3 April, 1203, either at Rouen or Cherbourg in Normandy. He certainly disappeared before Easter, 1203. He was buried at Notre Dame des Prés at Rouen, Normandy.

6? Philip

In 1611, the English antiquarian John Speed claimed in his History of Great Britain that Henry and Eleanor had a son called Philip, who was born between 1158 and 1162, but died young; there is no contemporary evidence for his existence, and Speed may have confused him with Richard I's bastard son Philip.

7 *Eleanor*

She was born on 13 October, 1161, at Domfront Castle, Normandy. She married Alfonso VIII, King of Castile (1156–1214), in September, 1177, at Burgos Cathedral, Castile, and had issue:

1. Sancho (*b.&d.* 1180).
2. Berengaria, Queen of Castile (1181–1234); she married Alfonso IX, King of Léon (1173–1230), and had issue.
3. Urracca (1182–1220); she married Alfonso II, King of Portugal (1185–1223), and had issue.
4. Blanche (1183?–1253); she married Louis VIII, King of France (1187–1226), and had issue.
5. Henry (*b.c.*1184; *d.* young).
6. Ferdinand (1189–1209 or 1211).
7. Eleanor (1190–1253); she married James I, King of Aragon (1205–1276), and had issue. She was divorced in 1229.
8. Constance, Abbess of Las Huelgas, Castile (*d.*1243).
9. Sanchia (*d.* young).
10. Matilda (*d.* young).
11. Henry I, King of Castile (1204–1217); he married Matilda (*d.*1257), daughter of Sancho I, King of Portugal. The marriage was later annulled.
12. Constance (*d.* young).

Eleanor died on 31 October, 1214, at Burgos, Castile, and was buried there in the Abbey of Las Huelgas.

8 *Joan*

She was born in October, 1165, at Angers Castle, Anjou. She married firstly William II, King of Sicily (1154–1189), on 13 February, 1177, at Palermo Cathedral, Sicily, and had issue:

1. Bohemond, Duke of Apulia (*b.&d.*1181).

Joan was crowned Queen of Sicily on 13 February, 1177, at Palermo Cathedral. She married secondly Raymond VI, Count of Toulouse (1156–1222) (who was the son of Constance of France, daughter-in-law of King Stephen), in October, 1196, at Rouen, Normandy, and had issue:

2 Raymond VII, Count of Toulouse (1197?–1249); he married firstly Sanchia, daughter of Alfonso II, King of Aragon, and had issue. They were divorced in 1241. He married secondly Margaret, daughter of Hugh X de Lusignan, Count of La Marche, by Isabella, widow of King John.

3 Mary or Wilhelmina (*b*.1198); she married Berald of Elbine, Prince of Orange.

4 Richard (or, less probably, Bertrand) (*b.&d*.1199).

After being veiled as a nun on her deathbed, Joan died on 4 September, 1199, at Fontevrault Abbey, France, either in childbirth or of injuries received in a fire; she was buried at Fontevrault, but her tomb was destroyed during the French Revolution.

9 *King John* (◊ page 67).

Henry II also had the following **illegitimate issue**:

By Ikenai, called 'a common prostitute', but probably the daughter of a knight:

1 Geoffrey (1151/3?–1212), Archbishop of York.

2 William Longespée, Earl of Salisbury (before 1170–1226); he may have been the son of Ikenai, but this is doubtful. He married Ela (1196?–1261), daughter of William FitzPatrick, Earl of Salisbury, and had issue. Ela later became Abbess of Lacock in Wiltshire.

3 Peter, called a brother of Geoffrey.

By Alice (*c*.1170–before 1225), daughter of Louis VII, King of France (she was at that time betrothed to Henry's son Richard):

4 Daughter (name not known) (*d*. young).

5 Child (name and sex not known) (*d*. young).

6 Child (name and sex not known) (*d*. young).

7 Child (name and sex not known) (*d*. young).

By Nesta, wife of Sir Ralph Bloet or Blewer:

8 Morgan, Provost of Beverley, Yorkshire, and Bishop-Elect of Durham.

By Alice de Porhoët:

9 Child (name and sex not known) (*b*.1168?); its fate is unknown.

By unknown mothers:

10 Matilda, Abbess of Barking, Essex (*d*. by 1202).

11 Hugh of Wells (?), Bishop of Lincoln (*d*.1235).

12 Richard (?).

HENRY II

He died on 6 July, 1189, at Chinon Castle in France, and was buried in Fontevrault Abbey, France.

He was succeeded by his son Richard.

Richard I

FATHER: *Henry II* (◊ page 59).
MOTHER: *Eleanor of Aquitaine* (◊ page 60, under *Henry II*).
SIBLINGS: (◊page 61, under *Henry II*).

RICHARD I

Known as 'Coeur de Lion' ('the Lionheart'), he was born on 8 September, 1157, at Beaumont Palace, Oxford. He was invested with the duchy of Aquitaine in 1172. He succeeded his father as King of England and Duke of Normandy on 2 September, 1189, being crowned on that day in Westminster Abbey. He was either crowned again, or (less probably) attended a formal crown-wearing on 17 April, 1194, at Winchester Cathedral, following his release from a foreign captivity during the Crusades. Richard I spent only 10 months of his 10 year reign in England.

Richard I married, on 12 May, 1191, at the Chapel of St George, Limassol, Cyprus:

Berengaria

She was the daughter of Sancho VI, King of Navarre, by Beatrice or Sanchia, daughter of Alfonso VII, King of Castile, and she was born *c.*1163/5 in Navarre. She was crowned Queen Consort on 12 May, 1191, in the Chapel of St George, Lemesnos, Limassol, Cyprus. It has often been said that Berengaria never set foot in England, but this was not so: during her widowhood, she paid several visits to the country of which she had been Queen. In 1230, she founded the Abbey of L'Espan in Le Mans, Anjou, and probably took the veil there as a nun, possibly assuming the name in religion of Juliana. The date of her death is not recorded. She was buried in l'Espan Abbey, Le Mans, France; her remains were removed to Le Mans Cathedral in 1821. There was no issue of her marriage to Richard I.

Richard I had the following **illegitimate issue**:

By Joan de St Pol (?):

1 Fulk(?).

By an unknown mother:

2 Philip, Lord of Cognac (*d.* after 1201); he perhaps married Amelia of Cognac.

RICHARD I

He died on 6 April, 1199, at Chalus in the Limousin, France, of the effects of an arrow wound received during the siege of Chalus. He was buried in Fontevrault Abbey, France.

He was succeeded by his brother John.

King John

FATHER: *Henry II* (◊ page 59).
MOTHER: *Eleanor of Aquitaine* (◊ page 60, under *Henry II*).
SIBLINGS: (◊ page 61, under *Henry II*).

KING JOHN

Known as 'Lackland' or 'Softsword', he was born on 24 December, 1166, at Beaumont Palace, Oxford. He was designated King of Ireland in 1177, and created Count of Mortain in 1189. He was styled Earl of Gloucester in right of his first wife from 29 August, 1189. He succeeded his brother Richard I as King of England and Duke of Normandy on 27 May, 1199, being crowned on that day in Westminster Abbey.

John married firstly, on 29 August, 1189, at Marlborough Castle, Wiltshire:

Isabella

Also called Hawise, Joan and Eleanor, she was the daughter of William, Earl of Gloucester, by Hawise, daughter of Robert de Beaumont, 3rd Earl of Leicester, and she was born before 1176. She was never styled Queen of England, but was divorced before 30 August, 1199, on grounds of consanguinity. There was no issue of the marriage. She married secondly Geoffrey de Mandeville, Earl of Essex and Gloucester (and Sussex?) (*d.*1216), between 16 and 26 January, 1214. She married thirdly Hubert de Burgh, Earl of Kent (*d.*1243) around September/October, 1217. Isabella died, probably suddenly, on 14 October or *c.*18 November, 1217, and was buried in Canterbury Cathedral, Kent.

John married secondly, on 24 August, 1200, at Bordeaux Cathedral, Gascony:

Isabella

She was the daughter of Aymer Taillefer, Count of Angoulême, by Alice, daughter of Peter de Courtenay, son of Louis VI, King of France, and she was born in *c.*1187. She was crowned Queen Consort on 8 October, 1200, in Westminster Abbey. She succeeded her father as Countess of Angoulême in the summer of 1202, but was not formally recognised as such until November, 1206. After the death of John, she married secondly Hugh X de Lusignan, Count of La Marche (*d.*1249), between 10 March and 22 May, 1220, and had issue:

1 Hugh XI, Count of La Marche and Angoulême (1221?–1250/60); he married Yolande (*d.*1272), daughter of Peter Mauclerk, Count of Brittany, and had issue.

2 Aymer, Bishop of Winchester (*d.*1260).

3 Guy, Lord of Cognac and Archiac (*d.*1264).

4 Henry, Count of La Marche (*d.*1260); he married Yolande of Penthiévre, and had issue.

5 Geoffrey, Lord of Jarnac (*d.* before 1263); he married Joan, Viscountess of Châtellérhault, and had issue.

6 William, Earl of Pembroke and Wexford (1225/30–1296); he married Joan (*d.*1307), daughter of Warin de Munchesni, Lord of Swanscombe, and had issue.

7 Alice (*d.*1256); she married John de Warenne, 6th Earl of Surrey (1231?–1304), and had issue.

8 Margaret (*d.*1283); she married firstly Raymond VII, Count of

Toulouse (son of Joan, daughter of Henry II). They were divorced in 1245. She married secondly Aymer, Viscount of Thouars, and thirdly Geoffrey, Seigneur de Châteaubriand.

9 Matilda; she married Humphrey de Bohun, 2nd Earl of Hereford and 1st Earl of Essex (1200?–1275), and had issue.

10 Isabella (*d.*1299); she married firstly Geoffrey, Seigneur de Taillebourg, and secondly Amaury, Seigneur de Craon.

11 Agatha or Agnes; she married William de Chauvigny, Seigneur de Châteauroux.

Isabella died on 31 May, 1246, at Fontevrault Abbey, France, where she was buried.

Issue of marriage:

1 *Henry III* (♢ page 74).

2 *Richard*

He was born on 5 January, 1209, at Winchester Castle, Hampshire. He was designated Count of Poitou before 14 August, 1225, and was first so styled on 21 August, 1227. He was created Earl of Cornwall on 30 May, 1227. He renounced the county of Poitou in *c.*December, 1243. He was elected King of Germany (Almayne) and King of the Romans on 13 January, 1257, and was crowned on 17 May, 1257, at Aachen Cathedral, Germany. He died on 2 April, 1272, at Berkhamstead Castle, Herts., and was buried in Hayles Abbey, Gloucs.

Richard had the following illegitimate issue:

By Jeanne de Valletort:

1 Richard de Cornwall (*d.* after 1280); he married and had issue.

By unknown mothers:

2 Walter de Cornwall.

3 Isabella de Cornwall; she married Maurice de Berkeley, and had issue.

Richard married firstly, on 13 or 30 March, 1231, at Fawley Church, Bucks.:

Isabella

She was the daughter of William Marshal, Earl of Pembroke, by Isabella, daughter of Richard FitzGilbert de Clare, 2nd Earl of Pembroke, and she was born on 9 October, 1200, at Pembroke Castle, Wales. She married firstly Gilbert de Clare, Earl of Hertford and Gloucester (1180?–1230) on 9 October, 1214 or 1217, at

Tewkesbury Abbey, Gloucs., and had issue:

1 Amice (1220?–1284); she married firstly Baldwin de Redvers, 6th Earl of Devon (d.1245), and secondly Robert of Guines.

2 Richard, Earl of Hertford and Gloucester (1222?–1262); he married firstly Margaret (Megotta) (d.1237), daughter of Hubert de Burgh, Earl of Kent. He married secondly Matilda (d. by 1289), daughter of John de Lacy, Earl of Lincoln, and had issue.

3 Agnes.

4 Isabella (1226–1254); she married Robert le Brus, Lord of Annandale (1210–1295), and had issue.

5 William (1228–1258).

6 Gilbert (b.1229); a priest (?).

Isabella died on 15 or 17 January, 1240, at Berkhamstead Castle, Herts., of jaundice contracted whilst in childbed, and was buried in Beaulieu Abbey, Hampshire.

Issue of marriage:

(i) *John*

He was born on 31 January or 2 February, 1232, at Marlowe-on-Thames, Bucks., and died on 22/23 September, 1233, at Marlowe-on-Thames, Bucks.; he was buried in Reading Abbey, Berkshire.

(ii) *Isabella*

She was born on 9 September, 1233, at Marlowe-on-Thames, Bucks., and died on 10 October, 1234, at Marlowe-on-Thames, Bucks.; she was buried in Reading Abbey, Berkshire.

(iii) *Henry*

He was born on 2, 4 or 12 November, 1235, at Haughley Castle, Suffolk. He was murdered by the sons of Simon de Montfort on 13 March, 1271, either in the Church of St Lorenzo, or the Church of St Silvestro, or the Cathedral of St Nicholas, Viterbo, Italy, and was buried in Hayles Abbey, Gloucs.

Henry married, on 5 or 15 May, 1269, at Windsor Castle:

Constance

She was the daughter of Gaston VII de Moncada, Viscount of Béarn, by Matilda, daughter of Boson de Mastas, Seigneur of Cognac. She married firstly Alfonso, Infante of Aragon (d.1260). Constance died in c.1299.

(iv) *Nicholas*

He was born on 17 January, 1240, at Berkhamstead Castle, Bucks., and died there the same day. He was buried in Beaulieu Abbey, Hampshire.

Richard married secondly, on 23 November, 1243, at Westminster Abbey:

Sanchia

She was the daughter of Raymond Berenger V, Count of Provence, by Beatrice, daughter of Thomas I, Count of Savoy; her sister Eleanor was the wife of Henry III. Sanchia was born in *c.*1225 at Aix-en-Provence, France. She was crowned Queen of the Romans and Queen of Germany with her husband on 17 May, 1257, at Aachen Cathedral, Germany. She died on 5 or 9 November, 1261, at Berkhamstead Castle, Bucks., and was buried in Hayles Abbey, Gloucs.

Issue of marriage:

(i) *Richard*

He was born in July, 1246, at Wallingford Castle, Berkshire; he died there on 15 August, 1246, and was buried at Grove Mile.

(ii) *Edmund*

He was born on 26 December, 1249, or 5 December, 1250 at Berkhamstead Castle, Bucks., and was invested as Earl of Cornwall on 13 October, 1272. He died on 24/25 September, or 1 October, 1300, at Ashridge Abbey, Herts., and was buried in Hayles Abbey, Gloucs.

Edmund married, on 6 October, 1272, at Ruislip Chapel, Middlesex:

Margaret

She was the daughter of Richard de Clare, Earl of Gloucester and Hertford, by Matilda, daughter of John de Lacy, Earl of Lincoln; her father was the son of Richard of Cornwall's first wife, Isabella Marshal. Margaret was born around 1249/50. She was either divorced or legally separated from her husband in February, 1293. She died in February, 1313 (or perhaps before 16 September, 1312), and was buried in Chertsey Abbey, Surrey. There was no issue of her marriage to Edmund.

(iii) *Richard* (?)

He may have been born in *c.*1252, although he has perhaps

been confused with Richard de Cornwall, Earl Richard's illegitimate son. He was killed in 1296, at the siege of Berwick, by iron shot in his head.

Richard married thirdly, on 16 June, 1269, at the Stiftkirche, Kaiserslauten, Germany:

Beatrice

She was the daughter of Dirk II, Count of Falkenburg, by Joan van Loon. (Her parentage is sometimes erroneously given as either (i) Walram de Fauquemont, Lord of Mountjoye, by Jutta, daughter of Otto, Count of Ravensburg, Westphalia, or (ii) Lothaire, Count of Hostade and Dalem, or (iii) Philip von Falkenstein, Arch-Chamberlain of the Empire. She was no connection of any of these.) Beatrice was born in *c.*1253, probably at Falkenburg Castle, Germany. She died on 17 October, 1277, and was buried in the Church of the Franciscan Friars Minor, Oxford.

3 *Joan* (◊ page 200, under *Alexander II, King of Scotland*).

4 *Isabella*

She was born in 1214. She married Frederick II, King of Sicily, and Emperor of Germany (*d.*1250), on 20 July, 1235, at Worms Cathedral, Germany, and had issue:

1 Jordan (?) (*b.*&*d.*1236).
2 Agnes (*b.*&*d.*1237).
3 Henry, King of Jerusalem (1238–1253).
4 Margaret (1241–1270); she married Albert I, Margrave of Meissen and Landgrave of Thuringia and Misnes (1240–1315), and had issue.

Isabella was crowned Empress of Germany on 20 July, 1235, at Worms Cathedral. She died on 1 or *c.*6 December, 1241, at Foggia, near Naples, Italy, in childbirth, and was buried at Andria, Sicily.

5 *Eleanor*

She was born in 1215. She married firstly William Marshal, 2nd Earl of Pembroke (*c.*1190–1231) (brother of Richard of Cornwall's first wife Isabella) on 23 April, 1224. Notwithstanding a vow of perpetual chastity entered into during her widowhood, she married secondly Simon de Montfort, Earl of Leicester (1208–1265: killed at the Battle of Evesham), on 7 January or 19 February, 1238, at the King's Chapel in the Palace of Westminster, and had issue:

1 Henry (1238–1265: killed at the Battle of Evesham).

2 Simon (1240–1271).

3 Guy, Count of Nola (1243?–1288?); he married Margaret, daughter of Aldobrandino Aldobrandeschi, Count of Anguillara, and had issue.

4 Amaury (d. after 1301); he was a canon at York, but later became a knight.

5 Richard (d. after 1266).

6 Eleanor (1252–1282); she married Llywelyn ap Gruffydd, Prince of Wales (killed 1282), and had issue.

After the death of her husband, Eleanor became a nun at Montargis Abbey in France. She died on 13 April, 1275, at Montargis Abbey, and was buried there.

King John also had the following **illegitimate issue**:

By a woman called Suzanne, or by a sister of William de Warenne, Earl of Surrey (Surrey's sister undoubtedly bore the King a child, but its identity is uncertain):

1 Richard FitzJohn of Dover, Baron of Chilham, Kent (d.1242/53); he married Rohese (d. by 1232), daughter of Fulbert of Dover, and had issue.

By Clementina, wife of Henry Pinel:

2 Joan (d.1237); she married Llywelyn ap Iorwerth, Prince of Wales (1173–1240), and had issue.

By Hawise, perhaps a member of the de Tracy family:

3 Oliver (d.1290); he was killed at the siege of Damietta, and was buried in Westminster Abbey.

By unknown mothers:

4 Osbert Gifford (d. after 1216).

5 Geoffrey FitzRoy (d.1205).

6 John FitzJohn or Courcy (d.1242); a knight; perhaps a clerk at Lincoln.

7 Odo or Eudo FitzRoy (d.1242?).

8 Ivo (confused with Odo?).

9 Henry; he married a minor heiress.

10 Richard, Constable of Wallingford Castle.

11 Matilda (?), Abbess of Barking.

12 Isabella la Blanche (?).

KING JOHN

He died on 18/19 October, 1216, at Newark Castle, Lincs., and was buried in Worcester Cathedral.

He was succeeded by his son Henry.

Henry III

FATHER: *King John* (◊ page 67).
MOTHER: Isabella of Angoulême (◊ page 68, under *King John*).
SIBLINGS: (◊ page 69, under *King John*)

HENRY III

He was born on 1 October, 1207, at Winchester Castle, Hampshire. He succeeded his father as King of England and Duke of Normandy and Aquitaine on 28 October, 1216, being crowned on that day in Gloucester Cathedral with his mother's circlet, the Crown Jewels having been lost in the River Wash. He was again crowned on 17 May, 1220, at Westminster Abbey. In December, 1259, he formally renounced the duchy of Normandy under the terms of the Treaty of Paris.

Henry III married, on 14 January, 1236, at Canterbury Cathedral, Kent:

Eleanor

She was the daughter of Raymond Berenger V, Count of Provence, by Beatrice, daughter of Thomas I, Count of Savoy; her sister Sanchia later married Henry's brother Richard. Eleanor was born between 1217 and 1226, perhaps in *c.*1223, at Aix-en-Provence, France, and was crowned Queen Consort on 19/20 January, 1236, at Westminster Abbey. She became a nun on 7 July, 1284, at Amesbury Abbey, Wiltshire. She died on 24/25 June, 1291, at Amesbury Abbey, and was buried there.

Issue of marriage:

1 *Edward I* (◊ page 82).
2 *Margaret* (◊ page 201, under *Alexander III, King of Scotland*).

3 *Beatrice*

She was born on 25 June, 1242, at Bordeaux, Gascony. She married John de Montfort of Dreux, Earl of Richmond, afterwards John II, Duke of Brittany (1239–1305), on 22 January, 1260, at the Abbey of St Denis, Paris, and had issue:

1 Arthur II, Duke of Brittany (1262–1312); he married firstly Beatrice (1260–1291), daughter of Guy VI, Viscount of Limoges, and had issue. He married secondly Yolande, daughter of Robert IV, Count of Dreux, and widow of Alexander III, King of Scotland, and had issue.

2 John, Earl of Richmond (1266?–1334).

3 Peter, Count of Léon (*d*.1312).

4 Mary (1268–1339); she married Guy de Châtillon, Count of St Pol, and had issue.

5 Eleanor or Alice (1274–1329?); she became a nun at Amesbury Abbey, Wiltshire, and later Abbess of Fontevrault, France.

6 Blanche (*d*.1327); she married Philip, Count of Artois, Lord of Conches and Domfront (*d*.1298), and had issue.

7 Henry (*d*. young, 1284).

Beatrice died on 24 March, 1275, in London; she was perhaps buried in Reading Abbey, Berkshire, and probably removed later to Greyfriars Church, Newgate, London. Her tomb was lost during the Reformation.

4 *Edmund*

Known as 'Crouchback', he was born on 16 January, 1245, in London. He was nominated King of Sicily by the Pope on 7 January, 1254, but deprived of that kingdom in 1263. He was created Earl of Leicester on 26 October, 1265, and Earl of Lancaster on 30 June, 1267. He became Count of Champagne and Brie in right of his second wife in 1276. Edmund died on 5 June, 1296, at Bayonne, and was buried in Westminster Abbey.

Edmund married firstly, on 8/9 April, 1269, in the newly-rebuilt Westminster Abbey:

Aveline

She was the daughter of William de Forz or Fortibus, 6th Earl of Aumale, by Isabella, daughter of Baldwin de Redvers, 7th Earl of Devon. She was born on 20 January, 1259, at Burstwick, Yorkshire, and succeeded her brother as Countess of Aumale before 6 April,

1269. She died on 10 November, 1274, at Stockwell, Surrey, and was buried in Westminster Abbey; hers was the first tomb in the new church. There was no issue of her marriage to Edmund.

Edmund married secondly, in January (before 3 February), 1276, or between 27 July and 29 October, 1276 (although no evidence exists as to where):

Blanche

She was the daughter of Robert I, Count of Artois, by Matilda, daughter of Henry II, Duke of Brabant, and she was born around *c.*1245/50. She married firstly Henry I, King of Navarre and Count of Champagne (*d.*1274), in 1269, and had issue:

1 Joan, Queen of Navarre (1273–1305); she married Philip IV, King of France (1268–1314), and had issue, including Isabella, wife of Edward II.

2 Theobald (*d.*young).

Blanche died on 2 May, 1302, in Paris, and was probably buried in the Minoresses Convent, Aldgate, London.

Issue of marriage:

(i) *Thomas*

He was born around 1277/80. He became Earl of Lincoln in right of his wife on or before 28 October, 1294. He succeeded his father as Earl of Lancaster and Leicester on 8 September, 1298. He was styled Earl Ferrers (Derby) from 1301. He renounced the earldom of Lincoln when he divorced his wife in *c.*1318. Thomas was executed on 22 March, 1322, at Pontefract, Yorkshire, by order of Edward II. He was buried in the Priory of St John at Pontefract.

Thomas married, on or before 28 October, 1294 (?), or perhaps as late as *c.*1310 (although no record exists as to where):

Alice

She was the daughter of Henry de Lacy, 3rd Earl of Lincoln, by Margaret, daughter of Sir William Longespée of Amesbury, Wiltshire, a descendant of Henry II. Alice was born on 25 December, 1281, probably at Denbigh Castle, Denbighshire, and succeeded her father as Countess of Lincoln on 5 February, 1311; she succeeded her mother as Countess of Salisbury before 20 September, 1311. Lancaster divorced her in *c.*1318 on account of her adultery with the Earl of Surrey's squire, Sir Eubulo Lestraunge, whom she married as her second husband before 10 November, 1324. Eubulo died in 1335. Alice married thirdly Hugh de Freyne, Baron Freyne (*d.*1336/7), before 23 March, 1336. She died on 2 October, 1348, and was buried in Barlings Abbey, Birling, Kent. She had no issue from any of her marriages.

(ii) *Henry*

He was born in *c.*1281 at Grosmont Castle, Monmouthshire. He was restored to the earldom of Leicester on 29 March, 1324, two years after his brother's execution for treason, and styled Earl of Lancaster from 26 October, 1326, being restored formally to that earldom on 3 February, 1327. He succeeded his brother John as Lord of Beaufort and Nogent in France in 1336 (?). Henry died on 22 September, 1345, at Leicester, and was buried in Newark Abbey, Leicester.

Henry married, before 2 March, 1297 (although no evidence exists as to where):

Matilda

She was the daughter of Sir Patrick de Chaworth of Kidwelly, by Isabella, daughter of William de Beauchamp, 1st Earl of Warwick. She was born in 1282 or 1288, and died before 3 December, 1322, being buried at Mottisfont Priory.

Issue of marriage:

(a) *Henry*

He was born between 1299 and 1314 at Grosmont Castle, Monmouthshire. He was created Earl of Derby on 16 March, 1337, and succeeded his father as Earl of Lancaster, Earl of Leicester and Lord of Beaufort and Nogent on 22 September, 1345. He was made a Knight of the Garter in 1348, created Earl of Lincoln on 20 August, 1349, and created Duke of Lancaster on 6 March, 1351. He was created Earl of Moray on 5 April, 1359, but never so styled. Henry died on 23/24 March, 1361, at Leicester Castle of the Black Death (bubonic plague), and was buried in Newark Abbey, Leicester.

Henry married, in *c.*1334/7 (although no record exists as to where):

Isabella

She was the daughter of Henry, 1st Baron de Beaumont and Earl of Buchan, by Alice, daughter of Sir Alexander Comyn. She died in 1361 at Leicester of the Black Death (bubonic plague), and was buried in Newark Abbey, Leicester.

Issue of marriage:

(i) *Matilda*

She was born on 4 April, *c.*1339 or 1341. She married firstly Ralph de Stafford (*d.*1347/9) on 1 November, 1344. She married secondly William V, Duke of Bavaria, Count of Holland, Hainault and Zeeland (1327–1389), in 1352 at the King's Chapel in the Palace of Westminster. She succeeded her father as Countess of Leicester on 23 March, 1361, but died on 10 April, 1362, in England, of the Black Death (bubonic plague) (although some sources say she was poisoned).

(ii) *Blanche*

She married John of Gaunt, Duke of Lancaster (◊ page 100, under Edward III).

(b) *Blanche*

She was born in *c.*1305, and married Thomas Wake, 2nd Baron Wake of Liddell (*d.*1349) before 9 October, 1316. She died on 10 July, 1380, and was buried in the Church of the Friars Minor, Stamford, Lincs.

(c) *Matilda*

She was born in *c.*1310. She married firstly William de Burgh, 3rd Earl of Ulster (1312–1333), after 1 May, 1327 (date of dispensation), and before 1330, and had issue:

1 Elizabeth; she married Lionel of Antwerp, Duke of Clarence (◊ page 96, under Edward III).

Matilda married secondly Ralph de Ufford (*d.*1346) before 8 August, 1343, and had issue:

2 Matilda (*d.*1413); she married Thomas de Vere, 8th Earl of Oxford (1336?–1371), and had issue.

Matilda became an Augustinian Canoness at Campsey Abbey, Suffolk (?), between 8 August, 1347, and 25 April,

1348; she transferred to the Poor Clares at Bruisyard Abbey, Suffolk (?), in 1364. She died before 5 May, 1377, at Campsey Abbey, Suffolk (?), and was buried in Bruisyard Abbey, Suffolk.

(d) *Joan*

She was born in *c.*1312. She married John, 3rd Baron Mowbray, Lord of Axholme, Bramber and Gower (1310–1361), after 28 February, 1327, and had issue:

1 John, 4th Baron Mowbray (1340–killed 1368); he married Elizabeth (1338–by 1368), daughter of John, 4th Baron de Segrave, by Margaret, Duchess of Norfolk (◊ page 87, under Edward I), and had issue.

2 Blanche (*d.*1409); she either married John de Segrave of Folkestone (*d.*1349) and had issue, or married firstly Robert, Baron Bertram of Bothall (*d.*1363/4), secondly Thomas, Baron Poynings (*d.*1375), thirdly Sir John Worth (*d.*1391) and fourthly Sir John Wiltshire.

3 Eleanor (*d.c.*1387); she married firstly Roger, Baron de la Warre (1326–1370), and secondly Sir Lewis de Clifford (*d.*1404).

Joan died on 7 July, 1345 (?) or 1349 (?), and was buried in Byland Abbey, Yorkshire.

(e) *Isabella*

She was born in *c.*1317, and perhaps married Henry de la Dale in her youth. She became a nun at Amesbury Abbey, Wiltshire, before 6 April, 1337, and was elected Prioress of Amesbury before 23 March, 1344. She died after 1 February, 1347.

(f) *Eleanor*

She was born in *c.*1318. She married firstly John, 2nd Baron de Beaumont (*d.*1342), before June, 1337, and had issue:

1 Henry, 3rd Baron de Beaumont (1340–1369); he married Margaret (*d.*1398), daughter of John de Vere, 7th Earl of Oxford, and had issue.

2 Joan (*d.* after 1400).

Eleanor married secondly Richard FitzAlan, 10th Earl of Arundel (1306/13–1376), on 5 February, 1345, at Ditton

Church, Stoke Poges, Bucks., and had issue:

3 Edmund (*c*.1346–*c*.1366).

4 Joan (*c*.1347–1419); she married Humphrey de Bohun, Earl of Hereford, Essex and Northampton (1342–1373), and had issue, including Mary, wife of Henry IV, and Eleanor, wife of Thomas, Duke of Gloucester (◊ page 115, under Edward III).

5 Richard, 11th Earl of Arundel (*c*.1348–executed 1397); he married firstly Elizabeth (*d*.1385), daughter of William de Bohun, Earl of Northampton, and had issue, and secondly Philippa Mortimer (◊ page 98, under Edward III).

6 Alice (*c*.1350–1414/16); she married Thomas Holland, 1st Earl of Kent (*c*.1355–1397), son of Joan, Princess of Wales (◊ page 93, under Edward III), and had issue, including Eleanor, Countess of March (◊ page 97, under Edward III).

7 John, Baron of Arundel (*c*.1351–drowned 1379); he married Eleanor (1346?–1405), daughter of Sir John Maltravers, and had issue.

8 Thomas, Archbishop of Canterbury (1353–1414).

9 Mary.

10 Eleanor (*c*.1354/6–before 1366).

Eleanor died on 11 January, 1372, at Arundel Castle, Sussex, and was buried in Lewes Priory, Sussex.

(g) *Mary*

She was born around 1320/21. She married firstly Henry Percy, 3rd Baron of Alnwick (1322?–1368), in *c*.September, 1334, at Tutbury Castle, and had issue:

1 Henry, 1st Earl of Northumberland (1341–1408); he married Matilda (*d*.1372), daughter of Ralph, Baron Neville of Raby, and had issue. He married secondly Matilda (*d*.1398), daughter of Thomas, Baron Lucy of Cockermouth.

2 Thomas, Earl of Worcester (1344?–executed 1403). Had illegitimate issue.

3 Mary (*b*.1360); she married John, Baron Ros of Helmsley.

Mary died on 1/2 September, 1362, and was buried at Alnwick, Northumberland.

Henry, Earl of Lancaster, married secondly, after 1322 (although no evidence exists as to where):
Alice
She was the daughter of John de Joinville, Seneschal of Champagne, by Alice, daughter of Gautier, Seigneur de Risnel. She married firstly John, Seigneur of Arcis-sur-Aube and Chacenay (*d.* by 1307). Nothing more is known of her.

(iii) *John*
He was born before May, 1286, and became Lord of Beaufort and Nogent-Lartauld on the death of his mother in May, 1302. He died unmarried in *c.*1327 (?) or 1336 (certainly by 1337) in France.

(iv) *Mary*
No dates are recorded. She died young, in France.

5 *Richard*
He was born in *c.*1247, and died before 1256. He was buried in Westminster Abbey.

6 *John*
He was born in *c.*1250 at Windsor Castle, and died before 1256. He was buried in Westminster Abbey.

7 *William*
He was born in *c.*1250/51, and died either at birth or in 1256. He was buried in the New Church of the Knights Templars, Fleet Street, London.

8 *Katherine*
She was born on 25 November, 1252/3, at the Palace of Westminster. A mute child, she died on 3 May, 1257, at Windsor Castle, and was buried in Westminster Abbey.

9 *Henry*
No dates are recorded. He died young, and was buried in Westminster Abbey.

HENRY III
He died on 16 November, 1272, at the Palace of Westminster, and was buried in Westminster Abbey.

He was succeeded by his son Edward.

Edward I

FATHER: *Henry III* (◊ page 74).
MOTHER: *Eleanor of Provence* (◊ page 74, under *Henry III*).
SIBLINGS: (◊ page 74 under *Henry III*).

EDWARD I
Known as 'Longshanks' and 'the Lawgiver', he was born on 17/18 June, 1239, at the Palace of Westminster. He was created Duke of Gascony in 1254, and Earl of Chester on 14 February, 1254. He resigned the earldom of Chester on 24 December, 1264, but was restored to it on 4 August, 1265. He succeeded his father as King of England on 20 November, 1272, and was crowned on 19 August, 1274, at Westminster Abbey.

Edward I married firstly, between 13 and 31 October, 1254, at the Abbey of Las Huelgas, Burgos, Castile:

Eleanor

She was the daughter of Ferdinand III, King of Castile, by Joan, daughter of Simon of Dammartin, Count of Ponthieu and Aumale. Eleanor was born around 1244/5 in Castile. She was crowned Queen Consort on 19 August, 1274, at Westminster Abbey. She succeeded her mother as Countess of Ponthieu and Montreuil in March, 1279. Eleanor died on 28 November, 1290, at the manor of Harby, Notts., of a fever, and was buried in Westminster Abbey.

Issue of marriage:

1 *Eleanor*

She was born *c.*17 June, 1264 (or possibly as late as 1269, although the Issue Rolls of 1302 describe her as Edward's eldest daughter), at Windsor Castle. She married firstly Alfonso III, King of Aragon (*d.*1291), by proxy on 15 August, 1290, at Westminster Abbey. The marriage was not consummated because of the bridegroom's early death. Eleanor married secondly Henry III, Count of Bar (*d.*1302), on 20 September, 1293, at Bristol, and had issue:

1 Edward I, Count of Bar (1294–1337); he drowned in a shipwreck. He married Mary (1298–c.1310), daughter of Robert, Duke of Burgundy, and had issue.

2 Joan (1295–1361); she married John de Warenne, Earl of Surrey (1286–1347), and had issue. She was divorced in 1315.

3 Eleanor (?); she is said to have married Llywelyn ap Owen of Deheubarth, and to have had issue, but this is doubtful.

Eleanor died on 12 October, 1298, at Ghent in Flanders, and was buried in Westminster Abbey.

2 *Joan*

She was born in the summer of 1265, either in Paris or perhaps at Abbeville, Ponthieu. She died before 7 September, 1265, in France, and was buried in Westminster Abbey.

3 *John*

He was born on 10 June or 10 July, 1266, either at Windsor Castle, or at Kenilworth Castle, Warwickshire, or at Winchester. He died on 1 or 3 August, 1271/2, at the Palace of Westminster, and was buried in Westminster Abbey.

4 *Henry*

He was born on 13 July, 1267/8, at Windsor Castle. He died on 14 October, 1274, either at Merton, Surrey, or at Guildford Castle, Surrey, and was buried in Westminster Abbey.

5 *Alice*

She is said to have been born at Woodstock Palace, Oxon., but the date of her birth is unknown. The Harleian MSS. say she died at the age of 12. Some historians have identified her with the child born to the King and Queen in March, 1279, but this cannot be correct, as that infant's funeral at Westminster Abbey took place during the same year (⌕ Isabella, below).

6 *Juliana* or *Katherine*

She was born in 1271 at Acre, Palestine, and died there on 28 May or 5 September, 1271. She is perhaps the daughter who is buried in the Church of the Friars Preachers, Bordeaux, Gascony.

7 *Joan*

She was born in Spring, 1272, at Acre, Palestine. She married firstly Gilbert de Clare, 3rd Earl of Gloucester and 7th Earl of Hertford (1243–1295), on 30 April, 1290, at Westminster Abbey, and had issue:

1 Gilbert, Earl of Gloucester and Hertford (1291–1314: killed at the Battle of Bannockburn); he married Matilda (d.1320), daughter of Richard de Burgh, Earl of Ulster, and had issue.

2 Eleanor (1292–1337); she married firstly Hugh le Despenser (executed 1326), and had issue. She married secondly Sir William la Zouche de Mortimer of Ashby, Leics. (d.1337).

3 Margaret (1293–1342); she married firstly Piers Gaveston, Earl of Cornwall (1284?–executed 1312), and had issue. She married secondly Hugh de Audley, Earl of Gloucester (1289?–1347), and had issue.

4 Elizabeth (1295–1360); she married firstly John de Burgh (d.1313), and had issue. She married secondly Sir Theobald de Verdon of Alton, Staffs. (1278–1316), and had issue. She married thirdly Roger, Baron d'Amory (d.1322), and had issue.

Joan married secondly Ralph, 1st Baron de Monthermer, Earl of Gloucester and Earl of Atholl (d.1325), before July, 1297, and had issue:

5 Thomas, 2nd Baron Monthermer (1301–1340: killed at the Battle of Sluys); he married Margaret Teyes (d.1349), and had issue.

6 Edward, 3rd Baron Monthermer (1304–1340).

7 Mary (1298–after 1371); she married Duncan, 10th Earl of Fife (1285–1353), and had issue.

8 Joan (b.1299); a nun at Amesbury Abbey, Wilts.

Joan died on 23 April, 1307, at her manor of Clare, Suffolk, and was buried in the Priory Church of the Austin Friars, Clare, Suffolk.

8 Alfonso

He was born on 24 November, 1273, either at Bayonne or at Bordeaux, Gascony, or in Maine. He was perhaps designated Earl of Chester in 1284. He died on 14 or 19 August, 1284, at Windsor Castle, and was buried in Westminster Abbey.

9 Margaret

She was born on 11 September, 1275, at Windsor Castle. She married John II 'the Peaceful', Duke of Brabant (d.1312), on 8 July, 1290, at Westminster Abbey, and had issue:

1 John III 'the Triumphant', Duke of Brabant (1300–1355); he married Mary (d.1335), daughter of Louis of France, Count of Evreux, and had issue.

Margaret died in 1318, and was buried in the Collegiate Church of St Gudule, Brussels.

10 *Berengaria* or *Berenice*

She was born in 1276 at Kempton Palace, Surrey, and died between 1276 and 1279. She was buried in Westminster Abbey.

11 *Mary*

She was born on 11 March or 22 April, 1278, at Windsor Castle. She entered Amesbury Abbey, Wiltshire, as a novice in 1284, being there professed as a nun on 15 August, 1285. She died before 8 July, 1332, at Amesbury Abbey, where she was buried.

12 *Isabella*

She was born on 12 March, 1279, probably at Woodstock Palace, Oxon., or at Windsor Castle, or at Marlborough Castle, Wiltshire. She died in 1279, and was buried in Westminster Abbey.

13 *Elizabeth*

She was born in August, 1282, at Rhuddlan Castle, Flintshire, Wales. She married firstly John I, Count of Holland and Zeeland (*d.*1299), on 18 January, 1296/7, at Ipswich Priory Church, Suffolk. She married secondly Humphrey de Bohun, 4th Earl of Hereford and Essex (1276?–1322), on 14 November, 1302, at Westminster Abbey, and had issue:

1 Hugh or Humphrey (1303?–1305).

2 Eleanor (1304–1363); she married firstly James Butler, 1st Earl of Ormonde (1305?–1338), and had issue. She married secondly Sir Thomas de Dagworth (1276–murdered 1350), and had issue.

3 Mary or Margaret (*b.&d.*1305).

4 John, Earl of Hereford and Essex (1306–1336); he married firstly Alice, daughter of Edmund FitzAlan, Earl of Arundel, and had issue, and secondly Margaret (*d.* after 1347), daughter of Ralph, Lord Bassett of Drayton.

5 Humphrey, Earl of Hereford and Essex (1309–1361).

6 William, Earl of Northampton (1310/12–1360); he married Elizabeth (1313–1356), daughter of Bartholemew de Badlesmere, and had issue.

7 Edward, twin of William (1310/12–drowned 1334); he married Margaret (*d.*1341), daughter of William, Baron de Ros.

8 Edmund; he married Matilda, daughter of Nicholas de Segrave,

Baron of Stowe.

9 Eneas (1313/15–before 1343).

10 Margaret (*d.*1391); she married Hugh de Courtenay, Earl of Devon (1303–1377), and had issue.

11 Isabella (*b.*&*d.*1316).

Elizabeth died on *c.*5 May, 1316 at Quendon, Essex, in childbirth, and was buried in Walden Abbey, Essex.

14 *Edward II* (◊ page 90).

15 *Beatrice*

She was born after August, 1286, either in Gascony or in Aquitaine. She died young.

16 *Blanche*

She was born in 1289/90, and died young.

Edward I married secondly, on 8 or 10 September, 1299, at Canterbury Cathedral, Kent:

Margaret

She was the daughter of Philip III, King of France, by Mary, daughter of Henry III, Duke of Brabant, and she was born around 1279/82 in Paris. Margaret was never crowned. She died on 14 February, 1317/18, at Marlborough Castle, Wiltshire, and was buried in Greyfriars Church, Newgate, London. Her tomb was lost during the Reformation.

Issue of marriage:

1 *Thomas*

He was born on 1 June, 1300, at Brotherton, Yorkshire, and was created Earl of Norfolk on 16 December, 1312. He died between 4 August and 20 September, 1338, and was buried in the Abbey of Bury St Edmunds, Suffolk.

Thomas married firstly, between *c.*1316 and 1320 (although no evidence exists as to where):

Alice

She was the daughter of Sir Roger Halys or Hales of Harwich, Essex. She died after 8 May, 1326, and before 1330.

Issue of marriage:

(i) *Edward*

He was born in *c.*1319/20, and died before 13 September, 1337, perhaps in 1332 (?).

Edward married, in May/June, 1328 (although no evidence

exists as to where):

Beatrice

She was the daughter of Roger Mortimer, Earl of March, by Joan, daughter of Peter de Genville. After the death of Edward, she married secondly Thomas de Braose, Lord Brewes, in *c*.1334 (before 13 September, 1337), and had issue:

1 Beatrice; she married William de Say, Baron Say (1340–1375), and had issue.
2 John, a knight (*d*.1367); he married Elizabeth de Montacute.
3 Thomas, a knight (*d*.1395).
4 Peter.
5 Elizabeth.
6 Joan.

Beatrice died on 16 October, 1383.

(ii) *Margaret*

Known as 'Margaret Marshal', as the Dukes of Norfolk have always held the office of Earl Marshal of England, she was born around 1320/22. She married firstly John de Segrave, 4th Baron de Segrave (1306 or 1315–1353), after 3 March, 1327, and probably in 1337/8, and had issue:

1 Elizabeth (1338–1375/6); she married John, 4th Baron Mowbray of Axholme, Lincs. (1340–killed 1368), and had issue.
2 Anne, Abbess of Barking (*d.c*.1377).

Margaret succeeded her father as Countess of Norfolk between 4 August and 20 September, 1338. She married secondly Walter, 1st Baron de Mauny or Manny (*d*.1372), before 30 May, 1354, and had issue:

3 Thomas (drowned in infancy before 1371/2).
4 Anne (1354–1384); she married John Hastings, 2nd Earl of Pembroke (1347–1375), who had married previously Margaret, daughter of Edward III, and had issue.

Margaret was created Duchess of Norfolk for life on 29 September, 1397. She died on 24 March, 1399/1400, and was buried either in the Charterhouse, London, or in Greyfriars Church, Newgate, London.

(iii) *Alice*

She was born in *c*.1324. She married Edward de Montacute,

1st Baron Montacute (c.1304–1361), before 16 January, 1339, and possibly before 29 August, 1338, and had issue:

1 Elizabeth (b.1344): she married either Walter de Ufford or Sir John de Braose (d.1367)
2 Margaret (c.1347–before 1351/2).
3 Joan (1349–1375); she married William de Ufford, 2nd Earl of Suffolk (1339?–1382), and had issue.
4 Matilda (c.1350–1394); a nun, later Abbess of Barking.

Alice died probably between 14 November, 1351, and 30 January, 1352 (certainly before 16 November, 1361), at Bungay, Suffolk, of wounds received as a result of an assault by her husband.

Thomas married secondly, in c.1328 (although no evidence exists as to where):

Mary

She was the daughter of Peter de Braose, and married firstly Ralph, Baron Cobham of Norfolk (d.1326), by whom she had issue:

1 John (1324–after 1378), Baron Cobham.

Mary died on 9 June, 1362 (or between 17 April, 1361, and 20 June, 1362).

Issue of marriage:

(i) *John*

No dates are recorded. He was a monk at Ely Abbey, Cambs.

2 Edmund

He was born on 5 August, 1301, at Woodstock Palace, Oxon., and was created Earl of Kent on 28 July, 1321. He was probably styled Earl of Arundel as well, as he held the castle and honour of Arundel, but he was never formally so created. He was executed for supporting his brother, the deposed Edward II, by order of the Regents Mortimer and Queen Isabella, on 19 March, 1330, outside Winchester Castle, and he was buried in the Church of the Dominican Friars, Winchester. His remains were later removed to Westminster Abbey.

Edmund married, in December, 1325 (after 6 October, date of dispensation) (although no record exists as to where):

Margaret

She was the daughter of John Wake, 1st Baron Wake of Liddell, by Joan, daughter either of William de Fenes or of John FitzBernard of

Kingsdown, Kent. Margaret was born around c.1299/1300. She married firstly John Comyn, Lord of Badenoch (killed 1314), and had issue:

1 Aymer (d.young before 1316).

Margaret succeeded her brother as Baroness Wake of Liddell on 30/31 May, 1349, being first so styled on 20 August, 1349. She died on 29 September, 1349, of the Black Death.

Issue of marriage:

 (i) *Edmund*

He was born in c.1326, and was restored to the earldom of Kent, which had been forfeited by his father, on 7 December, 1330. He died before 5 October, 1331, or on 5 January, 1333 (?).

 (ii) *Margaret*

She was born in 1327. She married Amanco, Seigneur d'Albret of Gascony, and died before 1352.

(iii) *Joan*

She married Edward of Woodstock, Prince of Wales (◊ page 93, under Edward III).

(iv) *John*

He was born on 7 April, 1330, at Arundel Castle, Sussex, his father's posthumous child. He succeeded his mother as Baron Wake of Liddell on 29 September, 1349. He was created Earl of Kent on 10 April, 1351. He died on 26/27 December, 1352, and was buried in the Church of the Greyfriars, Winchester, Hants.

John married, after 3 April, 1348 (date of dispensation) (although no evidence exists as to where):

Elizabeth

She was the daughter of William V, Margrave or Duke of Juliers, by Joan, daughter of William V, Count of Hainault and Holland, and sister of Philippa, wife of Edward III. After John's death, Elizabeth married secondly Sir Eustace d'Aubédcicourt (d.1372/3) on 29 September, 1360, at Wingham Church, Kent, and had issue:

1 Sanchez.

2 William.

After Eustace died, Elizabeth became a nun at Waverley Abbey. She died on 6 June, 1411, and was buried in the Church of the

Greyfriars, Winchester, Hants. There was no issue of her first marriage.

Note: There is no contemporary evidence that the marriage of Edmund, Earl of Kent, and Margaret Wake produced two other sons, Robert and Thomas, who are mentioned in later sources.

3 Eleanor

She was born on 4 May, 1306, at Winchester. She died in 1311 at Amesbury Abbey, Wilts., and was buried in Beaulieu Abbey, Hants.

Edward I is reputed to have had the following illegitimate issue (according to the Hayles Abbey Chronicle), and while this is possible, it is still subject to some doubt:

By an unknown mother,

1 John Botetourt, Lord of Mendlesham, Suffolk (*c.*1265–1324); he married Matilda, daughter of Thomas FitzOates, and had issue.

EDWARD I

He died on 7 July, 1307, at Burgh-on-Sands, Northumberland, and was buried in Westminster Abbey.

He was succeeded by his son Edward.

Edward II

FATHER: *Edward I* (◊ page 82).
MOTHER: *Eleanor of Castile* (◊ page 82, under *Edward I*).
SIBLINGS: (◊ page 82, under *Edward I*).

EDWARD II

He was born on 25 April, 1284, at Caernarvon Castle, Wales. He succeeded his mother as Count of Ponthieu and Montreuil on 28 November, 1290. He was created and invested as Earl of Chester and Prince of Wales on 7 February, 1301; he was the first English Prince of Wales, and since 1301 the title has usually been granted to the eldest son of the sovereign. The story of Edward being presented by his father to the Welsh on a shield, just after his birth in 1284, is a picturesque fabrication. He was created Duke of Aquitaine in May, 1306. He succeeded his father as King of England on 8 July, 1307, and was crowned on 24/25 February, 1308, in Westminster Abbey.

Edward II was deposed by an illegally-convened 'Parliament' on 20 January, 1327, and formally abdicated in favour of his son Edward on 25 January, 1327.

Edward II married, on 25 or 28 January, 1308, at Boulogne Cathedral, France:

Isabella

She was the daughter of Philip IV, King of France, by Joan I, Queen of Navarre, daughter of Blanche of Artois (◊ page 76, under Henry III). Isabella was born around 1292/5 in Paris. She was crowned Queen Consort on 24/25 February, 1308, in Westminster Abbey. She was instrumental in plotting the deposition and murder of her husband, and after his abdication she shared the Regency with her lover, Roger Mortimer, Earl of March. When Edward III attained his majority in 1330, the regents were overthrown. Mortimer was executed, and Isabella allowed an honourable retirement from public life. She died on 22 August, 1358, either at Castle Rising, Norfolk, or at Hertford Castle, and was buried in Greyfriars Church, Newgate, London. Her tomb was lost during the Reformation.

Issue of marriage:

1 *Edward III* (◊ page 92).

2 *John*

He was born on *c.*15 or 25 August, 1316, at Eltham Palace, Kent, and was created Earl of Cornwall between 16 and 31 October, 1328. He died on 13 September, 1336, at Perth, Scotland, and was buried in Westminster Abbey.

3 *Eleanor*

She was born on 18 June, 1318, at Woodstock Palace, Oxon.; she married Reginald II, Count of Gueldres and Zutphen (*d.*1343), in May, 1332, at Nimeguen, Gueldres, and had issue:

1 Reginald III, Count of Gueldres (1334–1371); he married Mary (*d.*1398), daughter of John III, Duke of Brabant.

2 Edward, Count of Gueldres (1336–1371); he married Katherine (*d.*1401), daughter of Albert, Duke of Holland and Hainault.

Eleanor may also have been the mother of the following, although it is more probable that they were the children of Reginald's first wife, Sophia of Malines (*d.*1329):

3 Margaret (*d.*1344).

4 Matilda (*d.*1380); she married firstly Godfrey, Count of Hennenburg, and secondly John, Duke of Cleves; she married thirdly John, Count of Châtillon, Blois.

5 Mary (*d.*1405); she married William VI, Duke of Juliers (*d.*1393), and had issue.

6 Isabella, Abbess of Graventhal.

Eleanor died on 22 April, 1355, at Deventer Abbey, Gueldres, where she was buried.

4 *Joan* (◊ page 212, under *David II of Scotland*).

Edward II also had the following **illegitimate issue:**

By an unknown mother:

1 Adam (*c.*1310–after 1322).

EDWARD II

He was murdered on 21 September, 1327, at Berkeley Castle, Gloucs., by having a red-hot spit thrust into his bowels; this was probably done on the orders of the Regent, Roger Mortimer, Earl of March, with the collusion of Queen Isabella, who was Mortimer's mistress. Edward was buried in Gloucester Cathedral.

He was succeeded by his son Edward, in whose favour he had abdicated on 25 January, 1327.

Edward III

FATHER: *Edward II* (◊ page 90).
MOTHER: *Isabella of France* (◊ page 91, under *Edward II*).
SIBLINGS: (◊ page 91, under *Edward II*).

EDWARD III

He was born on 13 November, 1312, at Windsor Castle. He was

created Earl of Chester on 24 November (?), 1312, and Count of Ponthieu and Montreuil on 2 September, 1325. He was created Duke of Aquitaine on 10 September, 1325. He succeeded his father as King of England on 25 January, 1327, Edward II having abdicated in favour of his son on that day. Edward III was crowned on 1 February, 1327, in Westminster Abbey. On 20 October, 1330, he assumed personal rule after overthrowing the regents, his mother Queen Isabella and her lover Roger Mortimer, Earl of March. He formally assumed the title King of France, which he claimed through his mother, in January, 1340, thus starting the Hundred Years War.

Edward III married, on 24 January, 1328, at York Minster:
Philippa

She was the daughter of William V 'the Good', Count of Hainault and Holland, by Joan, daughter of Charles of France, Count of Valois, and she was born in *c.*1313/14 either at Valenciennes or at Mons in Flanders. She was crowned on 2 or 20 February, 1328, at Westminster Abbey, and again on 4 March, 1330, also at Westminster Abbey. She died on 15 August, 1369, at Windsor Castle, of a dropsy-like illness, and was buried in Westminster Abbey.

Issue of marriage:

1 *Edward*

Known from the 16th century onwards as 'the Black Prince' (because of the colour of his armour), he was born on 15 June, 1330, at Woodstock Palace, Oxon. He was created Earl of Chester on 18 May, 1333, Duke of Cornwall on 3 March, 1337, and Prince of Wales on 12 May, 1343, being invested with the principality on the same day. He was made a Knight of the Garter when his father first founded the Order in 1348. He was created Prince of Aquitaine on 19 July, 1362, and was created Lord of Biscay and Castro Urdiales in Castile by Peter I, King of Castile, on 23 September, 1366. He resigned the principality of Aquitaine because of ill-health before 28 December, 1375. He died on 8 June, 1376, at the Palace of Westminster, and was buried in Canterbury Cathedral, Kent.

Edward married, on 10/11 October, 1361, probably at St Stephen's Chapel in the Palace of Westminster, or – less probably – at Canterbury Cathedral or at Windsor Castle:
Joan

She was the daughter of Edmund, Earl of Kent, son of Edward I, by

Margaret Wake, and she was born on 29 September, 1328. She married firstly Sir Thomas Holland or Holand of Broughton, Bucks. (d.1360), in c.1339 or in the Spring of 1340, according to her testimony of 1347. She then married secondly, and bigamously, William de Montacute, Earl of Salisbury (1328–1397), in c.1340/1 or 1346 (?) (probably before 10 February, 1341, and certainly by 15 October, 1348). Her marriage to Montacute was annulled by Papal Bull on 13 November, 1349, whilst her marriage to Holland was at the same time pronounced valid. The Pope accordingly ordered Joan to return to Holland and cohabit with him as his lawful wife, which she did around 1349, and had issue:

1 Edmund (b. before 1352; d. young).

2 Thomas, Earl of Kent (c.1355–1397); he married Alice (c.1350–1414/16), daughter of Richard FitzAlan, 10th Earl of Arundel and a descendant of Henry III, and had issue.

3 Joan (c.1356–1384); she married John de Montfort IV, Duke of Brittany (1339–1399) (who afterwards married Joan, later the wife of Henry IV).

4 John, Duke of Exeter (c.1358–executed 1400); he married Elizabeth, daughter of John of Gaunt, Duke of Lancaster (◊ page 101, below), and had issue.

5 Matilda (c.1359–1391); she married firstly Sir Hugh de Courtenay (d.1377), and secondly Waleran of Luxembourg, Count of St Pol and Ligny (d.1415), and had issue by her second husband.

Joan succeeded her brother John (◊ page 89, under Edward I) as Baroness Wake of Liddell and Countess of Kent on 26/27 December, 1352, and was confirmed in her new titles on 22 February, 1353. She was made a Lady of the Garter in 1378. She died on 7, 8 or 21 August, 1385, at Wallingford Castle, Berks., and was buried in Greyfriars Church, Stamford, Lincs. It is likely that her remains were shortly afterwards removed to London, although the site of their final resting place is not recorded.

Issue of marriage:

(i) *Edward*

He was born on 27 January, 1365, at Angoulême in France, and died in January, 1371/2, at Bordeaux, Gascony. He was buried at Bordeaux, but later removed to the Church of the Austin

Friars in London.

(ii) *Richard II* (◊ page 118).

Edward also had the following illegitimate issue:

By Edith de Willesford (*d.* after 1385):

1 Sir Roger de Clarendon (1345/60–executed 1402); he married Margaret (*d.*1382), daughter of John Fleming, Baron de la Roche.

By unknown mothers:

2 Edward (*b.c.*1349; *d.* young).

3 Sir John Sounders, or John de Galeis (Calais?).

2 *Isabella*

She was probably born in March (her mother was churched before 30 April), 1332, at Woodstock Palace, Oxon. She married Enguerrand II, Lord of Coucy, Count of Soissons and Earl of Bedford (1339?–1397), on 27 July, 1365 at Windsor Castle, and had issue:

1 Mary (1366–1404); she married Henry of Bar, Marquess of Pont-à-Mousson (*d.*1401), and had issue.

2 Philippa (1367–1411); she married Robert de Vere, Earl of Oxford and Duke of Ireland (1362–1392).

Isabella was made a Lady of the Garter in 1376. She died between 17 June and 5 October, 1382, and was buried in Greyfriars Church, Newgate, London.

3 *Joan*

She was probably born in February (certainly before 30 May), 1335, at Woodstock Palace, Oxon., not in the Tower of London as is sometimes stated. She died on 2 September, 1348, at Loremo, Bordeaux, Gascony, of the Black Death (bubonic plague), and was buried either at Loremo, or Bordeaux, or in Bayonne Cathedral, Gascony.

4 *William*

He was born around 1334/6, certainly before 16 February, 1337, at Hatfield, Yorkshire, where he died before 3 March, 1337. He was buried in York Minster.

5 *Lionel*

He was born on 29 November, 1338, at Antwerp in Brabant. He was styled Earl of Ulster in right of his wife from *c.*26 January, 1347. He was made a Knight of the Garter in *c.*April, 1361, and created Duke of Clarence on 13 November, 1362. He died on 17 October, 1368, at Alba, Piedmont, Italy, and was buried at Pavia, Italy. His remains were later removed to Clare Priory, Suffolk.

Lionel married firstly, on 15 August, 1342, in the Tower of London, and again on 9 September, 1342, at Reading Abbey, Berkshire:

Elizabeth

She was the daughter of William de Burgh, Earl of Ulster, by Matilda of Lancaster, a descendant of Henry III, and she was born on 6 July, 1332, probably at Carrickfergus Castle in Ulster. She succeeded her father as Countess of Ulster on 6 June, 1333. She died on 10 December (?), 1363, in Dublin, and was buried at Clare Priory, Suffolk.

Issue of marriage:

(i) *Philippa*

She was born on 16 August, 1355, at Eltham Palace, Kent. She married Edmund Mortimer, 3rd Earl of March (1352–1381) (grandson of the Regent Mortimer – ◊ page 91, under Edward II), after 15 February, 1359, and probably in May, 1368, at the Queen's Chapel, Reading Abbey, Berkshire. Philippa died between 21 November, 1378 (date of Will), and 9 February, 1381, and was buried at Cork in Ireland. Her remains were later removed to Wigmore, Herefordshire.

The House of York would one day base its claim to the throne on its descent from Edward III through Philippa, therefore her issue is included here in full:

(a) *Elizabeth*

She was born on 12 February, 1371, at Usk, Monmouthshire. She married firstly Sir Henry ('Hotspur') Percy (1361–1403: killed at the Battle of Shrewsbury) before 1 May, 1380, and had issue:

1 Henry, 2nd Earl of Northumberland (1394–1455); he married Eleanor (*d.*1472), daughter of Ralph Neville, 1st Earl of Westmorland, and had issue. Eleanor was a granddaughter of John of Gaunt, Duke of Lancaster (◊ page 111, below).

2 Elizabeth (*d.*1436); she married firstly John, 7th Baron Clifford (*d.*1421/2), and had issue, and secondly Ralph

Neville, 2nd Earl of Westmorland (1408–1485), and had issue.

Elizabeth married secondly Thomas, 1st Baron Camoys (*d*.1419), and had issue:

3 Son (name not known); he is said to have died young. Elizabeth died on 20 April, 1417, and was buried at Trotton, Sussex.

(b) *Roger*

He was born on 1 September, 1373, or 11 April, 1374, at Usk, Monmouthshire. He succeeded his mother as Earl of Ulster between 21 November, 1378, and 9 February, 1381, and his father as Earl of March on 27 December, 1381. He was killed on 20 July, 1398, at Kenlis during a skirmish with the Irish, and was buried at Wigmore, Herefordshire.

Roger married, on *c*.7 October, 1388 (although no record exists as to where):

Eleanor

She was the daughter of Thomas Holland, 1st Earl of Kent, by Alice, daughter of Richard FitzAlan, 10th Earl of Arundel and granddaughter of Eleanor of Lancaster, a descendant of Henry III, and she was born in *c*.1373. After Roger's death, she married secondly Edward de Cherleton, 4th Baron Cherleton of Powys (*d*.1421), after 19 June, 1399, and had issue:

1 Joan; she married Sir John Grey, Count of Tancarville (*d*.1421).

2 Joyce (1403?–1446); she married Sir John Tiptoft (*d*.1443), and had issue.

Eleanor died on 6, 18 or 23 October, 1405.

Issue of marriage:

(*i*) *Anne*

She married Richard, Earl of Cambridge (↷ page 112, below).

(*ii*) *Edmund*

He was born on 4 or 6 November, 1391, in the New Forest, Hampshire, and succeeded his father as Earl of March and Ulster on 20 July, 1398. He died on 18/19 January, 1425, at Trim Castle, Co. Meath,

Ireland, of plague, and was buried in the Collegiate Church of Stoke Clare, Suffolk.

Edmund married, in c.1415 (although no evidence exists as to where):

Anne

She was the daughter of Edmund, 5th Earl of Stafford, by Anne, Countess of Buckingham (◊ page 116, below), and was born in c.1398/1403. After the death of Edmund, she married secondly John Holland, Earl of Huntingdon and 3rd Duke of Exeter (1395?–1447), grandson of John of Gaunt (◊ page 101, below), before 5 March, 1427, and had issue:

1 Henry (1430–1475), 4th Duke of Exeter; he married Anne Plantagenet, sister of Edward IV, and had issue. Afterwards divorced.

Anne died on 20 or 24 September, 1432, and was buried in the Church of St Katherine-by-the-Tower, London.

(*iii*) *Roger*

He was born on 24 March or 23 April, 1393, at Netherwood, and died unmarried around c.1409/10.

(*iv*) *Eleanor*

She was born in c.1395. She married Edward, Baron Courtenay (*d.*1418), in 1408/9, and died after 1414, perhaps having become a nun after her husband's death.

(*v*) *Alice*

She is mentioned only by the Tudor chronicler Robert Fabyan, therefore her existence is doubtful.

(c) *Philippa*

She was born on 21 November, 1375, at Ludlow Castle, Shropshire. She married firstly John Hastings, 3rd Earl of Pembroke (1372–1389), in c.1385. She married secondly Richard FitzAlan, 11th Earl of Arundel (c.1348–executed 1397) (a descendant of Henry III), before 15 August, 1390, and had issue:

1 John (c.1394–*d.* young after 1397).

Philippa married thirdly Thomas Poynings, 5th Baron St

John of Basing (*d*.1429) before 24 November, 1399. She died around 24/26 September, 1400/1 at Halnaker, Sussex, and was buried in Boxgrove Priory, Lewes, Sussex.

(d) *Edmund*

He was born on 9 November, 1376/7, at Ludlow Castle, Shropshire, and was made a knight. He died before 13 May, 1411, possibly in 1409, at Harlech Castle, Wales.

Edmund married, in *c*.November, 1402, although no record exists as to where:

Katherine

She was the daughter of Owen Glendower by Margaret, daughter of Sir David Hanmer of Hanmer, Co. Flint. She died before 1 December, 1413, and was buried in St Swithun's Church, London.

Issue of marriage:

(*i*) Lionel (*d*. young).

(*ii*) Daughter (name not known) (*d*. young, 1413).

(*iii*) Daughter (name not known) (*d*. young, 1413).

(*iv*) Possibly more daughters who died young before 1413.

Lionel married secondly, on 28 May or 5 June, 1368, at the Church of St Maria Maggiore, Milan, Italy:

Yolande or Violante

She was the daughter of Galleazzo Visconti II, Duke of Milan, by Bianca Maria, daughter of Aimone, Count of Savoy, and she was born in *c*.1353. After the death of Lionel, she married secondly Ottone Paleologo, Marquess of Montferrat (murdered 1378), on 2 August, 1377, at Pavia, Italy. She married thirdly Ludovico Visconti, Lord of Lodi (1358–1381), on 18 April, 1381, and had issue:

1 John (Giovanni).

Yolande died in November, 1386.

6 *John*

Known as John of Gaunt, he was born in February or March (certainly before 28 May), 1340, at St Bavon's Abbey, Ghent, Flanders, and was created Earl of Richmond on 20 September, 1342. He was made a Knight of the Garter in *c*.April, 1361. He was first styled Earl of Derby, a title he held in right of his first wife, on

21 July, 1361. He was created Earl of Lancaster in right of his first wife before 14 August, 1361, and Lord of Beaufort and Nogent, also in right of his first wife, on 14 August, 1361. He succeeded his sister-in-law, Matilda of Lancaster (◊ page 77, under Henry III), as Earl of Derby, Earl of Leicester and Earl of Lincoln on 10 April, 1362, and was created Duke of Lancaster on 13 November, 1362. He was created Lord of Bergerac and Roche-sur-Yon on 8 October, 1370. He surrendered the earldom of Richmond on 5 June, 1372. He assumed the style and title of King of Castile and Léon, in right of his second wife, before 6 October, 1372. He was created Duke of Aquitaine on 2 March, 1390. He died on 3/4 February, 1399, probably at Leicester Castle, or – less probably – at Ely Place, Holborn, London, and was buried in Old St Paul's Cathedral, London.

John had the following illegitimate issue:

By Marie de St Hilaire (*d.* after 1399):

1 Blanche (before 1360–1388/9?); she married Sir Thomas Morieux.

John married firstly, on 19 May, 1359, at Reading Abbey, Berkshire:

Blanche

She was the daughter of Henry of Grosmont, Duke of Lancaster, by Isabella de Beaumont (◊ page 78, under Henry III), and she was born on 25 March, 1345. She died on 12 September, 1369, at Bolingbroke Castle, Lincs., of the Black Death (bubonic plague), and was buried in Old St Paul's Cathedral, London.

Issue of marriage:

(i) *Philippa*

She was born on 31 March, 1360, at Leicester Castle. She was made a Lady of the Garter in 1378. She married John I, King of Portugal (1357/8–1433), on 14 February, 1387, at Oporto Cathedral, Portugal, and had issue:

1 Blanche (1388–1389).

2 Alfonso (1390–1400).

3 Edward I, King of Portugal (1391–1438); he married Eleanor (*d.*1445), daughter of Ferdinand I, King of Aragon and Sicily, and had issue.

4 Peter, Duke of Coimbra (1392–1449); he married Isabella

(1409–1443), daughter of James II, Count of Urgel, and had issue.

5 Henry 'the Navigator', Duke of Viseu (1394–1460).

6 Isabella (1397–1471); she married Philip III, Duke of Burgundy (d.1467), and had issue.

7 John, Duke of Beja, Constable of Portugal (1400–1442); he married Isabella (d.1445), daughter of Alfonso I, Duke of Braganza, and had issue.

8 Ferdinand, Grand Master of Aviz (1402–1443).

Philippa died on 19 July, 1415, at Odivelas, near Lisbon, Portugal, of plague, and was buried in Odivelas Abbey. Her remains were later removed to Batalha Abbey, Portugal.

(ii) *John*

He was born in c.1362 or c.1364, and died young. He was buried in St Mary's Church, Leicester.

(iii) *Elizabeth*

She was born before 21 February, 1363, at Burford, Shropshire. She was made a Lady of the Garter in 1378. She married firstly John Hastings, 3rd Earl of Pembroke (1372–1389), in 1380 at Kenilworth Castle, Warwickshire, but the marriage was annulled after 24 September, 1383. Hastings afterwards married Philippa Mortimer (◊ page 98, above). Elizabeth married secondly John Holland, 1st Duke of Exeter (1352?–executed 1400) (son of Joan, Princess of Wales – ◊ page 94, above), on 24 June, 1386, at Plymouth, Devon, and had issue:

1 John, 3rd Duke of Exeter (1395–1447); he married firstly Anne, daughter of Edmund, 5th Earl of Stafford, by Anne, Countess of Buckingham (◊ page 116, below), and widow of Edmund Mortimer, Earl of March and Ulster (◊ page 98, above), and had issue. He married secondly Beatrice of Portugal (d.1439). He married thirdly Anne (d.1457), daughter of John de Montacute, 3rd Earl of Salisbury, and had issue.

2 Richard (d.1400 or 1416).

3 Constance (1387–1437); she married Thomas Mowbray, Earl of Norfolk (1385–executed 1405), and had issue. She married secondly Sir John Grey (d.1439), and had issue.

4 Edward, a knight (*c.*1399–after 1413).

5 Alice (*c.*1392–*c.*1406), she married Richard de Vere, 11th Earl of Oxford (1385–1417), and had issue.

Elizabeth married thirdly John Cornwall, 1st Baron Fanhope (*d.*1443), before 12 December, 1400, and had issue:

6 Constance (*d.* by 1429); she was married or betrothed to John Maltravers, Earl of Arundel (1407–1435).

Elizabeth died on 24 November, 1425/6, and was buried in Burford Church, Shropshire.

(iv) *Edward*

He was born in *c.*1365, and died the same year. He was buried in St Mary's Church, Leicester.

(v) *John*

He was born before 4 May, 1366, and died young. He was buried in St Mary's Church, Leicester.

(vi) *Henry IV* (↻ page 124).

(vii) *Isabella*

She was born in *c.*1368, and died young.

John married secondly, on 21 September, 1371, probably at Roquefort, Guienne, or – less probably – at St Andrew, Guienne:

Constance

She was the daughter of Peter I 'the Cruel', King of Castile, by Maria, daughter of John Garcias de Padilla, a handfast wife, and she was born in 1354 at Castro Kerez, Castile. She succeeded her father as 'de jure' Queen of Castile on 13 March, 1369, but was never Queen 'de facto', the throne having been usurped by Henry of Trastamara. She was made a Lady of the Garter in 1378. She died on 24 March, 1394, at Leicester Castle, and was buried in Newark Abbey, Leicester.

Issue of marriage:

(i) *Katherine*

She was born between 6 June, 1372, and 31 March, 1373, at Hertford Castle. She was made a Lady of the Garter in 1384. She married Henry III, King of Castile (1379–1406), in September, 1388, at the Church of St Antolin, Fuentarrabia, Castile, and had issue:

1 Mary (1401–1458); she married Alfonso V, King of Aragon and Sicily (1394–1458), and had issue.

2 John II, King of Castile (1406-1454); he married firstly Maria (*d*.1445), daughter of Ferdinand I, King of Aragon and Sicily, and had issue. He married secondly Isabella (1428?–1496), daughter of John, Duke of Beja in Portugal, and son of Philippa of Lancaster (◊ page 101, above), and had issue, including Isabella I, Queen of Spain, mother of Katherine of Aragon, first wife of Henry VIII.

3 Katherine (1406–1439); married Henry of Aragon, Duke of Villena (*d*.1445).

Katherine died on 2 June, 1418, and was buried at Toledo, Spain.

(ii) *John*

He was born in 1374 at Ghent in Flanders, and died in 1375.

John married thirdly, on 13 January, 1396, at Lincoln Cathedral:

Katherine

She was the daughter of Sir Payn Roët of Guienne, and she was born in *c*.1350. She married Sir Hugh Swynford of Coleby and Kettlethorpe, Co. Lincs. (1340–1372), before 1367 at St Clement Danes Church, Strand, London, and had issue:

1 Thomas (1368/72–1432), a knight; he married firstly Jane Crophill, and had issue. He married secondly Margaret (*d*.1454), daughter of Sir Henry Grey, and had issue.

2 Blanche (*b.c.*1370).

Katherine became the mistress of John of Gaunt in *c*.1371/2. She was made a Lady of the Garter in 1388. She died on 10 May, 1403, at Lincoln, and was buried in Lincoln Cathedral.

The issue of this marriage, all surnamed Beaufort after their father's French lordship, were all born before their parents were united in wedlock; they were legitimated by the Pope on 1 September, 1396, and also by Charter of Richard II on 9 February, 1397, but this same Charter also excluded them from the succession. Issue as follows:

(i) *John*

He was born around *c*.1371/3. He was made a Knight of the Garter in *c*.1397. He was created Earl of Somerset on 10 February, 1397, and Marquess of Somerset on 9 September, 1397. He was created Marquess of Dorset on 29 September, 1397, but deprived of this on 3 November, 1399. He died on 16

March, 1410, at the Hospital of St Katherine-by-the-Tower, London, and was buried in Canterbury Cathedral, Kent.

John married, before 28 September, 1397 (although no evidence exists as to where):

Margaret

She was the daughter of Thomas Holland, 1st Earl of Kent, son of Joan, Princess of Wales (♢ page 94, above), by Alice, daughter of Richard FitzAlan, 10th Earl of Arundel, a descendant of Henry III, and she was born around 1381/5. After the death of John, she married secondly Thomas, Duke of Clarence, son of Henry IV, after 10 November, 1411 (date of dispensation). She was made a Lady of the Garter in 1399. She died on 30/31 December, 1439, at St Saviour's Abbey, Bermondsey, London, and was buried in Canterbury Cathedral, Kent.

Issue of marriage:

(a) *Henry*

He was born on 26 November or, less probably, on 16 October, 1401, and succeeded his father as Earl of Somerset on 16 March, 1410. He died on 25 November, 1418.

(b) *John*

He was born before 25 March or in *c*.April, 1404. He succeeded his brother Henry as Earl of Somerset on 25 November, 1418, and was made a Knight of the Garter in 1440. He was created Duke of Somerset and Earl of Kendal on 28 August, 1443. He died, perhaps by suicide, on 27 May, 1444, and was buried in Wimborne Minster, Dorset.

John had the following illegitimate issue:

1 John, Bastard of Somerset (*d*. after 1453).

2 Jacinda or Thomasine (1434?–after 1469); she married Reginald, Baron Grey de Wilton (1421–1494), and had issue.

John married, in 1439 or *c*.1442 (although no record exists as to where):

Margaret

She was the daughter of John, 3rd Baron Beauchamp of Bletsoe, by Edith, daughter of Sir John Stourton. She married firstly Sir Oliver St John of Bletsoe, Beds. (*d*.1437), and had issue:

1 John of Bletsoe, a knight; he married Alice, daughter of Thomas Bradshaigh of Haigh, Co. Lancs., and had issue.

2 Oliver of Lidiard Tregos or of Ewell, Surrey (*d*.1497); he married Elizabeth, daughter of Henry, Baron Scrope of Bolton, and had issue.

3 Agnes; she married David Malpas.

4 Edith; she married Sir Geoffrey Pole of Medmenham, Bucks. (*d*.1474), and had issue, including Sir Richard Pole, who married Margaret Plantagenet (◊ page 138, under Edward IV).

5 Elizabeth; she married William, Baron Zouche of Haryngworth.

6 Mary; she married Richard Frogenhall.

After the death of John Beaufort, her second husband, Margaret married thirdly Leo, 6th Baron Welles (killed 1461), in *c*.April, 1447, and had issue:

7 John, 1st Viscount Welles (*d*.1498); he married Cecilia of York, daughter of Edward IV, and had issue.

Margaret died on 8 August, 1482, and was buried in Wimborne Minster, Dorset.

Issue of marriage:

(*i*) *Margaret* (◊ page 150, under *Henry VII*).

(c) *Thomas*

He was born in 1405, and was called Earl of Perche, although there is no record of any formal creation. He died unmarried in 1432.

(d) *Edmund*

He was born in *c*.1406. He was created Count of Mortain on 22 April, 1427, and made a Knight of the Garter before 5 May, 1436. He was styled Earl of Dorset from 1438, and formally created so on 18 or 28 August, 1442. He was created Marquess of Dorset on 24 June, 1443, and succeeded his brother John as Earl of Somerset on 27 May, 1444. He was created Duke of Somerset on 31 March, 1448. He was killed on 22 May, 1455, at the Battle of St

Albans, Herts., and was buried in St Albans Abbey.

Edmund married, around 1431/5, and before 7 March, 1436 (although no record exists as to where):

Eleanor

She was the daughter of Richard Beauchamp, 5th Earl of Warwick, by Elizabeth, daughter of Thomas, Lord Berkeley, and she was born in 1407/8 at Wedgenock, Co. Warwick. She married firstly Thomas, 9th Baron de Ros (1406–1430), and had issue:

1 Thomas (1427–1461); he married Philippa, daughter of John, Baron Tiptoft, and had issue.

After the death of Edmund Beaufort, her second husband, Eleanor married thirdly Walter Rokesley. She died around 4/6 or on 12 March, 1466/8, at Baynard's Castle, London. Issue of marriage:

(i) *Henry*

He was born on 26 January or in c.April, 1436, and was styled Earl of Dorset from 1448. He succeeded his father as Duke and Earl of Somerset, Marquess of Dorset and Count of Mortain on 22 May, 1455. He was attainted on 4 November, 1461, when all his honours and estates were declared forfeit, although he was restored to them all on 10 March, 1463. He was executed on 15 May, 1464, at Hexham, Northumberland, after the Battle of Hexham, and was buried either at Hexham Abbey or at Tewkesbury Abbey, Gloucs. He never married.

Henry had the following illegitimate issue:

By Joan Hill:

1 Charles Somerset, Earl of Worcester (1460?–1526); he married Elizabeth (1476?–1509/13), daughter of William Herbert, Earl of Huntingdon, and had issue. He married secondly Elizabeth, daughter of Thomas West, 8th Baron de la Warre, and had issue. He married thirdly Eleanor (*d.* by 1549), daughter of Edward Sutton, 2nd Baron Sutton. The present Dukes of Beaufort are descended from Charles Somerset.

(ii) *Edmund*

He was born in *c.*1439, and by 1440. He was styled Duke of Somerset after his father's death in 1455, but never formally restored to the title. He was executed on 6 May, 1471, at Tewkesbury, Gloucs., after the Battle of Tewkesbury, and buried in Tewkesbury Abbey.

(iii) *John*

He was killed on 4 May, 1471, at the Battle of Tewkesbury, Gloucs., and was buried in Tewkesbury Abbey.

(iv) *Thomas*

He died young before 1463.

(v) *Margaret*

She married firstly Humphrey Stafford (*d.*1457/8) in 1455, and had issue:

1 Henry, Duke of Buckingham (1455?–executed 1483); he married Katherine Woodville, sister of Elizabeth, wife of Edward IV, and had issue. (◊ page 127 under Henry IV).

2 Son.

Margaret married secondly Sir Richard Dayrell or Dayre of Lillingstone Dayrell, Bucks., and had issue:

3 Margaret; she married James Touchet, Baron Audley, and had issue.

Margaret died in 1474.

(vi) *Eleanor*

She married firstly James Butler, 5th Earl of Ormonde and 1st Earl of Wiltshire (*c.*1422–executed 1461), perhaps in April, 1458, at Woodsford, Dorset. She married secondly Sir Robert Spencer of Spencercombe, Devon (*d.* after 1492), in *c.*1470, and had issue:

1 Katherine (*d.*1542); she married Henry Percy, 5th Earl of Northumberland (1478–1527), and had issue.

2 Margaret; she married Thomas Carey of Chilton Foliot, and had issue.

Eleanor died on 16 August, 1501.

(vii) *Elizabeth*

She married Sir Henry Lewes, and had issue:

1 Mary

Elizabeth died before 1492.

(viii) *Mary* or *Margaret*

No dates are recorded. She married a man surnamed Burgh, and had issue:

1 Thomas.

2 Edward.

(ix) *Anne*

She married Sir William Paston of Norfolk (d.1496), and had issue:

1 William.

2 Mary (1469?–1489); she married Ralph Neville (d.1498).

3 Agnes. She is perhaps to be identified with Anne (◊ below).

4 Elizabeth; she married Sir John Saville of Thornhill, and had issue.

5 Margaret (b.&d.1474).

6 Anne; she married Sir Gilbert Talbot and had issue.

(x) *Joan*

She married first Robert Howth, Lord of Howth in Ireland, and secondly Sir Richard Fry. She died after 1492.

(e) *Joan* (◊ page 232, under *James I, King of Scotland*).

(f) *Margaret*

She married Thomas Courtenay, 5th Earl of Devon (1414–1458), and had issue:

1 Thomas, 6th Earl of Devon (1432–executed 1461).

2 John, 7th Earl of Devon (1435?–executed 1471).

3 Henry (executed 1466).

4 Joan; she married Sir Roger Clifford.

5 Elizabeth; she married Sir Hugh Conway.

(ii) *Henry*

He was born in *c*.1375, and entered the Church as a young

man. He became Dean of Wells Cathedral, Somerset, in 1397. He was provided to the See of Lincoln on 27 February, 1398, and was consecrated Bishop of Lincoln on 14 July, 1398. He was translated from Lincoln to Winchester on 19 November, 1404. He was nominated Cardinal-Priest of St Eusebius on 24 May, 1426. He died on 11 April, 1447, at Wolvesey Palace, Winchester, and was buried in Winchester Cathedral.

(iii) *Thomas*

He was born in *c.*January, *c.*1377. He was made a Knight of the Garter in *c.*1400. He was created Earl of Dorset on 5 July, 1411, and Duke of Exeter on 18 November, 1416. He was created Count of Harcourt and Lord of Lillebonne on 1 July, 1418. He died on 27 or 31 December, 1426, or on 1 January, 1427, at his manor of East Greenwich, Kent, and was buried in Bury St Edmunds Abbey, Suffolk.

Thomas married, before 15 February, 1403/4 (although no evidence exists as to where):

Margaret

She was the daughter of Sir Thomas Neville of Hornby, Lincs., by Joan Furnivall, and she was born in *c.*January, 1377, or in *c.*1383 (?). She was made a Lady of the Garter in 1408. She died between 1413 and 1426, probably before 9 April, 1424, and was buried in Bury St Edmunds Abbey, Suffolk.

Issue of marriage:

(a) *Henry*

No dates are recorded. He died young.

(iv) *Joan*

She was born in *c.*1379. She married firstly Robert, 2nd Baron Ferrers of Wemme (*d.*1396), before 30 September, 1394, and had issue:

1 Elizabeth (*c.*1394–1434); she married John de Greystoke, Baron Greystoke (1390–1436), and had issue.

2 Mary; she married Ralph Neville of Westmorland.

Joan married secondly Ralph Neville, 1st Earl of Westmorland (1364?–1425), before 29 November, 1396, and had issue:

3 Richard, Earl of Salisbury (1400?–killed 1460); he married Alice (1406–1462), daughter of Thomas de Montacute, 4th Earl of Salisbury, and had issue, including Richard Neville,

Earl of Warwick, father of Anne, Queen of Richard III, and Isabella, Duchess of Clarence (◊ page 137, under Edward IV).

4 William, Baron Fauconberg, Earl of Kent (d.1463); he married Joan, Baroness Fauconberg (1406–1490), and had issue.

5 George, Baron Latimer (d.1469) (?); he married Elizabeth (1417–1480), daughter of Richard Beauchamp, Earl of Warwick, and had issue.

6 Robert, Bishop of Salisbury and Durham (1404?–1457).

7 Edward, Baron Bergavenny (d.1476); he married Elizabeth (d.1448), daughter of Richard Beauchamp, Earl of Worcester, and had issue. He married secondly Katherine (d. after 1478), daughter of Sir Robert Howard, and had issue.

8 Cuthbert (d. young).

9 Thomas (d. young).

10 Henry (d. young).

11 Katherine (d. after 1483); she married firstly John Mowbray, Duke of Norfolk (1392–1432), and had issue. She married secondly Thomas Strangeways. She married thirdly John, Viscount Beaumont (killed 1460). She married fourthly John Woodville (1445?–executed 1469), brother of Elizabeth, wife of Edward IV (◊ page 126, under Henry IV).

12 Joan; a nun.

13 Anne (d.1480); she married firstly Humphrey, Earl of Stafford (1402–killed 1460), and had issue. She married secondly Walter Blount, 1st Baron Mountjoy (1420?–1474).

14 Eleanor (d.1472); she married firstly Richard le Despenser, Baron Burghersh (1396–1414), and had issue. She married secondly Henry Percy, 2nd Earl of Northumberland (1392–killed 1455), and had issue.

15 Cecily, Duchess of York (◊ page 135, under Edward IV).

16 One other, unnamed in the records.

Joan was made a Lady of the Garter in 1399. She died on 13 November, 1440 at Howden, Yorkshire, and was buried in

Lincoln Cathedral.

7 *Edmund*

He was born on 5 June, 1341, at Abbot's Langley (now King's Langley), Herts. He was made a Knight of the Garter in *c.*April, 1361, and was created Earl of Cambridge on 13 November, 1362. He was created Duke of York on 6 August, 1385. He died on 1 August, 1402, at King's Langley, Herts., and was buried there in the Church of the Mendicant Friars.

Edmund married firstly, between 1 January and 30 April, 1372, at Hertford Castle (?):

Isabella

She was the daughter of Peter I 'the Cruel', King of Castile, by Maria, daughter of John Garcias de Padilla, a handfast wife, and she was sister to Constance, wife of John of Gaunt (◊ page 102, above). Isabella was born in *c.*1355/6 at Morales or at Tordesillas, Castile. She was made a Lady of the Garter in 1379. She died on 23 November, 1392/3, and was buried in the Church of the Dominican Friars, King's Langley, Herts.

Issue of marriage:

(i) *Edward*

He was born in *c.*1373, perhaps at Norwich, Norfolk. He was made a Knight of the Garter in 1387. He was created Earl of Cork between 25 February, 1390, and 15 January, 1395, and Earl of Rutland on 25 February, 1390. He was created Duke of Aumale on 29 September, 1397, but deprived of the dukedom on 3 November, 1399. He succeeded his father as Duke of York on 1 August, 1402, and was confirmed in this dukedom on 5 November, 1402. He was restored to the dukedom of Aumale on 1 May, 1414. He was killed on 25 October, 1415, at the Battle of Agincourt, France, and was buried in the Collegiate Church of Fotheringhay, Northants.

Edward married, between 27 February, 1396, and 7 October, 1398:

Philippa

She was the daughter of John de Mohun, 2nd Baron of Dunster, by Joan, daughter of Sir Bartholemew de Burghersh of Ewyas Lacy, Co. Hereford. She married firstly Walter, 4th Baron FitzWalter (*d.*1386), before 27 June, 1385, and had issue:

1 Walter (*d*.1432); a knight; he married a lady called Elizabeth, and had issue.

Philippa married secondly Sir John Golafre of Langley, Oxon. (*d*.1396), before 13 November, 1389. She was made a Lady of the Garter in 1390. She died on 17 July, 1431, at Carisbrooke Castle, Isle of Wight, and was buried in Westminster Abbey.

(ii) *Constance*

She was born in *c*.1374. She married Thomas le Despenser, 1st Earl of Gloucester (1373–executed 1400), between 16 April, 1378 and 7 November, 1389 (possibly later, but certainly before 14 January, 1394), and had issue:

1 Edward (*d*. young).
2 Richard, Baron Burghersh (1396–1414); he married Eleanor (*d*.1472), daughter of Ralph Neville, 1st Earl of Westmorland by Joan Beaufort, daughter of John of Gaunt, Duke of Lancaster (↕ above, page 110).
3 Hugh (*d*. young, 1401).
4 Elizabeth (*b.c*.1398; *d*. young).
5 Isabella (1400–1439); she married firstly Richard de Beauchamp, Earl of Worcester (1397–1422), and had issue, and secondly Richard de Beauchamp, Earl of Warwick (1382–1439), and had issue.

Constance was made a Lady of the Garter in 1386. She died on 28 November, 1416, and was buried in Reading Abbey, Berkshire.

Constance may have had the following illegitimate issue (although the daughter in question always held that her parents had married in *c*.1404; however, this claim failed against the petition of her father's sisters):

By Edmund Holland, Earl of Kent (1383–1408):

1 Eleanor (?) (*b*.1406?); she married James Touchet, Baron Audley (1398?–1459), and had issue. She may have been the illegitimate issue of Edmund Holland by Elizabeth Burghersh, but this is unlikely.

(iii) *Richard*

He was born in *c*.September, *c*.1375/6, at Conisburgh Castle, Yorkshire. He was recognised as hereditary Earl of Cambridge on 1 May, 1414, but forfeited all his honours and estates on 5

August, 1415, on which day he was executed for treason at Southampton Green, Hampshire. He was buried in the Chapel of God's House, Southampton.

Richard married firstly, in c.May, 1406, or perhaps after 10 June, 1408 (date of dispensation) (although no record exists as to where):

Anne

She was the daughter of Roger Mortimer, Earl of March, by Eleanor Holland, and a great-great-granddaughter of Edward III ($\lozenge$ above), and it was through her that the House of York derived its claim to the throne. She was born on 27 December, 1390, and died in September, 1411, perhaps in childbirth. She was buried in King's Langley Church, Herts.

Issue of marriage:

(a) *Isabella*

She was born in 1409. She married firstly Sir Thomas Grey of Werke or Heton (*d.* by 1443) after February, 1413, but the marriage was annulled before 1426. She married secondly Henry Bourchier, 1st Earl of Essex (*c.*1409–1483), before 25 April, 1426, and had issue:

1 William, Viscount Bourchier (either killed 1471 or d.1483?); he married Anne (1438?–1489), daughter of Richard Woodville, 1st Earl Rivers, and sister of Elizabeth, wife of Edward IV, and had issue.

2 Henry (*d.*1462); he married Elizabeth, Baroness Scales (*d.*1473), daughter of Thomas, Baron Scales.

3 Humphrey (killed 1471); he married Joan (*d.*1490), daughter of Sir Richard Stanhope of Rampton.

4 John (*d.*1485 or 1494); he married firstly Elizabeth, Baroness Ferrers de Ruthyn, and secondly a daughter, whose name is not known, of John Chichele.

5 Thomas (*d.*1492); he married Isabella Barre.

6 Edward (killed 1460).

7 Fulk (*d.* young).

8 Hugh (*d.* young).

9 Isabella (*d.* young).

10 Florence (*d.*1525/6).

Isabella died on 2 October, 1484, and was buried in

Beeleigh Abbey, Maldon, Essex; her remains were later removed to Little Easton Church, Essex.

(b) *Richard*

He inherited the dukedom of York, and was the first of his line to adopt the surname Plantagenet. His laying claim to the throne of England led to the Wars of the Roses. For a full entry, ⇩ under Edward IV.

Richard married secondly, around 1411/15 (although no record exists as to where):

Matilda

She was the daughter of Thomas, 6th Baron Clifford, by Elizabeth, daughter of Thomas de Ros, Baron Ros of Hamlake. After the death of Richard, she married secondly (?) John Neville, 5th Baron Latimer of Danby (*d*.1430), from whom she was later divorced. She died on 26 August, 1446, and was buried in Roche Abbey, Yorkshire.

Edmund married secondly, before 4 November, 1393:

Joan

She was the daughter of Thomas Holland, 1st Earl of Kent, son of Joan, Princess of Wales (⇩ page 93, above), by Alice, daughter of Richard FitzAlan, Earl of Arundel, a descendant of Henry III. Her sister Margaret was married in turn to the sons of John of Gaunt (⇩ page 104, above) and Henry IV. Joan was born in *c*.1380. She was made a Lady of the Garter in 1399. After the death of Edmund, she married secondly William, 5th Baron Willoughby d'Eresby (*d*.1409) before 9 August, 1404. She married thirdly Henry, 3rd Baron Scrope of Masham (executed 1415), on 6 September, 1410, at Faxflete Chapel, Yorkshire, and had issue, although no details are available. She married fourthly Henry Bromflete, 1st Baron de Vesci (*d*.1469), between Michaelmas, 1415 and 27 April, 1416. Joan died on 12 April, 1434.

8 *Blanche*

She was born in March, 1342, in the Tower of London, and died there the same month. Hence she was known as Blanche de la Tour. She was buried in Westminster Abbey.

9 *Mary*

She was born on 10 October, 1344, at Waltham, near Winchester,

Hants. She married John de Montfort IV, Duke of Brittany (1339–1399), in the summer of 1361 at Woodstock Palace, Oxon. She died in the winter of 1361/2, and was buried in Abingdon Abbey, Oxon.

10 *Margaret*

She was born on 20 July, 1346, at Windsor Castle. She married John Hastings, 2nd Earl of Pembroke (1347–1375), on 19 May, 1359, at Reading Abbey, Berkshire. She died after 1 October, 1361, and was buried in Abingdon Abbey, Oxon.

11 *Thomas*

He was born probably in the summer of 1347, at Windsor Castle, and died young in 1348 (?). He was buried in King's Langley Church, Herts. Thomas has been overlooked by many historians who have confused him with his two brothers called William and his youngest brother, also called Thomas.

12 *William*

He was born before 24 June, 1348, at Windsor Castle, and died before 5 September, 1348. He was buried in Westminster Abbey.

13 *Thomas*

He was born on 7 January, 1355, at Woodstock Palace, Oxon. He was created Earl of Buckingham on 16 July, 1377, and became Earl of Essex in right of his wife on 22 June, 1380. He was made a Knight of the Garter between April, 1380, and April, 1381. He was called Duke of Aumale from before 3 September, 1385, although no record exists of his formal creation as such. He was created Duke of Gloucester on 6 August, 1385. He was murdered, probably on the orders of Richard II, at the Prince's Inn, Calais, France, on 8/9 September, 1397, and was buried in the Collegiate Church of the Holy Trinity, Pleshy, Essex; his remains were later removed to Westminster Abbey.

Thomas married, before 8 February, 1376, perhaps in 1374 (?) (although no record exists as to where):

Eleanor

She was the daughter of Humphrey de Bohun, Earl of Hereford, Essex and Northampton, by Joan, daughter of Richard FitzAlan, Earl of Arundel, a descendant of Henry III, and she was born in c.1366. She was made a Lady of the Garter in 1384. After her husband's murder in 1397, she is said to have lived as a nun at

Barking Abbey, Essex, but she did not renounce her property. She died on 3 October, 1399, at the Minoresses' Convent in Aldgate, London, and was buried in Westminster Abbey.

Issue of marriage:

(i) *Humphrey*

He was born in *c.*April, 1381/2, and styled Earl of Buckingham from his birth until his father's murder on 9 September, 1397. He died on 2 September, 1399, either at Chester, or Coventry, or Anglesey, of plague, and was buried in Walden Abbey, Essex.

(ii) *Anne*

She was born in April, 1383. She married firstly Thomas, 3rd Earl of Stafford (1368?–1392), in *c.*1390. She married secondly Edmund, 5th Earl of Stafford (1377–1403: killed at the Battle of Shrewsbury), before 28 June, 1398, and had issue:

1 Anne; she married Edmund Mortimer, Earl of March and Ulster (◊ page 98, above).

2 Humphrey, Earl of Stafford (1402–1460: killed at the Battle of Wakefield); he married Anne (*d.*1480), daughter of Ralph Neville, 1st Earl of Westmorland by Joan Beaufort (◊ page 110, above), and had issue.

3 Philippa (*d.* young).

Anne was recognised as Countess of Buckingham, Hereford and Northampton, and Lady of Brecknock and Holderness from 1399, and was so styled from that date. She also styled herself Countess of Stafford. She was made a Lady of the Garter in 1405. She married thirdly William Bourchier, Count of Eu (*d.*1420), before 20 November, 1405, and had issue:

4 Henry, Viscount Bourchier, Count of Eu, 1st Earl of Essex (*c.*1409–1483); he married Isabella Plantagenet (◊ page 113, above), and had issue.

5 Thomas, Cardinal of St Cirac, Archbishop of Canterbury (1413–1486).

6 William, Baron FitzWaryn (*c.*1412–before 1469); he married Thomasine Hankeford, Baroness FitzWaryn (1423–1453), daughter of Sir Richard Hankeford, and had issue. He married secondly Katherine (*d.*1467), daughter of John Affeton of Afton, Devon.

7 John, Baron Berners (c.1415–1474); he married Marjorie, daughter of Richard, Baron Berners, and had issue.

8 Eleanor (c.1417–1474); she married John Mowbray, Duke of Norfolk (1415–1461), and had issue.

Anne died between 16 and 24 October, 1438, and was buried in Llanthony Priory, Monmouthshire.

(iii) *Joan*

She was born in 1384. She perhaps married (or was betrothed to) Gilbert Talbot, Baron Talbot of Goderick Castle and Blackmere (d.1419), but there was no issue of the marriage.

Joan died on 16 August, 1400, perhaps in childbirth, and was buried in Walden Abbey, Essex.

(iv) *Isabella*

She was born on 12 March, 1385/6, and became a nun at the Minoresses' Convent in Aldgate, London, on 23 April, 1399. She died in c.April, 1402.

(v) *Philippa*

She was born in c.1389, and died before 3 October, 1399.

Edward III also had the following **illegitimate issue:**

By Alice Perrers (1348?–1400), wife of William de Windsor:

1 John de Southeray or Surrey (c.1364/5–after 1383:1384?); knighted 1377; he married Matilda, called a sister of Lord Henry Percy.

2 Joan; she married Robert Skerne of Kingston-upon-Thames, and perhaps had issue.

3 Joan or Jane; she married Richard Northland.

Perhaps by an unknown mother:

4 Nicholas Lytlington (?), Abbot of Westminster (d.1386). He did not claim to be the King's son, and was probably a member of the Despenser family.

EDWARD III

He died on 21 June, 1377, at Sheen Palace, Surrey, of a stroke, and was buried in Westminster Abbey.

He was succeeded by his grandson Richard.

Richard II

FATHER: *Edward, Prince of Wales* (◊ page 92, under *Edward III*).
MOTHER: *Joan of Kent* (◊ page 93, under *Edward III*).
SIBLINGS: (◊ page 94, under *Edward III*).

RICHARD II

He was born on *c.*6 January, 1367 (or 1366?), at Bordeaux, Gascony, France. He was created Prince of Wales, Earl of Cornwall and Earl of Chester on 20 November, 1376, and made a Knight of the Garter on 23 April, 1377. He succeeded his grandfather Edward III as King of England on 22 June, 1377, and was crowned at Westminster Abbey on 16 July, 1377.

Richard II was deposed on 19 August, 1399, by Henry of Bolingbroke, who usurped the throne as Henry IV when Richard formally abdicated on 29 September, 1399.

Richard II married firstly, on 14, 20 or 22 January, 1382, at St Stephen's Chapel in the Palace of Westminster:

Anne

She was the daughter of Charles IV, Holy Roman Emperor, by Elizabeth, daughter of Bogislaw V, Duke of Pomerania. Anne of Bohemia, as she was known, was born on 11 May, 1366, at Prague, Bohemia. She was crowned on 22 January, 1382, at Westminster Abbey, and was made a Lady of the Garter that same year. She died on 7 June, 1394, at Sheen Palace, Surrey, of the plague, and was buried in Westminster Abbey. There was no issue of the marriage.

Richard II married secondly, probably on 4 (less probably, 1) November, 1396, at St Nicholas' Church, Calais, France:

Isabella

She was the daughter of Charles VI, King of France, by Isabella, daughter of Stephen II, Duke of Bavaria-Ingolstadt. Her sister Katherine later married Henry V. Isabella was born on 9 November, 1389, at the Palace of the Louvre in Paris. She was made a Lady of the

Garter in 1396, and was crowned on 5, 7 or 8 January, 1397, at Westminster Abbey. After the death of Richard II, she married secondly Charles of Valois, Duke of Orleans (1394–1465), on 29 June, 1406, at Compiégne, France, and had issue:

1 Joan (1409–1432); she married John II, Duke of Alençon (1409–1476), and had issue.

Isabella died on 13 September, 1409, at the Château of Blois, France, in childbirth, and was buried in St Laumer's Abbey, Blois. Her remains were later removed to the Church of the Celestines, Paris. There was no issue of her marriage to Richard due to her extreme youth.

Richard II is said to have had the following **illegitimate issue**, but this is unlikely on chronological grounds:

1 Richard Maudelyn.

RICHARD II

He was probably murdered by being starved to death early in February, 1400, whilst being held prisoner in Pontefract Castle, Yorkshire; he was certainly dead by 17 February. He was buried in King's Langley Church, Herts., but was removed to Westminster Abbey in 1413.

He was succeeded by his cousin Henry of Bolingbroke.

CHAPTER FOUR

The Later Plantagenets: The Houses of Lancaster and York

The prolific Edward III sired eight sons, four of whom grew to maturity and had sons of their own. The eldest was the Prince of Wales, that Edward known to history as the Black Prince, who was the father of Richard II. Richard, although his entitlement to the throne was without dispute, was nevertheless a weak and unstable ruler. This led to his deposition by Henry of Bolingbroke in 1399, Bolingbroke's usurpation of the throne, and Richard's own probable murder the following year.

Bolingbroke, henceforth known as Henry IV, was the son of John of Gaunt, Duke of Lancaster, third surviving son of Edward III. In 1399, when Bolingbroke staged his successful coup, the rightful heir to the throne of England was Edmund Mortimer, Earl of March and Ulster, a child of nearly eight. Edmund was the great-grandson of Lionel of Antwerp, Duke of Clarence, second son of Edward III. Lionel's only child had been a daughter, Philippa, who was Edmund's grandmother, but in England there was no Salic Law to prevent the crown passing by way of inheritance to or through a female, and there is no doubt that Edmund had a better claim to the throne than Bolingbroke. However, Edmund was a child and Bolingbroke a grown man and a proven soldier: England needed a firm ruler, and so the claim of Edmund Mortimer was set aside while the House of Lancaster usurped the throne. Edmund died in 1425, and his claim to the throne was inherited by his surviving sister Anne's child, Richard, Duke of York. It was he who first used the surname Plantagenet.

For half a century, the House of Lancaster ruled England under Henry IV, Henry V, and Henry VI. Henry V executed Richard, Earl of Cambridge, who was the husband of Anne Mortimer and the son of

Edmund of Langley, Duke of York, fourth surviving son of Edward III; Richard of Cambridge had plotted to overthrow the fifth Henry, but his treason was discovered and he was eliminated on the eve of the campaign that would see the English victorious at Agincourt. Henry V died young, and the House of Lancaster came to grief under his son Henry VI, who was fitted rather for the clerical life than for kingship. Henry VI married the energetic and passionate Margaret of Anjou, but the marriage was childless for eight years. Then, in 1453, the queen produced a son whilst her husband was suffering one of his periodic fits of insanity, which Margaret's enemies interpreted as an admission that the Queen had foisted a bastard upon the royal line. Nevertheless, the infant was created Prince of Wales the following year. However, it was Henry VI's ineptitude as a ruler, rather than the rumours about his son's paternity, that precipitated the dynastic struggle that later came to be known as the Wars of the Roses, after the emblems of the two warring factions: the red rose of Lancaster, and the white rose of York.

York deeply resented the court party headed by the Queen, and promoted himself as the champion of good government; only later did he assert his superior claim to the throne. Thirty years of intermittent strife followed the outbreak of hostilities in 1455. Early battles in the conflict were indecisive. Then, in 1460, York was killed at the Battle of Wakefield, and his cause taken up by his son, Edward, Earl of March, who won a decisive victory at Towton the following Spring. This led to him being accepted as King of England and crowned at Westminster Abbey. Henry VI went into hiding, but was later taken into custody and imprisoned in the Tower.

Edward IV was a strong king, but he made the fatal mistake of making a very unpopular marriage to a commoner called Elizabeth Wydville, who brought instead of a dowry a host of rapacious relatives, eager for lands, honours and wealth. This marriage alienated the great Earl of Warwick, known as 'the kingmaker', who had been Edward's staunchest supporter. Warwick allied himself with Margaret of Anjou and brought about the 'readeption' of Henry VI, while Edward fled to the Low Countries. But he soon returned with an army, to march for the final time upon his enemies. Warwick was killed at the Battle of Barnet in April, 1471, and Margaret's Lancastrian forces routed in the bloody Battle of Tewkesbury in May.

On 21 May, Henry VI died in mysterious circumstances in the Tower of London. At last, the House of York was securely established upon the throne.

Edward IV died in 1483, worn out prematurely by the pleasures of the table and the bedchamber, leaving as his heir Edward V, a boy of twelve. The government of the realm was placed in the capable yet treacherous hands of Edward IV's brother, Richard, Duke of Gloucester. After securing the persons of Edward V and his brother Richard, Duke of York, in the Tower of London, and eliminating his enemies one by one, Gloucester had it announced, on the basis of questionable evidence, that his brother's marriage to Elizabeth Wydville had been bigamous, and that their children were therefore bastards and unfit to inherit the throne. As a result, the crown was offered to Gloucester, who was crowned King Richard III in July, 1483. Edward V and his brother, the 'Princes in the Tower', were never seen alive again, and controversy has raged ever since as to their fate. The evidence strongly suggests that they were murdered on the orders of Richard III, although this has often been disputed.

Richard III did not long enjoy his crown. His son died in 1484, and his wife in 1485. His heir was his sister's son, John de la Pole, Earl of Lincoln. Yet England was never destined to have a King John II. For although the great families who were descended from Edward III and had a strong claim to the throne of England had either died out or been barred from the succession by Act of Attainder, there yet remained in exile in France a scion of the Beauforts, who were the issue of John of Gaunt by his mistress (and later wife) Katherine Swynford. After their parents' marriage in 1396, the Beauforts were declared legitimate by a Statute of Richard II, but Henry IV added an amendment barring them from the throne, which was of dubious legality. This minor technicality did not, however, deter the 'unknown Welshman' called Henry Tudor, who in 1485 invaded England with a foreign army, defeated Richard III at the Battle of Bosworth, and had himself crowned on the battlefield as King Henry VII with the circlet that had fallen from the head of the last Plantagenet King of England and rolled under a hawthorn bush near to where Richard fell, hacked to death in the midst of the fray.

Thus was the Tudor dynasty founded, of whom we shall hear more in the next chapter. Henry VII united the rival Houses of York and

Lancaster by marrying Elizabeth, daughter of Edward IV. The Wars of the Roses ended in 1487 with the Battle of Stoke, when John, Earl of Lincoln, Richard III's nephew and heir, perished. But the tragedy of the House of York would be drawn out for a further eighty years, during which time its surviving members were either brutally eliminated or neutralised by the usurping, ever-suspicious Tudors.

Henry IV

FATHER: *John of Gaunt, Duke of Lancaster* (◊ page 99, under *Edward III*).
MOTHER: *Blanche of Lancaster* (◊ page 100, under *Edward III*).
SIBLINGS: (◊ page 100, under *Edward III*)

HENRY IV

He was born probably on 3 April, or – less probably – on 30 May, 1367, at Bolingbroke Castle, Lincs. He was made a Knight of the Garter on 23 April, 1377, and styled Earl of Derby from 16 July, 1377. He was created Earl of Northampton and (probably) Earl of Hereford in right of his wife on 22 December, 1384. He was created Duke of Hereford on 29 September, 1397, and succeeded his father as Duke of Lancaster, Earl of Leicester and Earl of Lincoln on 3 February, 1399. He usurped the throne of England upon the abdication of Richard II on 30 September, 1399, and was crowned on 13 October, 1399, at Westminster Abbey.

Henry IV married firstly, between 20 July, 1380, and 10 February, 1381, either at Rochford, Essex, or at Arundel Castle, Sussex:

Mary

She was the daughter of Humphrey de Bohun, Earl of Hereford, Essex and Northampton, by Joan, daughter of Richard FitzAlan, Earl of Arundel, a descendant of Henry III. Her sister Eleanor was married to Henry IV's uncle, Thomas, Duke of Gloucester (◊ page 115, under *Edward III*). Mary was born around 1369/70. She was made a Lady of the Garter in 1388. She died on 4 June, 1394, at Peterborough Castle, in childbirth, and was buried in St Mary's Church, Leicester. Her remains were later removed to Trinity Hospital, Leicester.

Issue of marriage:

1 *Edward*

He was born in April, 1382, and died aged 4 days. He was perhaps buried in Monmouth Castle Chapel.

2 **Henry V** (◊ page 130).

3 **Thomas**

He was born on 29 September, 1388, either at Kenilworth Castle, Co. Warwick, or in London. He was made a Knight of the Bath on 12 October, 1399, when the Order was founded by his father, and a Knight of the Garter in *c.*1400. He was created Duke of Clarence and Earl of Aumale on 9 July, 1412. He was killed on 22 March, 1421, at the Battle of Baugé, France, and was buried in Canterbury Cathedral.

Thomas had the following illegitimate issue:

1 John de Clarence; he was a knight, and was sometimes known as the Bastard of Clarence.

Thomas married, after 10 November, 1411 (date of dispensation) (although no evidence exists as to where):

Margaret

She was the daughter of Thomas Holland, Earl of Kent, son of Joan, Princess of Wales (◊ page 94, under Edward III), by Alice, daughter of Richard FitzAlan, Earl of Arundel, a descendant of Henry III. Margaret was born in *c.*1381/5. She married firstly John Beaufort, Marquess of Somerset, son of John of Gaunt, Duke of Lancaster (◊ page 103, under Edward III), and had issue. She was made a Lady of the Garter in 1399. She died on 30/31 December, 1439, at St Saviour's Abbey, Bermondsey, London, and was buried in Canterbury Cathedral, Kent.

4 **John**

He was born on 20 June, 1389. He was made a Knight of the Bath on 11 October, 1399, when the Order was founded by his father, and a Knight of the Garter in *c.*1400. He was created Earl of Kendal and Duke of Bedford on 16 May, 1414, and Earl of Richmond on 24 November, 1414. He died on the night of 14/15 September, 1435, at his house called 'Joyeux Repos' at Rouen, Normandy, and was buried in Rouen Cathedral, Normandy.

John had the following illegitimate issue:

1 Richard.

2 Mary (*d.* after 1458); she married Peter of Montferrat.

John married firstly by proxy on 13 or 17 April, 1423, at Montbar, France, and in person on 14 June, 1423, at Troyes Cathedral, France:

Anne

She was the daughter of John the Fearless, Duke of Burgundy, by Margaret, daughter of Albert of Bavaria, Count of Hainault, Holland and Zeeland, and she was born around 1404/5 at Arras, Burgundy, France. Anne died on 14 November, 1432, at the Hôtel de Bourgogne, Paris, in childbirth, and was buried in the Church of the Celestines, Paris. Her remains were later removed to the Chartreuse de Champnol, Dijon, Burgundy, France.

Issue of marriage:

(i) *Unnamed child*

It was born in November, 1432, in Paris, and died shortly after its birth.

John married secondly, on 20 or 22 April, 1433, at the Bishop's Palace, Thérouanne, France:

Jacquetta

She was the daughter of Peter of Luxembourg, Count of St Pol, by Margaret, daughter of Francis del Balso or Baux, Duke of Andria, and she was born in 1416 (?). After the death of Bedford, she married secondly Richard Woodville or Wydville, 1st Earl Rivers (1405?–executed 1469), between 16 September, 1435, and 23 March, 1436, and had issue:

1 Elizabeth; she married Edward IV (◊ page 139).

2 Anne (1438?–1489); she married firstly William, Viscount Bourchier (killed 1471 or *d.*1483?), son of Isabella Plantagenet (◊ page 113, under Edward III) and cousin of Edward IV, and had issue. She married secondly Sir Edward Wingfield, and thirdly George Grey, Earl of Kent (*d.*1503).

3 Margaret (1439?–1490/1); she married Thomas Maltravers, Earl of Arundel (1450?–1524).

4 Anthony, 2nd Earl Rivers (1440/2?–executed 1483); he married firstly Elizabeth (1436?–1473), daughter of Thomas, Baron Scales of Neucelles. He married secondly Mary, daughter of Sir Henry FitzLewes. Anthony had illegitimate issue.

5 Mary (1443?–by 1481); she married William Herbert, Earl of Pembroke and Huntingdon (*d.*1491), and had issue.

6 Jacquetta (1444/5?–1509); she married John le Strange, Baron Strange of Knockin (*d.*1479), and had issue.

7 John (1445–executed 1469); he married Katherine (*d.* after

1483), daughter of Ralph Neville, 1st Earl of Westmorland, by Joan Beaufort (◊ page 110, under Edward III).

8 Lionel, Bishop of Salisbury (1446?–1484).
9 Edward (killed 1488).
10 Richard, 3rd Earl Rivers (d.1491).
11 Thomas; he married Anne Holland.
12 John (d. young).
13 Lewis (d. young).
14 Katherine, Duchess of Buckingham and Bedford (◊ page 132, under Henry V).
15 Martha; she married Sir John Bromley.
16 Eleanor or Joan; she married Anthony Grey, Baron de Ruthin (d.1480), and had issue.

Jacquetta was made a Lady of the Garter in 1435. She died on 30 May, 1472.

5 *Humphrey*

He was born around August/September, or on 3 October, 1390. He was made a Knight of the Garter in c.1400, and created Duke of Gloucester and Earl of Pembroke on 16 May, 1414. In March, 1423, he assumed the style Count of Holland, Zeeland and Hainault in right of his first wife. He was created Count of Flanders on 30 July, 1436. He died, or was perhaps murdered, on 23 February, 1447, at Bury St Edmunds, Suffolk, and was buried in St Albans Abbey, Herts.

Humphrey had the following illegitimate issue:

1 Arthur (d.1447).
2 Antigone; she married firstly Henry Grey, Lord of Powys and Count of Tancarville in Normandy (1419?–1450), and had issue. She married secondly John d'Amancier.

Humphrey married firstly, before 7 March (perhaps in February?), 1422/3, at Hadleigh, Essex (?):

Jacqueline

She was the daughter of William IV, Duke of Bavaria, Count of Holland, Zeeland and Hainault, by Margaret, daughter of Philip the Hardy, Duke of Burgundy, and she was born on 25 July, 1401, at The Hague, Holland. She married firstly John of Viennois, Dauphin of France (1398–1417), in July, 1406 at Compiégne, France, and again in 1415 at The Hague, Holland. She succeeded her father as Duchess of Bavaria and Countess of Holland, Zeeland and Hainault in 1417. She married secondly John IV, Duke of Brabant (1400/3–1426), on 10 March, 1418. This marriage was annulled by the Anti-Pope, Benedict XIII, in 1421/2. She was made a Lady of the Garter in 1423. Her marriage to Humphrey was annulled on 9 July, 1428, by Papal Decree, which also pronounced as valid her marriage to Brabant. She married fourthly Francis or Floris van Borselen, Count of Ostrevant (d.1470), in July, 1432, at Ostende, Flanders. She was dispossessed by the Duke of Burgundy of all her territories save Ostrevant in 1433. She underwent a second marriage ceremony with her fourth husband in July, 1434, at Martensdijk Castle, Holland. Jacqueline died on 8/9 October, 1436, either at Leyden, or at Teilingen, Holland, and was buried at The Hague.

Issue of marriage:

(i) *Stillborn child*
   It was born in 1424.

Humphrey married secondly, in 1428 (?) (before 1431) (although no record exists as to where):

Eleanor

She was the daughter of Sir Reginald Cobham of Sterborough, Kent, by Eleanor, daughter of Sir Thomas Culpeper of Rayal. She was perhaps born at Sterborough Castle, Kent. She became Humphrey's mistress some time before their marriage, and may have borne him 2 bastard children, possibly those listed above, but no firm details are recorded, and the children, if they existed, may have died young before the marriage took place. Eleanor was made a Lady of the Garter in 1432. In 1441, she was convicted of practising witchcraft upon Henry VI, and was imprisoned for life. She died in either 1446 or 1457 in prison at Peel Castle, Isle of Man, where she is said to have been buried.

6 Blanche

She was born in the spring of 1392 at Peterborough Castle. She married Louis 'Barbatus', Duke of Bavaria and Count Palatine of the Rhine (d.1436) on 6 July, 1402, at Cologne Cathedral, Germany, and had issue:

1 Stillborn child (1407).
2 Rupert (1409–1426).

Blanche was made a Lady of the Garter in 1408. She died on 22

May, 1409, at Neustadt, Alsace, in childbirth, and was buried in the Church of St Mary, Neustadt, Alsace.

7 *Philippa*

She was born on or just before 4 June (not July, as is sometimes stated – her mother died giving birth to her in June), 1394, at Peterborough Castle. She married Eric of Pomerania, King of Sweden (Eric XIII), Denmark (Eric VII), and Norway (Eric III) (1382–1459), on 26 October, 1406, at Lund, Sweden, and had issue:

1 Stillborn child (1429).

Philippa was crowned Queen Consort of Sweden, Denmark and Norway on 1 November, 1406, at Lund, Sweden. She was made a Lady of the Garter in 1408. She died on 5 January, 1430, in the convent of Waldstena, Lingkoping, Sweden, where she was buried.

Henry IV is also said to have had the following **illegitimate issue**, although there is no contemporary evidence for this:

1 Edmund Labourde (*d.* young in 1401).

Henry IV married secondly, by proxy on 3 April, 1402, at Eltham Palace, Kent, and in person on 7 February, 1403, at Winchester Cathedral:

Joan

She was the daughter of Charles II, King of Navarre, by Joan, daughter of John II, King of France, and she was born in *c.*1370. She married firstly John de Montfort IV, Duke of Brittany (1339–1399) (who had previously been married to Mary, daughter of Edward III), either on 25 August, 1386, at Pampelina, Navarre, or on 11 September, 1386, at Saillé, Navarre, and had issue:

1 Joan (1387–1388).
2 Daughter (name not known) (*b.&d.*1388).
3 Peter, who took the name and style John V, Duke of Brittany (1389–1422); he married Joan (1391–1433), daughter of Charles VI, King of France, and sister to the wives of Richard II and Henry V, and had issue.
4 Mary (1391–1446); she married John I, Duke of Alençon (*d.*1415).
5 Arthur III, Duke of Brittany (1393–1458); he married firstly Margaret (*d.*1441), daughter of John the Fearless, Duke of Burgundy, and secondly Joan d'Albret, and thirdly Katherine of Luxembourg.

6 Giles, Lord of Chantocé (1394–1412).

7 Richard, Count of Éstampes (1395–1438); he married Margaret (*d.*1466), daughter of Louis of Valois, Duke of Orléans, and had issue.

8 Blanche (*c.*1396–*c.*1418); she married John or Lomagne, Count of Armagnac (*d.* after 1448).

9 Margaret (1397–1428); she married Alan, Viscount de Rohan.

Joan was crowned Queen Consort on 25/26 February, 1403, at Westminster Abbey. She was made a Lady of the Garter in 1405. She died on 2, 9 or 10 July, 1437, at the Dower House known as Pirgo, on the royal manor of Havering-atte-Bower, Essex, and was buried in Canterbury Cathedral, Kent. There was no issue of her marriage to Henry IV.

HENRY IV

He died on 20 March, 1413, in the Jerusalem Chamber in Westminster Abbey, of a disease resembling leprosy, and was buried in Canterbury Cathedral.

He was succeeded by his son Henry.

Henry V

FATHER: *Henry IV* (◊ page 124).
MOTHER: *Mary de Bohun* (◊ page 124, under *Henry IV*).
SIBLINGS: (◊ page 124, under *Henry IV*).

HENRY V

He was born probably on 9 August or 16 September, 1387, or – less probably – in August, 1386, at Monmouth Castle. He was created Prince of Wales, Duke of Cornwall and Earl of Chester, and Prince of Aquitaine on 15 October, 1399, and invested with these honours the same day. He was made a Knight of the Garter in 1399. He was created Duke of Aquitaine on 23 October or 10 November, 1399, and Duke of

Lancaster on 10 November, 1399. He succeeded his father as King of England on 21 March, 1413, and was crowned on 9 April, 1413, in Westminster Abbey. He was designated heir to the throne of France on 21 May, 1420, but did not live to enjoy his inheritance.

Henry V married, on 2 June, 1420, at Troyes Cathedral, France:
Katherine

She was the daughter of Charles VI, King of France, by Isabella, daughter of Stephen II, Duke of Ingolstadt-Bavaria. Her sister Isabella had been married to Richard II. Katherine was born on 27 October, 1401, at the Hôtel de St Pol, Paris. She was crowned in Westminster Abbey on 23/24 February, 1421. After the death of Henry V, she either secretly married, or formed a liaison with, a gentleman of her household, Owain ap Maredudd ap Tewdwr (Owen Tudor), son of Maredudd (Meredith) ap Tewdwr by his wife Margaret. This marriage, if it took place at all, was solemnised between 1425 and 1428. Owen Tudor was born in *c.*1400 at Plas Penmynydd, Wales, and he was executed on 3 February, 1461, by the Yorkists at Hereford. He was buried in Grey Friar's Church, Hereford. His union with Katherine produced issue as follows, and details are given in full as they are relevant to the succession:

(a) *Owen* or *Thomas* or *Edward*

He was born on 6 November, 1429, at the Palace of Westminster, and is perhaps to be identified with Edward Bridgewater, a monk at Westminster Abbey from 1468/9 to 1471/2. He died in 1502 at Westminster, and was buried in Westminster Abbey.

(b) *Edmund* (◊ page 150, under *Henry VII*).

(c) *Jaspar*

He was born in *c.*1431 at Hatfield, Herts. He was created Earl of Pembroke probably on 23 November, 1452, certainly before 30 January, 1453. He was made a Knight of the Garter before 23 April, 1459. He was attainted as a traitor by Act of Parliament on 4 November, 1461, and forfeited all his honours, but was styled Earl of Pembroke from October, 1470, until May, 1471, during the readeption of Henry VI. He was created Duke of Bedford on 27 October, 1485, and formally restored to all his honours on 12 December, 1485. He died on 21 or 26 December, 1495, and was buried in Keynsham Abbey, Somerset.

Jaspar had the following illegitimate issue:

By Mevanvy (*d.* by 1485?), a Welshwoman:

1 Helen or Ellen; she married William Gardiner of London, and had issue.

Jaspar married, before 7 November, 1485:

Katherine

She was the daughter of Richard Wydville, 1st Earl Rivers, by Jacquetta of Luxembourg (♀ page 126, under Henry IV), and sister to Elizabeth, wife of Edward IV. She was born before 1458. She married firstly Henry Stafford, 2nd Duke of Buckingham (1455?–executed 1483), in *c.*February, 1466, and had issue:

1 Edward, 3rd Duke of Buckingham (1478–executed 1521); he married Eleanor (*d.*1530), daughter of Henry Percy, 4th Earl of Northumberland, and had issue.

2 Henry, Earl of Wiltshire (1479?–1523); he married firstly Muriel or Margaret, daughter of Edward Grey, Viscount de Lisle, and secondly Cecilia (*d.*1529), daughter of William Bonville, Baron Harington.

3 Humphrey (*d.* young).

4 Anne; she married first Sir Walter Herbert (*d.*1507), and secondly George Hastings, Earl of Huntingdon (1488–1544), and had issue.

5 Elizabeth (*d.*1532); she married Robert Radcliffe, Earl of Sussex (*d.*1542). She was also the first recorded mistress of Henry VIII. After the death of Jaspar, Katherine married thirdly Sir Richard Wingfield of Kimbolton Castle, Hunts. (1468–1525). She died before 1513.

(d) *Daughter* (*name not known*)

Polydore Vergil, Henry VII's official historian, says she became a nun, and there is no reason to doubt this, although no other source mentions her.

(e) *Margaret* or *Katherine*

She was born in January, 1437, at the Abbey of St Saviour, Bermondsey, London, where she died shortly after her birth.

Katherine died on 3 January, 1437, at the Abbey of St Saviour, Bermondsey, London, in childbirth, and was buried in Westminster Abbey.

Issue of marriage:

1 *Henry VI* (♀ page 133).

HENRY V

He died on 31 August/1 September, 1422, at the Castle of Bois-de Vincennes, France, and was buried in Westminster Abbey.

He was succeeded by his son Henry.

Henry VI

FATHER: *Henry V* (◊ page 130).
MOTHER: *Katherine of France* (◊ page 131, under *Henry V*).
SIBLINGS: *Henry VI did not have any legitimate siblings.*

HENRY VI

He was born on 6 December, 1421, at Windsor Castle. He is said to have been designated Duke of Cornwall from birth. He succeeded his father Henry V as King of England on 1 September, 1422, and his grandfather, Charles VI of France, as King of France on 11 October, 1422, in accordance with the terms of the Treaty of Troyes (1420) which settled the French succession upon Henry V and his heirs. Henry VI was crowned at Westminster Abbey on 5/6 November, 1429, and at the Cathedral of Notre Dame in Paris on 16/17 December, 1431. He assumed personal rule on 12 November, 1437.

Henry VI was deposed in favour of Edward, Duke of York (Edward IV), on 4 March, 1461. He was restored to the throne on 30 October, 1470 – this was known as 'the Readeption' – but deposed again in favour of Edward IV on 11 April, 1471.

Henry VI married, by proxy on 24 May, 1444, at the Cathedral of St Martin, Tours, France, and in person on 23 April, 1445, at Titchfield Abbey, Hampshire:

Margaret

She was the daughter of René, Duke of Anjou and King of Naples and Sicily, by Isabella, Duchess of Lorraine, daughter of Charles I, Duke of Lorraine, and she was born on 23 March, 1429, at Pont-à-Mousson, Lorraine. She was crowned on 30 May, 1445, in

Westminster Abbey. She died on 25 August, 1482, at Château Dampierre, Anjou, and was buried in St Maurice's Cathedral, Angers, Anjou.

Issue of marriage:

1 *Edward*

He was born on 13 October, 1453, at the Palace of Westminster, and was Duke of Cornwall from birth. He was created Prince of Wales and Earl of Chester on 15 March, 1454, and invested with the principality of Wales on 9 June, 1454, at Windsor Castle. He was also made a Knight of the Garter. He was killed, or perhaps murdered by the Yorkists, on 4 May, 1471, at the Battle of Tewkesbury, and was buried in Tewkesbury Abbey, Gloucs.

Edward married on 13 December, 1470, at Château d'Amboise, France:

Anne

She was the daughter of Richard Neville, Earl of Warwick, by Anne, daughter of Richard de Beauchamp, Earl of Warwick, and she was born on 11 June, 1456, at Warwick Castle. After the death of Edward, she married Richard, Duke of Gloucester (⟡ page 144, under Richard III, for further details of her life).

HENRY VI

He was murdered on 21 May, 1471, almost certainly on the orders of Edward IV. Henry was buried in Chertsey Abbey, Surrey, but was removed to St George's Chapel, Windsor, in 1485. He had already been succeeded by his distant cousin Edward IV.

Edward IV

FATHER: *Richard*

He was the son of Richard, Earl of Cambridge (son of the fourth surviving son of Edward III), by Anne Mortimer (great-granddaughter of the second surviving son of Edward III), and he was born on 21 September, 1411/12. He married Cecily Neville before 18 October, 1424. Although the dukedom of York had been forfeited when his father was executed in 1415, Richard was allowed to style himself Duke of York from 2 February, 1425. He was not formally restored in blood to the dukedom of York until 19 May, 1426, and was recognised as Earl of March, Earl of Ulster and Earl of Cambridge by hereditary right on 12 May, 1432. He was made a Knight of the Garter on 22 April, 1433. In 1448, he assumed the surname Plantagenet, which had not been used since it was borne as a nickname by Geoffrey of Anjou, father of Henry II, in the 12th century; during the Wars of the Roses, York would use this surname to emphasise that his claim to the throne was stronger than that of Henry VI. York was attainted on 20 November, 1459, and all his titles and honours were declared forfeit. The Attainder against him was nullified in October, 1460, when he was restored to all his titles and honours, but he continued to press his claim to the throne, and was killed on 30 December, 1460, at the Battle of Wakefield. He was buried at Pontefract, but was later removed to the Collegiate Church of Fotheringhay, Northants.

MOTHER: *Cecily*

She was the daughter of Ralph Neville, 1st Earl of Westmorland, by Joan Beaufort, daughter of John of Gaunt, Duke of Lancaster (◊ page 110, under Edward III), and she was born on 3 May, 1415, at Raby Castle, Co. Durham. She died a Benedictine nun on 31 May, 1495, at Berkhamstead Castle, Herts., and was buried in the Collegiate Church of Fotheringhay, Northants.

SIBLINGS:

1 *Joan*

She was born in 1438, and died the same year.

2 *Anne*

She was born on 10/11 August, 1439, at Fotheringhay Castle, Northants. She married firstly Henry Holland, 4th Duke of Exeter (1430–drowned at sea 1475), before 30 July, 1447, and had issue.

1 Anne (c.1455–1475); she married Thomas Grey, 1st Marquess of Dorset (1455?–1501), son of Elizabeth Wydville, wife of Edward IV.

Anne was divorced from her first husband on 12 November, 1472. She married secondly Sir Thomas St Leger (executed 1483) in

1472/3, and had issue:

2 Anne (1476?–1526); she married George Manners, Lord Roos (*d.*1513).

Anne died on 12 or 14 January, 1476 (or 1482?), in childbirth (?), and was buried in St George's Chapel, Windsor.

3 *Henry*

He was born on 9/10 February, 1441, at Hatfield, Herts., and died young.

4 *Edmund*

He was born on 17 or 27 May, 1443, at Rouen, France. He was created Earl of Rutland on 29 January, 1446. He forfeited his earldom by Act of Attainder in 1459, but was restored to it in October, 1460. He was killed on 30 December, 1460, at the Battle of Wakefield, Yorks., and was buried at Pontefract. His remains were later removed to the Collegiate Church of Fotheringhay, Northants.

5 *Elizabeth*

She was born on 22 April, 1444, at Rouen, France. She married John de la Pole, 2nd Duke of Suffolk (*d.*1491), in *c.*August, 1461 (or, less probably, before October, 1460), and had issue:

1 John, Earl of Lincoln (1462/4?–1487: killed at the Battle of Stoke); he married Margaret (*d.* after 1493), daughter of Thomas FitzAlan, Earl of Arundel, and had issue.

2 Edmund, Earl of Suffolk (1471/2?–executed 1513); he married Margaret (*d.*1515), daughter of Sir Richard Scrope, and had issue.

3 Humphrey, Rector of Leverington, Cambs., and of Hingham, Norfolk (1474?–1513).

4 Edward, Archdeacon of Richmond, Yorks. (*d.*1485?).

5 Richard, styled 'Earl of Suffolk' or 'The White Rose' (killed at the Battle of Pavia in 1525).

6 Geoffrey.

7 William (1478?–1539), a knight; he married Katherine (*d.*1521), daughter of William, 2nd Baron Stourton.

8 Anne (*d.* after 1495); she was a nun at Sion Abbey, Middlesex.

9 Katherine; she is said to have married William, Baron Stourton (1457–1524).

10 Elizabeth (*d.* after 1489); she married Henry Lovell, Baron

Morley (*d.*1489).

11 Dorothy (*d.* unmarried).

Elizabeth died between 7 January, 1503, and 3 May, 1504, and was buried in Wingfield Church, Suffolk.

6 *Margaret*

She was born on 3 May, 1446, at Fotheringhay Castle, Northants., and married Charles the Bold, Duke of Burgundy (1433–killed at the Battle of Nancy, 1477), on 3 July, 1468, at Damme, Flanders. She died on 16 April or 28 November, 1503, at Malines, Flanders, and was buried in the Church of the Cordeliers, Malines.

7 *William*

He was born on 7 July, 1447, at Fotheringhay Castle, Northants., and died young.

8 *John*

He was born on 7 November, 1448, at The Neyte, a house near Westminster, and died young.

9 *George*

He was born on 21 October, 1449, at Dublin Castle, Ireland. He was made a Knight of the Garter in 1461, and a Knight of the Bath on 27 June, 1461. He was created Duke of Clarence on 28 June, 1461. He was created Earl of Salisbury and Earl of Warwick, in right of his wife, on 25 March, 1472. He was attainted on 8 February, 1478, and by this Act of Attainder forfeited all his estates and titles and the rights of himself and his heirs to the succession. He was privately executed on 18 February, 1478, in the Tower of London: tradition has it that he was drowned in a butt of Malmsey wine. He was buried in Tewkesbury Abbey, Gloucs.

George married, on 11 July, 1469, at the Church of Our Lady, Calais, France:

Isabella

She was the daughter of Richard Neville, Earl of Warwick, by Anne, daughter of Richard de Beauchamp, Earl of Warwick; her sister Anne married firstly Edward, Prince of Wales, son of Henry VI, and secondly Richard III. Isabella was born on 5 September, 1451, at Warwick Castle. She died, it was rumoured by poison, on 21 December, 1476, at Warwick Castle, and was buried in Tewkesbury Abbey, Gloucs.

Issue of marriage:

(i) *Anne* **(?)**

She was born on 16 April, 1470, in a ship off Calais. She was either born dead or died soon after birth, and was buried at Calais. Some sources state that the child born at sea in 1470 was a son.

(ii) *Margaret*

She was born on 14 August, 1473, at Farleigh Castle, near Bath, Wilts. She married Sir Richard Pole (*d.*1505) on 22 September, 1494, and had issue:

1 Henry, Marquess of Montagu (1495?–executed 1538); he married Jane (*d.*1538), daughter of George Neville, Lord Bergavenny, and had issue.

2 Reginald, Cardinal-Archbishop of Canterbury (1500–1558).

3 Geoffrey, a knight, of Lordington, Sussex (1501–1558); he married Constance, daughter of Sir John Pakenham, and had issue.

4 Ursula (*d.*1570); she married Henry, Lord Stafford (1501–1563), and had issue.

5 Arthur (*d.*1570); he married Jane, daughter of Sir Roger Lewkmor, and had issue.

Margaret was restored to her father's earldom of Salisbury on 14 October, 1513. She was attainted on 12 May, 1539, and all her titles were declared forfeit. She was executed on 28 May, 1541, in the Tower of London, and was buried in the Royal Chapel of St Peter ad Vincula within the Tower.

(iii) *Edward*

He was born on 21 or 25 February, 1475 (or 1474?), at Warwick Castle, and was styled Earl of Warwick from birth, in right of his mother. He succeeded his mother as Earl of Salisbury in December, 1476, but was never so styled. He was confirmed as Earl of Warwick in 1490. He spent the greater part of his life in confinement, Henry VII resenting his proximity to the throne, and was executed for treason on 24 or 28 November, 1499, on Tower Hill, London. He was buried in Bisham Abbey, Berks.

(iv) *Richard*

He was born on 6 October, 1476, at Tewkesbury Abbey,

Gloucs., and died on 1 January, 1477, at Warwick Castle. He was buried in Warwick Church, by the Castle.

10 *Thomas*

He was born in 1450/1, and died young.

11 *Richard III* (◊ page 144).

12 *Ursula*

Described as the youngest child, she was born on 22 July, 1455, at Fotheringhay Castle, Northants., and died young.

13 *Katherine* (?)

14 *Humphrey* (?)

Katherine and Humphrey are described by Cecily as her children in her will, although they are not included in any other contemporary list of the children of Richard, Duke of York. The entry in Cecily's will may therefore refer in fact to her grandchildren, Humphrey and Katherine de la Pole, the issue of Cecily's daughter Elizabeth.

EDWARD IV

He was born on 28 April, 1442, at Rouen, France. He was styled Earl of March during his father's lifetime. In November, 1459, he forfeited all his honours by Act of Attainder, but was restored to them in October, 1460. He succeeded his father as Duke of York, Earl of Ulster and Earl of Cambridge on 30 December, 1460. He was proclaimed King of England by Parliament on 4 March, 1461, after the deposition of Henry VI, and was crowned on 28 June, 1461, at Westminster Abbey.

Edward IV was deposed in favour of Henry VI on 3 October, 1470, but restored to the throne on 11 April, 1471.

Edward IV married, on 1 May, 1464, at the Manor of Grafton Regis, Northants.:

Elizabeth

She was the daughter of Richard Wydville (or Woodville), 1st Earl Rivers, by Jacquetta of Luxembourg (◊ page 126, under Henry IV), and she was born in *c.*1437 at Grafton Regis, Northants. She married firstly Sir John Grey of Groby (killed 1461) in *c.*1452, and had issue:

1 Thomas, Marquess of Dorset (*c.*1455–1501); he married firstly Anne (*c.*1455–1475), daughter of Henry Holland, Duke of Exeter, by Anne, sister of Edward IV. He married secondly Cecilia,

Baroness Bonville and Harington (d.1529), daughter of William Bonville, Baron Harington, and had issue.

2 Richard (1456?–executed 1483), a knight.

Elizabeth was crowned Queen Consort on 26 May, 1465, at Westminster Abbey. Her marriage to Edward IV was declared invalid by Act of Parliament in 1484, on the basis of Edward's alleged precontract to Lady Eleanor Butler; her children were at the same time declared illegitimate, and unfit to inherit the crown. The marriage was ultimately recognised as valid in October, 1485, by the first Parliament of Henry VII, and its issue were restored in blood accordingly. Elizabeth died on 8 June, 1492, at St Saviour's Abbey, Bermondsey, London, and was buried in St George's Chapel, Windsor.

Issue of marriage:

1 Elizabeth

(◊ page 151, under Henry VII, whom she married).

2 Mary

She was born on 11 August, 1467, at Windsor Castle. She was made a Lady of the Garter in 1480. She died on 23 May, 1482, at Greenwich Palace, Kent, and was buried in St George's Chapel, Windsor.

3 Cecily

She was born on 20 March, 1469, at the Palace of Westminster. She married firstly John Welles, 1st Viscount Welles, K.G. (d.1498), between 25 November, 1487, and 1 January, 1488, and had issue:

1 Elizabeth (d. young before 1498).

2 Anne (d. young in c.1499).

Cecily married secondly Thomas Kyme, Kymbe or Keme, either of Wainfleet and Friskney, Lincs., or of the Isle of Wight, between 13 May, 1502, and January, 1504, by whom she may have had issue, although the earliest evidence for this is as late as 1602, and may be suspect:

3 Richard; he married a lady called Agnes, and had issue.

4 Margaret or Marjorie; she married John Wetherby, and had issue.

Cecily was made a Lady of the Garter in 1480. She died on 24 August, 1507, at Quarr Abbey, Isle of Wight, where she was buried.

4 *Edward V* (◊ page 143).

5 *Margaret*

She was born on 10 April, 1472, at Windsor Castle, and died on 11 December, 1472. She was buried in Westminster Abbey.

6 *Richard*

He was born on 17 August, 1473, at the Dominican Friary, Shrewsbury, Shropshire. He was created Duke of York on 28 May, 1474, thereby establishing the tradition (which continues to this day) that the second son of the sovereign is always made Duke of York. He was made a Knight of the Garter on 15 May, 1475, and a Knight of the Bath during that same year. He was created Earl of Nottingham on 12 June, 1476, and Duke of Norfolk and Earl of Surrey and Warenne on 7 February, 1477. He was declared illegitimate and deprived of his titles by Act of Parliament in January 1484. York was probably murdered with his brother Edward V (◊ page 143) on the night of 3 September, 1483, in the Tower of London, on the orders of Richard III. In 1674, bones discovered in the Tower were thought to be those of the two Princes, and were reburied in 1678 in Westminster Abbey.

Richard married, on 15 January, 1478, at St Stephen's Chapel in the Palace of Westminster:

Anne

She was the daughter of John Mowbray, Duke of Norfolk, by Elizabeth, daughter of John Talbot, 2nd Earl of Shrewsbury, and she was born on 10 December, 1472, at Framlingham Castle, Suffolk. She was recognised and styled as Countess of Norfolk in her own right on 16/17 January, 1476, after the death of her father. She died between 16 January, and 19 November, 1481, at Greenwich Palace, and was buried in Westminster Abbey. When Henry VII's Chapel was under construction, her body was moved to the Minoresses' Convent at Stepney, where her coffin was found during excavations in 1965. She was then reburied in Westminster Abbey.

7 *Anne*

She was born on 2 November, 1475, at the Palace of Westminster. She married Lord Thomas Howard (afterwards Earl of Surrey, then Duke of Norfolk) (1473–1554) on 4 February, 1495, at Greenwich Palace, and had issue:

1 Thomas (c.1496 or 1508–1509).

2 Son (d. young before baptism).

3 Daughter (d. young before baptism).

4 Daughter (d. young before baptism).

Anne died after 22 November (23 November?), 1511, and before 1513, and was buried in Thetford Priory, Norfolk. Her remains were later removed to Framlingham Church, Suffolk.

8 *George*

He was born perhaps in March, 1477 (certainly before January, 1478), either at Windsor Castle, or at the Dominican Friary, Shrewsbury, Shropshire, and was perhaps styled Duke of Bedford. He died in March, 1479, at Windsor Castle, and was buried in St George's Chapel, Windsor.

9 *Katherine*

She was born on 14 August, 1479, at Eltham Palace, Kent. She married William Courtenay, later Earl of Devon (1475–1511), in c.October, 1495, and had issue:

1 Henry, Marquess of Exeter (1496?–executed 1538); he married firstly Elizabeth (d.1516?), daughter of John Grey, Viscount Lisle, and secondly Gertrude (d.1558), daughter of William Blount, 4th Baron Mountjoy, and had issue.

2 Edward (1497?–1502).

3 Margaret (1499?–1519?); she married William, Baron Herbert.

Katherine took a vow of perpetual chastity upon her widowhood in 1511. She died on 15 November, 1527, at Tiverton Castle, Devon, and was buried in Tiverton Parish Church.

10 *Bridget*

She was born on 10 or 20 November, 1480, at Eltham Palace, Kent. She became a nun at Dartford Priory, Kent, in c.1487 (and certainly before 1492). She died probably before 1513. John Weaver, writing in the 17th century, states she died in 1517, but Thomas More, writing in 1513, does not say that she is alive, although he mentions that her only surviving sister, Katherine, was then still living. Bridget was buried in Dartford Priory, Kent.

Edward IV also had the following **illegitimate issue:**

By Eleanor Talbot or Butler (d.1468), to whom Edward is alleged to have been precontracted:

1 Edward de Wigmore (d. in infancy, 1468).

By Elizabeth Lucy (née Waite), or Elizabeth (sometimes, but erroneously, called Jane) Shore:

2 Arthur Plantagenet, Viscount Lisle (1461/4–1542); he married firstly Elizabeth Grey, Baroness Lisle (*d*.1525/6), and had issue. He married secondly Honora (1493/5–1566), daughter of Sir Thomas Grenville.

3 Elizabeth (*b.c.*1464); she perhaps married Thomas Lumley. It is thought that Elizabeth Lucy was her mother.

By an unknown mother:

4 Grace (alive in 1492).

EDWARD IV

He died on 9 April, 1483, at the Palace of Westminster, and was buried in St George's Chapel, Windsor.

He was succeeded by his son Edward.

Edward V

FATHER: *Edward IV* (◊ page 134).
MOTHER: *Elizabeth Wydville* (◊ page 139, under *Edward IV*).
SIBLINGS:(◊ page 140, under *Edward IV*).

EDWARD V

He was born on 2 November, 1470, in the Sanctuary, Westminster Abbey. He was created Prince of Wales and Earl of Chester on 25/26 June, 1471, and Duke of Cornwall on 17 July, 1471. He was made a Knight of the Garter on 15 May, 1475, and created Earl of March and Earl of Pembroke on 8 or 18 July, 1479. He succeeded his father as King of England on 9 April, 1483.

Edward V was deposed on 25 June, 1483, and declared illegitimate by Act of Parliament in 1484 (◊ under *Edward IV*). He was probably murdered with his brother, Richard, Duke of York, on the night of 3 September, 1483, in the Tower of London, on the orders of Richard

III. In 1674, bones discovered in the Tower were thought to be those of the two Princes, and were reburied in 1678 in Westminster Abbey, by order of Charles II. Edward V was succeeded by his uncle, Richard of Gloucester.

Richard III

FATHER: *Richard Plantagenet, Duke of York* (◊ page 134, under *Edward IV*)
MOTHER: *Cecily Neville* (◊ page 135, under *Edward IV*)
SIBLINGS: (◊ page 135, under *Edward IV*)

RICHARD III

He was born on 2 October, 1452, at Fotheringhay Castle, Northants. He was created Duke of Gloucester on 1 November, 1461, and made a Knight of the Garter before 4 February, 1466. He acceded to the throne of England on 26 June, 1483, after the deposition of his nephew, Edward V, and was crowned on 6 July, 1483, in Westminster Abbey.

Richard III married, on 12 July, 1472, in Westminster Abbey or St Stephen's Chapel, Westminster:

Anne

She was the daughter of Richard Neville, Earl of Warwick, by Anne, daughter of Richard de Beauchamp, Earl of Warwick, and she was born on 11 June, 1456, at Warwick Castle. She married firstly Edward, Prince of Wales, son of Henry VI, probably on 13 December, 1470, at the Château of Amboise, France. She was crowned Queen Consort on 6 July, 1483, at Westminster Abbey. She died on 16 March, 1485, at the Palace of Westminster, probably of tuberculosis, and was buried in Westminster Abbey.

Issue of marriage:

1 *Edward*

He was born in Spring, 1476, at Middleham Castle, Yorkshire, and was created Earl of Salisbury on 15 February, 1478. He became Duke of Cornwall upon his father's accession to the throne on 26 June, 1483, and was created Prince of Wales and Earl of Chester on 24 August, 1483, being invested as such on 8 September, 1483, at York Minster. He died on 9 April, 1484, at Middleham Castle, Yorkshire, and was perhaps buried in Sheriff Hutton Church, Yorkshire.

Richard III also had the following **illegitimate issue:**

By unknown mothers:

1 John of Gloucester, or of Pontefract, Captain of Calais (c.1470–murdered? 1499?).
2 Richard Plantagenet of Eastwell, Kent (1469–1550).
3 Katherine; she married William Herbert, Earl of Huntingdon (1455?–1491).
4 Stephen Hawes (?).
5 Unnamed child (?).
6 Unnamed child (?).
7 Unnamed child (?).

RICHARD III

He was killed on 22 August, 1485, defending his crown and his kingdom against the forces of Henry Tudor at the Battle of Bosworth Field in Leicestershire. He was buried in the Collegiate Church of St Mary, Leicester. His grave was despoiled during the Reformation. Richard was the last Plantagenet King of England. He was succeeded by his distant cousin Henry Tudor.

CHAPTER FIVE

The Tudors

The Tudors came from bastard stock. Henry VII's mother, Margaret Beaufort, was a descendant of John Beaufort, the first of the natural children born to John of Gaunt, Duke of Lancaster, and his mistress, Katherine Swynford. Henry's father, Edmund Tudor, was the offspring of the liaison between Henry V's widow, Katherine of France, and the Welsh squire, Owen Tudor. Possibly these two married in secret, but no proof of this has ever been discovered; in the 15th century, their children were looked upon as bastards, with all the handicaps that imposed upon inheritance. Not for them a Statute conferring legitimacy, as had been the good fortune of the Beaufort bastards of Katherine Swynford when her lover Gaunt at long last made her his wife. Yet even to this there was a sting in the tail: for while the Beauforts were recognised as legitimate by a Statute of Richard II, they were soon afterwards debarred by Henry IV from ever inheriting the throne.

Henry VII was the only child of his parents; his father died before his birth and his mother remarried (she had been but 13 years old at the time of his birth, and never bore another child). Henry was exiled from England by Edward IV, while still a child, and spent his youth in the courts of France and Brittany with his uncle and staunch supporter, Jaspar Tudor. Both were loyal to Henry VI and the House of Lancaster, and after the death of Henry VI and his son Edward, Henry Tudor was seen by many as the natural heir to the Lancastrian claim to the throne of England, despite his legal ineligibility to fulfil such a role. There were no other heirs of the blood of Lancaster. And it was the crown of England that Henry meant to have. On Christmas Day, 1483, in the Cathedral of Rennes in Brittany, he vowed to marry

Elizabeth of York, daughter of Edward IV, and thus unite the red and white roses of Lancaster and York. Henry must have known at this date that Edward V and his brother were dead; Elizabeth had been declared a bastard, and if Henry was to claim the throne through marrying her, this could only be accomplished if her brothers had predeceased her. Two years later, in August, 1485, Henry Tudor defeated Richard III at the Battle of Bosworth and became King of England. In January, 1486, he kept his vow and married Elizabeth, who had been legitimated in his first Parliament; the slight delay between Henry's accession and his marriage served only to emphasise that Henry's crown was his by right of conquest and of descent (significantly, he dated his reign from the day before Bosworth), and not through union with Elizabeth of York.

Thus was founded the Tudor dynasty, a dynasty that, as if to compensate for its precarious claim to the throne, was to be the most splendid and successful of all the English Royal Houses. During the 118 years of Tudor rule, England emerged from the mediaeval world as a modern state, prosperous and proud of itself. It was, however, a revolutionary age and a brutal one. Henry VIII declared himself Head of the Church of England and severed for ever all links with the Church of Rome. Under Elizabeth, the Protestant Anglican Church became firmly established. Voyages of discovery were opening up the wider world and trade flourished. The old nobility found themselves being replaced by 'new men', who had risen through ability or wealth rather than noble lineage. Yet in this same age that witnessed the spread of the humanist 'new learning' and the flowering of the English Renaissance, thousands were executed for heresy or treason, often with appalling barbarity. There was no 'niceness' about the Tudor monarchs: they did what they saw as necessary thoroughly and ruthlessly, although by 1603, when Elizabeth I died, some of the power of government had devolved upon Parliament, so often consulted by successive Tudor monarchs to lend support and legality to revolutionary measures, and eventually insisting upon being consulted and giving approval as a right. The Tudors' parliamentary legacy to their successors was no easy one, and would in time, given the ineptitude and obstinacy of Charles I, lead to civil war.

Yet while they were powerful and capable monarchs, the Tudors were never quite secure on the throne. During the first fifty years of their rule, too many members of the House of York remained alive for the new dynasty to feel secure. Later, threats to the succession would be posed by the Grey family and by Mary, Queen of Scots. But it was the surviving members of the House of York who constituted the worst threat, as there was no doubt in the minds of many that their title to the throne was far more valid than that of the Tudors. In fact, in 1485, when Henry VII acceded to the throne, there were then living 18 people with a better right to it than he, including his own wife and mother. By 1510, this figure had increased by about 16 more persons, born with Yorkist blood in their veins.

Of course, many of these heirs of York were women. Although the Salic Law had no validity in England (unlike in France, where women were debarred from inheriting the throne), memories of the Empress Matilda, whose attempt in the 12th century to rule England had resulted in bloody civil war, had led to an enduring prejudice against the notion of a female sovereign. Women were considered unfit to rule over men, and no one seriously thought of espousing the cause of any of the Yorkist women. Ironically, it would be left to the Tudors themselves to demonstrate that a female sovereign could rule very successfully.

It was the male members of the House of York who were the thorn in the side of the Tudors. Some died young, and of the eight who survived to be serious contenders for the throne, two chose a life of retirement away from public life, and were not molested. Two died in battle, one of them an exile fighting under a foreign banner. Four were executed. Both Henry VII and Henry VIII were cognisant of the weakness of their claim to the throne, and dealt ruthlessly with any would-be rivals. Mention should be made of Margaret Pole, Countess of Salisbury, niece of Edward IV and Richard III, who, at the age of nearly 68, was beheaded in an horrific manner on the orders of Henry VIII, on a trumped-up charge of treason. Lesser members of her family were imprisoned by that monarch, and left to rot in the Tower. By then, the danger from the House of York had been virtually eliminated, although junior sprigs of the Plantagenet tree were being sent to the Tower as late as the reign of Elizabeth I.

To give his dynasty a sound title to the throne, Henry VII had to go back beyond the Plantagenets, the Normans, and the Saxon Kings, to the legendary Arthur, the ancient British kings, and the Welsh Prince

Cadwaladr, whose red dragon appeared on Henry's standard. He claimed descent from all these, through Rhys ap Tewdwr, Prince of Deheubarth in Wales, who died in 1093. Henry even named his eldest son after King Arthur to emphasise the link between the Tudors and ancient royalty. The message was clear: he was the true successor to Arthur and Cadwaladr and their ilk; all those who had come since were the real usurpers.

The dynasty survived, but it did not flourish. The succession was an ongoing problem, because the Tudors were not a fruitful family: many of its members were sickly, or died young. Henry VIII took drastic measures to get a male heir, taking six wives in the process, divorcing two, and beheading two more, as well as creating a schism in the Church. He was not just a man of lusts: nobody wanted a return to the dynastic warfare of the previous century, and Tudor prosperity had done much to make the new dynasty popular. Henry's only surviving son Edward VI did not live to marry, and there was then no alternative but for the country to turn to a female as its ruler. But Mary I, after suffering two tragic phantom pregnancies, did not live long. Her sister Elizabeth I had a long and glorious reign, but her solution to the succession problem was to remain unmarried, a choice she seems to have made for both political and personal reasons. For fear of factions forming around a designated successor, she kept her subjects guessing to the last whom she would name as her heir. It was, of course, her cousin, James VI of Scotland, a descendant of Henry VII, and founder of the House of Stuart in 1603.

Henry VII

FATHER: *Edmund*

He was the son of Owen Tudor by Katherine of France, widow of
Henry V, and he was born in *c.*1430, either at Much Hadham
Palace, Herts., or at Hadham, Beds. He was created Earl of
Richmond on 23 November, 1452. He married Margaret Beaufort
in October, 1455, at Bletsoe Castle, Beds. He died on 1 November,
1456, at Carmarthen Castle, Wales, and was buried in the Church
of the Grey Friars, Carmarthen. His remains were later transferred
to St David's Cathedral, Wales.

MOTHER: *Margaret*

She was the daughter of John Beaufort, Duke of Somerset (◊ page
105, under Edward III), by Margaret de Beauchamp, and she was
born on 31 May, 1443, at Bletsoe Castle, Beds. She married firstly
John de la Pole, later Duke of Suffolk (*d.*1491), between 28 January,
1449, and 18 August, 1450, but the marriage was annulled before 24
March, 1453, and de la Pole later married Elizabeth, sister of
Edward IV. Margaret married secondly Edmund Tudor. After his
death, she married thirdly Sir Henry Stafford (*d.*1471) between
*c.*1459 and 1464. She married fourthly Thomas Stanley, Earl of
Derby (1435?–1504), before October, 1473 (or October, 1482?),
although she had taken a vow of perpetual chastity. She was made
a Lady of the Garter in 1488. She died on 29 June, 1509, at the
Abbot's House, Cheyney Gates, Westminster Abbey, and was
buried in Westminster Abbey.

SIBLINGS: *Henry VII did not have any siblings.*

HENRY VII

He was born on 28 January, 1457, at Pembroke Castle in Wales, and
was Earl of Richmond from birth, being his father's posthumous
child. He was deprived of the earldom of Richmond before 12 August,
1462. He succeeded Richard III as King of England on 22 August,

1485, after the Battle of Bosworth (he dated his reign from 21 August, the day before Bosworth), and was crowned on 30 October, 1485, in Westminster Abbey.

Henry VII married, on 18 January, 1486, at Westminster Abbey:
Elizabeth

She was the daughter of Edward IV by Elizabeth Wydville, and she was born on 11 February, 1466, at the Palace of Westminster. She was crowned Queen Consort on 25 November, 1487, in Westminster Abbey. She died on 11 February, 1503, in the Tower of London, in childbed, and was buried in Westminster Abbey.

Issue of marriage:

1 *Arthur*

Called Arthur to emphasise the new dynasty's links with the Kings of ancient Britain, he was born on 19/20 September, 1486, at St Swithun's Priory, Winchester. He was Duke of Cornwall from birth. He was made a Knight of the Bath on 29 November, 1489. He was created Prince of Wales and Earl of Chester on 29 November, 1489, and was invested as such on 27 February, 1490, at the Palace of Westminster. He was made a Knight of the Garter on 8 May, 1491. He died on 2 April, 1502, at Ludlow Castle, Shropshire, and was buried in Worcester Cathedral.

Arthur married, by proxy on Whitsunday, 1499, at the manor of Bewdley, Worcs., again by proxy on 19 May, 1501, at Bewdley, and in person on 14 November, 1501, at St Paul's Cathedral, London:

Katherine

She was the daughter of Ferdinand V, King of Aragon, by Isabella I, Queen of Castile, a descendant of John of Gaunt, and she was born on 16 December, 1485, at Alcala de Henares in Spain. After the death of Arthur, she married secondly Henry VIII (◊ page 153, under Henry VIII for further details of her life).

2 *Margaret* (◊ page 240, under *James IV of Scotland*, whom she married).

3 *Henry VIII* (◊ page 153).

4 *Elizabeth*

She was born on 2 July, 1492, and died on 7 October or 14 November, 1495, at Eltham Palace, Kent, of 'atrophy'. She was buried in Westminster Abbey.

5 *Mary*

She was born on *c.*18 March, 1495/6, either at Richmond Palace, Surrey, or at the Palace of Westminster. She married firstly Louis XII, King of France (1462–1515), by proxy on 13 August, 1514, at Greyfriars Church, Greenwich Palace, again by proxy on 2 September, 1514, at the Church of the Celestines in Paris, and in person on 9 October, 1514, at Abbeville Cathedral, France. She was crowned on 5 November, 1514, at St Denis' Cathedral, Paris. She married secondly Charles Brandon, Duke of Suffolk (1484–1545), secretly on 3 March, 1515, at the Chapel in the Palais de Cluny, Paris, and in public on 13 May, 1515, in the Church of the Observant Friars, Greenwich, Kent, and had issue:

1 Henry, Earl of Lincoln (1516–1534).

2 Frances (◊ page 158, under *Queen Jane*).

3 Eleanor (1519–1547); she married Henry Clifford, Earl of Cumberland (1517–1570), and had issue.

Mary died on 25 June, 1533, at Westhorpe Hall, Suffolk, and was buried in the Abbey of Bury St Edmunds, Suffolk; her remains were later removed to St Mary's Church, Bury St Edmunds.

6 *Edmund*

He was born on 21 February, 1499, at Greenwich Palace, Kent; he was perhaps styled Duke of Somerset from birth, but was never formally so created. He died on 19 June, 1500, at the Old Palace, Hatfield, Herts., and was buried in Westminster Abbey.

7 *Edward*

He was the fourth and youngest son. The dates of his birth and death are not known. He died very young, and was buried in Westminster Abbey.

8 *Katherine*

She was born on 2 February, 1503, in the Tower of London, and died there on *c.*18 February, 1503. She was buried in Westminster Abbey.

Henry VII also had the following **illegitimate issue**:

By a Breton lady whose name is not known:

1 Roland de Velville, Constable of Beaumaris Castle, Anglesey; he married a Welshwoman, and had issue.

HENRY VII

He died on 21 April, 1509, at Richmond Palace, Surrey, and was buried in Westminster Abbey.

He was succeeded by his son Henry.

Henry VIII

FATHER: *Henry VII* (✷ page l50).
MOTHER: *Elizabeth of York* (✷ page 151, under *Henry VII*).
SIBLINGS: (✷ page 151, under *Henry VII*).

HENRY VIII

He was born on 28 June, 1491, at Greenwich Palace, Kent. He was made a Knight of the Bath on 31 October, 1491, and created Duke of York on 31st October, 1494. He was made a Knight of the Garter on 17 May, 1495. He succeeded his brother Arthur as Duke of Cornwall on 2 April, 1502, and was created and invested as Prince of Wales and Earl of Chester on 18 February, 1504, at the Palace of Westminster. He succeeded his father as King of England on 22 April, 1509, and was crowned on 24 June, 1509, in Westminster Abbey. In 1521, he added to the royal style the title 'Fidei Defensor' ('Defender of the Faith'), conferred upon him by Pope Leo X. This title is still borne by the Queen today. Henry styled himself King of Ireland from 1542.

Henry VIII married firstly, on 11 June, 1509, in the Queen's closet at Greenwich Palace, Kent:

Katherine

She was the daughter of Ferdinand V, King of Aragon, by Isabella I, Queen of Castile, a descendant of John of Gaunt, and she was born on 16 December, 1485, at Alcala de Henares in Spain. She married firstly Henry's elder brother Arthur, Prince of Wales, in 1501 (✷ page 151, under Henry VII). She was crowned Queen Consort on 24 June, 1509, in Westminster Abbey. Her marriage to Henry VIII was annulled on 23 May, 1533, by Thomas Cranmer, Archbishop of Canterbury, on the grounds that she had been the wife of her husband's brother and that, according to the Levitical Law, her second marriage was uncanonical and incestuous, and the Pope had no power to dispense in such a case. She died on 7 January, 1536, at Kimbolton Castle, Hunts., probably of cancer, and was buried in Peterborough Cathedral. Her original tomb was destroyed in 1642, but its site may still be seen, and her bones still lie beneath the flagstones.

Issue of marriage:

1 *Stillborn daughter*
She was born on 31 January, 1510.

2 *Henry*
He was born on 1 January, 1511, at Richmond Palace, Surrey, and was Duke of Cornwall from birth. He was also styled Prince of Wales. He died on 22 February, 1511, at Richmond Palace, and was buried in Westminster Abbey.

3 *Unnamed son*
He was born in November, 1513, at Richmond Palace, Surrey, and was Duke of Cornwall from birth. He died in November, 1513, and was buried in Westminster Abbey.

4 *Unnamed son*
He was born in February, 1515, at Greenwich, and died soon after birth. While he lived, he was Duke of Cornwall.

5 *Mary I* (◊ page 161).

6 *Unnamed daughter*
She was born on 10 November, 1518, and died the same day.

Henry VIII married secondly, in secret, on 25 January, 1533, at York Place, London:

Anne

She was the daughter of Thomas Boleyn or Bullen, 1st Earl of Wiltshire and Ormonde, by Elizabeth, daughter of Thomas Howard, 2nd Duke of Norfolk. She was born around 1500/1501 at Blickling Hall, Norfolk. She was created Lady Marquess of Pembroke in her own right (the first time a female had been created a peer in her own right) on 1 September, 1532. She was crowned Queen Consort on 1 June, 1533, in Westminster Abbey. On 15 May, 1536, Anne Boleyn was tried and found guilty of high treason, and condemned to death in the Great Hall of the Tower of London. Her marriage to Henry VIII was declared invalid on 17 May, 1536; the grounds for this are not known. She was executed on 19 May, 1536, on Tower Green, within the Tower of London, and was buried in the Chapel Royal of St Peter ad Vincula within the Tower of London.

Issue of marriage (declared illegitimate on 17 May, 1536):

1 *Elizabeth I* (◊ page 162).

2 *Stillborn child?* (sex unknown).

It was born in August/September, 1534; this was nearly a full-term pregnancy, but details of the birth were kept secret.

3 *Stillborn son*

He was born on 29 January, 1536, at Greenwich Palace.

Henry VIII married thirdly, on 30 May, 1536, at Whitehall Palace, London:

Jane

She was the daughter of Sir John Seymour by Margaret, daughter of Sir Henry Wentworth of Nettlestead, Suffolk, and she was born in 1507/8, probably at Wulfhall in Savernake Forest, Wiltshire. She was never crowned. She died on 24 October, 1537, at Hampton Court Palace, in childbed, and was buried in St George's Chapel, Windsor.

Issue of marriage:

1 *Edward VI* (◊ page 157).

Henry VIII married fourthly, on 6 January, 1540, at Greenwich Palace:

Anne

She was the daughter of John III, Duke of Cleves, by Mary, daughter of William III, Duke of Jülich and Berg, and she was born on 22 September, 1515, at Düsseldorf, Cleves, Germany. Her marriage to Henry VIII was not consummated, and it was annulled on 9 July, 1540, on the grounds of Anne's alleged precontract with the Duke of Lorraine. Anne died on 16 July, 1557, at Chelsea Old Palace, London, and was buried in Westminster Abbey. There was no issue of the marriage.

Henry VIII married fifthly, on 28 July, 1540, at Oatlands Palace, Surrey:

Katherine

She was the daughter of Lord Edmund Howard by Joyce or Jocasta, daughter of Sir Richard Culpeper, and she was born in *c.*1525, either at Lambeth in London, or at Horsham, Sussex. She was never crowned. Katherine was attainted for high treason, and was executed on 13 February, 1542, on Tower Green within the Tower of London. She was buried in the Chapel Royal of St Peter ad Vincula within the Tower of London. There was no issue of the marriage.

Henry VIII married sixthly, on 12 July, 1543, at Hampton Court Palace:

Katherine

She was the daughter of Sir Thomas Parr by Maud, daughter of Sir Thomas Green of Green's Norton, Northants., and she was born probably in 1512 at her father's house at Blackfriars, London. She married firstly Edward de Burgh, 2nd Baron Borough of Gainsborough (1463–1528) after 26 June, 1526. She married secondly John Neville, 3rd Baron Latimer (1493–1542), perhaps in 1530, and certainly before the end of 1533. After the death of Henry VIII, her third husband, she married fourthly Thomas Seymour, 1st Baron Sudely (1508?–executed 1549), brother of Queen Jane (♀ above), shortly before the end of April, 1547, and had issue:

1 Mary (1548–?); she either died young in c.1560, or grew up and married Sir Edward Bushel, and had issue. However, the evidence for this marriage dates from the 18th century only, and should therefore be regarded with caution.

Katherine died on 7 September, 1548, at Sudely Castle, Gloucs., in childbed, and was buried in Sudely Castle Chapel. There was no issue of her marriage to Henry VIII.

Henry VIII also had the following **illegitimate issue**:

By Elizabeth Blount (1502?–1539/41), daughter of Sir John Blount of Kinlet, Shropshire, afterwards wife of Gilbert, Lord Tailboys:

1 Henry FitzRoy, Duke of Richmond and Somerset (1519–1536); he married Mary (1519?–1557), daughter of Thomas Howard, 3rd Duke of Norfolk. He was the only bastard acknowledged by Henry VIII.

By Joan Dobson or Dingley:

2 Ethelreda or Audrey (d.1555); she married John Harington, and had issue.

By Mary Berkeley (?):

3 Sir John Perrot (1527?–1592) (?).

By an unknown mother:

4 Thomas Stucley or Stukely (1525?–1578) (?); he married Anne

Curtis. It is highly unlikely that Henry VIII was the father of Thomas or Sir John Perrot.

HENRY VIII

He died on 28 January, 1547, at Whitehall Palace, London, and was buried in St George's Chapel, Windsor.

He was succeeded by his son Edward.

Edward VI

FATHER: *Henry VIII* (◊ page 153).
MOTHER: *Jane Seymour* (◊ page 155, under *Henry VIII*).
SIBLINGS: *Edward VI did not have any full siblings.*

EDWARD VI

He was born on 12 October, 1537, at Hampton Court Palace, Surrey, and was Duke of Cornwall from birth. He succeeded his father as King of England on 28 January, 1547, and was crowned on 20 or 25 February, 1547, in Westminster Abbey.

EDWARD VI

He died unmarried on 6 July, 1553, at Greenwich Palace, Kent, and was buried in Westminster Abbey.

He was succeeded by his second cousin Lady Jane Grey.

Queen Jane

FATHER: *Henry*

He was the son of Thomas Grey, Marquess of Dorset, by Margaret, daughter of Sir Robert Wotton, and he was born on 17 January, 1517. He married firstly Katherine (*d.* after 1552), daughter of William FitzAlan, Earl of Arundel, before 1530. He succeeded his father as Marquess of Dorset, Baron Ferrers of Groby, Baron Harington and Baron Bonville on 10 October, 1530. He repudiated his first wife before 1533, and married secondly Frances Brandon in May, 1533, at Suffolk Place, Southwark, London. He was made a Knight of the Bath on 30 May, 1533, and a Knight of the Garter on 17 February, 1547, and was created Duke of Suffolk, in right of his wife, on 11 October, 1551. Henry was attainted, and his estates were declared forfeit, on 17 February, 1554, as a result of his treasonous involvement in Wyatt's rebellion against Mary I; he was executed on 23 February, 1554, on Tower Hill, London, and was buried in the Chapel Royal of St Peter ad Vincula within the Tower of London.

MOTHER: *Frances*

She was the daughter of Charles Brandon, Duke of Suffolk, by Mary, daughter of Henry VII, and she was born on 16 July, 1517, either at Bishop's Hatfield, Herts., or at Westhorpe Hall, Suffolk. After the execution of her first husband, the Duke of Suffolk, she married secondly Adrian Stokes (1533–1585), her Master of Horse, on 9 March, 1554, and had issue:

1 Elizabeth (*b.&d.*1554).

2 Son (*d.* young).

3 Son (*d.* young).

Frances died on 20 or 21 November, 1559, at the Charterhouse, Sheen, Surrey, and was buried in Westminster Abbey.

SIBLINGS:

1 *Unnamed brother*

He died young before 1537.

2 *Unnamed sister*

She died young before 1537.

3 *Katherine*

She was born in August, 1540, perhaps at Dorset House, Westminster. She married firstly Henry Herbert, 2nd Earl of Pembroke (after 1538–1601), on 25 May, 1553, at Durham House, Strand, London. The marriage was annulled in 1554, and Katherine married secondly Edward Seymour, 1st Earl of Hertford (1539–1621), in secret around November/December, 1560, at Hertford House, Cannon Row, Westminster, and had issue:

1 Edward, Baron Beauchamp (1561–1612); he married Honora (*d.* after 1608), daughter of Sir Richard Rogers of Bryanston, Dorset, and had issue.

2 Thomas (1563–1619); he married Isabella, daughter of Edward Onley of Catesby, Northants.

3 Edward (*d.*1602); his existence is doubtful.

4 Katherine (*d.* young); her existence is doubtful.

Katherine's union with Edward Seymour was declared 'no marriage' on 12 May, 1561, and deemed never to have taken place; it was, however, declared valid in 1608. Katherine died on 26/27 January, 1568, at Cockfield Hall, Yoxford, Suffolk, and was buried in Yoxford Church, Suffolk. Her remains were later removed to Salisbury Cathedral.

4 *Mary*

She was born in 1545, and was a hunchback. She married Thomas Keyes (*d.*1571) on 10 or 12 August, 1564/5, at the Water Gate Lodge, by the Palace of Westminster. She died on 20 April, 1578, at the Barbican, by Red Cross Street, London, and was buried either in St Botolph's Church, Aldersgate, London, or in Westminster Abbey.

QUEEN JANE

She was born in October, 1537, at Bradgate Manor, Leics. The Will of Henry VIII left the crown, in order of succession, to his children, Edward, Mary and Elizabeth, and then, if their lines failed, to the heirs of his sister Mary, Duchess of Suffolk. When Edward VI died on 6

July, 1553, the Duke of Northumberland, who had governed the country in the boy King's name as Lord Protector, wished to see the continuance of his own power and the maintenance of the newly-established Protestant religion in England. The next heir, Mary Tudor, was a staunch Catholic, therefore it had not been difficult for Northumberland to persuade the dying Edward – a fervent Protestant – to sign a Device changing his father's Will. Mary was set aside, and also Elizabeth, whose religious convictions were uncertain, and the crown was willed by Edward to Lady Jane Grey, bypassing her mother Frances, who was rightful Queen after Mary and Elizabeth. Jane was proclaimed Queen of England on 10 July, 1553.

Queen Jane married, on 25 May, 1553, at Durham House, Strand, London:

Guilford

He was the son of John Dudley, Duke of Northumberland, by Jane, daughter of Sir Edward Guilford, and he was born in 1536. He was executed on 12 February, 1554, on Tower Hill, London, and was buried in the Chapel Royal of St Peter and Vincula within the Tower of London. There was no issue of the marriage.

QUEEN JANE

She reigned for only nine days. The people of England rallied to the cause of Mary Tudor, and Jane, the usurper, was deposed on 19 July, 1553. She was executed on 12 February, 1554, on Tower Green, within the Tower of London, in the aftermath of Thomas Wyatt's rebellion. Jane was buried in the Chapel Royal of St Peter ad Vincula within the Tower of London.

She had already been succeeded by her second cousin Mary.

Mary I

FATHER: *Henry VIII* (◊ page 153).
MOTHER: *Katherine of Aragon* (◊ page 153, under *Henry VIII*).
SIBLINGS: (◊ page 154, under *Henry VIII*).

MARY I

She was born on 18 February, 1516, at Greenwich Palace, Kent. She was proclaimed Queen of England upon the deposition of Queen Jane on 19 July, 1553, although her regnal years were dated from 24 July. She was crowned on 1 October, 1553, at Westminster Abbey. She assumed the title Queen of Spain upon the accession of her husband, Philip II, to the throne of Spain on 16 January, 1556.

Mary I married, on 25 July, 1554, at Winchester Cathedral:
Philip

He was the son of Charles V, Holy Roman Emperor and King of Spain, by Isabella, daughter of Manuel I, King of Portugal, and he was born on 21 May, 1527, at Valladolid, Spain. He married firstly Mary (1527–1545), daughter of John III, King of Portugal, on 12 November, 1543, at Salamanca, Spain, and had issue:

1 Charles (Don Carlos) (1545–1568).

Philip was designated King of Naples, Jerusalem and Savoy in preparation for his marriage to Mary I (to give him equal rank), and was made a Knight of the Garter on 24 April, 1554. He succeeded his father as King of Spain on 16 January, 1556. After Mary's death, he married thirdly Elizabeth (1545–1568), daughter of Henry II, King of France, in 1559 at Toledo, Spain, and had issue:

1 Unnamed daughter (*b.*1564).

2 Unnamed daughter (*b.*1564).

3 Isabella Clara Eugenia (1566–1633); she married Albert, Archduke of Austria (1559–1621).

4 Katherine Michela (1567–1597); she married Charles Emmanuel I, Duke of Savoy (1562–1630).

5 Unnamed daughter (*b.&d.*1568).

Philip married fourthly Anne (1549–1580), daughter of Maximilian II, Holy Roman Emperor, in 1570 at Segovia, Spain, and had issue:

1 Ferdinand (1571–1578).

2 Edward (1575–1582).

3 Philip III, King of Spain (1578–1621); he married Marianna (1584–1611), daughter of Charles, Archduke of Austria, and had issue.

4 Mary.

Philip became King of Portugal in 1580. He died on 13 September, 1598, at the Palace of the Escorial, Madrid, Spain, where he is buried in the mausoleum. There was no issue of his marriage to Mary I.

MARY I

She died on 17 November, 1558, at St James's Palace, London, and was buried in Westminster Abbey.

She was succeeded by her half-sister Elizabeth.

Elizabeth I

FATHER: *Henry VIII* (◊ page 153).

MOTHER: *Anne Boleyn* (◊ page 154, under *Henry VIII*).

SIBLINGS: *Elizabeth I did not have any full siblings.*

ELIZABETH I

She was born on 7 September, 1533, at Greenwich Palace, Kent. She succeeded her half sister Mary I as Queen of England on 17 November, 1558, and was crowned on 15 January, 1559, at Westminster Abbey.

ELIZABETH I

She died unmarried and childless, and probably a virgin, on 24

March, 1603, at Richmond Palace, Surrey, and was buried in Westminster Abbey.

She was succeeded by her third cousin, James VI of Scotland. Elizabeth I was the last Tudor monarch.

CHAPTER SIX

The Kings and Queens of Scotland from the 9th century to 1603

Before proceeding chronologically to the royal House of Stuart, it is time to retrace our steps through history to the 9th century, when the kingdom of Scotland was first established. Prior to this date, details of the early rulers of Scotland are obscure; the Scottish monarchy is said to have been founded by Alpin, founder of the House of MacAlpin or MacAlpine, which provided Scotland with kings until 1034, when the succession passed to the House of Dunkeld via the marriage of Bethoc, daughter of Malcolm II. The House of Dunkeld held sovereignty until 1290, when Queen Margaret, 'the Maid of Norway', perished at sea. Her death led to a great contest for the throne, with thirteen 'competitors' all contending for the crown. Edward I of England was asked to arbitrate, and he chose John Balliol, a lightweight whom he could easily manipulate to England's advantage. The Scots naturally resented Edward's interference in their government, and Balliol was obliged to abdicate in 1296. There followed the Second Interregnum, when Scotland was without a King from 1296 until 1306. Edward I was making strenuous efforts to bring Scotland under English rule during this period, until the emergence of Robert le Brus (or 'the Bruce'), who declared himself King of Scotland in defiance of Edward in 1306, and who was destined to be one of the finest of Scotland's rulers. Bruce's dynasty did not long survive him; when his son died in 1371, the throne passed to Bruce's grandson Robert II, son of Marjorie Bruce by Walter the Steward, who gave his name to the House of Stewart.

The Stewarts ruled Scotland for more than two centuries, and Great Britain for another century, yet their hold on the throne was often a tenuous one. Throughout the 15th and 16th centuries, each Scottish monarch succeeded to the throne whilst still a child or a minor, and the country was subjected to continuous faction fights amongst power-hungry nobles. That the dynasty survived at all was nothing short of a miracle. Even the abdication of Queen Mary in 1567 did not ruin it, for her son James VI was guided by the magnates from his infancy along the Calvinist path they had marked out for him, and Elizabeth of England, of course, took care of the displaced Mary by first imprisoning and then executing her. Thus it was that the Stewarts – or Stuarts, as they had become when Mary had married into the French royal house – came to inherit also the throne of England. For Mary's grandfather, James IV, had married Margaret Tudor, daughter of Henry VII of England, and when Queen Elizabeth died without heirs in 1603, James VI of Scotland, the great-grandson of Margaret Tudor, was the English Queen's nearest surviving relative.

The succession of the earliest monarchs of Scotland is often confusing, as until Norman influence from England led to the adoption of succession by primogeniture in the late 11th century, the Scots favoured the ancient system of tanistry, whereby the crown passed back and forth from one branch of the family to the other. This system evolved in a time when life expectancy was short, society was violent, and a ruler might well die while his son was an infant: it ensured that the fittest, maturest male would inherit the throne. And until the reign of Malcolm II in the early 11th century, the kingdom of Scotland was shifting its borders all the time, incorporating earlier, smaller kingdoms, or being subdivided between rival rulers. Malcolm II could therefore be said to be the first monarch of modern Scotland. Yet our chapter begins two hundred years before his time, with Alpin, founder of the Scottish monarchy and its first dynasty.

PART ONE

The House of MacAlpine

King Alpin

FATHER: *Eochaid IV, King 'of Scotland'.*
MOTHER: *She was the sister and heiress of Constantine, King of the Picts.*
SIBLINGS: *Alpin is not known to have had any siblings.*

KING ALPIN
He succeeded his father as a King in Scotland, and became also King of Kintyre in March/August, 834, thus establishing his power over a wide area. There is no record of his coronation.
King Alpin married a Scottish Princess (whose name is not known) and had issue:
1 *Kenneth I* (◊ page 167).
2 *Donald I* (◊ page 168).

KING ALPIN
He died on 20 July or in August, 834; he was killed whilst fighting the Picts in Galloway. His place of burial is not recorded.
He was succeeded by his son Kenneth.

Kenneth I

FATHER: *King Alpin* (◊ page 166).
MOTHER: *a Scottish Princess.*
SIBLINGS: (◊ page 166), under *King Alpin*).

KENNETH I
He succeeded his father as King of Galloway and other parts of Scotland on 20 July or in August, 834, and became King of the area known as Dalriada in 841. In 843/4, he became King of the Picts, thus uniting the old Gaelic kingdoms of Alba for the first time, and by 846 he was firmly established as King of Scotland. There is no record of his coronation.

Kenneth I married a lady about whom no information exists, and had issue:

1 *Constantine I* (◊ page 168).
2 *King Aedh* (◊ page 169).
3 *Daughter* (name not known).
   She married Run Macarthagail, King of Strathclyde, and had issue:
   1 King Eochaid (◊ page 170).
4 *Daughter* (name not known).
   She married Olaf the White, King of Dublin.
5 *Daughter* (name not known).
   She married Aedh Finnliath, King of Ireland.

KENNETH I
He died in 859 at Forteviot, Perthshire, and was buried on the Isle of Iona.

He was succeeded by his brother Donald.

Donald I

FATHER: *King Alpin* (◊ page 166).
MOTHER: *a Scottish Princess.*
SIBLINGS: (◊ page 166, under *King Alpin*).

DONALD I
He succeeded Kenneth I in 859 as King of Scotland. There is no record of his coronation.

He was either killed in 863 in a battle at Scone, Perthshire, or died that year in his palace at Kinn Belachoir. He died unmarried and childless. His place of burial is not recorded.

He was succeeded by his nephew Constantine.

Constantine I

FATHER: *Kenneth I* (◊ page 167).
MOTHER: *Unknown.*
SIBLINGS: (◊ page 167, under *Kenneth I*).

CONSTANTINE I
He succeeded Donald I as King of Scotland in 863. There is no record of his coronation.
He married a lady about whom no information exists, and had issue:
1 *Donald II* (◊ page 170).

CONSTANTINE I

He was killed in 877 in a battle against the Danes at Inverdorat, the Black Cove, Angus. He was buried on the Isle of Iona.

He was succeeded by his brother Aedh.

King Aedh

FATHER: *Kenneth I* (◊ page 167).
MOTHER: *Unknown.*
SIBLINGS: (◊ page 167, under *Kenneth I*).

KING AEDH

He succeeded Constantine I as King of Scotland in 877. There is no record of his coronation.

He married a lady about whom no information exists, and had issue:
1 *Constantine II* (◊ page 171).
2 *Donald*
   He became King of Strathclyde in 908.

KING AEDH

He was killed in 878 at Strathallan, and was perhaps buried at Maiden Stone, Aberdeenshire.

He was succeeded by his nephew Eochaid.

King Eochaid

FATHER: *Run Macarthagail, King of Strathclyde.*
MOTHER: *A daughter of Kenneth I.*
SIBLINGS: *Eochaid is not known to have had any siblings.*

KING EOCHAID

He succeeded his father as King of Strathclyde before succeeding his uncle King Aedh as King of Scotland in 878. There is no record of his coronation.

King Eochaid was deposed in 889, and perhaps died unmarried and childless the same year. His place of burial is not recorded.

He was succeeded by his cousin Donald.

Donald II

FATHER: *Constantine I (♢ page 168).*
MOTHER: *Unknown.*
SIBLINGS: *Donald II did not have any siblings.*

DONALD II

He succeeded his cousin Eochaid as King of Scotland in 889. There is no record of his coronation.

He married a lady about whom no information exists, and had issue:

1 *Malcolm I* (♢ page 172).

DONALD II

He was killed in 900 at Dun-fother, and was buried on the Isle of Iona. He was succeeded by his cousin Constantine.

Constantine II

FATHER: *King Aedh* (◊ page 169).
MOTHER: *Unknown.*
SIBLINGS: (◊ page 169, under *King Aedh*).

CONSTANTINE II

He succeeded Donald II as King of Scotland in 900. There is no record of his coronation.

He married a lady about whom no information exists, and had issue:

1 *King Indulf* (◊ page 173).
2 *Cellach*
   He was killed in 937 at the Battle of Brunanburgh.
3 *Daughter* (*name not known*).
   She married Olaf Cuaran, King of Northumbria (*d*.981), in 937, and had issue:
   1 Gluniarainn, King of Dublin (*d*.989).
   2 Sihtric, King of Dublin (*d*.1042); he married and had issue.
   3 Reginald (killed 980); he married and had issue.

CONSTANTINE II

He abdicated in 942/3, and became a monk at the monastery of St Andrews, Fife, where he later became Abbot. He died at St Andrews in 952, and was probably buried there.

He was succeeded by his second cousin Malcolm.

Malcolm I

FATHER: *Donald II* (↻ page 170).
MOTHER: *Unknown.*
SIBLINGS: *Malcolm I did not have any siblings.*

MALCOLM I

He succeeded Constantine II as King of Scotland in 942/3. There is no record of his coronation.

He married a lady about whom no information exists, and had issue:

1 *King Duff* (↻ page 174).
2 *Kenneth II* (↻ page 176).

Malcolm I is also said to have had the following **illegitimate issue:**

1 Kenneth (?).

MALCOLM I

He was killed in 954 by the men of Moray, and was buried on the Isle of Iona.

He was succeeded by his second cousin Indulf.

King Indulf

FATHER: *Constantine II* (↷ page 171).
MOTHER: *Unknown.*
SIBLINGS: (↷ page 171, under *Constantine II*).

KING INDULF

He succeeded Malcolm I as King of Scotland in 954. There is no record of his coronation.

He married a lady about whom no information exists, and had issue:

1 *King Colin* (↷ page 175).
2 *Eochaid*
   He was killed in 971 by the King of Strathclyde.
3 *Olaf*
   He was killed in *c.*977 by Kenneth II.

KING INDULF

He abdicated in 962 and became a monk. He was killed the same year by Viking invaders at the Battle of the Bauds at the Muir of Findochty, Banffshire. His place of burial is not recorded.

He was succeeded by his third cousin Duff.

King Duff

FATHER: *Malcolm I* (◊ page 172).
MOTHER: *Unknown.*
SIBLINGS: (◊ page 172, under *Malcolm I*).

KING DUFF
He succeeded Indulf as King of Scotland in 962. There is no record of his coronation.

He married a lady about whom no information exists, and had issue:

1 *Kenneth III* (◊ page 177).

2 *Malcolm*
Styled Prince of Cumbria (a title borne in the early middle ages by the sons of the Kings of Scotland) in his youth, he became King of Strathclyde in 973, and died in 990/1.

KING DUFF
He was killed in 967 at Forres by the men of Moray. His place of burial is not recorded.

He was succeeded by his third cousin Colin.

King Colin

FATHER: *King Indulf* (↷ page 173).
MOTHER: *Unknown.*
SIBLINGS: (↷ page 173, under *King Indulf*).

KING COLIN

Also called Cuilean, he succeeded Duff as King of Scotland in 967. There is no record of his coronation.

He married a lady about whom no information exists, and had issue:

1 *Constantine III* (↷ page 177).

2 *Malcolm*

   He was alive in 1002. Nothing more is known of him.

KING COLIN

He was killed in 971 by Riderch of Strathclyde. His place of burial is not recorded.

He was succeeded by his third cousin Kenneth.

Kenneth II

FATHER: *Malcolm I* (◊ page 172).
MOTHER: *Unknown.*
SIBLINGS: (◊ page 172, under *Malcolm I*).

KENNETH II
He succeeded Colin as King of Scotland in 971. There is no record of his coronation.

He is said to have married a Princess of Leinster (whose name is not known), and had issue:

1 *Malcolm II* (◊ page 178).
2 *Dungal*
   He was killed in 999 by his cousin Gillacomgain, son of Kenneth III.
3 *Donada* (?)
   She is also described as the daughter of Malcolm II. She married firstly (?) Finlay (Findlaech) MacRory, Mormaer of Moray (*d.c.*1004/5), and had issue:
   (i) *King Macbeth* (◊ page 183).
   Donada married secondly Sigurd II Digri, Jarl of Orkney and Caithness (killed 1014), in *c.*1005/8, and had issue:
   1 Thorfinn, Jarl of Orkney and Caithness (*c.*1009–*c.*1056/65?); he married Ingibiorg of Halland, afterwards the wife of Malcolm III, and had issue.

KENNETH II
He died (perhaps murdered on behalf of his successor) in 995 at Finella's Castle, probably at Fettercairn, and was buried on the Isle of Iona.

He was succeeded by his fourth cousin Constantine.

Constantine III

FATHER: *King Colin* (◊ page 175).
MOTHER: *Unknown*.
SIBLINGS: (◊ page 175, under *King Colin*).

CONSTANTINE III

He succeeded Kenneth II as King of Scotland in 995. There is no record of his coronation.

He married a lady about whom no information exists. There was no issue of the marriage.

CONSTANTINE III

He was killed in 997 at Rathinveramon. His place of burial is not recorded.

He was succeeded by his fourth cousin Kenneth.

Kenneth III

FATHER: *King Duff* (◊ page 174).
MOTHER: *Unknown*.
SIBLINGS: (◊ page 174, under *King Duff*).

KENNETH III

He succeeded Constantine III as King of Scotland in 997. There is no record of his coronation.

He married a lady about whom no information exists, and had issue:

1 *Beoedhe*

Also known as Bodhe or Boite, he married a lady about whom no information exists, and had issue:

(i) *Son (name not known)*

He married a lady about whom no information exists, and fathered a son (name not known) who was murdered in infancy in 1033.

(ii) *Gruoch* (◊ page 183, under *King Macbeth, whom she married*).

Beoedhe died before 1033.

2 *Giric*

A Mormaer, or 'Subregulus', he was killed on *c*.25 March, 1005, at the Battle of Monzievaird.

3 *Gillacomgain*

He lived to maturity, but nothing more is known of him.

KENNETH III

He was killed on *c*.25 March, 1005, at the Battle of Monzievaird (?).

His place of burial is not known.

He was succeeded by his cousin Malcolm.

Malcolm II

FATHER: *Kenneth II* (◊ page 176).
MOTHER: *a Princess of Leinster*.
SIBLINGS: (◊ page 176, under *Kenneth II*).

MALCOLM II

He was born in *c*.954. In his youth, he was styled Prince of Cumbria. He succeeded his cousin Malcolm, son of King Duff, as King of Strathclyde in *c*.990/1, and ruled Strathclyde until 995, when he was deposed. He was restored in 997, and succeeded Kenneth III as King of Scotland on 25 March, 1005. In *c*.1016, he became King of Lothian, thus becoming the first effective ruler of the whole of Scotland. There is no record of his coronation.

Malcolm II married a lady whose name is not recorded, said to have been an Irishwoman from Ossory, and had issue:

1 *Bethoc*

Known as the Lady of Atholl, she married Crinan the Thane, Mormaer of Atholl, Abthane of Dule, Steward of the Western Isles, and Lay Abbot of Dunkeld (*c.*975–killed 1045 in battle against Macbeth), son of Duncan, Mormaer of Atholl. The marriage took place before 1008, perhaps in 1000, and they had issue, through whom they were founders of the Royal House of Dunkeld:

(i) *Duncan I* (◊ page 181).

(ii) *Maldred*

He was created Lord of Allerdale, and was appointed Regent of the Kingdom of Strathclyde in 1034. He was probably killed in battle in 1045.

Maldred married (no record exists of the date or the place): *Edith*

She was the daughter of Uhtred, Earl of Northumbria, by Elgiva, daughter of Ethelred II, King of England.

Issue of marriage:

(a) *Gospatrick*

He was born in *c.*1040. He was created Earl of Northumbria before 1071, possibly in 1068, but was deprived of this earldom in 1072, when he was created Earl of Dunbar. He died on 15 December, but the year is unspecified, at Ubbanford (modern Norham), Scotland, and was buried in Norham Church; however, another tradition states that he became a monk at Durham Cathedral, where he died and was buried.

Gospatrick married an unknown lady, and had issue:

1 Dolfin, Earl of Cumberland (*d.* after 1092); he married an unknown lady and had issue.

2 Waltheof, 1st Baron of Allerdale, Abbot of Crowland (*d.*1138?); he married a lady called Sigrid, and had issue.

3 Gospatrick, 2nd Earl of Dunbar (killed at the Battle of the Standard, 1138); he married an unknown lady, and had issue.

    4 Octreda; she married Waldeve, son of Gillemin.

    5 Gunhilda; she married Orm, son of Ketil.

    6 Matilda; she married Dolfin, son of Aylward.

    7 Ethelreda; she married Duncan II.

(b) *Maldred*

He married a lady about whom no information exists, and had issue:

    1 Robert.

    2 Uhtred.

    3 Ulkil(?).

(iii) *Daughter (name not known)*

She married a man about whom no information exists, and had issue:

    1 Moddan, Earl of Caithness (killed 1040).

(iv) *Daughter (name not known)*

Nothing is known about her.

2 *Donada* (?)

She has also been described as the daughter of Kenneth II, and the details of her life appear on page 176.

3 *Daughter (name not known)*

This may have been the daughter married to Sigurd, Jarl of Orkney, in *c.*1005/8; some sources identify her with Donada.

MALCOLM II

He died on 25 November, 1034, at Glamis Castle, Angus, mortally wounded by his kinsmen, and was buried on the Isle of Iona. He was the last sovereign of the House of MacAlpine.

He was succeeded by his grandson Duncan.

PART TWO

The House of Dunkeld

Duncan I

FATHER: *Crinan, Lay Abbot of Dunkeld* (◊ page 179, under *Malcolm II*).
MOTHER: *Bethoc, daughter of Malcolm II.*
SIBLINGS: (◊ page 179, under *Malcolm II*).

DUNCAN I
Known as the Gracious, he was born in *c*.1001, and became King of Strathclyde in 1018. He succeeded his grandfather, Malcolm II, as King of Scotland on 25 November, 1034, thus becoming the first sovereign of the House of Dunkeld, named after his father's abbacy. There is no record of his coronation.

Duncan I married, in *c*.1030 (although no record exists as to where):
Sybilla

She was either the daughter of Bjorn Bearsson and sister of Siward Digera, Earl of Northumbria, or the daughter of Siward by Elfleda, daughter of Ealdred, Earl of Northumbria.

Issue of marriage:
1 *Malcolm III* (◊ page 185).
2 *Donald III* (◊ page 187).
3 *Maelmuire*

He was born in c.1035.

Maelmuire married a lady about whom no information exists, and had issue:

(i) *Madach*

Also known as Matad, he was created Earl of Atholl before 1115 (or later, before 1136?). He died between 1139 and 1159, perhaps in 1152.

Madach married Margaret, daughter of Haakon Paulsson, and had issue:

(a) Malcolm, Earl of Atholl (*d*.1186/98); he married firstly an unknown lady, and had issue, and secondly, Hextilda, daughter of Huctred of Tynedale by Bethoc, daughter of Donald III.

(b) Harold, Jarl of Orkney, Earl of Caithness (*d*.1206); he married Afrika, sister of Duncan, Earl of Fife, and had issue. He married secondly Gormlath or Hvarlod, daughter of Malcolm MacHeth, 1st Earl of Ross.

Madach married secondly, in c.1133 (although no record exists as to where):

Margaret

She was the daughter of Haco, Jarl of Orkney. After the death of Madach, she married secondly Erland Ugni, Jarl of Orkney (killed 1156).

4 *Daughter* (*name not known*) (?)

Her existence is doubtful. She is said to have married one Bertolf or Bartholemew (*d*.1121?), and had issue.

DUNCAN I

He was either murdered by Macbeth, or killed in battle against him, on 14 August, 1040, at Bothganowan (now Pitgaveny), near Elgin, or at Burghead. He was buried on the Isle of Iona.

He was succeeded by his cousin Macbeth.

King Macbeth

FATHER: *Finlay MacRory, Mormaer of Moray.*
MOTHER: *Donada, daughter either of Kenneth II or Malcolm II.*
SIBLINGS: (◊ page 176, under *Kenneth II*).

KING MACBETH

He was born in *c.*1005, and became Mormaer of Moray around 1029/32. He succeeded Duncan I as King of Scotland on 14 August, 1040. No record exists of his coronation.

Macbeth married, after 1032 (although no record exists as to where):
Gruoch

She was the daughter of Beoedhe, son of Kenneth III. She was born in *c.*1015. She married firstly Gillacomgain, Mormaer of Moray (burned alive in 1032), and had issue:
(a) King Lulach (◊page 184).
There was no issue of her marriage to Macbeth.

KING MACBETH

He was killed on 15 August, 1057, at the Battle of Lumphanan, Aberdeenshire, by the future Malcolm III, son of Duncan I, and was buried on the Isle of Iona.

He was succeeded by his stepson Lulach.

King Lulach

FATHER: *Gillacomgain, Mormaer of Moray.*
MOTHER: *Gruoch (◊ page 183, under Macbeth).*
SIBLINGS: *King Lulach did not have any siblings.*

KING LULACH
Known as 'the Simple', he was born around *c.*1029/32. He succeeded his stepfather Macbeth as King of Scotland on 15 August, 1057, and was crowned that same month on the Coronation Stone at Scone Abbey, Perthshire. This is the first recorded instance of the coronation of a King of Scotland.

King Lulach married (no record exists of the date or place):
Finnghuala (?)
She was the daughter of Sinill, Mormaer of Angus. Her dates are not recorded.

Issue of marriage:

1 *Malsnechtai*
He was perhaps created Mormaer of Moray at some stage, although he certainly became a monk later on. He died in 1085.

2 *Daughter (name not known)*
She married Aedh, Mormaer of Moray, and had issue:
  1 Gruaidh; she married William, Lord of Egremont (◊ page 188, under *Duncan II*).
  2 Angus, King of Moray (*d.*1130); he married and had issue.

KING LULACH
He was killed on 17 March, 1058, at Essie in Strathbogie by his distant cousin and successor, Malcolm III. He was buried on the Isle of Iona.
He was succeeded by Malcolm, son of Duncan I.

Malcolm III

FATHER: *Duncan I* (◊ page 181).
MOTHER: *Sybilla of Northumbria* (◊ page 181, under *Duncan I*).
SIBLINGS: (◊ page 181, under *Duncan I*).

MALCOLM III

Known as 'Canmore' (or 'Bighead'), he was born in *c.*1031, and became King of Strathclyde and Prince of Cumbria in 1034. He succeeded Lulach as King of Scotland on 17 March, 1058, and was crowned on 25 April, 1058, at Scone Abbey, Perthshire.

Malcolm III married firstly, in *c.*1059 or *c.*1066 (although no record exists as to where):

Ingibiorg

She was the daughter of Finn Arnasson of Vrjar, Jarl of Halland, by Bergljot, daughter of Halfdan Sigurdsson. She married firstly Thorfinn II, Earl of Caithness and Jarl of Orkney (1009–1056/65?), before 1038, and had issue:

1 Paul, Jarl of Orkney (*d.*1099); he married an unnamed daughter of Haakon Ivarsson, and had issue.

2 Erlend, Jarl of Orkney (*d.*1099); he married Thora, daughter of Somerled Uspaksson, and had issue.

Ingibiorg died before 1070.

Issue of marriage:

1 *Duncan II* (◊ page 188).

2 *Malcolm*
He died in *c.*1094.

3 *Donald*
He died in 1085.

Malcolm III married secondly, in *c.*1069, at Dunfermline Abbey, Fife:

St Margaret

She was the daughter of Edward the Atheling, son of Edmund II,

King of England, by Agatha of Hungary, and she was born in c.1045/6 in Hungary. She died on 16 November, 1093, at Edinburgh Castle, and was buried in Dunfermline Abbey, Fife. Her remains were later translated to the Escorial in Madrid, Spain, her head being buried in the Jesuit College at Douai, France. She was canonised as a saint in 1250.

Issue of marriage:

1 *Edward*

He died on 16 November, 1093, at Edwardsisle, near Jedburgh, of wounds received at the Battle of Alnwick.

2 *King Edmund* (↷ page 190).

3 *King Edgar* (↷ page 191).

4 *Alexander I* (↷ page 191).

5 Edith, *later called* Matilda

(↷ page 47, under *Henry I of England,* whom she married).

6 *David I* (↷ page 192).

7 *Ethelred*

He became Lay Abbot of Dunkeld. He was also styled Earl of Fife, probably posthumously, and probably before 1107 (although the date is uncertain). He died before c.1097, and was buried in Kilremont Church.

8 *Duncan*

Nothing is known of him. He may have become confused with Duncan II, Malcolm's son by Ingibiorg.

9 *Mary*

She married Eustace III, Count of Boulogne, in c.1101/2, and had issue:

1 Unnamed son (*d.* young).

2 Matilda; she married Stephen, King of England.

Mary died on 31 May, 1115/16, and was buried in the Abbey of St Saviour, Bermondsey, London.

MALCOLM III

He was killed on 13 November, 1093, in a battle near Alnwick, Northumberland, and was buried at Tynemouth. His remains were later removed to Dunfermline Abbey, Fife, and, later still, to the Escorial, Madrid, Spain.

He was succeeded by his brother Donald, a usurper.

Donald III

FATHER: *Duncan I* (◊ page 181).
MOTHER: *Sybilla of Northumbria* (◊ page 181, under *Duncan I*).
SIBLINGS: (◊ page 181, under *Duncan I*).

DONALD III

Known as 'Donaldbane', he was born in *c.*1033, and was probably created Mormaer or Earl of Gowrie in *c.*1060. He usurped the throne of Scotland on 13 November, 1093, upon the death of his brother, Malcolm III, but was deposed by Malcolm's son Duncan II in May, 1094. When Duncan II died on 12 November, 1094, Donald III was restored to the throne as joint monarch with his nephew King Edmund, Donald ruling north of the Forth/Clyde line, and Edmund ruling south of it. Both Donald and Edmund were deposed in favour of King Edgar in October, 1097. No record exists of Donald ever being crowned.

Donald III married a lady about whom no information exists, and had issue:

1 *Bethoc*
   She married Huctred of Tynedale, and had issue:
   1 Hextilda; she married firstly Richard Comyn, and had issue. She married secondly Malcolm, 2nd Earl of Atholl (*d.*1186/98).

DONALD III

He was deposed in October, 1097, and imprisoned. He died in 1099 in prison at Rescobie, Forfarshire, and was buried in Dunkeld Abbey. His remains were later removed to the Isle of Iona.

He was succeeded by King Edgar.

Duncan II

FATHER: *Malcolm III* (◊ page 185).
MOTHER: *Ingibiorg of Halland* (◊ page 185, under *Malcolm III*).
SIBLINGS: (◊ page 185, under *Malcolm III*).

DUNCAN II
He was born in *c.*1060. He proclaimed himself King of Scotland after deposing his uncle, Donald III, in May, 1094. There is no record of his coronation.

Duncan II married, in *c.*1090/94 (although no record exists as to where):

Ethelreda or *Octreda*
She was the daughter of Gospatrick, Earl of Northumbria and Dunbar, a great-grandson of Malcolm II. She was buried in Dunfermline Abbey, Fife.

Issue of marriage:

1 *William*
He adopted the surname FitzDuncan, and is said to have been created Earl of Moray. He became Lord of Skipton and Craven, in right of his wife, in 1138 (?). He died in *c.*1154.

William had the following illegitimate issue:
1 Donald
William married, in 1138 (?) (although no record exists as to where):
Alice
She was the daughter of William le Meschin, Lord of Copeland, by Cecilia de Rumely, Lady of Skipton. She married firstly a man called William. She married secondly Alexander FitzGerold. She succeeded her mother as Lady of Skipton and Craven.
Issue of marriage:
(i) *William*
He adopted the surname MacWilliam, and was called Lord of

Egremont. He was drowned at Bolton Wharf after 1155.

William married firstly (no record exists of the date or place):

Gruaidh

She was the daughter of Aedh, Mormaer of Moray, by a daughter of King Lulach.

Issue of marriage:

(a) *Donald MacWilliam*

He was killed on 31 July, 1187, on Mangarnia Moor, Speyside. Donald married an unknown lady, and had issue:

(*i*) Godfrey MacWilliam (executed in 1213 at Kincardine).

(*ii*) Donald MacWilliam (killed on 15 June, 1215, in Morayshire).

(*iii*) Unnamed daughter; she married a man surnamed MacEwen, and had issue.

(b) *Gospatrick MacWilliam*

He was created Lord of Airton, Yorks. He married and had issue, but no details are available. He died before 1208.

William married secondly (no record exists of the date or place):

Octreda

She was the daughter of Alan, Lord of Allerdale.

(ii) *Cecilia*

She married William le Gros, 3rd Earl of Aumale (*d.*1179), and had issue.

(iii) *Amabel*

She married Reginald de Lucy (*d.*1179), and had issue, although no details are available.

(iv) *Alice*

She married firstly Gilbert Pipard, and secondly Robert de Courtenay. She died in 1215.

DUNCAN II

He was killed on 12 November, 1094, at the Battle of Monthechin (Mondynes), Kincardineshire, and was buried in Dunfermline Abbey, Fife.

He was succeeded by the man he had deposed, Donald III.

King Edmund

FATHER: *Malcolm III* (◊ page 185).
MOTHER: *St Margaret* (◊ page 185, under *Malcolm III*).
SIBLINGS: (◊ page 186, under *Malcolm III*).

KING EDMUND
He was styled Prince of Cumbria in his youth. He became joint King of Scotland with Donald III, his uncle, on 12 November, 1094, following the death of his half-brother, Duncan II. Edmund's authority was confined to the area south of the Forth/Clyde line, while Donald III ruled north of it. There is no record of Edmund's coronation.

KING EDMUND
He was deposed (along with Donald III) in October, 1097, in favour of his brother Edgar. Edmund became a monk at Montacute Abbey, Somerset, where he later died (the date of his death is unknown). He was probably buried in Montacute Abbey. He never married, or had children.

He was succeeded by his brother Edgar.

King Edgar

FATHER: *Malcolm III* (◊ page 185).
MOTHER: *St Margaret* (◊ page 185, under *Malcolm III*).
SIBLINGS: (◊ page 186, under *Malcolm III*).

KING EDGAR
He was born around *c.*1072/4. He succeeded Donald III and Edmund (joint rulers) as King of Scotland in October, 1097. There is no record of his coronation.

KING EDGAR
He died unmarried and childless on 8 January, 1107, either at Dundee, or at Edinburgh Castle, and was buried in Dunfermline Abbey, Fife.
    He was succeeded by his brother Alexander.

Alexander I

FATHER: *Malcolm III* (◊ page 185).
MOTHER: *St Margaret* (◊ page 185, under *Malcolm III*).
SIBLINGS: (◊ page 186, under *Malcolm III*).

ALEXANDER I
Known as 'the Fierce', he was born in *c.*1077/8. He succeeded his brother Edgar as King of Scotland on 8 January, 1107. There is no record of his coronation.
Alexander I married, in *c.*1107 (although no record exists as to where):

Sybilla

She was an illegitimate daughter of Henry I, King of England, by Sybilla Corbet, and she was born around *c.*1092 at Domfront, Normandy. She died on 12/13 July, 1122, on the Island of the Woman (Eilean ham Bam), Loch Tay, Perthshire, and was buried in a church there. There was no issue of the marriage.

Alexander I had the following **illegitimate issue:**

1 Malcolm MacHeth, Earl of Ross (1105/15?–1168); he married a sister of Somerled, Lord of Argyll, and had issue.

ALEXANDER I

He died on 23, 25 or 27 April, 1124, at Stirling Castle, and was buried in Dunfermline Abbey, Fife.

He was succeeded by his brother David.

David I

FATHER: *Malcolm III* (◊ page 185).
MOTHER: *St Margaret* (◊ page 185, under *Malcolm III*).
SIBLINGS: (◊ page 186, under *Malcolm III*).

DAVID I

He was born around 1080/85, and was designated Prince of Cumbria in 1107. He was styled Earl of Huntingdon in right of his wife, and possibly also Earl of Northampton from *c.*1113/14. He succeeded his brother Alexander I as King of Scotland on 23, 25 or 27 April, 1124. There is no record of his coronation.

David I married, in 1113/14 (although no record exists as to where):
Matilda

She was the daughter of Waltheof, Earl of Huntingdon and Northampton, by Judith, daughter of Lambert of Boulogne, Count of Lens, by Adeliza, sister of William I, King of England, and she was born in *c.*1074. She married firstly Simon de St Liz, Earl of

Huntingdon and Northampton (*d.* after 1111), in *c.*1090, and had issue:

1 Simon, Earl of Huntingdon and Northampton (after 1103–1153); he married Isabella, daughter of Robert de Beaumont, 1st Earl of Leicester, and had issue.

2 St Waltheof, Abbot of Melrose (*c.*1100–1159/60).

3 Matilda (*d.*1140); she married Robert FitzRichard (*d.*1134), and had issue.

Matilda died between 23 April, 1130, and 22 April, 1131 (although she appears in a charter of 1147, now thought to be spurious), and was buried in Scone Abbey, Perthshire.

Issue of marriage:

1 *Malcolm*

Probably the firstborn. He died young. He is said to have been strangled in infancy by Donald III, although this is chronologically impossible, as Donald died in 1099, and Malcolm was not born until 1113 or later.

2 *Henry*

He was born in *c.*1114/15, and succeeded to the earldom of Huntingdon upon his father's resignation in *c.*February, 1136. He was created Earl of Northumberland in 1139. He died on 12 June, 1152, and was buried in Kelso Abbey, Roxburghshire.

Henry had the following illegitimate issue:

1 Margaret or Marjorie; she married John de Lindsay, and had issue.

Henry married, in 1139 (although no record exists as to where):

Ada

Also called Adama or Adeline, she was the daughter of William de Warenne, 2nd Earl of Surrey, by Isabella, daughter of Hugh, Count of Vermandois. She died in 1178.

Issue of marriage:

(i) *Malcolm IV* (◊ page 197).

(ii) *King William the Lyon* (◊ page 198).

(iii) *David*

He was born in *c.*1143/52. He succeeded his father as Earl of Huntingdon, Earl of Northumberland, Earl of Carlisle and Earl of Doncaster on 12 June, 1152 (his succession being confirmed in 1185). He was created Earl of Garioch in *c.*1180, and

Earl of Cambridge and Earl of Lennox in 1205. He was deprived of all his English honours in 1215/16, but restored to them on 13 March, 1218. He died on 17 June, 1219, at Yardley, Northants., and was buried in Sawtrey Abbey, Hunts.

David had the following illegitimate issue:

1 Henry of Stirling.
2 Henry of Brechin (d.1238); he married Juliana, probably the daughter of Ralph de Cornhill, and had issue.
3 Ada; she married Malise, son of Ferteth, Earl of Strathearn.
4 David (?).

David married, on 26 August, 1190 (although no record exists as to where):

Matilda

She was the daughter of Hugh de Kevilloc, Earl of Chester, by Bertrada, daughter of Simon de Montfort, Count of Evreux, and she was born in 1171. She died on 6 January, 1233.

Issue of marriage:

(a) *Robert*

He died young, and was buried in Lindores Abbey, Fife.

(b) *Isabella*

She was born in 1206, and was known as 'Isabella the Scot'.

She married Robert le Brus, 'the Noble', Lord of Annandale (d.1245), and had issue:

1 Robert, Lord of Annandale, a Competitor for the Crown of Scotland in 1292 (1220–1295); he married firstly Isabella (1226–1254), daughter of Gilbert de Clare, Earl of Hertford and Gloucester, and secondly Christina (d.c.1305), daughter of Sir William de Ireby, by whom he had issue:

1 Robert le Brus (♭ page 207, under *Robert I*).
2 Beatrice; she married Hugh de Neville.

Isabella died in c.1251, and was buried in Saltre Abbey, near Stilton, Gloucs.

(c) *John*

Known as 'the Scot', he was born in c.1207, and succeeded his father as Earl of Huntingdon and Garioch on 17 June, 1219. He was created Earl of Chester on 21 November,

1232. He died shortly before 6 June, 1237, at Darnal, and was buried in the Church of St Werburg, Chester.

John married, in *c.*1220/22 (although no record exists as to where):

Helen

She was the daughter of Llywelyn ap Iorwerth, Prince of Wales, by Joan, illegitimate daughter of John, King of England. After the death of John the Scot, she married secondly Robert de Quincy (*d.*1257) in 1237, and had issue:

1 Hawise (1250?–1295?); she married Baldwin Wake (*d.*1282), and had issue.

2 Joan (*d.*1283); she married Humphrey de Bohun (*d.*1265).

Helen died in 1253.

(d) *Henry*

He died young after 1215, and was buried in Lindores Abbey, Fife.

(e) *Ada*

She married Henry de Hastings (*d.*1250?) before 7 June, 1237, and had issue:

1 Henry, 1st Baron Hastings (*d.*1269); he married Joan de Cantelou (*d.*1271), and had issue.

Ada died after 1241.

(f) *Margaret*

She married Alan, Lord of Galloway (*d.*1234), in 1209, and had issue:

1 Devorguilla (◊ page 204, under King John Balliol).

2 Christina (*d.*1246); she married William de Forz, 5th Earl of Aumale (*d.*1241).

Margaret died in 1228.

(g) *Matilda*

She died unmarried.

(iv) *Ada*

She was born after 1139. She married Florence III, Count of Holland (*d.c.*1191), in 1162, and had issue:

1 Florence IV, Count of Holland, and Competitor for the Crown of Scotland in 1192 (murdered 1206?).

Ada died after 1206.

(v) *Margaret*

She married firstly Conan IV, Duke of Brittany (*d.*1171), in 1159/60, and had issue:

1 Constance, Duchess of Brittany (◊ page 62, under Henry II of England).

Margaret married secondly Humphrey de Bohun (*d.*1182) before Easter, 1175, and had issue:

2 Henry, 1st Earl of Hereford (1176?–1220); he married Matilda (*d.*1236), daughter of Geoffrey FitzPiers, Earl of Essex, and had issue.

(vi) *Isabella*

She married Robert, Baron Ros of Wark (*d.*1174), and had issue, but no details are recorded.

(vii) *Matilda*

She died young in 1152.

(viii) *Marjorie* (?)

She is said to have been Earl Henry's daughter by his wife Ada, but is now thought to have been more probably the daughter of one of the bastard sons of David, Earl of Huntingdon (◊ above), both of whom were called Henry. In 1291, Robert de Pinkeney, one of the Competitors for the Crown of Scotland, claimed to be her great-grandson, but there is no contemporary evidence for her parentage. She is said to have married Sir David de Lindsay, Lord of Luffness (*d.c.*1214), and to have had issue:

1 David, a knight (*d.*1241); he married a lady called Christina.

2 Gerard, a knight (*d.*1249).

3 Walter; he is said to have married Christina Huse, and to have had issue.

4 William.

5 Alice; she married Sir Henry de Pinkeney, Lord of Wedon-Pinkeney, and had issue.

3 *Claricia*

She died unmarried.

4 *Hodierna*

She died young and unmarried.

DAVID I

He died on 24 May, 1153, at Carlisle in Cumbria, and was buried in Dunfermline Abbey, Fife. He was known as 'the Saint', and was popularly reputed as one after his death.

He was succeeded by his grandson Malcolm.

Malcolm IV

FATHER: *Henry, Earl of Huntingdon* (◊ page 193, under *David I*).
MOTHER: *Ada de Warenne* (◊ page 193, under *David I*).
SIBLINGS: (◊ page 193, under *David I*).

MALCOLM IV

Known as 'the Maiden', he was born on 20 March, 1141/2. He succeeded his grandfather David I as King of Scotland on 24 May, 1153, and was crowned soon afterwards (the date is unknown) at Scone Abbey, Perthshire.

Malcolm IV is said, with reservations, to have had the following **illegitimate issue:**

1 Henry (*d.*1152 sic.). His existence rests only upon very obscure evidence, and he has perhaps been confused with King Malcolm's father, Henry. The date of his death, 1152, is impossible, as his alleged father was then no more than 11 years old.

MALCOLM IV

He died unmarried on 9 December, 1165, at Jedburgh Castle, and was buried in Dunfermline Abbey, Fife.

He was succeeded by his brother William.

King William

FATHER: *Henry, Earl of Huntingdon* (◊ page 193, under *David I*).
MOTHER: *Ada de Warenne* (◊ page 193, under *David I*).
SIBLINGS: (◊ page 193, under *David I*).

KING WILLIAM
Known as 'the Lyon', he was born in *c*.1142/3. He succeeded his father as Earl of Northumberland on 12 June, 1152, but surrendered this earldom in 1157. He succeeded his brother Malcolm IV as King of Scotland on 9 December, 1165, and was crowned on 24 December, 1165, at Scone Abbey, Perthshire.

King William married, on 5 September, 1186, at Woodstock Palace, Oxon.:

Ermengarde
She was the daughter of Richard, Viscount of Beaumont-le-Maine, by Constance, illegitimate daughter of Henry I, King of England. She died on 11 February, 1233/4, and was buried in Balmerino Abbey, Fife.

Issue of marriage:

1 *Margaret*
She was born in *c*.1193. She married Hubert de Burgh, 1st Earl of Kent (*d*.1243), on 19 June, 1221, and had issue:

1 Margaret (Megotta) (1222?–1237); she married Richard de Clare, Earl of Hertford and Gloucester (1222?–1262).

Margaret died in 1259, and was buried in the Church of the Black Friars, London.

2 *Alexander II* (◊ page 200).

3 *Isabella*
She married Roger Bigod, 4th Earl of Norfolk (1212?–1270), in May, 1225, at Alnwick, Northumberland. She was repudiated by her husband on grounds of consanguinity in 1245, but was reconciled to him in 1253. The date of her death is not known. She was

buried in the Church of the Black Friars, London.

4 *Marjorie*

She married Gilbert Marshal, 4th Earl of Pembroke (*d.*1241), either before 14 July, or on 1 August, 1235, at Berwick-upon-Tweed. She died on 17 November, 1244, and was buried in the Church of the Black Friars, London.

King William also had the following **illegitimate issue**:

By the daughter of Adam de Hythus:

1 Margaret (*d.* after 1226); she married Eustace de Vesci (1169–1216), and had issue.

By a daughter of Robert Avenal:

2 Isabella; she married firstly Robert le Brus (*d.* before 1191), and had issue. She married secondly Robert de Ros, 1st Baron Ros of Helmsley (*d.*1226), and had issue.

By unknown mothers:

3 Robert de London.

4 Henry Galightly; he married and had issue.

5 Ada (*d.*1200); she married Patrick, 4th Earl of Dunbar (1152–1232), and had issue.

6 Aufrica; she married William de Say and had issue.

7 Unnamed child.

8 Unnamed child.

9 Unnamed child. No information exists about these three children.

KING WILLIAM

He died on 4 December, 1214, at Stirling, and was buried in Arbroath Abbey, Scotland.

He was succeeded by his son Alexander.

Alexander II

FATHER: *King William the Lyon* (◊ page 198).
MOTHER: *Ermengarde de Beaumont* (◊ page 198, under *King William*).
SIBLINGS: (◊ page 198, under *King William*).

ALEXANDER II

He was born on 24 August, 1198, at Haddington, East Lothian. He succeeded his father as King of Scotland on 4 December, 1214, and was crowned on 6 December, 1214, at Scone Abbey, Perthshire.

Alexander II married firstly, on 18 or 25 June, 1221, at York Minster:
Joan

She was the daughter of John, King of England, by Isabella of Angoulême, and she was born on 22 July, 1210 (or, far less probably, in 1203 in Normandy). She died on 4, 5 or 12 March, 1238, at Havering-atte-Bower, Essex, and was buried in Tarrant Crawford Abbey, Dorset. There was no issue of the marriage.

Alexander II married secondly, on 15 May, 1239, at Roxburgh:
Mary

She was the daughter of Enguerrand III, Lord of Coucy, by Mary, daughter of John, Lord of Montmirel-en-Brie. After the death of Alexander II, she married secondly John of Brienne, son of the King of Jerusalem, before 6 June, 1257. The date of her death is not known. She was buried at Newbottle, Scotland.

Issue of marriage:

1 *Alexander III* (◊ page 201)

Alexander II also had the following **illegitimate issue**:

1 Marjorie; she married Alan Durward, and had issue.

ALEXANDER II

He died on 6 July, 1249, on the Isle of Kerrara in the Bay of Oban, and was buried in Melrose Abbey, Roxburghshire.

He was succeeded by his son Alexander.

Alexander III

FATHER: *Alexander II* (◊ page 200).
MOTHER: *Mary de Coucy* (◊ page 200, under *Alexander II*).
SIBLINGS: *Alexander III did not have any legitimate siblings.*

ALEXANDER III

Known as 'the Glorious', he was born on 4 September, 1241, at
Roxburgh. He succeeded his father as King of Scotland on 8 July,
1249, and was crowned on 13 July, 1249, at Scone Abbey, Perthshire.
Alexander III married firstly, on 26 December, 1251, at York
  Minster:
Margaret
  She was the daughter of Henry III, King of England, by Eleanor of
Provence, and she was born on 29 September or 5 October, 1240, at
Windsor Castle. She died on 26/27 February, 1275, at Cupar Castle,
Fife, and was buried in Dunfermline Abbey, Fife.
Issue of marriage:
1 *Margaret*
  She was born on 28 February, 1261, at Windsor Castle. She married
Eric II, King of Norway (1268–1300), on *c.*31 August, 1281 at
Bergen, Norway, and had issue:
  (i) *Queen Margaret* (◊ page 203).
  Margaret died on 9 April, 1283, at Tönsberg, Norway, in childbed,
and was buried in Christ Kirk, Bergen, Norway.
2 *Alexander*
  He was born on 21 January, 1264, at Jedburgh, Roxburghshire. He
died on 17 or 28 January, 1284, at Lindores Abbey, Fife, and was
buried in Dunfermline Abbey, Fife.
    Alexander married on 15 November, 1282, at Roxburgh:
Margaret
  She was the daughter of Guy of Dampierre, Count of Flanders.
After the death of Alexander, she married secondly Reginald I,

Count of Gueldres in c.1290, and had issue:

1 Reginald II, Count of Gueldres (d.1343); he married firstly Sophia of Malines (d.1329) and had issue, and secondly Eleanor, daughter of Edward II of England (◊ page 91), and had issue.

2 Margaret; she married Thierry VIII, Count of Cleves.

3 Isabella; a nun.

4 Philippa; a nun.

5 Guy(?).

6 Philip (?).

Margaret died in 1330.

3 David

He was born on 20 March, 1273. He died at the end of June, 1281, at Stirling Castle, and was buried in Dunfermline Abbey, Fife.

Alexander III married secondly, on 1 November, 1285, at Jedburgh Abbey:

Yolande or *Joletta*

She was the daughter of Robert IV, Count of Dreux. After the death of Alexander III, she married secondly Arthur II de Montfort, Duke of Brittany (1262–1312), in May, 1294, and had issue:

1 Joan (1294–1363); she married Robert, Lord of Cassel (d.1331).

2 Beatrice (1295–1384); she married Guy, Lord of Laval (d.1347).

3 John III, Duke of Brittany (d.1345); he married Joan of Flanders, and had issue.

4 Alice (1297–1377); she married Bouchard VI, Count of Vendôme (d.1353).

5 Blanche (b.1300; d. young).

6 Mary (1302–1371); a nun.

Yolande died in 1323. There was no issue of her marriage to Alexander III.

ALEXANDER III

He was killed on 16 or 19 March, 1286, when his horse plunged over a cliff between Burntisland and Kinghorn, Fife. He was buried in Dunfermline Abbey, Fife.

He was succeeded by his granddaughter Margaret.

Queen Margaret

FATHER: *Eric II, King of Norway.*
MOTHER: *Margaret, daughter of Alexander III.*
SIBLINGS: *Queen Margaret did not have any siblings.*

QUEEN MARGARET

Known as 'the Maid of Norway', she was born before 9 April, 1283, at Tönsberg, Norway. She succeeded her grandfather Alexander III, as Scotland's first Queen Regnant on 19 March, 1286, but was never crowned.

QUEEN MARGARET

She died in May (?) or on *c.*26 September, 1290, on board a ship passing by the Orkneys, whilst on her way to Scotland. She was buried at Bergen, Norway.

The death of the Maid of Norway left Scotland without a monarch, and at the mercy of Edward I of England. In 1290 began the First Interregnum, and the contest for the throne between the 13 Competitors. From these, Edward I, called upon to decide which had the most lawful claim to the crown, chose John Balliol as Scotland's next king.

PART THREE

The House of Balliol

King John

FATHER: *John*

He was the son of Hugh de Balliol of Barnard Castle. He married Devorguilla of Galloway in 1233. He died in 1268/9.

MOTHER: *Devorguilla*

She was the daughter of Alan, Lord of Galloway, by Margaret, daughter of David, Earl of Huntingdon, grandson of David I. She died on 28 January, 1290, and was buried in Sweetheart Abbey, Kirkland.

SIBLINGS:

1 *Hugh*

He was born in *c.*1238 at Barnard Castle, and rose to the rank of knight. He married Agnes (*d.*1310), daughter of William de Valence, Earl of Pembroke. He died in 1271.

2 *Alan*

He was born at Barnard Castle. His dates are not recorded.

3 *Alexander*

He was born at Barnard Castle, and rose to the rank of knight. He married Eleanor of Geneva (*d.c.*1303), a kinswoman of Henry III, King of England. He died in 1278.

4 *Eleanor* or *Mary*

She married Sir John Comyn of Badenoch, and had issue, although no details are recorded.

5 *Cecilia*

She married John de Burgh (*d.*1280), and had issue:

1 Devorguilla; she married Robert FitzWalter (*d.*1326), and had issue.

2 Hawise; she married Robert de Grelley (*d.*1282), and had issue.

3 Marjorie; a nun at Chicksands Priory.

Cecilia died before 1273.

6 *Ada*

She married William de Lindsay of Lamberton (1250–killed 1283), and had issue:

1 Christina; she married Enguerrand de Guisnes, Seigneur de Coucy.

KING JOHN

Known as 'Toom Tabard' (or 'Turncoat'), he was born either in *c.*1240, or in 1249/50. He was created Baron of Bywell in Northumberland, but forfeited this honour in 1285. He was elected King of Scotland by Edward I of England on 17 November, 1292, thus bringing to an end the First Interregnum. He was crowned on 30 November, 1292, at Scone Abbey, Perthshire.

King John married, before 7 February, 1281 (although no evidence exists as to where):

Isabella

She was the daughter of John de Warenne, 6th Earl of Surrey, by Alice, daughter of Hugh X de Lusignan, Count of La Marche, by Isabella of Angoulême, widow of John, King of England, and she was born in 1253. The date of her death is not known.

Issue of marriage:

1 *King Edward* (↷ page 214).

2 *Henry*

He was killed on 16 December, 1332, at the Battle of Annan.

3 *Margaret*

She died unmarried.

4 *Anne* (?)

There is doubt that she ever existed. She is said to have married Brian FitzAlan of Bedale.

KING JOHN

He abdicated on 10/11 July, 1296, at Brechin. Scotland was left without a King, and thus began the Second Interregnum, which lasted until 1306, when Robert Bruce seized the throne in defiance of Edward I, who had tried during the years it stood vacant to take it himself, and make Scotland a fief of England.

King John died between 4 March, 1313, and 4 January, 1314, either at Château Gaillard, Normandy, or at Bailleut-en-Gouffern, Normandy. He was probably buried in the Church of St Waast, Normandy.

For further details of the House of Balliol, ◊ page 214, after the House of Bruce.

PART FOUR:

The House of Bruce

Robert I

FATHER: *Robert*

He was the son of Robert le Brus, Lord of Annandale (*d.*1295) (who was the son of Isabella 'the Scot' of Huntingdon, a great-granddaughter of David I), by Christina (*d.c.*1305), daughter of Sir William de Ireby, and he was born in July, 1243. He married Margaret, Countess of Carrick, in 1271 at Turnberry Castle, and became Earl of Carrick in right of his wife. He resigned this earldom in favour of his son Robert on 27 October, 1292. After Margaret died, he married secondly, after 1292, a lady called Eleanor, whose origins are unknown. (After his death, she married secondly Sir Richard le Waleys of Burgh Wallis, Yorks., (*d.* after 1336) between 2 December, 1304, and 8 February, 1306, and had issue, although no details are available. She died between 13 April and 8 September, 1331.) Robert le Brus succeeded his father as Lord of Annandale before 4 July, 1295, and died shortly before 4 April, 1304, either in England or in Palestine. He was buried in the Abbey of Holm Cultram.

MOTHER: *Margaret* or *Marjorie*

She was the daughter of Neil, 2nd Earl of Carrick, by Margaret, daughter of Walter, High Steward of Scotland. She succeeded her father to the earldom of Carrick, in 1256. She married firstly Adam de Kilconquhar, 3rd Earl of Carrick (*d.*1268), before 4 October, 1266. She died before 9 November, 1292.

SIBLINGS:

1 *Isabella*

She was born in *c.*1275. She married Eric II, King of Norway (1268– 1300) (who had previously been married to Margaret, daughter of Alexander III, and by her had been the father of the Maid of Norway), before 25 September, 1293, and had issue:

1 Ingibiorg (1297?–?); she married Waldemar, Duke of Finland (murdered 1318).

Isabella died in 1358.

2 *Edward*

He was created Lord of Galloway before 16 March, 1309, and Earl of Carrick before 24 October, 1313. He became King of Ireland, and was crowned on 2 May, 1316. He was killed on 14 October, 1318, at the Battle of Dundall, Ireland.

Edward had the following illegitimate issue (and ◊ also below):

1 Thomas de Bruce.

Edward is said to have married firstly (although no evidence exists as to where):

Isabella

She was the daughter of John of Strathbogie, Earl of Atholl, by Margaret, daughter of Donald, 6th Earl of Mar. There is little sound evidence for her marriage to Edward, and it is thought likely that she was only his mistress. She died before 1 June, 1317.

Issue of marriage or liaison:

(i) Alexander de Bruce, Earl of Carrick (killed 1333); he married Eleanor, daughter of Sir Archibald Douglas.

Edward married secondly, after 1 June, 1317 (date of dispensation) (although no evidence exists as to where):

Isabella

She was the daughter of William, 5th Earl of Ross. No further details of her are recorded.

3 *Neil*

He was executed in 1306 at Berwick by the English.

4 *Thomas*

He rose to the rank of knight, and was executed in 1307 at Carlisle Castle by the English.

Thomas married (although no record exists of the date or the place):

Helen

She was the daughter of Sir John Erskine. Her dates are not recorded.

5 *Alexander*

He was appointed Dean of Glasgow, and executed in 1307 at Carlisle Castle by the English.

6 *Mary*

She married firstly Sir Neil Campbell of Lochawe (*d.c.*1316), probably after Michaelmas, 1312, and had issue:

1 John of Lochawe, Earl of Atholl (1313?–killed 1333); he married Joan, daughter of Sir John Menteith of Rusky and Knapdale.

2 Dougal; he married and had issue.

3 Duncan (?); he is said to have married and had issue, but the evidence for his existence is unsatisfactory.

Mary married secondly Sir Alexander Fraser (killed 1332) in *c.*1316, and had issue:

1 John of Touch Fraser (1317?–died in early manhood); he married an unknown lady and had issue.

2 William, a knight (1318?–killed 1346); he married Margaret (*d.*1364), said to have been the daughter of Sir Andrew Moray of Bothwell, and had issue.

Mary died before 22 September, 1323.

7 *Christina* or *Christian*

She married firstly Gartnait, Earl of Mar (*d.*1305), in *c.*1292, and had issue:

1 Donald, 8th Earl of Mar (killed 1332); he married Isabella (*d.*1347), perhaps the daughter of Sir Alexander Stewart of Bonkyll, and had issue.

2 Helen (*d.* after 1342); she married firstly Sir John Menteith, Lord of Arran, and had issue, and secondly Sir James Garioch (?).

Christina married secondly Christopher Seton (executed 1306) in 1305/6. She married thirdly Sir Andrew Murray of Bothwell (1298–1338) after 12 October, 1325 (date of dispensation), and had issue:

1 John, a knight (*d.*1352); he married Margaret Graham, Countess of Menteith (◊ page 217, under Robert II).

2 Thomas, a knight (*d.*1361); he married Joan, daughter of Maurice Moray, Earl of Strathearn.

Christina died in 1356/7 'at a great age'.

8 *Margaret*

She married Sir William de Carlyle (*d.* by 1329), and had issue:

1 William, a knight (*d.*1347).

2 John (*d.*1347); married and had issue.

9 *Matilda*

She married Hugh, 6th Earl of Ross (killed 1333), in *c.*1308, and had issue:

1 Matilda or Marjorie (*d.* after 1350); she married Malise, Earl of Strathearn and Caithness (*d.*1344/57).

2 William, 7th Earl of Ross (*d.*1372); he married Mary, daughter of Angus Og, Lord of the Isles, and had issue.

Matilda died between 1323 and 1329, and was buried at Fearn, Scotland.

10 *Son (name not known)*

He probably died young.

ROBERT I

Known as 'the Bruce', he was born on 11 July, 1274, probably at Writtle, near Chelmsford, Essex. He succeeded his father as Earl of Carrick on 27 October, 1292, and as Lord of Annandale either in 1295 (?) or in 1304. On 25 or 27 March, 1306, he assumed the Crown and Royal Dignity of Scotland, thus bringing to an end the Second Interregnum. This he did in defiance of Edward I of England, who had declared his English estates forfeit on 20 February, 1305/6. Robert I was crowned on 27 March, 1306, at Scone Abbey, Perthshire.

Robert I married firstly, in *c.*1295 (although no evidence exists as to where):

Isabella

She was the daughter of Donald, 6th Earl of Mar, by his wife Helen, who was said to have been an illegitimate daughter of Llywelyn the Great, Prince of Wales. Isabella was dead by 1302.

Issue of marriage:

1 *Marjorie*

She was born in *c.*1297. (◊ page 216, under Robert II).

Robert I married secondly, in *c.*1302 (although no evidence exists as to where):

Elizabeth

She was the daughter of Richard de Burgh, Earl of Ulster and Connaught, by Margaret, daughter of John de Burgh. She died on 26 October, 1327, at Cullen Castle, Banffshire, and was buried in Dunfermline Abbey, Fife.

Issue of marriage:

1 *Margaret*

She married William, 5th Earl of Sutherland (*d.*1371), between 2 August and 28 September, 1345, and had issue:

1 John, Master of Sutherland (1346?–1361).

Margaret died between 30 March, 1346, and 9 November, 1347 in childbed.

2 *Matilda*

She married Thomas Isaac, and had issue:

1 Joan; she married John, Lord of Lorne.

2 Katherine.

Matilda died on 20 July, 1353, at Aberdeen, and was buried in Dunfermline Abbey, Fife.

3 *David II* (◊ page 212).

4 *John*

He was born in October, 1327, and died young. He was buried in Restennet Priory, Forfarshire.

Robert I also had the following **illegitimate issue:**

1 Robert, Baron of Liddesdale (killed 1332).

2 Neil or Nigel of Carrick, a knight (*d.*1346).

3 Walter of Odistoun (?); probably spurious.

4 Christina of Carrick.

5 Margaret (*d.* after 1364); she married Robert Glen.

6 Elizabeth; she married Sir Walter Oliphant of Aberdalgie (*d.* after 1378), and had issue.

ROBERT I

He died on 7 June, 1329, at Cardross Castle, Dumbartonshire, and was buried in Dunfermline Abbey, Fife.

He was succeeded by his son David.

David II

FATHER: *Robert I* (◊ page 207).
MOTHER: *Elizabeth de Burgh* (◊ page 211, under *Robert I*).
SIBLINGS: (◊ page 211, under *Robert I*).

DAVID II

He was born on 5 March, 1324, at Dunfermline Palace, Fife, and was created Earl of Carrick between 17 March and 17 July, 1328, thus establishing the tradition that the title of Earl of Carrick is always borne by the eldest son of the sovereign in Scotland. David succeeded his father as King of Scotland on 7 June, 1329, and was crowned on 24 November, 1331, at Scone Abbey, Perthshire. He was overthrown by Edward Balliol (◊ page 214) in August, 1332, at the Battle of Dupplin Moor, near Perth, but restored to the throne the following December. He was again deposed by Edward Balliol in 1333, and finally restored in 1336.

David II married firstly, on 17 July, 1328, at Berwick-upon-Tweed, Northumberland:

Joan

She was the daughter of Edward II, King of England, by Isabella of France, and she was born on 5 July, 1321, at the Tower of London. She was crowned Queen Consort on 24 November, 1331, at Scone Abbey, Perthshire, this being the first time that a Scottish Queen Consort was crowned. Joan died on 7 September, 1362, at Hertford Castle, and was buried in Greyfriars Church, Newgate, London. There was no issue of her marriage to David II.

David II married secondly, in April or December, 1363 (or, less probably, 13 or *c*.20 February, 1364), either at Inchmurdach Manor, Fife, or at Inchmahome Priory, Perthshire:

Margaret

She was the daughter of Sir Malcolm Drummond by a daughter of Sir Patrick de Graham. She married firstly Sir John Logie, and had issue:

1   John of Logie.
David II divorced Margaret on *c.*20 March, 1370. She died soon after
31 January, 1375, perhaps at Avignon, France. There was no issue of
the marriage.

DAVID II
He died on 22 February, 1371, at Edinburgh Castle, and was buried in
Holyrood Abbey, Edinburgh.
   He was succeeded by his nephew Robert Stewart.

CONTINUATION OF PART THREE

The House of Balliol

King Edward

FATHER: *King John* (◊ page 204).
MOTHER: *Isabella de Warenne* (◊ page 205, under *King John*)
SIBLINGS: (◊ page 205, under *King John*).

KING EDWARD

His date of birth is unknown. He claimed the throne of Scotland as his father's successor, and defeated David II in August, 1332, at the Battle of Dupplin Moor, near Perth. He was crowned King of Scotland on 24 September, 1332, at Scone Abbey, Perthshire. He was deposed in favour of David II on 16 December, 1332, and expelled from Scotland, but was restored to the throne in March, 1333. He was again deposed in 1334, and fled to England, yet was restored once more in 1335. He was finally deposed in 1336. He never married, and had no children.

KING EDWARD

He surrendered all claims to the throne of Scotland on 20 January, 1356. He probably died between May, 1363, and September, 1365, perhaps in January, 1364, at Wheatley, near Doncaster, Yorks., but one source at least hints that he was still alive in 1370. His place of burial is not known. He was succeeded in 1336 by David II (◊ page 212), who was in turn succeeded by Robert Stewart.

PART FIVE

The House of Stewart

Robert II

FATHER: *Walter*

He was the son of James, 5th High Steward of Scotland, by Cecilia, daughter of Patrick, 7th Earl of Dunbar and March. He was born in 1292, and in due course succeeded his father as 6th High Steward of Scotland, from which title derived the royal surname of Stewart, adopted by his successors. Walter married firstly, it is said, Alice, daughter of Sir John Erskine (although there is no proof of this), by whom he is said to have had issue:

1 Jean; she married Hugh, 6th Earl of Ross (*d.*1333), and had issue.

Walter married secondly Marjorie Bruce in 1315, thus founding the Royal House of Stewart. He married thirdly Isabella, daughter of Sir John Graham of Abercorn, and had issue:

1 John of Railston or Cunningham, a knight; he married and had issue.

2 Andrew; a knight.

3 Egidia (*d.* by 1406); she married firstly Sir James Lindsay of Crawford (*d.*1358), and had issue. She married secondly Sir Hugh of Eglinton, and thirdly Sir James Douglas of Dalkeith (*d.*1420).

Walter died on 9 April, 1326/7.

MOTHER: *Marjorie*

She was the daughter of Robert I, King of Scotland, by Isabella of Mar, and she was born in *c.*1297. She died on 2 March, 1316, at Paisley, Renfrewshire, in childbed, after falling from her horse, and was buried in Paisley Abbey.

SIBLINGS: *Robert II did not have any siblings.*

ROBERT II

He was born on 2 March, 1316, at Paisley, Renfrewshire. He was created Earl of Atholl on 16 February, 1342, and Earl of Strathearn around 6/13 November, 1357/8. He resigned the earldom of Atholl on 31 May, 1367, and either resigned, or was deprived of, the earldom of Strathearn on 18 April, 1369; he was formally deprived of it on 16 September, 1369, although he was restored in blood to the earldom of Strathearn around 4/7 April, 1370. He succeeded David II as King of Scotland – the first Stewart King – on 22 February, 1371, and was crowned either on 22 February or 26 March, 1371, at Scone Abbey, Perthshire.

Robert II married firstly, in 1336, and again after 22 November, 1347 (date of dispensation), perhaps in 1349 (because the first marriage ceremony was uncanonical) (although no record exists as to where):
Elizabeth

She was the daughter of Sir Adam Mure of Rowallan, Ayrshire, by Joan Cunningham, his first wife, or Janet Mure, his second wife. The children of this marriage, most of whom were born before the second ceremony of marriage, were looked upon by many as not quite legitimate, although one of the sons succeeded his father as King. This uncertainty surrounding their status led to bitter conflict in after years between them and the unquestionably legitimate children of their father's second marriage (◊ below). Elizabeth Mure died before 1355.

Issue of marriage:

1 *John, who styled himself **Robert III*** (◊ page 228).

2 *Walter*

He was styled Earl of Fife in right of his wife before 14 August, 1362. He died between 14 August, 1362, and 10 January, 1363.

Walter married, before 1362 (although no record exists as to where):

Elizabeth

She was the daughter of Duncan, 10th Earl of Fife, by Mary, daughter of Ralph de Monthermer, Earl of Gloucester, by Joan, daughter of Edward I, King of England, and she was born before 1332. She succeeded her father as Countess of Fife in 1353, and was so styled from 1359. She married firstly Sir William Ramsay of Colluthie, Earl of Fife (*d.* after 1360). Walter Stewart was her second husband; there was no issue of the marriage. After his death, she married thirdly Sir Thomas Bisset of Upsetlington, Earl of Fife (*d.*1365), between 10 January, 1363, and April (?) or 8 June, 1363. She married fourthly John de Dunbar, Earl of Fife (*d.* by 1371). She resigned the earldom of Fife to Robert, Duke of Albany, her brother-in-law (◊ below), on 30 March, 1371, but was again created Countess of Fife before 6 March, 1372. She died after 12 August, 1389.

3 Robert

He was born in *c.*1340/41, and was created Earl of Menteith on 28 February, 1361, pending his forthcoming marriage to the heiress of Menteith. He was created Earl of Fife between 4 December, 1371, and 6 March, 1372, following the resignation of Elizabeth, his sister-in-law (◊ above), but resigned the earldom to her on 6 March, 1372. He was created Duke of Albany on 28 April, 1398. He was created Earl of Atholl for life on 2 September, 1403, but was never so styled, so it may be that he resigned at once. He was created Earl of Buchan before 20 September, 1406, following the death of his brother, Alexander (◊ below), but resigned it the same day. Robert died on 3 September, 1420, at Stirling Castle, and was buried in Dunfermline Abbey, Fife.

Robert married firstly, after 9 September, 1361 (date of dispensation) (although no record exists as to where):

Margaret

She was the daughter of Sir John Graham by Mary, Countess of Menteith, and she was born before 1334. She married firstly Sir John Murray, Lord of Bothwell (*d.*1352) (son of Christina, sister of Robert I), after 21 November, 1348 (date of dispensation). She married secondly Thomas, Earl of Mar (1330?–1374), between 15 August, 1352 ,and 29 May, 1354, but he divorced her in *c.*1359, on the grounds that she was barren. She married thirdly Sir John

Drummond of Concraig (*d.*1360/61) in *c.*1359. She succeeded her mother as Countess of Menteith on 29 April, 1360. Robert Stewart was her fourth husband. She died between 20 July, 1372, and 4 May, 1380, and was buried in Inchmahome Priory, Perthshire.

Issue of marriage:

(i) *Murdoch*

He was born in 1362 (?), and succeeded his father as Duke of Albany, Earl of Fife and Earl of Menteith on 3 September, 1420. He forfeited all his honours on 25 May, 1425, and was executed the same day on Castle Hill, Stirling. He was buried in the Church of the Black Friars, Stirling.

Murdoch had the following illegitimate issue:

1 Daughter (name not known) (?); she is said to have married Archibald Campbell (*d.* by 1440), son of Marjorie Stewart (daughter of Robert, Duke of Albany by his second wife), but the evidence for her existence is unsatisfactory.

Murdoch married, between 17 February and 8 November, 1392 (although no record exists as to where):

Elizabeth

She was the daughter of Duncan, 8th Earl of Lennox, by Helen, daughter of Gillespic Campbell of Lochawe, and she was born in *c.*1370. She was styled Countess of Lennox in her own right from 12 May, 1437. She died between 7 October, 1456, and 4 May, 1458, at Inchmurrah Castle, Loch Lomond.

Issue of marriage:

(a) *Robert*

He was known as the Master of Fife. He died between 1416 and July, 1421.

(b) *Walter*

He rose to the rank of knight. He was executed on 24 May, 1425, on Castle Hill, Stirling, and was buried in the Church of the Black Friars, Stirling.

Walter had the following illegitimate issue:

By a lady surnamed Campbell:

1 Andrew Stewart, Lord of Avandale (*d.*1488) (?); he married a lady about whom no information exists.

2 Arthur.

By an unknown mother:

    3 Mariott (?); she is said to have married Colin Campbell, Earl of Argyll (1406?–1475), but there is little evidence to support this.

By Janet, daughter of Sir Robert Erskine (Walter was granted a dispensation to marry her on 24 April, 1424, but there is no evidence to show that the marriage ever took place):

    4 Walter of Morphie; he married and had issue.

Note: All Walter's bastards were legitimated on 17 April, 1479.

(c) *Alexander*

He rose to the rank of knight. He was executed on 25 May, 1425, on Castle Hill, Stirling, and was buried in the Church of the Black Friars, Stirling.

(d) *James*

He died before 18 May, 1451, in exile in Ireland.

James had the following illegitimate issue:

By an Irish lady surnamed MacDonald:

1 Andrew, Lord of Avandale (?).

2 Arthur.

3 Walter.

4 James Beg.

5 Matilda; she married William Edmonston of Duntreath.

6 Son (name not known).

7 Son (name not known).

(e) *Isabella*

She married Sir Walter Buchanan, and had issue, although no details are recorded.

(ii) *Janet*

She was contracted in marriage on 20 July, 1372, to David de Loen, but no evidence exists to show that the wedding ever took place. She probably died unmarried.

(iii) *Mary*

She married Sir William Abernethy of Saltoun (*d.*1420), and had issue:

1 Son.

2 Son.

3 etc. Other children.

(iv) *Margaret*

She married Sir John de Swinton of Swinton (killed in battle in 1402) in *c*.1392, and had issue, although no details are available. She perhaps married secondly Sir Robert Stewart, Lord of Lorne and Innermeath (*d*.1449), but she may have been confused in the records with her sister Joan (◊ below). Details of the issue of this possible marriage are not recorded.

(v) *Joan*

She married Robert Stewart, Lord of Lorne and Innermeath (*d*.1449), after 27 September, 1397 (date of dispensation), and had issue:

1 John, Lord of Lorne (killed 1463).

2 Walter, 1st Lord Innermeath (*d*. by 1488/9); he married Margaret Lindsay (*d*. after 1481), and had issue.

3 Alan (*d.c*.1463).

4 David.

5 Robert.

6 Daughter (name not known); she is said to have married Robert, 8th Lord Erskine (*d*. by 1452), but there is no evidence for this.

(vi) *Beatrice*

She married James Douglas, Earl of Douglas and Avandale (*d*.1443). She died in *c*.1424.

(vii) *Isabella*

She married firstly Alexander Leslie, 9th Earl of Ross (*d*.1402) (◊ page 223, under Euphemia, Countess of Ross) before 1398, and had issue:

1 Euphemia, Countess of Ross (*d*. after 1424); she became a nun at North Berwick, and renounced her inheritance.

Isabella married secondly Walter Haliburton of Dirleton between 1402 and 2 February, 1408, and had issue:

1 Walter (*d*. by 1447); he married Marjorie (◊ page 229, under Robert III), daughter of Archibald Douglas, 3rd Earl of Douglas, and had issue.

2 Christina; she married George Leslie, 1st Earl of Rothes (1417?–1490), and had issue.

Robert married secondly, after 4 May, 1380 (date of dispensation) (although no evidence exists as to where):

Muriella

She was the daughter of Sir William Keith by Margaret, daughter of John Fraser. She died shortly before 1 June, 1449.

Issue of marriage:

(i) *John*

He was born in 1381 (?), and succeeded his father as Earl of Buchan before 20 September, 1406. He was killed on 17 August, 1424, at the Battle of Verneuil, France.

John married, in November, 1413 (although no evidence exists as to where):

Elizabeth

She was the daughter of Archibald Douglas, 4th Earl of Douglas and Duke of Touraine, by Margaret, daughter of Robert III. She married secondly Sir Thomas Stewart (*d.* by 1435), and thirdly William Sinclair, 3rd Earl of Orkney (*d.*1476/82), by whom she had issue:

1 William; he married Christina, daughter of George Leslie, Earl of Rothes, and had issue.

2 Katherine, Duchess of Albany (◊ page 236, under James II).

Elizabeth died before 1451.

Issue of marriage:

(a) *Margaret*

She married George Seton, 1st Lord Seton (*d.*1478), before 1436, and had issue:

1 John, Master of Seton (*d.* by 1478); he married Christina (*d.*1496), daughter of John, 1st Lord Lindsay of the Byres, and had issue.

2 Dougal (?).

(ii) *Andrew*

He died before 1413.

(iii) *Robert*

He is said to have been killed on 17 August, 1424, at the Battle of Verneuil, France, but this is impossible as he was recorded as alive in 1431.

(iv) *Marjorie*

She married Duncan, 1st Lord Campbell of Lochawe (*d.*1453), and had issue:

1 Archibald or Celestine (*d.* by 1440); he married Elizabeth, daughter of John, 3rd Lord Somerville of Carwath. He is said to have married secondly a daughter of Murdoch, Duke of Albany (⟡ above), but this is improbable.

Some sources name Marjorie as the mother of Colin, 1st Earl of Argyll (1431?–1493), and state that she died, possibly in childbed, before August, 1432. Colin was almost certainly the son of Lord Campbell by his second wife whom he married shortly after Marjorie's death in *c.*1406.

(v) *Elizabeth*

She married Sir Malcolm Fleming of Biggar and Cumbernauld (executed 1440) before 28 June, 1413, and had issue:

1 Malcolm (*d.* after 1432).
2 Robert, Lord Fleming (*d.*1491); he married firstly Janet, daughter of James Douglas, 7th Earl of Douglas, and had issue. He married secondly Margaret, daughter of John Lindsay of Covington.
3 Margaret; she married Patrick, Master of Gray.

4 *Alexander*

Known as 'the Wolf of Badenoch', he was born in *c.*1343, and created Lord of Badenoch on 30 March, 1371. He was created Earl of Buchan on 22 July, 1382, and was styled Earl of Ross in right of his wife from July, 1382. Alexander died before 1406: a possible date is 24 July, 1394. However, he may have died as late as 25 March, 1406. Other possible dates are 20 February, 1395 (but here there is possible confusion with the date of his wife's death), 1 August, 1405, or any date between August, 1405, and March, 1406. He was buried in Dunkeld Cathedral, Perthshire.

Alexander had the following illegitimate issue:

By Margaret Atheyn:

1 Alexander, Earl of Mar (1375?–1435); he married Elizabeth, Countess of Mar (1360?–1408).
2 Duncan.
3 Andrew of Sandhauch, Banffshire; a knight.
4 Walter.
5 James.
6 Robert of Atholl.
7 Margaret; she married Robert, Earl of Sutherland (*d.*1427), and

had issue.

Alexander married, on or before 22/24 July, 1382 (although no evidence exists as to where):

Euphemia

She was the daughter of William, 7th Earl of Ross, by Mary, daughter of Angus Og, Lord of the Isles, and she was born after 1342/5. She married firstly Sir Walter Leslie, Earl of Ross (*d.*1382), between 1357 and 13 September, 1366, and had issue:

1 Alexander, 9th Earl of Ross (*d.*1402); he married Isabella Stewart, daughter of Robert, Duke of Albany (♭ above), and had issue.

2 Mary, Countess of Ross (*d.c.*1435); she married Donald Macdonald, Lord of the Isles (*d.*1423) (son of Margaret, daughter of Robert II), and had issue.

Euphemia was styled Lady of Ross from 9 February, 1372, following the death of her father; she was styled Countess of Ross during her second marriage to Alexander Stewart. She died between 5 September, 1394, and 20 February, 1395, and was buried in Fortrose Cathedral, Ross and Cromarty. There was no issue of her marriage to Alexander.

5 *Elizabeth*

She married Sir Thomas de la Haye, 7th Lord of Erroll (*d.*1406), before 7 November, 1372, and had issue:

1 William, a knight (*d.*1436); he married Margaret, daughter of Sir Patrick Gray of Broxmouth, and had issue.

2 Gilbert of Dronlaw, a knight; he married Elizabeth Reid, and had issue.

3 Elizabeth; she married Sir George Leslie of Rothes (1350–after 1412), and had issue.

4 Alice; she married Sir William Hay of Locharret.

5 Daughter (name not known); she married Norman (?), son of Andrew Leslie, and had issue.

6 *Isabella*

She married firstly James Douglas, 2nd Earl of Douglas (1358?–killed 1388), after 24 September, 1371 (date of dispensation), perhaps in 1373 (?), and had issue:

1 Son (name not known) (*d.* young).

Isabella married secondly Sir John Edmondston of Duntreath in 1388/90, and had issue:

1 Son (name not known).

Isabella died in c.1410.

7 *Jean*

She married firstly Sir John Keith (*d*.1375) on 17 January, 1373/4, and had issue:

1 Robert (*d*. by 1404).

2 Robert, Lord of Strathkyn (*d*.1430); he married the heiress of Troup, and had issue.

Jean married secondly Sir John Lyon of Glamis (killed 1382) between 27 June and 4 October, 1376, and had issue:

3 John, a knight (*d*.1435); he married Elizabeth, daughter of Sir Patrick Graham of Dundaff and Kilpont, by Euphemia, Countess Palatine of Caithness and Strathearn (◊ page 225, below), and had issue.

Jean married thirdly Sir James Sandilands of Calder in c.November, 1384, and had issue:

4 James of Calder, a knight (*d.c.*1426); he married a lady called Janet, and had issue.

Jean died after 1404, and was buried in Scone Abbey, Perthshire.

8 *Katherine* (?)

She may have been a daughter of Robert II by Elizabeth Mure. She married Sir Robert Logan of Restalrig, by whom she may have had issue, although no details are recorded. She died after 1394 (?).

9 *Margaret*

She married John MacDonald, Lord of the Isles (1326?–1387), after 14 June, 1350 (date of dispensation), and had issue:

1 Donald, Lord of the Isles (*d*.1423); he married Mary (*d.c.*1435), daughter of Sir Walter Leslie by Euphemia, Countess of Ross (◊ page 223 above), and had issue.

2 John, known as Ian Mor Tanisteir (murdered 1427); he married Marjorie, daughter of Sir Hugh Bisset, and had issue.

3 Alexander, known as Alastair Carrach; he married and had issue.

4 Angus.

5 Hugh, Thane of Glentilt; he married and had issue.

6 Marcus.

7 Mary; she married Lachlan Maclean of Duart.

8 Elizabeth or Margaret; she married Angus Duff Mackay of Strathnaver.

10 *Marjorie*

She married firstly John de Dunbar, Earl of Moray (*d.*1391/2), after 11 July, 1370 (date of dispensation), and had issue:

1 Thomas, Earl of Moray (*d.*1415/22); he married a lady called Margaret (*d.*1422), and had issue.

2 Alexander; he is said to have married Matilda, daughter of James Fraser of Frendraught, and to have had issue.

3 James (*b.*1390).

4 Euphemia; she married Alexander Cumming and had issue (?).

Marjorie married secondly Sir Alexander Keith of Grandown before 24 April, *c.*1403, and perhaps had issue:

5 Christina (?); she married Sir Patrick Ogilvy (drowned 1429), and had issue.

Marjorie died after 6 May, 1417.

Robert II married secondly, after 2 May, 1355 (date of dispensation) (although no evidence exists as to where):

Euphemia

She was the daughter of Hugh, 6th Earl of Ross, by Margaret Graham. She married firstly John Randolph, 3rd Earl of Moray (*d.*1346). She was crowned Queen Consort in 1372 at Scone Abbey, Perthshire. She died in 1387.

Issue of marriage:

1 *David*

He was born around 1356/60. He was created Earl Palatine of Strathearn on 26/27 March, 1371, and Earl of Caithness between 21 November, 1375, and 28 December, 1377. He died before 5 March, 1389, perhaps in February (?), 1389 (?), or perhaps as early as 1382.

David married a lady whose name is not recorded:

She was the daughter of Sir Alexander Lindsay of Glenesk, by Katherine, daughter of Sir John Stirling of Glenesk.

Issue of marriage:

(i) *Euphemia*

She was born before 1375, and succeeded her father as Countess Palatine of Caithness and Strathearn before 5 March, 1389. She resigned the earldom of Caithness before July, 1402. She married firstly Sir Patrick Graham of Dundaff and Kilpont (*d.*1413) before December (and perhaps by 24 August), 1406, and had issue:

1 Malise, Earl of Strathearn and Menteith (c.1407–1490); he married a lady called Janet (d.c.1477), and had issue. He married secondly Marion (d.1530), possibly a Campbell of Glenorchy, and had issue.

2 Euphemia (d.1468); she married firstly Archibald Douglas, 5th Earl of Douglas (1390–1439), and had issue. She married secondly James, 1st Lord Hamilton (1415–1479) (he married secondly Mary, daughter of James II).

3 Elizabeth or Anne; she married Sir John Lyon (d.1435) (son of Jean, daughter of Robert II).

Euphemia married secondly Sir Patrick Dunbar of Bele (d. after 1438), and had issue:

4 Patrick.

5 George.

Euphemia died on 15 October, c.1434.

2 Walter

He was born in c.1360, and was created Baron of Brechin in 1378. He was created Earl of Caithness before July, 1402, and Earl of Atholl on c.28 April, 1404. He was created Baron Cortachy on 22 September, 1409, and Earl Palatine of Strathearn on 22 July, 1427. He resigned the earldom of Caithness in favour of his son Alexander around c.1428/30: 13 December, 1429, is the most probable date. He succeeded Alexander as Earl of Caithness in late summer, 1431. His honours and estates were declared forfeit on 26 March, 1437, and he was executed with appalling barbarity on the same day in Edinburgh as punishment for his part in the murder of James I.

Walter married, before 19 October, 1378 (although no evidence exists as to where):

Margaret

She was the daughter of Sir David de Barclay, Lord of Brechin, by Janet, daughter of Sir Edward Keith of Synton. She died before 1 August, 1404.

Issue of marriage:

(i) *Alexander* or *Alan*

He was created Earl of Caithness around c.1428/30. He was killed in 1431 in a foray at Inverlochy, Inverness-shire.

(ii) *David*

He died after February, 1433, in England.

David married an Englishwoman whose identity is unknown, and had issue:

(a) *Robert*

He rose to the rank of knight, and was known as the Master of Atholl. He was granted a dispensation to marry one Margaret Ogilvy on 29 January, 1428/9, but there is no evidence to show that the marriage ever took place. He was executed in March, 1437, in Edinburgh for his part in the murder of James I.

On 1 August, 1404, Walter Stewart was granted a dispensation to marry Elizabeth, daughter of Sir William Graham of Kincardine, but no evidence exists to show that the marriage actually took place. Elizabeth married Sir John Stewart of Dundonald, bastard son of Robert II, in 1407/8.

3 *Elizabeth*

She married David Lindsay, 1st Earl of Crawford (1360?–1407), in 1380 or 1384 (dispensation granted on 22 February, 1374/5), and had issue:

1 Alexander, 2nd Earl of Crawford (1387?–1438); he married Marjorie Dunbar (*d.* after 1429), perhaps a daughter of the Earl of Dunbar, and had issue.
2 David, Lord of Newdosk; he later became a priest.
3 Gerard (*d.* before 1421).
4 Ingelram (?), Bishop of Aberdeen (*d.*1458).
5 Marjorie; she married Sir William Douglas of Lochleven.
6 Elizabeth; she married Sir Robert Keith.
7 Elizabeth; she married Robert, Lord Erskine (*d.*1451/2); she may have been confused with her sister of the same name, and it is possible that they were one and the same person.
8 Isabella; she married Sir John Maxwell of Pollok, and had issue.

4 *Egidia or Jill*

She married Sir William Douglas of Nithsdale in *c.*1387, and had issue:

1 William, Lord of Nithsdale (*d.* after 1419).
2 Egidia (*d.* after 1438); she married Henry St Clair, Earl of Orkney (*d.*1421), and had issue.

Egidia died after 1388.

Robert II also had the following **illegitimate issue**:

By Moira Leitch (according to tradition):

1 John Stewart of Dundonald, a knight (*d.*1445/9); he married firstly Janet, daughter of John Sympil of Elistoun, and had issue. He married secondly Elizabeth, daughter of Sir William Graham of Kincardine.

By unknown mothers:

2 John Stewart, Lord of Burley (killed 1425).
3 John Stewart of Cairdney, a knight.
4 Alexander Stewart, Canon of Glasgow.
5 Alexander Stewart of Inverlunan, a knight.
6 Thomas Stewart, Archdeacon of St Andrews, Dean of Dunkeld.
7 James Stewart of Kinfauns.
8 Walter Stewart.

ROBERT II

He died on 19 April, 1390, at Dundonald Castle, Ayrshire, and was buried in Scone Abbey, Perthshire.

He was succeeded by his son John, who took the name Robert upon his accession.

Robert III

FATHER: *Robert II* (↷ page 215).
MOTHER: *Elizabeth Mure* (↷ page 216, under *Robert II*).
SIBLINGS: (↷ page 216, under *Robert III*).

ROBERT III

He was christened John, and took the name Robert upon his accession. He was born around *c.*1337/40. He was created Earl of Carrick on 22 June, 1368, and styled Earl of Atholl on 17 October (?), *c.*1379, for this occasion only. He succeeded his father as King of Scotland on 19 April, 1390, and was crowned on 14 August, 1390, at Scone Abbey, Perthshire.

Robert III married, in c.1366/7 (although no evidence exists as to where):

Annabella

She was the daughter of Sir John Drummond of Stobhall by Mary, daughter of Sir William Montifex, and she was born in c.1350. She was crowned Queen Consort on 15 August, 1390, at Scone Abbey, Perthshire. She died in c.October ('Harvest-tide'), 1401, at Scone Palace, Perthshire, and was buried in Dunfermline Abbey, Fife.

Issue of marriage:

1 David

He was born on 24 October, 1378. He was created Earl of Carrick between 19 April, 1390, and 2 January, 1391, and Duke of Rothesay (a title borne henceforth by the eldest son of a Scottish sovereign) on 28 April, 1398. He was created Earl of Atholl on 6 September, 1398. He died on 26/27 March, 1402, in prison at Falkland Palace, Fife; he is said to have been starved to death, but he probably succumbed to dysentery. He was buried in Lindores Abbey, Fife.

David married, in February, 1399/1400, at Bothwell Church:

Marjorie

She was the daughter of Archibald Douglas, 3rd Earl of Douglas, by Joan, daughter of Thomas Moray of Bothwell. David Stewart was her first husband. She married secondly Sir Walter Haliburton of Dirleton (*d.* by 1447) (son of Isabella Stewart of Albany, granddaughter of Robert II) in 1403, and had issue:

1 John, Lord Haliburton (*d.*1452/4); he married Janet (*d.* after 1493), daughter of Sir William Seton of Seton, and had issue.

2 Walter (*d.* after 1433); he married Katherine, daughter of Alexander Chisholme.

3 Robert.

4 William (*d.* after 1439).

Marjorie died before 11 May, 1421.

2 James I (⇨ page 232).

3 Robert

He died young.

4 Margaret

Known as the Lady of Galloway, she married Archibald Douglas, 4th Earl of Douglas and Duke of Touraine (1370?–killed 1424), before 1390, and had issue:

1 Archibald, 5th Earl of Douglas (1390–1439); he married Euphemia (d.1468), daughter of Sir Patrick Graham by Euphemia, granddaughter of Robert II, and had issue.

2 William; he married Marjorie Stewart, and had issue.

3 Elizabeth; she married John Stewart, Earl of Buchan (◊ page 221, under Robert II).

4 James, a knight (killed 1424).

Margaret died between 26 January, 1449, and September, 1456, probably at Thrieve Castle, Galloway, and was buried in the Collegiate Church of Lincluden, Dumfries.

5 *Mary or Mariot*

She married firstly George Douglas, 13th Earl of Angus (d.1402/5), after 24 May, 1397 (date of dispensation and contract), and had issue:

1 William, Earl of Angus (1398?–1437); he married Margaret (d. after 1484), daughter of Sir William Hay of Yester, and had issue.

2 Elizabeth; she married Alexander Forbes, 1st Lord Forbes (d.1448), and had issue. She married secondly Sir David Hay of Yester.

Mary married secondly Sir James Kennedy of Dunure (killed 1408) in 1404 (?), and had issue:

3 James, Bishop of Dunkeld and St Andrews (1405/6–1465).

4 Gilbert, Lord Kennedy (1406?–1480?); he married firstly Katherine, daughter of Herbert, 1st Lord Maxwell, and had issue. He married secondly Isabella (d.1484), daughter of Sir Walter Ogilvy of Lintrathen.

5 John, a knight (d. after 1434).

In July, 1409, Mary was granted a dispensation to marry Sir William Cunningham (d.1413/15), but it is doubtful whether the marriage ever took place. She married thirdly William, 1st Lord Graham of Kincardine (d.1424), on 13 November (?), 1413 (?) (certainly before 15 May, 1416), and had issue:

6 Patrick, Archbishop of St Andrews (d.1478).

7 Robert of Strathcarron and Fintry; he married firstly Janet, daughter of Sir Richard Lovel of Ballumbie, and had issue. He married secondly Matilda, daughter of Sir James Scrymgeour of Dudhope, and had issue.

8 Son (name not known).

9 Son (name not known).

10 Son (name not known).

Mary married fourthly Sir William Edmondston of Duntreath in 1425, and had issue, although no details are recorded. She died in c.1458, and was buried in Strathblane Church, Scotland.

6 *Egidia*

She died unmarried.

7 *Elizabeth*

She married Sir James Douglas, 1st Lord of Dalkeith (*d.*1441), before 10 November, 1387, and perhaps as early as 24 March, 1381/2, and had issue:

1 William (1390–1425); he perhaps married Margaret Borthwick, although this is unlikely.

2 James, 2nd Lord of Dalkeith (*d.*1456/8); he married Elizabeth (*d.* after 1456), daughter of James Gifford of Sheriffhall, and had issue, including James, who married Joan, daughter of James I.

3 Henry of Dalkeith (*d.* by 1456); he married Margaret (*d.*1473), daughter of James Douglas, 7th Earl of Douglas, and had issue.

Elizabeth died before 1411.

Robert III also had the following **illegitimate issue**:

1 James Stewart of Kilbride.

ROBERT III

He died on 4 April, 1406, at Dundonald Castle, Ayrshire, and was buried in Paisley Abbey, Renfrewshire.

He was succeeded by his son James.

James I

FATHER: *Robert III* (◊ page 228).
MOTHER: *Annabella Drummond* (◊ page 229, under *Robert III*).
SIBLINGS: (◊ page 229, under *Robert III*).

JAMES I
He was born on 25 July (?) (or in December), 1394, at Dunfermline
Palace, Fife. He was created Duke of Rothesay and Earl of Carrick on
10 December, 1404. He succeeded his father as King of Scotland on 4
April, 1406 (although he was not proclaimed until June), whilst being
held in captivity in England. He was not released to govern his
kingdom until 1424, when he was crowned on 2 or 21 May at Scone
Abbey, Perthshire.

James I married, on 2, 10 or 13 February, 1424, at the Priory Church
of St Mary Overy, Southwark, London:

Joan
She was the daughter of John Beaufort, Earl of Somerset, a
grandson of Edward III, King of England, by Margaret Holland. She
was crowned Queen Consort on 2 or 21 May, 1424, at Scone Abbey,
Perthshire. She married secondly Sir James Stewart ('the Black
Knight') of Lorne (*d.c.*1448) before 21 September, 1439, and had
issue:

1 John, Earl of Atholl (1440?–1512); he married firstly Margaret
(*d.c.*1475), daughter of Archibald Douglas, 5th Earl of Douglas, and
had issue. He married secondly Eleanor (*d.*1518), daughter of
William Sinclair, Earl of Orkney and Caithness, and had issue.

2 James, Earl of Buchan (*d.*1498/1500); he married Margaret,
daughter of Sir Alexander Ogilvy of Auchterhause, and had issue.

3 Andrew, Bishop of Moray (*c.*1443–1501).

Joan died on 15 July, 1445, at Dunbar Castle, and was buried in the
Monastery of the Charterhouse, Perth.

Issue of marriage:

1 *Margaret*

She was born around Christmas, 1424. She married Louis, Dauphin of Viennois (afterwards Louis XI, King of France: *d.* 1483) on 24 June, 1436, at Tours Cathedral, France, and again on 25 June, 1436, at Rheims Cathedral, France. She died on 16 August, 1445, at Châlons, France, and was buried in Châlons Cathedral. Her remains were later removed to the Church of St Léon, Thouars, France.

2 *Isabella*

She married Francis I, Duke of Brittany (*d.*1450), on 30 October, 1442, and had issue:

1 Mary; she married John, Viscount de Rohan.

2 Margaret; she married Francis II, Duke of Brittany, and had issue.

Isabella died in 1494.

3 *Eleanor*

She was born on 26 October, 1427. She married Sigismund von Tirol, Archduke of Austria (*d.*1496), around 12/24 February, 1449. She died in 1480.

4 *Joan*

A mute, she was born in *c.*1428. She is alleged to have married James Douglas, Earl of Angus (*d.*1446), and she was certainly contracted to him on 18 October, 1440, but there is no evidence to show that the marriage ever took place. She did marry James Douglas, Earl of Morton (*d.*1493), before 15 May, 1459, and had issue:

1 John, Earl of Morton (by 1466–1513); he married Janet (*d.* after 1515), daughter of Patrick Crichton of Cranston-Riddell, and had issue.

2 Janet (*d.* by 1490); she married Patrick Hepburn, 1st Earl of Bothwell (*d.*1508), and had issue.

3 James (*d.* after 1480).

4 Elizabeth (*d.* after 1479).

Joan died after 16 October, 1486, and was buried in Dalkeith Church, Midlothian.

5 *Alexander*

He was born on 16 October, 1430, at Holyrood Palace, Edinburgh, the elder of twins. He was Duke of Rothesay from birth. He died in 1430.

6 *James II* (◊ page 235).

7 *Mary*

She was designated Countess of Buchan, either at birth or upon her marriage. She married Wolfert van Borssele, Count of Grandpré and Lord of Campveere in Zeeland (*d.*1487), in 1444 at ter Veere, Zeeland, and had issue:

1 Unnamed son (*d.* young).

2 Unnamed son (*d.* young).

Mary died on 20 March, 1465, and was buried at Sandenburg-ter-Veere, Zeeland.

8 *Annabella or Jean*

She married firstly Louis of Savoy, Count of Geneva, afterwards King of Cyprus (*d.* 1482), on 14 December, 1447 (or possibly 1455), at Stirling Castle. They divorced in 1458. Annabella married secondly George Gordon, 2nd Earl of Huntly (*d.*1501), before 10 March, 1459/60, and had issue:

1 Isabella (*d.* by 1485); she married William Hay, 3rd Earl of Erroll (*d.*1507).

Annabella was also possibly, but improbably, the mother of the following:

2 Janet (*d.*1559); she married Alexander Lindsay, Master of Crawford (*d.*1489), and had issue. She married secondly Patrick Grey, 3rd Lord Grey (*d.*1541); they were later divorced. She married thirdly Patrick Butler of Gormock, and fourthly James Halkerstoun of Southwood.

3 Elizabeth (*d.* after 1525); she married William Keith, 2nd Earl Marischal (*d.* 1527), and had issue.

4 Margaret; she married Patrick Hepburn, 1st Earl of Bothwell (*d.*1508), and had issue.

5 Agnes; she married Sir Gilbert Hay of Kilmalamak.

6 (Highly improbable) Alexander, Earl of Huntly (*d.*1524); he married firstly Janet (*d.*1510), daughter of John Stewart, 1st Earl of Atholl, and had issue. He married secondly Elizabeth (*d.*1529/30), daughter of Andrew, 2nd Lord Hay.

Annabella was divorced from her second husband on 24 July, 1471, on grounds of consanguinity.

JAMES I

He was assassinated on 21 February, 1437, in the monastery of the Friars Preachers at Perth (or at Edinburgh), and was buried at Perth, either in the monastery of the Carthusians, or the monastery of the Black Friars, or the monastery of the Dominican Friars.

He was succeeded by his son James.

James II

FATHER: *James I* (◊ page 232).
MOTHER: *Joan Beaufort* (◊ page 232, under *James I*).
SIBLINGS: (◊ page 233, under *James I*).

JAMES II

He was born on 16 October, 1430, at Holyrood Palace, Edinburgh, the younger of twins. He succeeded his brother Alexander as Duke of Rothesay, probably in 1430, being first so styled on 22 April, 1431. He succeeded his father as King of Scotland on 21 February, 1437, and was crowned on 25 March, 1437, at Holyrood Abbey, Edinburgh.

James II married, on 3 July, 1449, at Holyrood Abbey, Edinburgh:

Mary

She was the daughter of Arnold, Duke of Gueldres, by Katherine, daughter of Adolf, Duke of Cleves, and she was born in 1433. She was crowned Queen Consort on 3 July, 1449, at Holyrood Abbey, Edinburgh. She died on 16 November or 1 December, 1463, and was buried in Holy Trinity Church, Edinburgh.

Issue of marriage:

1 *Unnamed child*

It was born on 19 May, 1450, and died the same day.

2 *Mary*

She was probably born in the summer of 1451 (?), certainly before 16 May, 1452. She married firstly Thomas Boyd, 1st Earl of Arran (*d.*1473/4), before 26 April, 1467/8, and had issue:

1 James, 2nd Lord Boyd (killed 1484).

2 Margaret or Grizelda (1468/73–after 1516); she married Alexander Forbes, 4th Lord Forbes (*d.* by 1491). She married secondly David Kennedy, 1st Earl of Cassilis (killed at Flodden, 1513).

Mary's marriage to Arran was declared null and void in *c.*February/March, 1473/4 (or, much less probably, in 1469). She married secondly James, 1st Lord Hamilton (1398?–1479), in *c.*February/March, and before April, 1474, and had issue:

1 James, Earl of Arran (1475?–1529); he married firstly Elizabeth (*d.*1544), daughter of Alexander, 2nd Lord Home; they were later divorced. He married secondly Janet (*d.*1522), daughter of Sir David Beaton of Creich, and had issue.

2 Robert, Seigneur d'Aubigny (*d.*1543).

3 Elizabeth (*d.* after 1531); she married Matthew Stewart, 2nd Earl of Lennox (killed at Flodden, 1513), and had issue.

Mary died in *c.*May, 1488 (?).

3 *James III* (♢ page 239).

4 *Alexander*

He was born in *c.*1454/5, certainly before 8 July, 1455. He was created Baron of Annandale and styled Earl of March before 4 August (on 8 July?), 1455, and was created Duke of Albany between 4 July, 1457, and 3 July, 1458. His titles and estates were all declared forfeit on 4 October, 1479, but he was restored in blood between June and December, 1482, and was created Earl of Mar and Garioch between 29 September and 10 October, 1482. His titles and estates were again declared forfeit on 27 June, 1483. He was killed in 1485 (?) in France at a tournament, and was buried in the Church of the Celestines, Paris.

Alexander married firstly, in *c.*1475 (although no evidence exists as to where):

Katherine

She was the daughter of William Sinclair, 3rd Earl of Orkney and Caithness, by Elizabeth, daughter of Archibald Douglas, 4th Earl of Douglas, by Margaret, daughter of Robert III. She was divorced on 2 or 9 March, 1478, on grounds of propinquity, and her issue declared illegitimate. The divorce was ratified by Act of Parliament on 15 November, 1516.

Issue of marriage:

(i) *Margaret*

She married Sir Patrick Hamilton of Kincavil (*d.*1520), and was said to have had issue, but this is improbable. She died after 5 July, 1542.

(ii) *Andrew*

Nothing is known of him.

(iii) *Son (name not known)*

He was born in 1477, and died before 1479.

(iv) *Alexander*

He was born in the late 1470s. He took Holy Orders, and was appointed Prior of Whitehorn. He later became Abbot of Inchaffray. He was nominated Bishop of Moray on 31 May, 1528, and consecrated on 16 April, 1532. He died on 19 December, 1537, and was buried in Scone Abbey, Perthshire.

Alexander had the following illegitimate issue:

1 Alexander; he was legitimated in 1550.

2 Alexander.

3 Margaret; she married first Patrick Graham of Inchbrakie (*d.*1536), and had issue. She married secondly Colin Campbell of Glenurchy.

Alexander married secondly, between 16 January and 4 December, 1479 (and not on 10 February, 1480, as is sometimes stated), in France:

Anne

She was the daughter of Bertrand de la Tour, Count of Auvergne, by Louise, daughter of George de la Trémouille, Seigneur of Trémouille in Poitou. After the death of Alexander, she married secondly Louis, Count of La Chambre in Savoy (*d.*1517), on 17 February, 1487. She died on 13 October, 1512, at La Rochette Castle, Savoy, and was buried in the Carmelite monastery at La Rochette.

Issue of marriage:

(i) *John*

He was born around 1481/5. He was first styled Duke of Albany in June, 1505, and was formally restored to the duchy between 8 April, 1514, and May, 1515. He died on 2 June, 1536, at

Mirefleur in the Auvergne, France, and was buried in the chapel of the Palace of Vic-le-Comte, France.

John had the following illegitimate issue:

By Jean Abernethy:

1 Eleanor; she married John de l'Hôpital, Comte de Choisy, and had issue.

John married, after 13 July, 1505 (date of dispensation) (although no evidence exists as to where):

Anne

She was the daughter of John de la Tour, Count of Auvergne and Lauraguais, by Joan, daughter of John of Bourbon, Count of Vendôme, and she was born after 1495. She became Countess of Auvergne and Boulogne in her own right. She died in June, 1524, at the Castle of St Saturnin, France.

5 *David*

He was born after 1454 and before 12 February, 1456. He was created Earl of Moray on 12 February, 1456, and died before 18 July, 1457.

6 *John*

He was born after October, 1456, perhaps in c.July, 1457, or in 1459 (?). He was created Earl of Mar and Garioch between 21 June, 1458, and 25 June, 1459. He forfeited all his estates in 1479/80, and died, or was murdered, either on 9 July, 1479, or – more probably – some time in 1480, at Craigmillar Castle, Edinburgh.

7 *Margaret*

Some sources state that she became the wife of William, Lord Crichton (*d.*1493), but this is almost certainly a fabrication. He abducted and seduced her to spite her brother, James III; there is no contemporary evidence for their marriage. Their clandestine union produced the following illegitimate issue:

1 Margaret Crichton (*d.* by 1546); she married firstly William Todrik of Edinburgh (*d.* by 1507), and secondly George Halkerstoun (killed at Flodden, 1513), and had issue. She married thirdly George Leslie, 2nd Earl of Rothes (*d.*1513), and had issue.

James II also had the following **illegitimate issue:**

1 John Stewart of Sticks and Ballechin; he married and had issue.

JAMES II

He was killed on 3 August, 1460, when a cannon burst at the siege of Roxburgh; he was buried in Holyrood Abbey, Edinburgh.

He was succeeded by his son James.

James III

FATHER: *James II* (◊ page 235).
MOTHER: *Mary of Gueldres* (◊ page 235, under *James II*).
SIBLINGS: (◊ page 235, under *James II*).

JAMES III

He was born either in May, or on 10 July, 1452 (or, less probably, on 20 July, 1451), either at the Castle of St Andrews, Fife, or at Stirling Castle. He was Duke of Rothesay from birth. He succeeded his father as King of Scotland on 3 August, 1460, and was crowned on 10 August, 1460, at Kelso Abbey, Roxburghshire.

James III married, on 10 or 13 July, 1469, at Holyrood Abbey, Edinburgh:

Margaret

She was the daughter of Christian I, King of Denmark, Norway and Sweden, by Dorothea, daughter of John III, Margrave and Elector of Brandenburg, and she was born in *c.*1456/7. She died on 14 July, 1486, at Stirling Castle, and was buried in Cambuskenneth Abbey, Stirlingshire.

Issue of marriage:

1 *James IV* (◊ page 240).
2 *James*

He was born in March, 1476 (?), and is said to have been created Marquess of Ormonde at his baptism that year. He was created Duke of Ross on 23 January, 1481, or 29 January, 1488. He was created Earl of Ardmannoch and Baron of Brechin and Nevar, and perhaps Duke of Ross, on 29 January, 1488. He was nominated

Archbishop of St Andrews on 20 September, 1497, but was never consecrated. He died around 12/17 January, 1504, in Edinburgh, and was buried in St Andrews Cathedral, Fife.

3 John

He was born between 16 July, 1479, and 12 July, 1480, perhaps in December, 1479. He was created Earl of Mar on 2 March, 1486. He died unmarried on 11 March, 1503.

JAMES III

He was assassinated on 11 June, 1488, in a cottage at Milltown, near Bannockburn, and was buried in Cambuskenneth Abbey, Stirlingshire.

He was succeeded by his son James.

James IV

FATHER: *James III* (◊ page 239)
MOTHER: *Margaret of Denmark* (◊ page 239, under *James III*).
SIBLINGS: (◊ page 239, under *James III*).

JAMES IV

He was born on 17 March, 1473, and was Duke of Rothesay, Earl of Carrick and Lord of Cunningham probably from birth. He succeeded his father as King of Scotland on 11 June, 1488, and was crowned on 26 June, 1488, at Scone Abbey, Perthshire.

James IV married, by proxy on 25 January, 1502, at Richmond Palace, Surrey, and in person on 8 August, 1503, at Holyrood Abbey, Edinburgh:

Margaret

She was the daughter of Henry VII, King of England, by Elizabeth of York, and she was born on 28, 29 or 30 November, 1489, at the Palace of Westminster. She was crowned Queen Consort on 8 August, 1503, at Holyrood Abbey, Edinburgh. After the death of James, she married secondly Archibald Douglas, 6th Earl of Angus (1490?–1557), on 4, 5 or 6 August, 1514, at Kinnoul Church, and had issue:

1 Margaret (1515–1578); she married firstly Lord Thomas Howard (*d.*1537). She married secondly Matthew Stewart, 4th Earl of Lennox (1516–murdered 1571), and had issue, including Henry, Lord Darnley, who married Mary, Queen of Scots.

Margaret divorced her second husband on 11 March, 1527/8. She married thirdly Henry Stewart, 1st Lord Methven (1495/1500?–1552), before 2 April, perhaps in March, 1528, and may have had issue (although this is improbable):

1 Dorothea (?); (*d.* young).

Margaret died on 8 or 18 October, or on 24 November, 1541, at Methven Castle, Perthshire, of 'palsy', and was buried in the Carthusian Abbey of St John, Perth.

Issue of marriage:

1 *James*

He was born on 21 February, 1507, at Holyrood Palace, Edinburgh, and was Duke of Rothesay from birth. He died on 27 February, 1508, at Stirling Castle.

2 *Daughter* (*name not known*)

She was born on 15 July, 1508, at Holyrood Palace, Edinburgh, where she died the same day.

3 *Arthur*

He was born on 20/21 October, 1509, at Holyrood Palace, Edinburgh, and was Duke of Albany from birth. He died on 14/15 July, 1510, at Edinburgh Castle, and was buried in Holyrood Abbey, Edinburgh.

4 *James V* (♀ page 243).

5 *Daughter* (*name not known*)

She was born in November, 1512, at Holyrood Palace, Edinburgh, and died the same month.

6 *Alexander*

His father's posthumous son, he was born on 12 or 30 April, 1514, at Stirling Castle, and was styled Duke from birth: perhaps Duke of Ross. He died on 18 December, 1515, at Stirling Castle, and was buried in Cambuskenneth Abbey, Stirlingshire.

James IV also had the following **illegitimate issue:**

By Marion Boyd of Bonshaw:

1 Alexander Stewart, Archbishop of St Andrews (1493?–1513); he

was killed at Flodden.

2 Katherine (d. after 1554); she married James Douglas, 3rd Earl of Morton (d.1548), and had issue.

By Janet Kennedy:

3 James Stewart, Earl of Moray (1499?–1544/5); he married Elizabeth, daughter of Colin Campbell, 3rd Earl of Argyll, and had issue.

4 Unnamed child (d. young).

5 Unnamed child (d. young).

By Margaret (murdered by poison, 1502), daughter of John, Lord Drummond:

6 Margaret (b.1497?); she married firstly John, Lord Gordon, Master of Huntly (d.1517), and had issue. She married secondly Sir John Drummond of Innerpeffray, and had issue.

By Isabella (d.1557), daughter of James Stewart, Earl of Buchan:

7 Janet or Joan (d.1560/63); she married Malcolm, 3rd Lord Fleming, and had issue.

JAMES IV

He was killed on 9 September, 1513, at the Battle of Flodden Field, Northumberland. He was perhaps buried in Sheen Abbey, Surrey, and his head may be interred in the Church of St Michael, Wood Street, City of London. A body said to be his was found at Hume Castle, but the identification is dubious. The only certain evidence of the fate of the King's body is the report that it was kept in a lumber room at Richmond Palace, Surrey, during the reign of Henry VIII. Reports that James IV was seen alive on the evening after Flodden and thereafter went on pilgrimage to the Holy Land, whence he never returned, are not to be trusted, although in 1527 Queen Margaret petitioned for a divorce from her second husband on the grounds that James was still alive in 1514 when her second marriage took place. James was succeeded by his son James.

James V

FATHER: *James IV* (◊ page 240)
MOTHER: *Margaret Tudor* (◊ page 240, under *James IV*).
SIBLINGS: (◊ page 241, under *James IV*).

JAMES V

He was born on 10, 11 or 15 April, 1512, at Linlithgow Palace, Fife, and was Duke of Rothesay from birth. He succeeded his father as King of Scotland on 9 September, 1513, and was crowned on 21 September, 1513, at the Chapel Royal, Stirling Castle. He was made a Knight of the Garter on 20 January, 1535.

James V married firstly, on 1 January, 1537, at the Cathedral of Notre Dame, Paris:

Madeleine

She was the daughter of Francis I, King of France, by Claude, daughter of Louis XII, King of France, and she was born on 10 August, 1520, at the Château of St Germain-en-Laye, Paris. She died on 2 or 7 July, 1537, at Holyrood Palace, Edinburgh, and was buried in Holyrood Abbey, Edinburgh. There was no issue of the marriage.

James V married secondly, by proxy in May, 1538, and in person on 12 June, 1538, at St Andrews Cathedral, Fife:

Mary

She was the daughter of Claude I, Duke of Guise-Lorraine, by Antoinette, daughter of Francis de Bourbon, Duke of Vendôme, and she was born on 22 November, 1515, at Bar-le-Duc, France. She married firstly Louis II, Duke of Longueville (*d.*1537), on 4 August, 1534, and had issue:

1 Francis, Duke of Longueville (1535–1551).
2 Louis (*b.&d.*1537).

Mary was crowned Queen Consort on 22 February, 1540, at Holyrood Abbey, Edinburgh. She died on 11 June, 1560, at Edinburgh Castle, and was buried in Rheims Cathedral, France.

Issue of marriage:

1 James

He was born on 22 May, 1540, at St Andrews, Fife, and was Duke of Rothesay from birth. He died in April, 1541, at St Andrews, and was buried in Holyrood Abbey, Edinburgh.

2 Arthur or Robert

He was born in April, 1541, at Falkland Palace, Fife, where he died, aged 8 days, the same month. He was styled Duke of Albany during his lifetime. He was buried in Holyrood Abbey, Edinburgh.

3 Queen Mary (◊ page 245).

James V also had the following **illegitimate issue**:

By Elizabeth or Katherine, daughter of Sir John Carmichael:

1 John, Prior of Coldingham (1531/2–1563); he married Jean, daughter of Patrick Hepburn, 3rd Earl of Bothwell, and had issue.

By Margaret, daughter of John, 4th Lord Erskine:

2 James Stewart, Earl of Moray and Mar (1531?–murdered 1570); he married Agnes, daughter of William Keith, 3rd Earl Marischal, and had issue.

By Euphemia, daughter of Alexander, 1st Lord Elphinstone:

3 Robert, Earl of Orkney and Prior of Holyrood (1533–1591); he married Janet (d.1598), daughter of Gilbert Kennedy, 3rd Earl of Cassilis, and had issue.

By Elizabeth Shaw of Sauchie:

4 James Stewart, Abbot of Kelso and Melrose (1529?–1557).

By Christine Barclay:

5 James Stewart.

By Elizabeth, daughter of John Stewart, 3rd Earl of Lennox:

6 Adam, Prior of the Charterhouse (d.1606); he married Janet, daughter of William Ruthven.

By Elizabeth Bethune or Beaton:

7 Jean; she married Archibald Campbell, 5th Earl of Argyll (d.1573), from whom she was later divorced.

By unknown mothers:

8 Robert, Prior of Whithorn (d.1581).

9 Margaret.

JAMES V

He died on 14 December, 1542, at Falkland Palace, Fife, and was buried in Holyrood Abbey, Edinburgh.

He was succeeded by his daughter Mary.

Queen Mary

FATHER: *James V* (◊ page 243).
MOTHER: *Mary of Guise* (◊ page 243, under *James V*).
SIBLINGS: (◊ page 244, under *James V*).

QUEEN MARY

She was born on 8 December, 1542, at Linlithgow Palace. She succeeded her father as Queen of Scotland on 14 December, 1542, and was crowned on 9 September, 1543, at Stirling Castle. She became Queen Consort of France on 6 July, 1559, upon the accession of her first husband to the French throne.

Queen Mary married firstly, on 24 April, 1558, at the Cathedral of Notre Dame, Paris:

Francis II

He was the son of Henry II, King of France, by Catherine, daughter of Lorenzo de' Medici, Duke of Florence, and he was born on 16 January, 1544, at the Château of Fontainbleau-sur-Loire, France. He became King Consort of Scotland upon his marriage to Queen Mary. He succeeded his father as King of France on 6 July, 1559, and was crowned on 18 September, 1559, at Rheims Cathedral. He died on 5 December, 1560, at Orléans, France, and was buried in the Cathedral of St Denis, Paris. There was no issue of the marriage.

Queen Mary married secondly, on 29 July, 1565, in the Chapel of Holyrood Palace, Edinburgh:

Henry

He was the son of Matthew Stewart (who had adopted the French form of his surname, Stuart), 4th Earl of Lennox, by Margaret, daughter of Archibald Douglas, 6th Earl of Angus, by Margaret Tudor, daughter of Henry VII of England and widow of James IV. He was born on 7 December, 1546, at Temple Newsham, Yorkshire, and was styled Lord Darnley from birth. He was created Baron Ardmannoch and Earl of Ross on 15 May, 1565, and Duke of Albany on 20 July. He was proclaimed King of Scotland on 28 July, 1565. He was murdered, probably suffocated or strangled before his house was blown up, on 10 February, 1567, at the old Provost's Lodging, Kirk o' the Field, Edinburgh, and buried in the Chapel Royal, Holyrood Palace.

Issue of marriage:

1 *James VI & I* (◊ page 247).

Queen Mary married thirdly, on 15 May, 1567, at Holyrood Palace, Edinburgh:

James

He was the son of Patrick Hepburn, 3rd Earl of Bothwell, and he was born in *c.*1535. He succeeded his father as 4th Earl of Bothwell in September, 1556. He married firstly Jean, daughter of George Gordon, 4th Earl of Huntly, on 24 February, 1566; they were divorced on 3 May, 1567, in the Protestant Commissary Court of Edinburgh, on grounds of his adultery; the marriage was also annulled on 7 May, 1567, on grounds of consanguinity. James was created Duke of Orkney and Earl of Shetland on 12 May, 1567. His titles and estates were all declared forfeit on 20 December, 1567. He died on 14 April, 1578, in prison at Dragsholm Castle, Denmark, and was buried in Faarevejle Church, Dragsholm, Denmark.

Issue of marriage:

2 & 3 *Stillborn twins*

They were born between 18 and 24 July, 1568, at Lochleven Castle.

QUEEN MARY

She was forced by the lords of Scotland to abdicate in favour of her son on 24 July, 1567. She fled to England, where she was kept a prisoner for 18 years by Elizabeth I. She plotted to take the English crown, and was executed on 8 February, 1587, at Fotheringhay Castle, Northants. She was buried in Peterborough Cathedral; her remains were removed to Westminster Abbey in 1612.

She was succeeded by her son James.

James VI

FATHER: *Henry Stuart, Lord Darnley* (◊ page 245, under *Queen Mary*).
MOTHER: *Mary, Queen of Scots* (◊ page 245).
SIBLINGS: *James VI did not have any siblings.*

JAMES VI

Christened Charles James, he was born on 19 June, 1566, at Edinburgh Castle, and was Duke of Rothesay from birth. He succeeded his father as Duke of Albany, Earl of Ross and Baron Ardmannoch on 10 February, 1567. He succeeded his mother as King of Scotland on 24 July, 1567, and was crowned on 29 July, 1567, at the Church of the Holy Rude, Stirling.

JAMES VI

He succeeded Elizabeth I, last of the Tudor sovereigns, as King of England, on 24 March, 1603, thus founding the Royal House of Stuart (now using the French version of the name) and uniting for the first time the Crowns of England and Scotland under one monarch. Henceforth, the kingdom incorporating England and Scotland would be known as Great Britain.

For further details of the life of James VI and I, ◊ under James I.

CHAPTER SEVEN

The House of Stuart

England and Scotland became one united kingdom in 1603 when James VI of Scotland became James I of England, and thus finally fulfilled Edward I's dream of the two countries being joined together.

The Stuart century was to see dramatic changes in the nature of the monarchy. James I believed in the Divine Right of Kings, a doctrine which held that the King was God's mouthpiece on earth, and could do and say no wrong. This was a view also held by James's son, Charles I, who, when thwarted by Parliament – a Parliament grown used to being consulted to an increasingly greater degree by successive Tudor monarchs – tried to rule without it. He failed, and the country was plunged into a great civil war, which ended with the King's execution and the declaration of a Republic or 'Commonwealth' under Oliver Cromwell, who became Lord Protector.

Against the odds, the monarchy did survive. Charles II lived in exile at the courts of Holland and France while Cromwell governed, but the Lord Protector's hold on the country died with him in 1658. His son Richard was weak and ineffectual, and it was not long before Parliament sent for Charles II, whose Restoration took place in May, 1660. Yet by then, the balance of power had been tipped firmly on the side of Parliament, and no British monarch after that date would ever enjoy the autonomy exercised by his predecessors. In fact, it was in the late 17th century that 'constitutional' monarchy came into being in Britain; this meant that, instead of actually ruling the country, the sovereign reigned over it. The real power lay with an elected Parliament. In 1688, James II, a professed Catholic, realised that he could not hold the throne in the face of Protestant opposition, and fled the country. Parliament deemed that this act was tantamount to abdication, and invited William of Orange, husband of James's daughter Mary, to take the throne of Britain with his wife. In what was known as the 'Bloodless' or 'Glorious' Revolution, he accepted, and thus became the first 'constitutional' monarch.

The unpopularity of James II, mainly due to his Catholicism, made King and Parliament realise that never again could Britain be successfully ruled by a monarch not of the Protestant faith of the Church of England. Thus, in 1701 was passed the Act of Settlement, barring any Roman Catholic from ascending the throne, and any British sovereign from marrying a Roman Catholic. This same Act also settled the succession, in default of Stuart heirs, upon the successors of Sophia of Bohemia, a granddaughter of James I, who had married the Protestant Ernest Augustus, Elector of Hanover, in Germany.

The Stuarts, like the Tudors, were not dynastically robust. Many of their children died young or were miscarried – poor Queen Anne suffering the most losses in this respect – and those who did grow to maturity died in the flower of youth of smallpox. Charles II's wife was barren, so was Mary II. Anne's children had all died by the time she ascended the throne. James II's only surviving son was rumoured, falsely, to have been a changeling, and spent his life in exile, plotting to regain the throne from which he, a Catholic, was debarred by the Act of Settlement. Therefore, when Queen Anne died in 1714, there was no suitable heir of the House of Stuart to succeed her. Thus it came about that Prince George, Elector of Hanover, a bucolic German who could speak no English, succeeded to the throne of Britain and founded the Hanoverian dynasty.

James I

JAMES I

He succeeded Elizabeth I as King of England on 24 March, 1603, thus founding the Royal House of Stuart and uniting the crowns of England and Scotland under one monarch. (For details of his earlier life, ♦ page 247, under James VI of Scotland in the previous chapter.) James was crowned on 25 July, 1603, in Westminster Abbey.

James VI & I married, by proxy on 20 or 24 August, 1589, at Kronborg Castle, Copenhagen, Denmark, and in person on 23 November, 1589, at Oslo, Norway, and again in person on 21 January, 1590, at Kronborg Castle:

Anne

She was the daughter of Frederick II, King of Denmark and Norway, by Sophia, daughter of Ulrich III, Duke of Mecklenburg-Güstrow. She was born on 14 October (date on coffin plate) (although the date is sometimes incorrectly given as 12 December), 1574, at Skanderborg Castle, Jutland, Denmark. She was crowned Queen Consort of Scotland on 17 May, 1590, at Holyrood Abbey, Edinburgh, and Queen Consort of England on 25 July, 1603, in Westminster Abbey. She died on 4 March (date on coffin plate) (although other sources state 1 or 12 March), 1619, at Hampton Court Palace, and was buried in Westminster Abbey.

Issue of marriage:

1 *Henry Frederick*

He was born on 19 February, 1594, at Stirling Castle, and was Duke of Rothesay, Earl of Carrick, and Lord of the Isles from birth. He became Duke of Cornwall upon the accession of his father to the throne of England on 24 March, 1603. He was made a Knight of the Garter on 14 June, 1603. He was created, and invested as, Prince of Wales and Earl of Chester on 4 June, 1610, at Westminster Abbey. He died on 6 (or, less probably, 12 or 16)

November, 1612, at St James's Palace, London, of typhoid, and was buried in Westminster Abbey.

2 *Stillborn child*

It was born at the end of July, 1595.

3 *Elizabeth*

She was born on 19 August, 1596, at Dunfermline Palace, Fife. She married Frederick Henry of Wittelsbach, Elector Palatine of the Rhine and later Frederick V, King of Bohemia (1596–1632), on 14 February, 1613, at the Chapel Royal, Whitehall Palace, London, and had issue:

1 Frederick Henry (1614–drowned 1629).

2 Charles Louis, Duke of Bavaria, Elector Palatine of the Rhine (1618–1680); he married firstly Charlotte (1627–1687), daughter of William V, Landgrave of Hesse-Cassel, and had issue, although they were later divorced. He married secondly, morganatically, Marie Susanne Louise (1634–1677), Raugräfin of Degenfeld, daughter of Baron Martin Christopher von Degenfeld, and had issue.

3 Elizabeth, Abbess of Hervorden (or Herford) (1618–1680).

4 Rupert, Duke of Cumberland (1619–1682); he married, morganatically, Frances Baird (*d.*1708). He also had illegitimate issue.

5 Maurice (1621–drowned 1654).

6 Louise Hollandine, Abbess of Maubisson, Pontoise (1622–1709).

7 Louis (1623–1624).

8 Edward (1625–1663); he married Anne (1616–1684), daughter of Charles I de Gonzaga, Duke of Nevers and Mantua, and had issue.

9 Henrietta Maria (1626–1651); she married Sigismund Ragotski, Prince of Siebenbürgen, Transylvania (1623?–1652).

10 John Philip Frederick (1627–killed 1650).

11 Charlotte (1628–1631).

12 Sophia; she married Ernest Augustus, Elector of Hanover, and became the mother of George I (⟡ page 273, under George I).

13 Gustavus Adolphus (1632–1641).

Elizabeth became Queen Consort of Bohemia upon the accession of her husband to the throne of Bohemia on 27 August, 1619, and was crowned as such on 7 November, 1619, at Prague Cathedral, Bohemia. She was driven into exile with her husband in 1620 after he was deposed, and was afterwards known as 'the Winter Queen'. There is no foundation in the rumour that, after Frederick's death, she married secondly William Craven, Earl of Craven. She died on 3, 12, 14 or 23 February, 1662, at Leicester House, Leicester Fields, London, and was buried in Westminster Abbey.

4 *Margaret*

She was born on 24 December, 1598, at Dalkeith Palace, Scotland, and died in March, 1600, at Linlithgow Palace, Fife. She was buried in Holyrood Abbey, Edinburgh.

5 *Charles I* (◊ page 253).

6 *Robert Bruce*

He was born on 18 January or 18 February, 1602, at Dunfermline Palace, Fife. He was designated Duke of Kintyre and Lorne, Marquess of Wigtown, Earl of Carrick and Lord of Annerdail (Annandale?) on 2 May, 1602. He died on 27 May, 1602, at Dunfermline Palace, Fife, and was buried in Dunfermline Abbey.

7 *Stillborn son*

He was born in May, 1603, at Stirling Castle.

8 *Mary*

She was born on 8 April, 1605, at Greenwich Palace, Kent. She died on 16 September or 16 December, 1607, at Stanwell Park, Staines, Middlesex, and was buried in Westminster Abbey.

9 *Sophia*

She was born on 22 June, 1606, at Greenwich Palace, Kent, and died there on 23 June, 1606. She was buried in Westminster Abbey.

Queen Anne also suffered at least three other miscarriages.

JAMES I & VI

He died on 27 March, 1625, at Theobalds Park, Herts., and was buried in Westminster Abbey.

He was succeeded by his son Charles.

Charles I

FATHER: *James I* (◊ page 250).
MOTHER: *Anne of Denmark* (◊ page 250, under *James I*).
SIBLINGS: (◊ page 250, under *James I*).

CHARLES I

He was born on 19 November, 1600, at Dunfermline Palace, Fife. He was created Duke of Albany, Marquess of Ormonde, Earl of Ross and Baron of Ardmannoch on 23 December, 1600. He was created Duke of York and made a Knight of the Bath on 6 January, 1605. He was made a Knight of the Garter on 24 April, 1611. He succeeded his brother Henry as Duke of Cornwall and Rothesay on 6 November, 1612, and was created and invested as Prince of Wales and Earl of Chester on 4 November, 1616, at Whitehall Palace, London. He succeeded his father as King of Great Britain on 27 March, 1625, and was crowned on 2 February, 1626, at Westminster Abbey. He was crowned in Scotland on 15 or 18 June, 1633, at Holyrood Abbey, Edinburgh.

Charles I married, by proxy on 1 or 11 May, 1625, at the Cathedral of Notre Dame, Paris, and in person on 13 June, 1625, at St Augustine's Church, Canterbury, Kent:

Henrietta Maria

She was the daughter of Henry IV (of Bourbon), King of France, by Mary, daughter of Francis I de' Medici, Grand Duke of Tuscany, and she was born on 26 November, 1609, at the Palace of the Louvre, Paris. She was not crowned Queen Consort; as a Roman Catholic, she would not allow herself to participate in the Anglican coronation ritual. She died on 21 August (O.S.) or 31 August (N.S.), 1669, at the Château of St Colombes, near Paris, and was buried in the Cathedral of St Denis, Paris.

Issue of marriage:

1 *Charles James*

He was born on 13 May, 1629, at Greenwich Palace, Kent, and was

Duke of Cornwall and Rothesay from birth. He died the same day, and was buried in Westminster Abbey.

2 *Charles II* (◊ page 255).

3 *Mary Henrietta*

She married William II of Orange, and became the mother of William III. (◊ page 265, under *William III*).

4 *James II* (◊ page 259).

5 *Elizabeth*

She was born on 29 December, 1635, at St James's Palace, London. She died on 8 September, 1650, in prison at Carisbrooke Castle, Isle of Wight, and was buried in St Thomas's Church, Newport, Isle of Wight.

6 *Anne*

She was born on 17 March, 1637, at St James's Palace, London. She died on 5 November, 1640, at Richmond Palace, Surrey, of consumption, and was buried in Westminster Abbey.

7 *Katherine*

She was born on 29 June, 1639, at Whitehall Palace, London, and died the same day. She was probably buried in Westminster Abbey.

8 *Henry*

He was born on 8 July, 1640, probably at Oatlands Palace, Surrey, and was probably styled Duke of Gloucester from birth. He was made a Knight of the Garter on 4 April, 1653, and is said to have been created Duke of Gloucester and Earl of Cambridge on 13 May, 1659. He died on 13 (O.S.) or 23 (N.S.) September, 1660, at Whitehall Palace, London, and was buried in Westminster Abbey.

9 *Henrietta Anne*

Known as 'Minette', she was born on 16 June, 1644, at Bedford House, Exeter, Devon. She married Philip of Bourbon, Duke of Orléans (1640–1701), on 21 (O.S.) or 31 (N.S.) March, 1661, at the Chapel of the Palais Royale, Paris, and had issue:

1 Marie Louise (1662–1689); she married Charles II, King of Spain (1661–1700).

2 Miscarriage (1663).

3 Philip Charles, Duke of Valois (1664–1666).

4 Unnamed daughter (*b.&d.*1665).

5 Miscarriage (1666).

6 Miscarriage (1667).

7 Miscarriage (1668).

8 Anne Marie (1669–1728); she married Victor Amadeus II, Duke of Savoy and King of Sardinia (1666–1732), and had issue, from whom descends the present day Stuart claimant to the throne of Great Britain (who is a Roman Catholic and therefore barred from the succession).

Henrietta Anne died on 15 or 30 June, 1670, at the Palace of St Cloud, near Paris, and was buried in the Cathedral of St Denis, Paris.

CHARLES I

He was tried and condemned to death by an illegally convened Parliament following the conclusion of the Civil War between the Cavaliers (supporters of the King) and the Roundheads (Parliamentarians), the latter being led by Oliver Cromwell. Charles I was convicted of treason against the state, and was executed on 30 January, 1649, outside Whitehall Palace, London. He was buried in St George's Chapel, Windsor. After his death, Britain was declared a Republic (for the only time in its history) with Oliver Cromwell as Lord Protector. Charles I was succeeded in name only by his son Charles, then in exile in France.

Charles II

FATHER: *Charles I* (◊ page 253).
MOTHER: *Henrietta Maria of France* (◊ page 253, under *Charles I*).
SIBLINGS: (◊page 253, under *Charles I*).

CHARLES II

He was born on 29 May, 1630, at St James's Palace, London, and was Duke of Cornwall and Rothesay from birth. He was made a Knight of the Garter on 21 May, 1638, and around the same time was designated

Prince of Wales and Earl of Chester, although he was never formally so created. He succeeded his father as King of Great Britain in name only on 30 January, 1649; Charles I was executed on that day, and Charles II was then an exile in France, whilst Cromwell took up the reins of government in Britain under the title Lord Protector. The Scots rallied to Charles' cause, and he was crowned on 1 January, 1651, at Scone Abbey, Perthshire. He was formally restored to the throne of Great Britain, Cromwell having died, on 29 May, 1660, and was crowned on 23 April, 1661, at Westminster Abbey.

Charles II married, on 21/22 May, 1662, at the Church of St Thomas à Becket, Portsmouth:

Katherine Henrietta

She was the daughter of John IV, Duke of Braganza and King of Portugal, by Louisa Maria, daughter of John Manuel Domingo Perez de Guzman, 8th Duke of Medina-Sidonia, and she was born on 15 (O.S.) or 25 (N.S.) November, 1638, at Vila Viçosa, Lisbon, Portugal. She was never crowned as Queen Consort because she was a Roman Catholic and could not take part in the Anglican coronation ritual. She died on 30 November or 1 December, 1705, at Belém Palace or at Bemposta Palace, Lisbon, Portugal, and was buried in the monastery of Belém, Lisbon.

Issue of marriage:

1 *Miscarriage*
   This occurred in 1662.

2 *Stillborn child*
   It was born in February, 1666, at Oxford.

3 *Stillborn child*
   It was born on 7 May, 1668.

4 *Stillborn child*
   It was born on *c.*7 June, 1669.

Charles II also had the following **illegitimate issue**:

By Margaret de Carteret of Jersey:

1 James, a Jesuit (1646–1667?).

By Lucy (1630?–1658), daughter of Richard Walter of Haverfordwest:

2 James Crofts, who took his wife's surname of Scott upon marriage, Duke of Monmouth (1649–executed 1685); he married Anne (1651–1732), daughter of Francis Scott, Earl of Buccleuch, and had issue.

Monmouth always claimed that his parents had been married, and that he was therefore legitimate; he also claimed to possess their marriage lines, but never produced them.

Lucy Walter bore another child, Mary, but Charles II was not her father.

By Elizabeth, afterwards Lady Shannon, daughter of Sir Robert Killigrew:

3 Charlotte Jemima Henrietta Maria FitzRoy (1650–1684); she married firstly James Howard, Earl of Suffolk (d.1669). She married secondly William Paston, 2nd Earl of Yarmouth (1653–1732), and had issue.

By Katherine, daughter of Thomas Pegge of Yeldersley, Derbyshire:

4 Charles FitzCharles, Earl of Plymouth (1657–1680); he married Bridget (d.1718), daughter of Thomas Osborne, 1st Duke of Leeds.

5 Katherine (1658–1759); she was a nun at Dunkirk, France.

6 Unnamed daughter (?) (Katherine?); her existence is conjectural. She is said to have died young.

By Barbara (1641–1709), daughter of William Villiers, 2nd Viscount Grandison, and wife of Roger Palmer, Earl of Castlemaine; she was later created Duchess of Cleveland in her own right:

7 Anne FitzRoy (1661–1722); she married Thomas Lennard, Earl of Sussex (1654–1715). She was possibly the daughter of Roger Palmer, although the King acknowledged her as his own.

8 Charles FitzRoy, Duke of Southampton and Cleveland (1662–1730); he married firstly Mary (1664–1680), daughter of Sir Henry Wood. He married secondly Anne (1663–1745), daughter of Sir William Poultney of Misterton, Leics., and had issue.

9 Henry FitzRoy, Duke of Grafton (1663–1690); he married Isabella (d.1723), daughter of Henry Bennett, 1st Earl of Arlington, and had issue.

10 Charlotte FitzRoy (1664–1717); she married Edward Henry Lee, Earl of Lichfield (1663–1716), and had issue.

11 George FitzRoy, Duke of Northumberland (1665–1716); he married firstly Katherine (d.1714), daughter of Robert Wheatley of Bracknell, Berks., and secondly Mary (d.1738), daughter of Henry Dutton.

12 Barbara (who later assumed the name Benedicte when she entered the religious life) Prioress of Hôtel Dieu, Pontoise, France (1672–1737). She had illegitimate issue. Although Lady Castlemaine claimed that Charles II was Barbara's father, other evidence makes it more probable that she was the daughter of John Churchill, 1st Duke of Marlborough.

By Eleanor, known as 'Nell' (1650–1687), daughter of Thomas Gwyn or Gwynne:

13 Charles Beauclerk, Duke of St Albans (1670–1726); he married Diana (d.1742), daughter of Aubrey de Vere, 20th Earl of Oxford, and had issue.

14 James, Lord Beauclerk (1671–1680).

By Louise Renée de Penencoët de Quérouialle (or Kérouaille), Duchess of Portsmouth in her own right (1649–1734):

15 Charles Lennox, Duke of Richmond, and Duke of Aubigny in France (1672–1723); he married Anne, daughter of Francis, Lord Brudenell, and had issue.

By Mary, or 'Moll', Davies, an actress:

16 Mary Tudor (1673–1726); she married firstly Edward Ratcliffe, 2nd Earl of Derwentwater (1655–1705), and had issue. She married secondly Henry Graham of Levens (d.1707), and thirdly James Rooke.

CHARLES II

He died on 6 February, 1685, at Whitehall Palace, London, of the effects of a stroke, and was buried in Westminster Abbey.

He was succeeded by his brother James.

James II

FATHER: *Charles I* (◊ page 253).
MOTHER: *Henrietta Maria of France* (◊ page 253, under *Charles I*).
SIBLINGS: (◊ page 253, under *Charles I*).

JAMES II

He was born on 14 (O.S.) or 24 (N.S.) October, 1633, at St James's Palace, London, and was designated Duke of York from birth. He was made a Knight of the Garter on 20 April, 1642. He was created Duke of York on 27 January, 1644, and Earl of Ulster on 10 May, 1659. He was created Duke of Normandy by Louis XIV of France on 31 December, 1660. He succeeded his brother Charles II as King of Great Britain on 6 February, 1685. Having converted to Roman Catholicism sometime previously, he was privately crowned by Catholic rites on 22 April, 1685, at Whitehall Palace, London; he was crowned by the traditional Anglican ritual on 23 April, 1685, at Westminster Abbey.

James II married firstly, in secret in November or on 24 December, 1659, at Breda, Holland (although doubts exist as to whether this ceremony ever took place), and publicly on 3 September, 1660, at Worcester House, The Strand, London:

Anne

She was the daughter of Edward Hyde, 1st Earl of Clarendon, by Frances, daughter of Sir Thomas Aylesbury, and she was born on 12 or 22 March, 1637, at Cranbourne Lodge, Windsor. She died on 31 March, 1671, at St James's Palace, London, of cancer, and was buried in Westminster Abbey.

Issue of marriage:

1 *Charles*

He was born on 22 October, 1660, at Worcester House, The Strand, London, and was designated Duke of Cambridge. He died on 5 May, 1661, at Whitehall Palace, London, and was buried in Westminster Abbey.

2 *Mary II* (◊ page 266).

3 *James*

He was born on 11 or 12 July, 1663, at St James's Palace, London. He was created Duke and Earl of Cambridge and Baron of Dauntsey, Wilts., on 23 August, 1664, and was made a Knight of the Garter on 3 December, 1666. He died on 20 June, 1667, at Richmond Palace, Surrey, and was buried in Westminster Abbey.

4 *Queen Anne* (◊ page 267).

5 *Charles*

He was born on 4 July, 1666, at St James's Palace, London, and was designated Duke of Kendal, Earl of Wigmore and Baron Holdenby; there is no evidence of any formal creation. He died on 22 May, 1667, at St James's Palace, London, and was buried in Westminster Abbey.

6 *Edgar*

He was born on 14 September, 1667, at St James's Palace, London. He was created Duke and Earl of Cambridge and Baron of Dauntsey, Wilts., on 7 October, 1667. He died on 8 June, 1671, at Richmond Palace, Surrey, and was buried in Westminster Abbey.

7 *Henrietta*

She was born on 13 January, 1669, at Whitehall Palace, London. She died on 15 November, 1669, at St James's Palace, London, and was buried in Westminster Abbey.

8 *Katherine*

She was born on 9 February, 1671, probably at Whitehall Palace, London (less probably at Richmond Palace, Surrey). She died on 5 December, 1671, at St James's Palace, London, and was buried in Westminster Abbey.

James II married secondly, by proxy on 20 (O.S.) or 30 (N.S.) September, 1673, at the Ducal Palace, Modena, Italy, and in person on 21 November, 1673, at Dover, Kent:

Mary Beatrice Eleanor Anne Margaret Isabella

Baptised Maria, but called Mary from the time of her marriage, she was the daughter of Alfonso d'Este III, Duke of Modena, by Laura, daughter of Girolamo Martinozzi, and she was born on 25 September (O.S.) or 5 October (N.S.), 1658, at the Ducal Palace, Modena, Italy. She was crowned Queen Consort by Catholic rites on 22 April, 1685, at Whitehall Palace, London, and by Anglican rites on 23 April, 1685, at Westminster Abbey. She died on 7/8 May, 1718, at the Château of St Germain-en-Laye, Paris, of cancer, and was buried in the Abbey of the Visitation of St Mary, Chaillot, France (although her body was later destroyed during the French Revolution).

Issue of marriage:

1 *Stillborn child*

It was born in March or May, 1674.

2 *Katherine Laura*

She was born on 10 January, 1675, at St James's Palace, London. She died on 3 October, 1675, at St James's Palace, London, of convulsions, and was buried in Westminster Abbey.

3 *Stillborn child*

It was born in October, 1675.

4 *Isabella*

She was born on 18 (O.S.) or 28 (N.S.) August, 1676, at St James's Palace, London. She died on 2 or 4 March, 1681, at St James's Palace, and was buried in Westminster Abbey.

5 *Charles*

He was born on 7 November, 1677, at St James's Palace, London, and was designated Duke of Cambridge. He died on 12 December, 1677, at St James's Palace, of smallpox, and was buried in Westminster Abbey.

6 *Elizabeth*

She was born and died in *c.*1678.

7 *Stillborn child*

It was born in February, 1681.

8 *Charlotte Maria*

She was born on 16 August, 1682, either at St James's Palace, London, or at Windsor Castle. She died on 6 October, 1682, at St James's Palace, of convulsions, and was buried in Westminster Abbey.

9 *Stillborn child*

It was born in October, 1683.

10 *Stillborn child*

It was born in May, 1684.

11 *James Francis Edward*

Called 'James III', according to Roman Catholic doctrine, he was also known as the 'Chevalier de St George' or 'The Old Pretender'. He was born on 10 June, 1688, at St James's Palace, London. There were widespread rumours at the time that he was a changeling, smuggled into the Queen's bed in a warming pan, but this was mere political invention. What is certain is that the birth of a Catholic heir ensured that James II's days as King were numbered. James was Duke of Cornwall and Rothesay from birth, and was styled Prince of Wales and Earl of Chester from birth. His father abdicated when he was a baby, and he spent his life in exile in France or Italy. He was made a Knight of the Garter in 1692. He succeeded his father as Stuart pretender to the throne of Great Britain (from which he was barred by the Act of Settlement) on 16 September, 1701, and was proclaimed in France as 'James III of England and VIII of Scotland'. He was attainted by Act of Parliament on 2 March, 1702, and forfeited all his British titles. He died on 1 January, 1766, in Rome, where he was buried in St Peter's Basilica in the Vatican.

James married, by proxy on 9 (O.S.) or 19 (N.S.) May, 1719, at Bologna, Italy, and in person on 1 or 3 September, 1719, at Montefiascone Cathedral, Italy:

Maria Casimire Clementina

She was the daughter of Prince James Louis Henry Sobieski of Poland, by Hedwig Elizabeth Amelia, daughter of Philip William, Elector of Pfalz-Neuburg, and she was born on 6 (O.S.) or 17/18 (N.S.) July, 1702. She was called 'Queen of Great Britain' by adherents of the Stuarts. She died on 12 or 18 January, 1735, at the Apostolic Palace, Rome, and was buried in St Peter's Basilica in the Vatican.

Issue of marriage:

(i) *Charles Edward Louis John Philip Casimir Sylvester Maria*
Called 'Charles III' by his adherents, he was also known as the 'Chevalier de St George', 'The Young Pretender' and 'Bonnie Prince Charlie'. He was born on 31 December, 1720, at the Palazzo Muti, Rome, and was styled 'Prince of Wales' from birth. He sometimes styled himself 'Count of Albany'. On the death of his father on 1 January, 1766, he succeeded him as Stuart pretender to the throne of Great Britain, styling himself 'Charles III'. He died on 30/31 January, 1788, at the Palazzo Muti, Papazurri, Rome, and was buried in Frascati Cathedral, Italy. His remains were later removed to St Peter's Basilica in the Vatican.

Charles had the following illegitimate issue:
By Clementina Maria Sophia Walkinshaw, Countess of Alberstroff (d.1802):

1 Charlotte, Countess of Albany in her own right (1753–1789). She had illegitimate issue.

Charles married, by proxy on 28 March, 1772, in Paris, and in person on 17 April, 1772, at the Chapel of the Palazzo Compagnani, Marefoschi, Macerata, Ancona, Italy:

Louise Maximiliana Caroline Emanuèle

She was the daughter of Gustavus Adolphus, Prince of Stolberg-Gedern, by Elizabeth Philippine Claudine, daughter of Maximilian Emanuel, Prince of Hornes and of the Empire. She was born on 20 or 21 September, 1752, at Mons, Hainault, Flanders. After her marriage, she was styled 'Queen of Great Britain' by adherents of the Jacobite cause. It is possible, but not probable, that she made a second marriage, either with Count Vittorio Alfieri, or with Francis Xavier Fabre. She died on 29 January, 1824, at Florence, Italy, and was buried in the Church of Santa Croce, Florence.

(ii) *Henry Benedict Maria Clement Thomas Francis Xavier*

He was born on 6 or 21 March, 1725, at the Palazzo Muti, Papazurri, Rome, Italy, and was styled 'Duke of York' from birth by adherents of the Jacobite cause. He entered the Roman Catholic Church, and was ordained Cardinal Deacon on 30 June, 1747, and Cardinal of Santa Maria, Portici, on 3 July, 1747, before being ordained as a priest on 1 September, 1748. He was known thereafter as 'Cardinal York'. He was provided to the Archbishopric of Corinth on 19 November, 1758, but was translated to the Bishopric of Frascati, Italy, on 13 July, 1761. He succeeded his brother Charles as Pretender to the throne of Great Britain on 30/31 January, 1788, styling himself 'Henry IX'. He died on 13 July, 1807, at Frascati, Italy, and was buried in St Peter's Basilica in the Vatican, Rome, after being briefly laid to rest in the church of St Andrea della Valle, Rome.

12 *Louisa Maria Theresa*

She was baptised Louisa Maria, and received the name Theresa at her confirmation. She was born on 18 (O.S.) or 28 (N.S.) June,

1692, at the Château of St Germain-en-Laye, Paris, and died there on 8 (O.S.) or 18 (N.S.) April, 1712. She was buried in the Chapel of St Edmund in the Church of the English Benedictines, Rue St Jacques, Paris, but later transferred to St Germain-en-Laye by order of George IV.

James II also had the following **illegitimate issue**:

By Arabella (1648–1730), daughter of Sir Winston Churchill and sister of John Churchill, 1st Duke of Marlborough:

1 Henrietta FitzJames (1667–1730); she married firstly Henry, 1st Baron Waldegrave of Chewton, Somerset (1661–1690), and had issue. She married secondly Piers Butler, 2nd Viscount of Galmoye (*d.*1740).

2 James FitzJames (1670–1734), Duke of Berwick; he married firstly Honora (1674–1697), daughter of William Bourke, Earl of Clanricarde, and had issue. He married secondly Anne (*d.*1751), daughter of Henry Bulkely, and had issue.

3 Henry FitzJames, Duke of Albemarle (1673–1702); he married Marie Gabrielle (1675–1741), daughter of John d'Audibert, Count of Lussan, and had issue.

4 Arabella (1674–1704); she became a nun at Pontoise, France, under the name Ignatia.

Arabella Churchill may have borne James other children who died young prior to 1670.

By Katherine, Countess of Dorchester (1657–1717), daughter of Sir Charles Sedley:

5 Katherine Darnley (1679/81–1743); she married firstly James Annesley, Earl of Anglesey (*d.*1702), but they later divorced. She married secondly John Sheffield, Duke of Buckingham and Normanby (1647–1721), and had issue.

6 James Darnley (1684–1685).

7 Charles Darnley (*d.* young).

JAMES II

He was deemed by Parliament to have abdicated on 11 December, 1688, by fleeing the country to exile in France. He was formally deposed by Parliament on 23 December, 1688. He died on 16 September, 1701, at the Château of St Germain-en-Laye, near Paris. His body was temporarily buried in the Chapel of St Edmund in the

Church of the English Benedictines in the Rue St Jacques, Paris, whilst hopefully awaiting eventual transportation to England for burial in Westminster Abbey. The body seems to have disappeared, however, during the French Revolution, although there are reports that it was found and reinterred at St Germain-en-Laye by order of George IV.

An Interregnum followed the deposition of James II, who was succeeded two months later by his son-in-law William of Orange and his daughter Mary as joint sovereigns.

William III and Mary II

WILLIAM III

FATHER: *William (II)*

He was the son of Frederick Henry, Prince of Orange, by Amalia, daughter of John Albert I, Count of Solms-Braunfels, and he was born on 27 May, 1626, at The Hague, Holland. He married Mary Stuart on 2 May, 1641, at the Chapel Royal, Whitehall Palace, London. He was made a Knight of the Garter on 2 March, 1645. He succeeded his father as William II, Stadtholder of the United Provinces of the Netherlands, in March, 1647. He died on 6 November, 1650, at the Binnenhof Palace at The Hague, of smallpox, and was buried at Delft, Holland.

MOTHER: *Mary Henrietta*

She was the daughter of Charles I, King of Great Britain, by Henrietta Maria of France, and she was born on 4 or 29 November, 1631, at St James's Palace, London. She was designated Princess Royal in *c.*1642, thus establishing the tradition that the eldest daughter of a British sovereign bears the title Princess Royal. She died on 24 December, 1660, at Whitehall Palace, London, of smallpox, and was buried in Westminster Abbey.

SIBLINGS: *William III did not have any siblings.*

WILLIAM III

Baptised William Henry, he was born on 4 (O.S.) or 14 (N.S.) November, 1650, at the Binnenhof Palace, The Hague, Holland. He was Stadtholder of Holland from birth, his father having predeceased him, but was deprived of the title during his childhood. He was made a Knight of the Garter on 25 April, 1653. He was designated Count of Nassau-Dillenburg, and reinstated as Stadtholder of Holland in 1672. He acceded to the throne of Great Britain as joint sovereign with his wife Mary (the rightful heir) on 13 February, 1689, following the Interregnum after the abdication and deposition of his father-in-law James II. William was crowned on 11 April, 1689, at Westminster Abbey. He died on 8 March, 1702, at Kensington Palace, London, and was buried in Westminster Abbey.

William III married, on 4 November, 1677, either at St James's Palace or at Whitehall Palace, London:

MARY II

FATHER: *James II* (◊ page 259).
MOTHER: *Anne Hyde* (◊ page 259, under *James II*).
SIBLINGS: (◊ page 259, under *James II*).

MARY II

She was born on 30 April, 1662, at St James's Palace, London. She was proclaimed Queen of Great Britain on 13 February, 1689, following the deposition of her father and the Interregnum; she reigned as joint sovereign with her husband, with whom she was crowned on 11 April, 1689. She died on 28 December, 1694, at Kensington Palace, London, of smallpox, and was buried in Westminster Abbey.

Issue of marriage:

1 *Stillborn child*
   It was born in *c.*April, 1678, at Breda, Holland.
2 *Stillborn child*
   It was born in September, 1678, at Hanserlaersdyck, Holland.
3 *Stillborn child*
   It was born in February, 1680, at The Hague, Holland.

WILLIAM III

After **Mary II**'s death, **William III** reigned alone, the rightful heir,

Anne Stuart, having given up her place in the succession to him for the term of his life.

William was succeeded by Anne in 1702.

Queen Anne

FATHER: *James II* (◊ page 259).
MOTHER: *Anne Hyde* (◊ page 259, under *James II*).
SIBLINGS: (◊ page 259, under *James II*).

QUEEN ANNE

She was born on 6 February, 1665, at St James's Palace, London. She succeeded her brother-in-law William III as Queen of Great Britain on 8 March, 1702, and was crowned on 23 April, 1702, at Westminster Abbey. In 1707, she adopted the royal style Queen of Great Britain, France and Scotland, following the Act of Union.

Queen Anne married, on 28 July, 1683, at the Chapel Royal, St James's Palace, London:

George

He was the son of Frederick III of Oldenburg, King of Denmark, by Sophia Amelia, daughter of George, Duke of Brunswick-Lüneberg, and he was born on 2 April (date on coffin plate), 29 February, 11 November or 21 April, 1653, at Copenhagen, Denmark. He was naturalised as an English subject on 20 September, 1683, and made a Knight of the Garter on 1 January, 1684. He was created Duke of Cumberland, Earl of Kendal and Baron Wokingham ('Ockingham') on 6 April, 1689. During Queen Anne's reign he was styled Prince George, never King Consort. He died on 28 October, 1708, at Kensington Palace, London, and was buried in Westminster Abbey.

Issue of marriage:

1 *Stillborn daughter*

She was born on 12 May, 1684, and was buried in Westminster Abbey.

2 *Mary or Marie*

She was born on 2 June, 1685, at Whitehall Palace, London. She died on 8 February, 1687, at Windsor Castle of 'an acute infection', and was buried in Westminster Abbey.

3 *Anne Sophia*

She was born on 12 May, 1686, at Windsor Castle. She died there on 2 February, 1687, and was buried in Westminster Abbey.

4 *Stillborn child*

It was born between 20 January and 4 February, 1687, probably on 21 January, and was buried in Westminster Abbey.

5 *Stillborn son*

He was born on 22 October, 1687, and was buried in Westminster Abbey on the day of his birth.

6 *Miscarriage*

It occurred on 16 April, 1688.

7 *Stillborn child (?)*

It was perhaps born late in 1688.

8 *William Henry*

He was born on 24 July, 1689, at Hampton Court Palace, and was styled Duke of Gloucester from birth, although he was never formally so created. He was made a Knight of the Garter on 6 January, 1695. He died on 30 July, 1700, at Windsor Castle, of hydrocephalus, and was buried in Westminster Abbey.

9 *Mary*

She was born on 14 October, 1690, at St James's Palace, London, where she died, aged 2 hours, the same day. She was buried in Westminster Abbey.

10 *George*

He was born on 17 April, 1692, at Syon House, Brentford, Middlesex, where he died, aged a few minutes, the same day. He was buried in Westminster Abbey.

11 *Stillborn daughter*

She was born on 23 March, 1693, at Berkely House, St James's Street, London, and was buried in Westminster Abbey.

12 *Stillborn child*

It was born on 21 January, 1694, and may have been a daughter.

13 *Stillborn daughter*

She was born on 17 or 18 February, 1695.

14 Stillborn son

Of six months' growth, he was born on 25 March, 1696.

15 Stillborn twins

A male foetus of 2 or 3 months' growth and a male foetus of 7 months' growth were born on 25 March, 1697, and were buried in St George's Chapel, Windsor.

16 Stillborn son

He was born in early December (before 10 December), 1697.

17 Stillborn son

He was born on 15 September, 1698, at Windsor Castle, and was buried in St George's Chapel, Windsor.

18 Stillborn son

He was born on 25 January, 1700, and was buried in Westminster Abbey.

QUEEN ANNE

She died on 1 August, 1714, at Kensington Palace, London, and was buried in Westminster Abbey. Although she conceived 19 children, none survived her, and she was the last Stuart sovereign.

She was succeeded by her third cousin, Prince George of Hanover.

CHAPTER EIGHT

The House of Hanover

When Queen Anne died in 1714, her nearest living Protestant relative was her third cousin, Prince George of Hanover, who was the grandson of Elizabeth Stuart, the Winter Queen of Bohemia and daughter of James I; Elizabeth's daughter Sophia had married the Elector of Hanover. When the Act of Settlement was passed in 1701, investing the succession in the House of Hanover, Sophia was still alive and hopeful of becoming Queen of Great Britain herself in the fullness of time; this was not to be, as she died only weeks before Queen Anne passed away, and it was her son George who succeeded instead.

There were, however, still living in France at that time, members of the House of Stuart, the children of James II, notably Prince James Francis Edward, the Old Pretender (as he later came to be called). He was a Roman Catholic, and therefore barred from the succession, yet he maintained all his life the belief that he was the rightful King of Great Britain, and his adherents, known as Jacobites, led an uprising on his behalf in 1715 in an ill-fated attempt to restore him to the throne. It failed miserably, and James never took up arms again in his cause. It was left to his son, known to history as Bonnie Prince Charlie, to uphold the Jacobite claims, and in 1745 a further uprising saw the young Prince at first victorious. The bloody defeat of his supporters at Culloden, however, put an end once and for all to any hopes the Stuarts had of ever regaining the throne. In exile in Italy, they quietly continued to style themselves Kings of Great Britain: James III, Charles III, and lastly Henry IX (brother of Charles), but they were no longer a threat to the House of Hanover, and their line came to an end in 1807.

The Hanoverians reigned over Great Britain for nearly 200 years, with the succession passing peacefully from father to son, or grandson, and, finally, to the girl who became the illustrious Queen Victoria. Yet the sovereigns of this particular dynasty all manifested a peculiar resentment against their heirs designate: George I, George II and George III all disliked their eldest sons vehemently; George IV had a poor relationship with his only daughter, Princess Charlotte; and Queen Victoria never understood and was irritated by the future Edward VII. It was not, on a personal level, a happy dynasty.

Furthermore although it was a fruitful dynasty, it was fraught with marital scandals. George I divorced his wife for adultery, and shut her up in a castle for the rest of her life. Several brothers and sons of George III made morganatic, or unofficial, and therefore unsuitable, marriages, most notably the future George IV. Some Hanoverian males lived openly in sin with their mistresses, many for years. It was the marriages of his brothers that shocked George III, a moral-minded man, into passing the Royal Marriages Act in 1772. This Act, which still applies to the royal family today, provides that any marriage made by any of the descendants of George II without the consent of the sovereign automatically becomes null and void. Should the sovereign withhold consent to a projected marriage, the Prince or Princess wishing to make it may wait until he or she reaches the age of 25 and then apply to the Privy Council for assent. This being given, the marriage may be lawfully entered into. It will be seen in the following chapters what effect the Act had upon the personal lives of members of the House of Hanover.

Modern monarchy evolved during the Hanoverian period. Increasingly, the sovereign reigned, rather than ruled, over his/her people. The rights of the sovereign became confined to the rights of being informed, of advising, and of warning those in whom actual power was invested, i.e. the government.

The monarch came to be seen more as a figurehead than as a participant; George II was the last king to lead his troops into battle, at Dettington in 1747. Later sovereigns confined their martial activities to reviewing their armed forces, and undertaking military training. As Head of the Church of England, the monarch was expected to set a moral example. Few of the Hanoverians were capable of this. It was left to George III and Queen Charlotte, Queen Adelaide, and Queen Victoria and Prince Albert to set moral standards acceptable to their people, and which we now think of as Victorian. In this way, the monarchy became very much a domestic institution, and to this day a constitutional sovereign leading an exemplary family life has a very much better chance of achieving popularity than one who might be described as 'playboy'. One is reminded, when reflecting upon this, of the Victorian lady who went to watch a performance of Shakespeare's *Antony and Cleopatra:* 'So unlike the home life of our own dear Queen!' she commented.

The Hanoverians were very much a German dynasty; even Queen Victoria spoke with a German accent. They married German princes or princesses. Apart from George IV and Victoria, they had little time for the arts, although George I and George II patronised Handel. They were not popular monarchs, and suffered scathing portrayals by the caricaturists of their time. They were licentious and uncouth; even Victoria was highly sexed, and in her youth revelled in being 'decadent'. George I and George II saw Britain as secondary in importance to Hanover, which did not endear them to their new subjects. Yet this dynasty, which began so unpromisingly with George I, ended in a blaze of glory as Victoria, the Queen-Empress, celebrated her Diamond Jubilee four years before her death in 1901, amidst scenes of unprecedented adulation and reverence. Thus was the monarchy pulled from the mire to the pinnacle of respectability where it has remained, almost constantly, to this very day.

George I

FATHER: *Ernest Augustus*

He was the son of George, Duke of Brunswick-Lüneberg, by Anne Eleanor, daughter of Louis, Landgrave of Hesse-Darmstadt, and he was born on 20 or 30 November, 1629/30, at Herzberg, Germany. He married Sophia of Bohemia on 30 September, 1658, at the Castle Chapel, Heidelberg, Germany. He was elected Prince Bishop of Osnabrück in 1661, and succeeded his father as Duke of Hanover and Brunswick-Lüneberg in 1679; he was created Elector of Hanover in 1692 (this conferred upon him the right to elect the German Emperor). He died on 23 January, 1698, at Schloss Herrenhausen, Hanover, and was buried in the Chapel of the Leine Schloss, Hanover. His remains were later removed to the Chapel of Schloss Herrenhausen, Hanover.

Ernest perhaps had the following illegitimate issue:

By Clara Elizabeth Meisenburg, wife of Francis Ernest, Count von Platen:

1 Sophia Charlotte, Countess of Platen, Baroness von Kielmansegge, Countess of Leinster, Baroness of Brentford, and Countess of Darlington (1673?–1725). She later became the mistress of her half-brother, George I.

2 George Louis.

3 Charles Augustus.

4 Caroline.

By the Marchesa Paleotti of Bologna:

5 Unnamed son.

6 Laura (?).

MOTHER: *Sophia*

She was the daughter of Frederick V, King of Bohemia and Elector Palatine of the Rhine, by Elizabeth, daughter of James I, and she was born on 13/14 October, 1630, at the Wassenaer Court Palace,

The Hague, Holland. She died on 8 or 14 June, 1714, at Schloss Herrenhausen, Hanover, and was buried in the Chapel of the Leine Schloss, Hanover. Her remains were later removed to the family vault in the Chapel of Schloss Herrenhausen, Hanover.

SIBLINGS:

1 *Frederick Augustus*

He was born on 3 October, 1661, at Hanover, Germany. He was killed on 31 December, 1690 (O.S.) or 10 January, 1691 (N.S.), fighting the Turks at the Battle of St Georgen, Siebenbürgen, Transylvania.

2 *Stillborn twins*

They were born in February, 1664, at Heidelberg, Germany.

3 *Maximilian William*

He was born on 13 (O.S.) or 23 (N.S.) December, 1666, at Schloss Iburg, Hanover, and died on 16 (O.S.) or 27 (N.S.) July, 1726, at Vienna, Austria.

4 *Stillborn son*

He was the twin of Maximilian, and was born in December, 1666, at Schloss Iburg, Hanover.

5 *Sophia Charlotte*

She was born on 12 October, 1668, at Schloss Iburg, Hanover. She married Frederick III of Brandenburg, later Frederick I King of Prussia (1657–1713), on 8 or 28 September, 1684, at Schloss Herrenhausen, Hanover, and had issue:

1 Frederick Augustus (1685–1686).

2 Unnamed son (*b.&d.*1687).

3 Frederick William I, King of Prussia (1688–1740); he married Sophia Dorothea, daughter of George I, and had issue.

Sophia died on 21 January (O.S.) or 1 February (N.S.), 1705, at Hanover, and was buried in the Royal Chapel, Berlin, Germany.

6 *Charles Philip*

He was born on 3 or 13 October, 1669, at Schloss Iburg, Hanover. He was killed on 31 December, 1690, or 1 January, 1691, fighting the Turks at the Battle of Pristina, Albania.

7 *Christian*

He was born on 19 or 29 September, 1671, at Schloss Iburg, Hanover. He drowned on 31 July, 1703, in the River Danube, near Ulm, during the Battle of Munderkingen.

8 *Ernest Augustus*

He was born on 7 (O.S.) or 17 (N.S.) September, 1674, at Osnabrück, Hanover. He was elected Prince Bishop of Osnabrück in 1715. He was made a Knight of the Garter on 3 July, 1716, and was created Duke of York and Albany and Earl of Ulster on 5 July, 1716. He died on 14 August, 1728, at Osnabrück, Hanover.

GEORGE I

Baptised George Louis, he was born on 28 May (O.S.) or 7 June (N.S.), 1660, at Osnabrück, Hanover. He succeeded his father as Duke and Elector of Hanover on 23 January, 1698. He was made a Knight of the Garter on 18 June, 1701, and was naturalised as a British subject in 1705. He succeeded his third cousin, Queen Anne, as King of Great Britain on 1 August, 1714, and adopted the style King of Hanover also on the same day. He was crowned on 20 October, 1714, in Westminster Abbey.

George I married, on 21 November, 1682, at Celle Castle Chapel, Germany:

Sophia Dorothea

She was the daughter of George William, Duke of Brunswick-Lüneberg-Celle, by Eleanor, Countess of Williamsburg, daughter of Alexander II d'Olbreuse, Marquess of Desmiers, and she was born on 3 February, 5 September or 15 September, 1666, at Celle Castle, Germany. She was divorced by Prince George on 28 December, 1694, on the grounds of her adultery with Count Philip Christopher von Königsmarck. She was forbidden to remarry, and was confined to the Castle of Ahlden for the rest of her life, being styled Duchess of Ahlden from February, 1695. She was never Queen of England. She died on 2 (O.S.) or 13 (N.S.) November, 1726, at the Castle of Ahlden, Hanover, Germany, and was buried in Celle Church, Germany.

Issue of marriage:

1 *George II* (↻ page 277).

2 *Sophia Dorothea*

She was born on 16 (O.S.) or 26 (N.S.) March, 1685 or 1687, at Hanover. She married Frederick William of Prussia, later Frederick William I, King of Prussia (1688–1740), firstly on 17 November, 1706, at Hanover, and secondly on 28 November, 1706, at Berlin, Prussia, and had issue:

1 Frederick Louis (1707–1708).

2 Frederica Sophia Wilhelmina (1709–1758); she married Henry or Frederick, Margrave of Bayreuth (1711–1763), and had issue.

3 Frederick William, Prince of Orange (1710–1711).

4 (Charles) Frederick II 'the Great', King of Prussia (1712–1786); he married Elizabeth Christina (1715–1797), daughter of Ferdinand Albert II, Duke of Brunswick-Wolfenbüttel.

5 Charlotte Albertine (1713–1714).

6 Frederica Louisa (1714–1784); she married Charles William Frederick, Margrave of Brandenburg-Ansbach (1712–1757), and had issue.

7 Philippina Charlotte (1716–1801); she married Charles I, Duke of Brunswick-Wolfenbüttel (1713–1780), and had issue.

8 Louis Charles William (1717–1719).

9 Sophia Dorothea Maria (1719–1765); she married Frederick William, Margrave of Brandenburg-Schwedt (1700–1771), and had issue.

10 Louisa Ulrica (1720–1782); she married Adolphus Frederick of Gottorp, King of Sweden (1710–1771), and had issue.

11 Augustus William (1722–1758); he married Louisa Amelia (1722–1780), daughter of Ferdinand Albert II, Duke of Brunswick-Wolfenbüttel, and had issue.

12 Anne Amalia, Abbess of Quedlinburg (1723–1787).

13 Frederick Henry Louis (1726–1802); he married Wilhelmina (1726–1808), daughter of Maximilian, Landgrave of Hesse-Cassel.

14 Augustus Ferdinand (1730–1813); he married Louisa (1738–1820), daughter of Frederick William, Margrave of Brandenburg-Schwedt, and had issue.

Sophia Dorothea died on 28 or 29 June, 1757, at Monbijou Palace near Berlin, Prussia, and was buried at Potsdam, Germany.

George I also had the following **illegitimate issue**:

By Ermengarde Melusina (1667–1743), Baroness von der Schulenberg, Duchess of Kendal, daughter of Gustavus Adolphus, Baron von der Schulenberg:

1 Petronilla Melusina, Baroness of Aldborough and Countess of Walsingham (1693?–1778); she married Philip Stanhope, Earl of

Chesterfield (1694–1773).

2 Margaret Gertrude (1703–1773); she married Count von Lippe.

GEORGE I

He died on 28 May (O.S.) or 11 June (N.S.), 1727, near Osnabrück, Hanover, of the effects of a stroke. He was buried in the Chapel of the Leine Schloss, Hanover, but was transferred to the Chapel vaults of Schloss Herrenhausen after the Second World War. He was succeeded by his son George.

George II

FATHER: *George I* (◊ page 273).
MOTHER: *Sophia Dorothea of Celle* (◊ page 275, under *George I*).
SIBLINGS: (◊ page 275, under George I).

GEORGE II

Baptised George Augustus, he was born on 30 October (O.S.) or 9 November (N.S.), 1683, at Schloss Herrenhausen, Hanover. He was naturalised as a British subject in 1705, and was made a Knight of the Garter on 4 April, 1706. He was created Duke and Marquess of Cambridge, Earl of Milford Haven, Viscount Northallerton and Baron of Tewkesbury on 9 November, 1706. He became Duke of Cornwall and Rothesay when his father succeeded to the throne of Great Britain on 1 August, 1714, and was created and invested Prince of Wales and Earl of Chester on 27 September, 1714, at the Palace of Westminster. He succeeded his father as King of Great Britain on 28 May (O.S.) or 11 June (N.S.), 1727, and was crowned on 11 October, 1727, at Westminster Abbey.

George II married, on 22 August (O.S.) or 2 September (N.S.), 1705, at Schloss Herrenhausen, Hanover:
(Wilhelmina Charlotte) Caroline
Known by her last Christian name, she was the daughter of John

Frederick, Margrave of Brandenburg-Ansbach, by Eleanor Erdmuthe Louisa, daughter of John George, Duke of Saxe-Eisenach. She was born on 1/2 (O.S.) or 11 (N.S.) March, 1683, at Ansbach, Germany. She was crowned on 11 October, 1727, at Westminster Abbey. She died on 20 November, 1737, at St James's Palace, London, and was buried in Westminster Abbey.

Issue of marriage:

1 *Frederick Louis*

He was born on 20 January (O.S.) or 1 February (N.S.), 1707, at Hanover, Germany. He was made a Knight of the Garter on 3 July, 1716, and was created Duke of Gloucester on 10 January, 1717. He became Duke of Cornwall and Rothesay when his father succeeded to the throne of Great Britain on 11 June, 1727. He was created Duke of Edinburgh, Marquess of the Isle of Ely, Earl of Eltham, Viscount of Launceston, and Baron of Snowdon on 26 July, 1727. He was created Prince of Wales and Earl of Chester on 8 January, 1729. He died on 20 (O.S.) or 31 (N.S.) March, 1751, at Leicester House, St Martin's-in-the-Fields, London, and was buried in Westminster Abbey.

Frederick had the following illegitimate issue:

By Anne (1705–1736), daughter of Gilbert Vane, Baron Barnard:

1 FitzFrederick Vane (1732–1736).

By Margaret, Comtesse de Marsac:

2 Charles Marsack (1736–1820).

Frederick married, on 27 April (O.S.) or 8 May (N.S.), 1736, at the Chapel Royal, St James's Palace, London:

Augusta

She was the daughter of Frederick II, Duke of Saxe-Gotha-Altenburg, by Magdalena Augusta, daughter of Charles William, Prince of Anhalt-Zerbst, and she was born on 20 (O.S.) or 30 (N.S.) November, 1719, at Gotha, Germany. She died on 8 February, 1772, at Carlton House, London, of cancer, and was buried in Westminster Abbey.

Issue of marriage:

  (i) *Augusta*

    She was born on 31 July, 1737, at St James's Palace, London. She married Charles II (William Ferdinand), Duke of Brunswick-Wolfenbüttel (1735–1806), at the Chapel Royal, St

James's Palace, on 16 January, 1764, and had issue:

1 Augustina Caroline Frederica Louise (1764–1788); she married Frederick I (William Charles), King of Württemberg (1754-1816) (who afterwards married Charlotte, daughter of George III), and had issue.

2 Charles George Augustus (1766–1806); he married Frederica Louise Wilhelmina (1770–1819), daughter of William V, Prince of Orange.

3 Caroline Amelia Elizabeth; she married George IV, King of Great Britain (◊ page 301, under George IV).

4 George William Christian (1769–1811).

5 Augustus (1770–1820).

6 Frederick William, Duke of Brunswick-Wolfenbüttel (1771–1815); he married Mary Elizabeth Wilhelmina (1782–1808), daughter of Prince Charles Louis of Baden, and had issue.

7 Amelia Caroline Dorothea Louise (1772–1773).

Augusta died on 23 March, 1813, at her house in Hanover Square, London, and was buried in St George's Chapel, Windsor.

(ii) *George III* (◊ page 286).

(iii) *Edward Augustus*

He was born on 14 March, 1739, at Norfolk House, St James's Square, London. He was made a Knight of the Garter on 13 March, 1752, and was created Duke of York and Albany and Earl of Ulster on 1 April, 1760. He died on 17 September, 1767, at Monaco, and was buried in Westminster Abbey.

(iv) *Elizabeth Caroline*

She was born on 30 December, 1740, at Norfolk House, St James's Square, London. She died on 4 September, 1759, at Kew Palace, Surrey, and was buried in Westminster Abbey.

(v) *William Henry*

He was born on 14 November, 1743, at Leicester House, St Martin's-in-the-Fields, London. He was made a Knight of the Garter on 27 May, 1762, and was created Duke of Gloucester and Edinburgh and Earl of Connaught on 19 November, 1764. He died on 25 August, 1805, at Gloucester House, Grosvenor Street, London, and was buried in St George's Chapel, Windsor.

William had the following illegitimate issue:

By Lady Almeria Carpenter:

1 Louisa Maria (1762–1835); she married Godfrey Bosville MacDonald, 3rd Baron of Slate, and had issue.

William married, on 6 September, 1766, at her father's house in Pall Mall, London:

Maria

She was the illegitimate daughter of Sir Edward Walpole by Dorothy, daughter of Hammond Clement of Darlington or Durham, and she was born shortly before 10 July, 1736, at Westminster, London. She married firstly James Waldegrave, 2nd Earl Waldegrave (1714–1763), on 15 May, 1759, at her father's house in Pall Mall, London, and had issue:

1 Elizabeth Laura (1760–1816), Countess Waldegrave; she married George Waldegrave, 4th Earl Waldegrave (1751–1789), and had issue.

2 Charlotte Maria (1761–1808); she married George Henry FitzRoy, Duke of Grafton (1760–1844), and had issue.

3 Anne Horatia (1762–1801); she married Admiral Sir Hugh Seymour (1759–1801), and had issue.

Maria died on 22/23 August, 1807, at Oxford Lodge, Brompton, Middlesex, and was buried in St George's Chapel, Windsor.

Issue of marriage:

(a) *Sophia Matilda*

She was born on 29 May, 1773, at Gloucester House, Grosvenor Street, London. She died on 29 November, 1844, at the Ranger's House, Blackheath, Kent, and was buried in St George's Chapel, Windsor.

(b) *Caroline Augusta Maria*

She was born on 24 June, 1774, at Gloucester House, Grosvenor Street, London, and died there on 14 March, 1775. She was buried in St George's Chapel, Windsor.

(c) *William Frederick*

He was born on 15 January, 1776, at the Tedoli Palace, Rome, Italy. He was made a Knight of the Garter on 16 July, 1794. He succeeded his father as Duke of Gloucester and Edinburgh and Earl of Connaught on 25 August,

1805. He died on 30 November, 1834, at Bagshot Park, Surrey, and was buried in St George's Chapel, Windsor.

William married, on 22 July, 1816, at the Private Chapel, Buckingham Palace, London:

Mary

She was the daughter of George III, King of Great Britain, by Charlotte of Mecklenburg-Strelitz, and she was born on 25 April, 1776, at Buckingham Palace. She died on 30 April 1857, at Gloucester House, Piccadilly, London, and was buried in St George's Chapel, Windsor. There was no issue of the marriage.

(vi) *Henry Frederick*

He was born on 27 October, 1745, at Leicester House, St Martin's-in-the-Fields, London. He was created Duke of Cumberland and Strathearn and Earl of Dublin on 22 October, 1766, and was made a Knight of the Garter on 21 December, 1767. He died on 18 September, 1790, at Cumberland House, Pall Mall, London, and was buried in Westminster Abbey.

Henry is alleged, on circumstantial evidence, to have married privately, either on 4 March (?), 1767, or in 1770:

Olivia

She was the daughter of the Reverend D. James Wilmot. She died on 5 December, 1774.

Alleged issue of marriage:

(a) *Olivia*

Known as 'Princess Olivia of Cumberland'; she was born on 3 April, 1772. She married John Thomas Serres on 1 September, 1791, and had issue:

1 Lavinia Janetta Horton (1797–1871); she married Antony Thomas Ryves, and had issue.

2 Daughter.

Olivia died before 3 December, 1834 (date of burial), and was buried in St James's Church, Westminster.

Henry certainly did marry, on 2 October, 1771, at her house in Hertford Street, Mayfair, London (the which marriage was bigamous if Henry had actually married Olivia Wilmot):

Anne

She was the daughter of Simon Luttrell, 1st Earl of Carhampton, by Judith Maria, daughter of Sir Nicholas Lawes, and she was born on 24 January, 1742/3, in the Parish of St Marylebone, London. She married firstly Christopher Horton of Catton Hall, Derbyshire, on 4 August, 1765, and had issue:

1 Son (name not known) (*d.* young).

Anne died on 28 December, 1808, or in February, 1809, at Trieste, Italy. There was no issue of her marriage to Henry.

(vii) *Louisa Anne*

She was born on 8 March, 1749, at Leicester House, St Martin's-in-the-Fields, London. She died on 13 May, 1768, at Carlton House, Mayfair, London, and was buried in Westminster Abbey.

(viii) *Frederick William*

He was born on 13 May, 1750, at Leicester House, St Martin's-in-the-Fields, London. He died there on 29 December, 1765, and was buried in Westminster Abbey.

(ix) *Caroline Matilda*

She was born on 11 July, 1751, at Leicester House, St Martin's-in-the-Fields, London. She married Christian VII, King of Denmark (1749–1808), by proxy on 1 October, 1766, at Carlton House, London. and in person on 8 November, 1766, at Schloss Frederiksberg, or at Christianborg, Denmark, and had issue:

1 Frederick VI, King of Denmark (1768–1839); he married Mary Sophia Frederica (1767–1852), daughter of Charles, Landgrave of Hesse-Cassel, and had issue.

2 Louise Augusta (1771–1843); she married Frederick Christian II, Duke of Schleswig-Holstein (1765–1814), and had issue. Although recognised as the legitimate daughter of Christian VII, Louise was without doubt the daughter of Queen Caroline by her lover, Count Struensee: her portraits bear this out most strikingly when compared to those of Struensee.

Caroline was crowned Queen Consort of Denmark on 1 May, 1767. She was divorced on 6 April, 1772, on the grounds of her adultery with Count John Frederick Struensee (1737–executed

1772). She died on 10 May, 1775, at Celle Castle, Hanover, and was buried in Celle Church.

2 *Anne*

She was born on 9 or 22 (O.S.) October or 2 November (N.S.), 1709, at Schloss Herrenhausen, Hanover. She was styled Princess Royal from c.30 August, 1727. She married William IV (Charles Henry Friso), Prince of Orange (1711–1751) on 14 (O.S.) or 24/25 (N.S.) March, 1734, at the Chapel Royal St James's Palace, and had issue:

1 Unnamed son (*b.&d.*1735).
2 Unnamed daughter (*b.&d.*1736).
3 Unnamed daughter (*b.&d.*1739).
4 Wilhelmina Caroline (1743–1787); she married Charles Christian, Duke of Nassau-Weilburg (1735–1788), and had issue.
5 Anne Marie (*b.&d.*1746).
6 William V (Batavus), Prince of Orange (1748–1806); he married Frederica Sophia Wilhelmina (1751–1820), daughter of Prince Augustus William of Prussia, and had issue.

Anne died on 2 (O.S.) or 12 (N.S.) January, 1759, at The Hague, Holland.

3 *Amelia Sophia Eleanor*

Known as Emily, she was born on 30 May (O.S.) or 10 June (N.S.), 1711, at Schloss Herrenhausen, Hanover. She died on 31 October, 1786, at her house in Cavendish Square, London, and was buried in Westminster Abbey.

4 *Caroline Elizabeth*

She was born on 30 May (O.S.) or 10 June (N.S.), 1713, at Schloss Herrenhausen, Hanover. She died on 28 December, 1757, at St James's Palace, London, and was buried in Westminster Abbey.

5 *Stillborn son*

He was born on 9 November, 1716, at St James's Palace, London.

6 *George William*

He was born on 2/3 November, 1717, at St James's Palace, London. He is sometimes referred to as the Duke of Gloucester, but there is no evidence that he was ever so styled, designated or formally created. He died on 6 February, 1718, at Kensington Palace, London, and was buried in Westminster Abbey.

7 *Miscarriage*

This occurred in 1718.

8 *William Augustus*

He was born on 15 April, 1721, either at Leicester House, St Martin's-in-the-Fields, London, or – less probably – at St James's Palace, London. He was made a Knight of the Bath on 27 May, 1725, and was created Duke of Cumberland, Marquess of Berkhamstead, Earl of Kennington, Viscount Trematon, and Baron of Alderney on 27 July, 1726. He was made a Knight of the Garter on 18 May, 1730. He died unmarried on 31 October, 1765, at his house in Upper Grosvenor Street, London, and was buried in Westminster Abbey.

William is said, without reliable evidence, to have had three illegitimate children by the daughter of a Scottish soldier.

9 *Mary*

She was born on 22 February (O.S.) or 5 March (N.S.), 1723, at Leicester House, St Martins-in-the-Fields, London. She married Frederick II, Landgrave of Hesse-Cassel (1720–1785), by proxy on 8 (O.S.) or 19 (N.S.) May, 1740, at St James's Palace, London, and in person on 28 June, 1740, at Cassel, Germany, and had issue:

1 William (1741–1742).
2 William IX, Landgrave and Elector of Hesse-Cassel (1743–1821); he married Wilhelmina Caroline (1747–1820), daughter of Frederick V, King of Denmark by Louisa, daughter of George II (◊ page 277), and had issue.
3 Charles, Landgrave of Hesse-Cassel (1744–1836); he married Louisa (1750–1831), daughter of Frederick V, King of Denmark, by Louisa, daughter of George II (◊ below), and had issue.
4 Frederick III, Landgrave of Hesse-Cassel (1747–1837); he married Caroline Polyxena (1762–1823), daughter of Charles William, Prince of Nassau-Usingen, and had issue, including Augusta, wife of Adolphus, Duke of Cambridge, son of George III.

Mary died on 14 or 16 January, 1772, at Hanau, Germany.

10 *Louisa*

She was born on 7 December, 1724, at Leicester House, St Martin's-in-the-Fields, London. She married Frederick V, King of Denmark and Norway (1723–1766), by proxy on 27 or 30 October, 1743, at

Hanover, Germany, and in person on 11 December, 1743, at Altona, near Hamburg, Germany and had issue:

1 Christian (1745–1747).

2 Sophia Magdalena (1746–1813); she married Gustavus III, King of Sweden (1746–1792), and had issue.

3 Wilhelmina Caroline (1747–1820); she married William I, Elector of Hesse-Cassel (son of Mary, daughter of George II – ◊ above) (1747–1821), and had issue.

4 Christian VII, King of Denmark (1749–1808); he married Caroline Matilda of Wales, granddaughter of George II (◊ page 282).

5 Louisa (1750–1831); she married Charles, Landgrave of Hesse-Cassel (1744–1836) (son of Mary, daughter of George II – ◊ above), and had issue.

Louisa died on 8 or 19 December, 1751, at Christianborg Castle, Copenhagen, Denmark.

George II may have had the following illegitimate issue, although the King never acknowledged him as such:

By Amalia Sophia Marianne, Countess von Walmoden and Countess of Yarmouth (1704–1765):

1 John Louis, Count von Walmoden-Gimborn (1736–1811).

GEORGE II

He died on 25 October, 1760 at Kensington Palace, London, and was buried in Westminster Abbey.

He was succeeded by his grandson George.

George III

FATHER: *Frederick, Prince of Wales* (◊ page 277, under *George II*).
MOTHER: *Augusta of Saxe-Gotha* (◊ page 278, under *George II*).
SIBLINGS: (◊ page 278, under *George II*).

GEORGE III
Baptised George William Frederick, he was born on 24 May (O.S.) or
4 June (N.S.), 1738, at Norfolk House, St James's Square, London. He
was made a Knight of the Garter on 22 June, 1749. He succeeded his
father as Duke of Cornwall and Rothesay, Duke of Edinburgh,
Marquess of the Isle of Ely, Earl of Eltham, Viscount of Launceston
and Baron of Snowdon on 20 March, 1751. He was created Prince of
Wales and Earl of Chester on 20 April, 1751. He succeeded his
grandfather George II as King of Great Britain on 25 October, 1760,
and was crowned on 21/22 September, 1761, at Westminster Abbey.
On 1 January, 1801, he relinquished for ever the title 'King of France',
held by English Kings since Edward III laid claim to the French crown
in 1340.

George III is alleged to have married secretly, on 17 April, 1759, a
Quakeress called Hannah Lightfoot, daugher of a Wapping shoe-
maker, who is said to have borne him three children. Documents
relating to the alleged marriage, bearing the Prince's signature, were
impounded and examined in 1866 by the Attorney General. Learned
opinion at that time leaned to the view that these documents were
genuine. They were then placed in the Royal Archives at Windsor; in
1910, permission was refused a would-be author who asked to see
them. If George III did make such a marriage when he was Prince of
Wales, before the passing of the Royal Marriages Act in 1772, then his
subsequent marriage to Queen Charlotte was bigamous, and every
monarch of Britain since has been a usurper, the rightful heirs of
George III being his children by Hannah Lightfoot, if they ever
existed.

George III married, bigamously or not, on 8 September, 1761, at the
Chapel Royal, St James's Palace, London:
(Sophia) Charlotte

Known as Charlotte, she was the daughter of Charles Louis
Frederick, Duke of Mecklenburg-Strelitz, by Elizabeth Albertine of
Saxe-Hildburghausen, and she was born on 19 May, 1744, at Mirow,
Mecklenburg-Strelitz, Germany. On 7 March, 1760, she was invested
as a Protestant canoness of Herford (or Hervorden) in Westphalia,
Germany. She was crowned Queen Consort on 21/22 September,
1761. She died on 17 November, 1818, at Kew Palace, Surrey, and was
buried in St George's Chapel, Windsor.

Issue of marriage:

1 *George IV* (◊ page 301).

2 *Frederick Augustus*

He was born on 16 August, 1763, at St James's Palace, London (or,
less probably, at Buckingham Palace). He was elected Prince Bishop
of Osnabrück on 27 February, 1764, and was made a Knight of the
Garter on 19 June, 1771. He was created Duke of York and Albany
and Earl of Ulster on 29 November, 1784. He died on 5 January,
1827, at Rutland House, Arlington Street, London, and was buried
in St George's Chapel, Windsor.

Frederick had the following illegitimate issue (?):

1 Charles, Captain Hesse. There is no certain proof that Frederick
actually was his father, although he was generally reputed to be.
Charles was killed in a duel with Count Léon, bastard son of
Napoleon I, Emperor of the French.

Frederick married, on 28 September, 1791, at Charlottenburg,
Berlin, Prussia, and again on 23 November, 1791, at Buckingham
Palace:
Frederica Charlotte Ulrica Katherine

She was the daughter of Frederick William II, King of Prussia, by
Elizabeth Christine Ulrica, daughter of Charles, Duke of Brunswick-
Wolfenbüttel, and she was born on 7 May, 1767, either at
Charlottenburg or at Potsdam, Prussia. She died on 6 August, 1820,
at Oatlands Park, Weybridge, Surrey, and was buried in Weybridge
Churchyard, Surrey. There was no issue of the marriage.

3 *Miscarriage*

This occurred in the summer of 1764 at Richmond Lodge, Surrey.

4 William IV (◊ page 303).

5 Charlotte Augusta Matilda

She was born on 29 September, 1766, at Buckingham Palace, and was styled Princess Royal from October, 1766; she was officially designated Princess Royal on 22 June, 1789. She married Frederick William Charles, Duke of Württemburg, afterwards Frederick I, King of Württemburg (1754–1816), on 18 May, 1797, at the Chapel Royal, St James's Palace, London, and had issue:

1 Stillborn daughter; she was born on 27 April, 1798.

Charlotte became Queen Consort when her husband acceded to the throne of Württemburg on 1 January, 1806, and was crowned as such on the same day at Stuttgart, Germany. She died on 6 October, 1828, at Ludwigsburg Palace, Stuttgart, Germany, and was buried there in the Ludwigsburg family vault.

6 Edward Augustus

He was born on 2 November, 1767, at Buckingham Palace. He was made a Knight of the Garter on 2 June, 1786, and was created Duke of Kent and Strathearn and Earl of Dublin on 23 or 24 April, 1799. He died on 23 January, 1820, at Woodbrook Cottage, Sidmouth, Devon, and was buried in St George's Chapel, Windsor. His remains were later removed to the Kent Mausoleum, Frogmore, Windsor.

Edward had the following illegitimate issue:

By Adelaide Dubus:

1 Adelaide Victoria Augusta (1789–1790).

By Julie de St Laurent (?):

2 A son or sons, said to have been adopted at birth in Canada (?).

Edward married, on 29 May, 1818, at Schloss Ehrenburg, Coburg, Germany, and again on 13 July, 1818, at Kew Palace, Surrey:

(Mary Louisa) Victoria

Known as Victoria, she was the daughter of Francis I (Frederick Anthony), Duke of Saxe-Coburg-Saalfield, by Augusta Caroline Sophia, daughter of Henry XXIV, Count of Reuss-Ebersdorf, and she was born on 17 August, 1786, at Coburg, Germany. She married firstly Emich Charles, 2nd Prince of Leiningen (1763–1814), on 21 December, 1803, and had issue:

1 Charles Frederick William Ernest, 3rd Prince of Leiningen (1804–1856); he married Mary, Countess of Kleklesburg

(1806–1880), daughter of Maximilian, Count of Kleklesburg, and had issue, although they were afterwards divorced.

2 Anne Feodora Augusta Charlotte Wilhelmina (1807–1872); she married Ernest, Prince of Hohenlohe-Langenburg (1794–1860), and had issue.

Victoria died on 16 March, 1861, at Frogmore House, Windsor, and was buried in St George's Chapel, Windsor. Her remains were later removed to the Kent Mausoleum, Frogmore, Windsor.

Issue of marriage:

(i) *Queen Victoria* (⟡ page 305).

7 *Augusta Sophia*

She was born on 8 November, 1768, at Buckingham Palace. She perhaps married Major General Sir Brent Spencer (*d.*1828) in *c.*1811, but there is no substantiating evidence for this. She died on 22 September, 1840, at Clarence House, London, and was buried in St George's Chapel, Windsor.

8 *Elizabeth*

She was born on 22 May, 1770, at Buckingham Palace. Some documentary evidence exists to suggest that she either married or was the mistress of a page called George Ramus in *c.*1785, and that they had a daughter Eliza, born in *c.*1786/7, who married a man called James Money. Although such a marriage would have been illegal under the Royal Marriages Act 1772, other evidence would seem to indicate that it did not take place at all, and that there was no connection whatsoever between Elizabeth and 'George Ramus': among 6 or 7 pages surnamed Ramus, not one was called George. Furthermore, the known details of the Princess's illness in 1786/7 are not identifiable with the symptoms of pregnancy. Elizabeth did marry Frederick (Joseph) VI, Landgrave and Prince of Hesse-Homburg (1769–1829) on 7 April, 1818, at the Private Chapel, Buckingham Palace. She died on 10 January, 1840, at Frankfurt-am-Main, Germany, and was buried in the Mausoleum of the Landgraves at Homburg, Germany.

9 *Ernest Augustus*

He was born on 5 June, 1771, at Buckingham Palace. He was made a Knight of the Garter on 2 June, 1786, and was created Duke of Cumberland and Teviotdale and Earl of Armagh on 24 April, 1799. He succeeded his brother William IV as King of Hanover on 20

June, 1837, adopting the style Ernest I; the Salic Law governed the Hanoverian succession, thus preventing the accession of Queen Victoria. Ernest died on 18 November, 1851, at Schloss Herrenhausen, Hanover, and was buried there in the Chapel vaults.

Ernest had the following illegitimate issue:

1 George FitzErnest (*d.*1828).

Ernest married, on 29 May, 1815, at the parish church of Neu Strelitz, Germany, and again on 29 August, 1815, at Carlton House, London:

Frederica Louisa Caroline Sophia Alexandrina

She was the daughter of Charles Louis Frederick V, Grand Duke of Mecklenburg-Strelitz, by Frederica Caroline Louise, daughter of George William, Landgrave of Hesse-Darmstadt, and she was born on 2 March, 1778, at Hanover, Germany. She married firstly Prince Frederick Louis Charles of Prussia (1773–1796) on 26 December, 1793, at the Royal Palace, Berlin, Prussia, and had issue:

1 Frederick William Louis (1794–1863); he married Louise (1799–1882), daughter of Alexis, Duke of Anhalt-Bernbourg, and had issue.

2 Charles George (1795–1798).

3 Frederica Wilhelmina Louise (1796–1850); she married Leopold Frederick, Duke of Anhalt-Dessau (1794–1871).

Frederica was divorced from her first husband in 1796. She married secondly Frederick William, Prince of Solms-Braunfels (1770–1814) on 7 or 10 January, 1798/9, or 10 December, 1798, at Berlin, Prussia, and had issue:

4 Frederick William Henry Casimir George Charles Maximilian (1801– 1868); he married Mary Anne (1809–1892), daughter of Francis, Count of Kinsky, and had issue.

5 Son (name not known); (*b.*1801; *d.* young).

6 Augusta Louisa Theresa Matilda (1804–1865); she married Albert, Prince of Schwarzbourg-Roudolstadt (1798–1869).

7 Alexander Frederick Louis (1807–1867); he married Louise (*b.*1835), daughter of Engelbert, Baron Landsberg-Steinfürt, and had issue.

8 Frederick William Louis George Alfred Alexander (1812–1875); he married Marie Josephine Sophie, daughter of Prince Constantine of Löwenstein-Wertheim-Rochefort, and had issue.

Frederica became Queen of Hanover upon the accession of her third husband, Prince Ernest, to the throne of Hanover, on 20 June, 1837. She died on 29 June, 1841, at Hanover, and was buried in the Chapel at Schloss Herrenhausen, Hanover. Issue of marriage:

(i) *Frederica*

She was stillborn on 27 January, 1817, at St James's Palace, London. She was buried in Westminster Abbey, but was later removed to St George's Chapel, Windsor.

(ii) *Stillborn Daughter*

She was born in April, 1818. There is no record of her burial.

(iii) *George Frederick Alexander Charles Ernest Augustus*

He was born on 27 May, 1819, in a house on the Unter-den-Linden Strasse, Berlin, Prussia. He was made a Knight of the Garter on 15 August, 1835. He succeeded his father as King of Hanover, Duke of Cumberland and Teviotdale, and Earl of Armagh on 18 November, 1851; he was styled George V of Hanover. He was deposed on 20 September, 1866, by the Prussians, and formally abdicated on the same day. He died on 12 June, 1878, at 7, Rue Presbourg, Paris, and was buried in St George's Chapel, Windsor.

(Note: King George went blind following an accident in 1834).

George married, on 18 February, 1843, at Hanover, Germany:

(Alexandrina) Mary Wilhelmina Katherine Charlotte Theresa Henrietta Louisa Pauline Elizabeth Frederica Georgina

Known as Mary, she was the daughter of Joseph George Frederick Ernest Charles, Duke of Saxe-Altenburg, by Amelia Theresa Louise Wilhelmina Philippina, daughter of Louis Alexander, Duke of Württemburg, and she was born on 14 April, 1818, at Hildburghausen, Germany. She died on 9 January, 1907, at Gmunden, Austria, where she was buried.

Issue of marriage:

(a) *Ernest Augustus William Adolphus George Frederick*

He was born on 21 September, 1845, at Hanover, and was Crown Prince of Hanover until his father's abdication on 20 September, 1866. He succeeded his father as Duke of Cumberland and Teviotdale and Earl of Armagh on 12 June, 1878, and was made a Knight of the Garter on 23

June, 1878. He was created Duke of Brunswick-Lüneberg on 18 October, 1884. He died on 14 November, 1923, at Gmunden, Austria.

Ernest married, on 21 December, 1878, at Copenhagen, Denmark:

Thyra Amelia Caroline Charlotte Anne

She was the daughter of Christian IX, King of Denmark, by Louise Wilhelmina Frederica Caroline Augusta Julie, daughter of William X, Landgrave of Hesse-Cassel, and she was also sister to Alexandra, Queen of Edward VII. She was born on 29 September, 1853, at Copenhagen, Denmark. She died on 26 February, 1933, at Gmunden, Austria, where she was buried.

Issue of marriage:

(i) *Marie Louise Victoria Caroline Amelia Alexandra Augusta Frederica*

She was born on 11 October, 1879, at Gmunden, Austria. She married Maximilian, Prince and Margrave of Baden (1867–1929), on 10 July, 1900, at Gmunden, Austria, and had issue:

1 Marie Alexandra Thyra Victoria Louisa Carola Hilda (1902–1944); she married Wolfgang Moritz, Prince of Hesse (*b.*1896).

2 Berthold Friedrich William Carl, Margrave of Baden (1906–1963); he married Theodora (*b.*1906), daughter of Prince Andrew of Greece and Denmark, and sister of Prince Philip, Duke of Edinburgh, and had issue.

Marie died on 31 January, 1948, at Salem Castle, Germany.

(ii) *George William Christian Albert Edward Alexander Frederick Waldemar Ernest Adolphus*

He was born on 28 October, 1880, at Gmunden, Austria, and was styled Duke of Armagh. He was killed on 20 May, 1912, in a motor accident at Nackel, Brandenburg, Germany.

(iii) *Alexandra Louise Marie Olga Elizabeth Theresa Vera*

She was born on 29 September, 1882, at Gmunden,

Austria. She married Frederick Francis IV, Grand Duke of Mecklenburg-Schwerin (1882–1945) on 7 June, 1904, at Gmunden, Austria, and had issue:

1 Frederick Francis V, Grand Duke of Mecklenburg-Schwerin (b.1910); he married Karen Elizabeth (b.1920), daughter of Walter von Schaper.

2 Christian Louis, Grand Duke of Mecklenburg-Schwerin (b.1912); he married Barbara (b.1920), daughter of Prince Sigismund of Prussia, and had issue.

3 Thyra (b.1919).

4 Anastasia (b.1922); she married Frederick Ferdinand, Prince of Schleswig-Holstein-Sonderburg-Glücksburg (b.1913), and had issue.

Alexandra died on 30 August, 1963, at Glucksburg Castle, Germany.

(iv) *Olga Adelaide Louise Marie Alexandrina Agnes*

She was born on 11 July, 1884, at Gmunden, Austria, and died on 21 September, 1958, either at Linz, or at Hubertibus, Gmunden, Austria.

(v) *Christian Frederick William George Peter Waldemar*

He was born on 4 July, 1885, at Gmunden, Austria, and died there on 3 September, 1901.

(vi) *Ernest Augustus Christian George*

He was born on 17 November, 1887, at Penzing Hall, near Vienna, Austria. He succeeded his father as Duke of Brunswick-Lüneberg on 14 November, 1923. He died on 30 January, 1953, at Marienburg Castle, Hanover, Germany.

Ernest married, on 24 May, 1913, at Berlin, Germany:

Victoria Louise

She was the daughter of William II, Emperor of Germany, by Augusta Victoria, daughter of Frederick, Duke of Schleswig-Holstein-Sonderburg-Augustenburg, and she was born on 13 September, 1892, at the Marble Palace, Potsdam, Germany. She died in 1980.

Issue of marriage:

1 Ernest Augustus George William Christian Louis Francis Joseph Nicholas (b.1914); he married firstly Ortrud (1925–1980), daughter of Prince Albert of Schleswig-Holstein-Sonderburg-Glücksburg, and had issue. He married secondly Monica (b.1929), daughter of George Frederick, Duke of Solms-Laubach.

2 George William Ernest Augustus Frederick Axel (b.1915); he married Sophia (b.1914), daughter of Prince Andrew of Greece and Denmark, and sister of Prince Philip, Duke of Edinburgh, and had issue.

3 Frederica Louise Thyra Victoria Margaret Sophia Olga Cecilia Isabella Christa (1917–1981); she married Paul I, King of Greece (1901–1964), and had issue.

4 Christian Oscar Ernest Augustus William Victor George Henry (1919–1981); he married Mireille (b.1946), daughter of Armand Dutry, and had issue, although they were divorced in 1976.

5 Welf Henry Ernest Augustus George Christian Berthold Frederick William Louis Ferdinand (b.1923); he married Alexandra (b.1938), daughter of Otto Frederick, Fürst of Ysenburg and Büdingen.

(b) *Frederica Sophia Marie Henrietta Amelia Theresa*

She was born on 9 January, 1848, at Hanover, Germany. She married Liutbert Alexander George Lionel Alphonse, Baron von Pawel-Rammingen (1843–1932), on 24 April, 1880, at St George's Chapel, Windsor, and had issue:

1 Victoria Georgina Beatrice Maud Anne, Baroness von Pawel-Rammingen (b.&d.1881).

Frederica died on 16 October, 1926, at Biarritz, France.

(c) *Mary Ernestine Josephine Adolphine Henrietta Theresa Elizabeth Alexandra*

She was born on 3 December, 1849, at Hanover, Germany, and died on 4 June, 1904, at Gmunden, Austria, where she was buried.

10 *Augustus Frederick*

He was born on 27 January, 1773, at Buckingham Palace. He was made a Knight of the Garter on 2 June, 1786, and was created Duke of Sussex, Earl of Inverness and Baron Arklow on 27 November, 1801. He died on 22 April, 1843, at Kensington Palace, London, and was buried in Kensal Green Cemetery, London.

Augustus had the following illegitimate issue:

By Miss Tranter of Windsor:

1 Lucy Beaufoy Tranter; she married Charles George Tranter, and had issue, from whom was descended the actress Dame Anna Neagle.

Augustus married firstly, privately, and in contravention of the Royal Marriages Act 1772, on 4 April, 1793, at the Hotel Sarmiento, Rome, and again on 5 December, 1793, at St George's Church, Hanover Square, London:

Augusta

She was the daughter of John Murray, 4th Earl of Dunmore, by Charlotte, daughter of Alexander Stewart, 6th Earl of Galloway, and she was born on 27 January (?), 1763 (or, less probably, 1768), in London. Her marriage to Augustus was declared null and void by the Arches Court of Canterbury on 14 July, 1794, and again by the Prerogative Court on 3 August, 1794, although she did not separate from Augustus until 1801. She assumed the style 'Duchess of Sussex' in 1801. On 13 October, 1806, she assumed instead, by Royal Licence, the surname and title Lady de Ameland. She died on 5 March, 1830, at her house on the East Cliff, Ramsgate, Kent, and was buried in St Lawrence's Church, Isle of Thanet, Kent.

Issue of marriage:

(i) *Augustus Frederick*

He was born on 13 January, 1794, at 16, Lower Berkeley Street, London. He adopted the surname 'd'Este', and was knighted. He died on 28 December, 1848, at Ramsgate, Kent, of disseminated sclerosis, and was buried in St Lawrence's Church, Isle of Thanet, Kent.

(ii) *Augusta Emma*

She was born on 9 August, 1801, in Grosvenor Street, London, and was styled 'Mademoiselle d'Este'. She married Thomas Wilde, 1st Baron Truro of Bowes (1782–1855) on 13 August,

1845, in London. She died on 21 May, 1866, at 83, Eaton Square, London, and was buried in St Lawrence's Church, Isle of Thanet, Kent.

Augustus married secondly, also privately and in contravention of the Royal Marriages Act 1772, on *c.*2 May, 1831, at Great Cumberland Place, London:

Cecilia Laetitia

She was the daughter of Arthur Saunders Gore, 2nd Earl of Arran, by Elizabeth, daughter of Richard Underwood of Dublin, and she was born in 1778, or 1785, or 1788, or 1789. She married firstly Sir George Buggin of Thetford, Norfolk (1760–1825), on 14 May, 1815, at her father's house in Dover Street, London. She assumed her mother's maiden surname of Underwood by Royal Licence on 2 May, 1831, the day her second marriage is thought to have taken place. She was created Duchess of Inverness in her own right on 5 April, 1840. She died on 1 August, 1873, at Kensington Palace, London, and was buried in Kensal Green Cemetery, London. There was no issue of the marriage.

11 *Adolphus Frederick*

He was born on 24 February, 1774, at Buckingham Palace. He was made a Knight of the Garter on 2 June, 1786, and was created Duke of Cambridge, Earl of Tipperary, and Baron of Culloden on 27 November, 1801. He died on 8 July, 1850, at Cambridge House, Piccadilly, London, and was buried at Kew. His remains were later removed to St George's Chapel, Windsor.

Adolphus married, on 7 May, 1818, at Cassel, Prussia, and again on 1 June, 1818, at Kew Palace, Surrey:

Augusta Wilhelmina Louisa

She was the daughter of Frederick III, Landgrave of Hesse-Cassel (son of Mary, daughter of George II), by Caroline Polyxena, daughter of Charles William, Prince of Nassau-Usingen, and she was born on 25 July, 1797, at Rumpenheim Castle, Cassel, Germany. She died on 6 April, 1889, at St James's Palace, London, and was buried at Kew. Her remains were later removed to St George's Chapel, Windsor.

Issue of marriage:

(i) *George William Frederick Charles*

He was born on 26 March, 1819, at Cambridge House,

Hanover, Germany. He was made a Knight of the Garter on 15 August, 1835, and succeeded his father as Duke of Cambridge, Earl of Tipperary and Baron of Culloden on 8 July, 1850. He died on 17 March, 1904, at Gloucester House, Piccadilly, London, and was buried in Kensal Green Cemetery, London.

George married, privately and in contravention of the Royal Marriages Act 1772, on 8 January, 1847, at St John's Church, Clerkenwell, London:

Sarah Louisa

She was the daughter of John Fairbrother by an unnamed daughter of Thomas Freeman of Wylcot, Shrewsbury, and she was born in 1816 at Bow Street, Covent Garden, London. An actress, she was known as 'Mrs FitzGeorge' after her marriage. She died on 12 January, 1890, at 6, Queen Street, Mayfair, London, and was buried in Kensal Green Cemetery, London.

Sarah Louisa had the following illegitimate issue:

1 Charles Manners Sutton Fairbrother (?) (1836–1901).
2 Louisa Katherine (*b*.1839?); she married a Captain Hamilton.

Issue of marriage, all surnamed 'FitzGeorge' (the first two were actually born before their parents entered wedlock):

(a) *George William Adolphus*

He was born on 27 August, 1843, in London. He died on 2 September, 1907, at Lucerne, Switzerland.

George married, on 28 November, 1885, in Paris:

Rosa Frederica

She was the daughter of William Baring of Norman Court, Hants., by Elizabeth Hammersley, and she was born on 9 March, 1854, at Norman Court, Hants. She married firstly Frank Wigsell Arkwright of Sanderstead Court, Surrey, on 29 August, 1878, and had issue:

1 Mabel Iris (*b*.1886); she married firstly Robert Shekelton Balfour (1869–1942), and had issue, and secondly Vladimir Emanuellovitch, Prince Galitzine (1884–1954).
2 George Daphné (1889–1954); she married Sir George Foster Earle (1890–1965), although they later divorced.
3 George William Frederick (1892–1960); he married

297

firstly Esther Vignon (1888–c.1935), from whom he was later divorced, and secondly Frances (b.1911), daughter of Robert Bellenger.

Rosa was divorced from her first husband, prior to marrying George FitzGeorge. She died on 10 March, 1927, either at Cannes or in London. There was no issue of her marriage to George.

(b) *Adolphus Augustus Frederick*

He was born on 30 January, 1846, in London, and rose to the rank of knight. He died on 17 December, 1922, in London.

Adolphus married firstly, on 21 September, 1875, either at Hull or at Hessle, Yorkshire:

Sophia Jane

She was the daughter of Thomas Holden of Winestead Hall, Hull, and she was born in 1857 at Hull. She died on 3 February, 1920, in London.

Issue of marriage:

(*i*) *Olga Mary Adelaide*

She was born in 1877. She married firstly Sir Archibald Hamilton (1876–1939), and had issue: 1 George Edward Archibald Augustus FitzGeorge (1898–killed in action 1918). She was divorced from her first husband in 1902, and married secondly Robert Charlton Lane (1873–1943), and had issue, although again, I have been unable to obtain details of such. She died in 1920.

Adolphus married secondly, on 28 October, 1920, at Pimlico, London:

Margaret Beatrice Daisy

She was the daughter of John Watson, and she was born in 1863. She died on 26 February, 1934, in London. There was no issue of the marriage.

(c) *Augustus Charles Frederick*

He was born on 12 June, 1847, in London, and rose to the rank of knight. He died unmarried on 30 October, 1933, in London.

(ii) *Augusta Caroline Charlotte Elizabeth Mary Sophia Louise*

She was born on 19 July, 1822, at the Palace of Montbrilliant, Hanover. She married Frederick William, Grand Duke of Mecklenburg-Strelitz (1819–1904), on 28 June, 1843, at Buckingham Palace, and had issue:

1 Unnamed son (*b.&d.*1845).
2 George Adolphus Frederick Augustus Victor Ernest Adalbert Gustavus William Wellington, Grand Duke of Mecklenburg-Strelitz (1848–1914); he married Elizabeth Marie Frederica Amelia Agnes of Anhalt (1857–1933), and had issue.

Augusta died on 4/5 December, 1916, at Neustrelitz, Germany, where she was buried.

(iii) *Mary Adelaide Wilhelmina Elizabeth*

She was born on 27 November, 1833, at Hanover, Germany.
She married Francis Paul Charles Louis Alexander, Duke of Teck (1837–1900), on 12 June, 1866, at Kew Church, Surrey, and had issue:

1 Queen Mary, wife of George V. (◊ page 320, under George V.)
2 Adolphus Charles Alexander Albert Edward George Philip Louis Ladislaus, 1st Marquess of Cambridge (1868–1927); he married Margaret Evelyn (1873–1929), daughter of Hugh Lupus Grosvenor, 1st Duke of Westminster, and had issue.
3 Francis Joseph Leopold Frederick (1870–1910).
4 Alexander Augustus Frederick William Alfred George, Earl of Athlone (1874–1957); he married Princess Alice of Albany, daughter of Prince Leopold, Queen Victoria's youngest son, and had issue.

Mary Adelaide died on 27 October, 1897, at White Lodge, Richmond Park, Surrey, and was buried in St George's Chapel, Windsor.

12 *Mary*

She was born on 25 April, 1776, at Buckingham Palace. She married her cousin, William Frederick, Duke of Gloucester (◊ page 281, under George II) (1776–1834), on 22 July, 1816, at the Private Chapel, Buckingham Palace. She died on 30 April, 1857, at Gloucester House, Piccadilly, London, and was buried in St George's Chapel, Windsor.

13 *Sophia Matilda*

She was born on 3 November, 1777, at Buckingham Palace. She

died on 27 May, 1848, at her house in Vicarage Place, Kensington, London, and was buried in Kensal Green Cemetery.

Sophia had the following illegitimate (?) issue:

By General Thomas Garth (*d.*1829):

1 Thomas Garth (1800–after 1839). He left issue. He was born before August, 1800, in Weymouth, Dorset. It is possible that Sophia and General Garth had been married soon after her arrival in Weymouth that year, as his family lived nearby. However, there is no evidence to support a story that they were married in Puddletown Church, Dorset. A portrait of Sophia in old age shows her wearing a wedding ring.

14 *Octavius*

He was born on 23 February, 1779, at Buckingham Palace. He died on 3 May, 1783, at Kew Palace, Surrey, and was buried in Westminster Abbey. His remains were later removed to St George's Chapel, Windsor.

15 *Alfred*

He was born on 22 September, 1780, at Windsor Castle. He died on 20 August, 1782, at Windsor Castle, and was buried in Westminster Abbey. His remains were later removed to St George's Chapel, Windsor.

16 *Amelia*

She was born on 7 August, 1783, at The Lodge, Windsor Castle. It is possible that she married, at some unknown date, the Hon. Charles FitzRoy (1762–1831), but the evidence is conflicting. She died on 2 November, 1810, at Augusta Lodge, St Albans Street, Windsor, of erysipelas, and was buried in St George's Chapel, Windsor.

GEORGE III

He suffered from the disease porphyria, which led his contemporaries to believe he was mad. The death of his youngest daughter Amelia in 1810 broke his health for good, and he became unfit to reign. In 1811, his son George was created Prince Regent, and remained so until his father's death, when he succeeded him.

George III died on 29 January, 1820, at Windsor Castle, and was buried in St George's Chapel, Windsor.

He was succeeded by his son George.

George IV

FATHER: *George III* (◊ page 286).
MOTHER: *Charlotte of Mecklenburg-Strelitz* (◊ page 287, under *George III*).
SIBLINGS: (◊ page 287, under *George III*).

GEORGE IV

Baptised George Augustus Frederick, he was born on 12 August, 1762, at St James's Palace, London, and was Duke of Cornwall and Rothesay, Earl of Carrick, Baron Renfrew and Lord of the Isles from birth. He was created Prince of Wales and Earl of Chester on 17 or 19 August, 1762. He was created Prince Regent of the United Kingdom by Act of Parliament on 5 February, 1811, because of his father's incapacity; he held this title until his accession. He succeeded his father as King of Great Britain on 29 January, 1820, and was crowned on 19 July, 1821, at Westminster Abbey.

George IV married firstly, privately and in contravention of the Act of Settlement 1701 and the Royal Marriages Act 1772, on 15 September, 1785, at her house in Park Lane, Mayfair, London:

Maria Anne

She was the daughter of Walter Smythe of Brambridge, Hants., by Mary, daughter of John Errington of Red Rice, Andover, Hants., and she was born on 26 July, 1756, at Brambridge, Hants. She married firstly Edward Weld (*d.*1775), of Lulworth Castle, Dorset, in 1775, and secondly Thomas FitzHerbert of Norbury, Derby, and Swynnerton, Staffs. (*d.*1781), in 1778. Her marriage to the Prince of Wales was invalid under British Law, but was recognised by Papal Brief in 1800 (Mrs FitzHerbert was a Roman Catholic). Maria formally adopted the following children:

1 Mary ('Minnie') Seymour, orphaned daughter of Lord Hertford, who later married Colonel Dawson Darner.

2 Mary Anne Smythe, the illegitimate daughter of Maria's brother; she later married Captain Jerningham.

Maria spent most of her married life living apart from her husband. She died on 27 or 29 March, 1837, at Brighton, Sussex, and was buried in the R.C. Church of St John the Baptist, Brighton, Sussex. There was no issue of her marriage to George IV.

George IV married secondly, on 8 April, 1795, at the Chapel Royal, St James's Palace, London:

Caroline Amelia Elizabeth

She was the daughter of Charles II (William Ferdinand), Duke of Brunswick-Wolfenbüttel, by Princess Augusta of Wales, granddaughter of George II. She was born on 17 May, 1768, at Brunswick, Germany. The King tried unsuccessfully to divorce her for adultery (then a treasonable crime on the part of his Consort), and she was refused admission to his coronation in 1821. She died on 7 August, 1821, at Brandenburg House, Hammersmith, London, and was buried at Brunswick.

Issue of marriage:

1 *Charlotte Augusta*

She was born on 7 January, 1796, at Carlton House, London. She married Prince Leopold George Frederick of Saxe-Coburg-Saalfield (1790–1865) (later to become Leopold I, King of the Belgians) on 2 May, 1816, at Carlton House, London, and had issue:

1 Miscarriage; this occurred in July, 1816, at Camelford House, London.

2 Stillborn son; he was born on 5 November, 1817, at Claremont House, Esher, Surrey, and was buried in St George's Chapel, Windsor.

Charlotte died on 6 November, 1817, at Claremont House, Esher, Surrey, in childbed, and was buried in St George's Chapel, Windsor.

George IV also had the following **illegitimate issue**:

By Grace Darymple, Mrs Elliott:

1 Georgina Frederica Augusta (?) (*b*.1782). She may have been the daughter of Lord Cholmondeley.

By Elizabeth Milbanke, Viscountess Melbourne (*d*.1818):

2 George (*b*.1784). Perhaps died young.

GEORGE IV

He died on 26 June, 1830, at Windsor Castle, and was buried in St George's Chapel, Windsor.

He was succeeded by his brother William.

William IV

FATHER: *George III* (◊ page 286)
MOTHER: *Charlotte of Mecklenburg-Strelitz* (◊ page 287, under *George III*).
SIBLINGS: (◊ page 287, under *George III*).

WILLIAM IV

Baptised William Henry, he was born on 21 August, 1765, at Buckingham Palace. He was made a Knight of the Thistle on 5 April, 1770, and a Knight of the Garter on 19 April, 1782. He was created Duke of Clarence and St Andrews, and Earl of Munster on 20 May, 1789. He succeeded his brother George IV as King of Great Britain on 26 June, 1830, and was crowned on 8 September, 1831, at Westminster Abbey.
William IV married, on 13 July, 1818, at Kew Palace, Surrey:
Adelaide Louisa Theresa Caroline Amelia

She was the daughter of George I (Frederick Charles), Duke of Saxe-Meiningen, by Louisa Eleanor, daughter of Christian Albert Louis, Prince of Hohenlohe-Langenburg, and she was born on 13 August, 1792, at Meiningen, Thuringia, Germany. She was crowned Queen Consort on 8 September, 1831, at Westminster Abbey. She died on 2 December, 1849, at Bentley Priory, Stanmore, Middlesex, and was buried in St George's Chapel, Windsor.

Issue of marriage:

1 *Charlotte Augusta Louise*

She was born on 27 March, 1819, at the Fürstenhof Palace, Hanover, and died the same day. She was buried at Hanover, Germany.

2 *Stillborn child*

It was born on 5 September, 1819, at Dunkirk, France.

3 *Elizabeth Georgina Adelaide*

She was born on 10 December, 1820, at St James's Palace, London, where she died on 4 March, 1821. She was buried in St George's Chapel, Windsor.

4 *Stillborn child*

It was born in the spring of 1822 at Bushey Park, Middlesex.

5 *Stillborn twins*

They were born in 1824.

William IV also had the following **illegitimate issue:**

By Caroline von Linsingen (who alleged that William married her in 1784/5 or c.1790, in secret; this is very unlikely, although not impossible):

1 William (1784/5–drowned 1807).

By Dorothea Bland, Mrs Jordan (1761–1816):

2 George Augustus Frederick FitzClarence, Earl of Munster (1794–committed suicide 1842); he married Mary, illegitimate daughter of George Wyndham, 3rd Earl of Egremont, and had issue.

3 Henry Edward FitzClarence (1795–1817).

4 Sophia FitzClarence (1796–1837); she married Philip Charles Sidney, 1st Baron de Lisle and Dudley of Penshurst (1800–1851).

5 Mary FitzClarence (1798–1864); she married Charles Richard Fox.

6 Frederick FitzClarence (1799–1854); he married Augusta Boyle.

7 Elizabeth FitzClarence (1801–1856); she married William George Hay, 18th Earl of Erroll (1801–1846), and had issue.

8 Adolphus FitzClarence (1802–1856).

9 Augusta FitzClarence (1803–1865); she married firstly John Kennedy Erskine, and had issue, and secondly John, Lord Gordon.

10 Augustus FitzClarence, Rector of Mapledurham (1805–1854); he married Sarah Elizabeth Katherine Gordon.

11 Amelia FitzClarence (1807–1858); she married Lucius Bentinck Carey, 10th Viscount Falkland (1803–1884), and had issue.

WILLIAM IV

He died on 20 June, 1837, at Windsor Castle, and was buried in St George's Chapel, Windsor.

He was succeeded by his niece Victoria.

Queen Victoria

FATHER: *Edward, Duke of Kent* (◊ page 288, under *George III*).
MOTHER: *Victoria of Saxe-Coburg-Saalfield* (◊ page 288, under *George III*).
SIBLINGS: *Queen Victoria did not have any full siblings.*

QUEEN VICTORIA

Baptised Alexandrina Victoria, she was born on 24 May, 1819, at Kensington Palace, London. She succeeded William IV, her uncle, as Queen of Great Britain on 20 June, 1837, and was crowned on 28 June, 1838, at Westminster Abbey. She was declared Empress of India on 1 May, 1876, and proclaimed as such on 1 January, 1877, at Delhi, India.

Queen Victoria married, on 10 February, 1840, at the Chapel Royal, St James's Palace, London:

Albert Francis Charles Augustus Emmanuel

He was the son of Ernest I, Duke of Saxe-Coburg and Gotha, by Louise of Saxe-Gotha-Altenburg, and he was born on 26 August, 1819, at the Marble Hall, Schloss Rosenau, Coburg, Germany. He was made a Knight of the Garter on 16 December, 1839. He was created Prince Consort by Letters Patent on 26 June, 1857, and proclaimed as such the same day. He died on 14 December, 1861, at Windsor Castle, of typhoid, and was buried in St George's Chapel Windsor (in the Albert Memorial Chapel). His remains were later removed to the Royal Mausoleum, Frogmore, Windsor.

Issue of marriage:

1 *Victoria Adelaide Mary Louise*

She was born on 21 November, 1840, at Buckingham Palace, and was designated Princess Royal from birth. She married Prince Frederick William Nicholas Charles of Prussia, afterwards Frederick III, Emperor of Prussia (1831–1888), on 25 January, 1858, at the Chapel Royal, St James's Palace, London, and had issue:

1 William II (Frederick William Albert Victor), Emperor of Germany (1859–1941); he married Augusta Victoria Louisa Feodora Jenny (1858–1921), daughter of Frederick, Duke of Schleswig-Holstein, and had issue. He married secondly, Hermine (1887–1947), daughter of Henry XXII, Duke of Reuss.

2 Victoria Elizabeth Augusta Charlotte (1860–1919); she married Bernhard III, Duke of Saxe-Meiningen (1851–1928), and had issue.

3 Albert William Henry (1862–1929); he married Irene Louise Mary Anne (1866–1953), daughter of Louis IV, Grand Duke of Hesse-Darmstadt, by Alice, daughter of Queen Victoria (◊ below), and had issue.

4 Francis Frederick Sigmund (1864–1866).

5 Frederica Wilhelmina Amelia Victoria (1866–1929); she married firstly Prince Adolphus William of Schaumburg-Lippe (1856–1916), and secondly Alexander Alexandrovich Zubka (1900–1936).

6 Joachim Frederick Ernest Waldemar (1868–1879).

7 Sophia Dorothea Ulrica Alice (1870–1932); she married Constantine I, King of Greece (1868–1923), and had issue.

8 Margaret Beatrice Feodora (1872–1954); she married Frederick Charles, Landgrave of Hesse (1868–1940), and had issue.

Victoria died on 5 August, 1901, at the Friedrichshof Palace, Krönberg, Germany, of cancer, and was buried in the Friedenskirche, Potsdam, Germany.

2 *Edward VII* (◊ page 318).

3 *Alice Maud Mary*

She was born on 25 April, 1843, at Buckingham Palace. She married Louis IV, Grand Duke of Hesse-Darmstadt and the Rhine, and Duke of Saxony (1837–1892) on 1 July, 1862, at Osborne House, Isle of Wight, and had issue:

1 Ernest Louis Albert Charles William (1868–1937), Grand Duke of Hesse-Darmstadt and the Rhine; he married Princess Victoria of Edinburgh (1876–1936), granddaughter of Queen Victoria (◊ page 309, below), and had issue, although they were afterwards divorced. He married secondly Eleanor Ernestine Marie of Solms-Hohensolmslich (1871–1937), and had issue. Both he and his second wife were killed in air crashes.

2 Frederick William Augustus Victor Leopold Louis (1870–1873). He was killed falling out of an upstairs window.

3 Victoria Alberta Elizabeth Matilda Mary (1863–1950); she married Prince Louis Alexander of Battenberg (who changed his name to Mountbatten in 1917), 1st Marquess of Milford Haven (1854–1921), and had issue, including Lord Louis Mountbatten, 1st Earl Mountbatten of Burma (1900 – assassinated by the I.R.A. in 1979).

4 Elizabeth Alexandra Louise Alice (assumed name Elizabeth Federovna upon marriage) (1864–assassinated 1918 during the Russian Revolution); she married Grand Duke Serge of Russia (1857–murdered 1905).

5 Irene Louise Marie Anne (1866–1953); she married Prince Albert William Henry of Prussia (1862–1929), son of the Princess Royal, eldest daughter of Queen Victoria (◊ page 306, above), and had issue.

6 Alice Victoria Helena Louise Beatrice (assumed name Alexandra Federovna upon marriage) (1872–1918: murdered during the Russian Revolution); she married Nicholas II, Tsar of all the Russias (1868–assassinated 1918 by the Bolsheviks), and had issue, all of whom were assassinated during the Russian Revolution.

7 Mary Victoria Feodora Leopoldine (1874–1878); she died of diphtheria.

Alice died on 14 December, 1878, at Darmstadt, of diphtheria, and was buried in the Mausoleum of Rosenhöhe, Hesse-Darmstadt, Germany.

4 Alfred Ernest Albert

He was born on 6 August, 1844, at Windsor Castle. He was made a Knight of the Garter on 24 May, 1863, and was created Duke of Edinburgh, Earl of Kent and Earl of Ulster on 24 May, 1866. He succeeded his father's brother Ernest as reigning Duke of Saxe-Coburg and Gotha on 22 August, 1893. He died on 30 July, 1900, at Schloss Rosenau, Coburg, Germany, of cancer, and was buried in the cemetery of Coburg.

Alfred married, on 23 January, 1874, at the Winter Palace, St Petersburg, Russia:

Marie Alexandrovna

She was the daughter of Alexander II, Tsar of all the Russias, by Marie Alexandrovna, daughter of Louis II, Grand Duke of Hesse and the Rhine, and she was born on 5 or 17 October, 1853, at Tsarskoie-Selo, Russia (or, less probably, at St Petersburg, Russia). She died on 5 or 24 October, 1920, at Zürich, Switzerland.

Issue of marriage:

(i) *Alfred Alexander William Ernest Albert*

He was born on 15 October, 1874, either at Buckingham Palace, or at Eastwell Park, Kent. He became a Prince of Saxe-Coburg and Gotha upon the accession of his father to the ducal throne on 22 August, 1893, and he was made a Knight of the Garter on 23 April, 1894. He never married. He shot himself on 6 February, 1899, at Meran, in the Austrian Tyrol (or, much less probably, at Coburg), and was buried in the Castle church at Friedenstein, near Gotha, Germany.

(ii) *Marie Alexandra Victoria*

She was born on 29 October, 1875, at Eastwell Park, Kent. She married Ferdinand I (Albert Meinrad), King of Romania (1865–1927), on 10 January, 1893, at Sigmaringen Castle, Romania, and had issue:

1 Charles II, King of Romania (1893–1953); he married firstly Joanna Maria Valentina (known as Zizi) (1898–1953), daughter of Constantine Lambrino; they were divorced in 1919. He married secondly Helen (1896–1982), daughter of Constantine I, King of Greece, and had issue; they were divorced in 1928. He married thirdly Elena Magda (1902–1977), daughter of Nicholas Lepescu.

2 Elizabeth Charlotte Josephine Victoria Alexandra (1894–1956); she married George II, King of Greece (1890–1947), but they were divorced in 1935.

3 Marie (1900–1961); she married Alexander I, King of

Yugoslavia (1891–murdered 1934), and had issue.

4 Nicholas (b.1903); he married firstly Joanna Dolete (1909–1963), daughter of John Dumitrescu-Tohani, and secondly Theresa Lisboa Figueria (b.1913), daughter of Jeronymo de Avellar Figueira de Mello.

5 Ileana (b.1909); she married firstly Anton, Archduke of Austria-Tuscany (b.1901), and had issue; they were divorced in 1954. She married secondly Stephen Issarescu (b.1906). She is now a nun, and is known as Mother Alexandra of the Monastery of the Transfiguration, Ellwood City, P.A., U.S.A.

6 Mircea (1913–1916).

Marie died on 18 July, 1938, at Peles Castle, Sinaia, Romania.

(iii) *Victoria Melita*

She was born on 25 November, 1876, at the Palace of San Antonio, Malta. She married firstly Ernest Louis, Grand Duke of Hesse-Darmstadt and the Rhine (1868–1937) (son of Alice, daughter of Queen Victoria – ↊ above) on 19 April, 1894, at Schloss Ehrenburg, Coburg, Germany, and had issue:

1 Elizabeth Mary Alice Victoria (1895–1903).

2 Unnamed son (b.&d. 1900).

3 Miscarriage.

Victoria was divorced from Ernest on 21 December, 1901. She married secondly Grand Duke Kyrill Vladimirovitch of Russia (1876–1938) on 8 October, 1905, at Tegernsee, and had issue:

1 Marie Kirillovna (1907–1951); she married Frederick Charles Edward Erwin, 6th Fürst of Leiningen (1898–1946), and had issue.

2 Kira Kirillovna (1909–1967); she married Louis Ferdinand, Prince of Prussia (b.1907), and had issue.

3 Vladimir Kirillovitch (b.1917); he married Leonida Georgievna, Princess Bagration-Monkhransky (b.1913), and had issue.

Victoria died on 2 March, 1936, at Amorbach, Germany.

(iv) *Alexandra Louise Olga Victoria*

She was born on 1 September, 1878, at Coburg, Germany.

She married Ernest William Frederick Charles Maximilian, 7th Prince of Hohenlohe-Langenburg (1863–1950), on 20 April,

1896, at Coburg, and had issue:

1 Godfrey Victor Hermann Alfred Paul Maximilian, 8th Prince of Hohenlohe-Langenburg (1897–1960); he married Margaret (1905–1981), daughter of Prince Andrew of Greece and Denmark and sister of Prince Philip, Duke of Edinburgh, and had issue.

2 Marie Melita Leopoldine Victoria Feodora Alexandra Sophia (1899–1967); she married William Frederick, Duke of Schleswig-Holstein-Glücksburg, and had issue.

3 Alexandra Beatrice Leopoldine (1901–1963).

4 Irma Helena (*b*.1902).

5 Alfred (*b*.&*d*.1911).

Alexandra died on 16 April, 1942, at Schwäbisch-Hall, Württemburg, Germany.

(v) *Unnamed daughter*

She was born on 13 October, 1879, at Eastwell Park, Kent, and died the same day. She may have been stillborn.

(vi) *Beatrice Leopoldine Victoria*

She was born on 20 April, 1884, at Eastwell Park, Kent. She married Alfonso Maria Francisco Antonio Diego, Infante of Spain and 3rd Duke of Galliera (1886–1975), on 15 July, 1909, at Schloss Rosenau, Coburg, Germany, and had issue:

1 Alvaro Antonio Fernando Carlos Felipe, Prince of Orléans (*b*.1910); he married Carla Delfino (*b*.1909), and had issue.

2 Alonso Maria Cristino Justo (1912–killed 1936).

3 Ataulfo Alejando Isabelo Carlos (*b*.1913).

Beatrice died on 13 July, 1966, at Sanlucar de Barrameda, Spain.

5 *Helena Augusta Victoria*

She was born on 23 or 25 May, 1846, at Buckingham Palace. She married Christian, Prince of Schleswig-Holstein-Sonderburg-Augustenburg (1831–1917), on 5 July, 1866, at the Private Chapel, Windsor Castle, and had issue:

1 Christian Victor Albert Louis Ernest Anthony (1867–1900).

2 Albert John Charles Frederick Alfred George, Duke of Schleswig-Holstein (1869–1931).

3 Victoria Louise Sophia Augusta Amelia Helena (1870–1948).

4 Franzisca Josepha Louise Augusta Marie Christina Helena (known as Princess Marie Louise) (1872–1956); she married

Aribert Joseph Alexander, Prince of Anhalt (1864–1933); they were divorced in 1900.

5 Frederick Christian Augustus Leopold Edward Harold (*b.&d.*1876).

6 Unnamed son (*b.&d.*1877).

Helena died on 9 June, 1923, at Schomberg House, Pall Mall, London, and was buried at Frogmore, Windsor.

6 *Louise Caroline Alberta*

She was born on 18 March, 1848, at Buckingham Palace. She married John George Edward Henry Douglas Sutherland Campbell, Marquess of Lorne, later 9th Duke of Argyll (1845–1914), on 21 March, 1871, at St George's Chapel, Windsor. She died on 3 December, 1939, at Kensington Palace, London, and was cremated at Golders Green Crematorium, her ashes being buried at Frogmore, Windsor.

7 *Arthur William Patrick Albert*

He was born on 1 May, 1850, at Buckingham Palace. He was made a Knight of the Garter on 24 May, 1867, and a Knight of the Thistle on 24 May, 1869. He was created Duke of Connaught and Strathearn and Earl of Sussex on 24 May, 1874. He died on 16 January, 1942, at Bagshot Park, Surrey, and was buried in the Royal Mausoleum, Frogmore, Windsor.

Arthur married, on 13 March, 1879, at St George's Chapel, Windsor:

Louise Marguerite Alexandra Victoria Agnes

She was the daughter of Prince Frederick Charles Nicholas of Prussia by Mary Anne, daughter of Leopold Frederick, Duke of Anhalt-Dessau, and she was born on 25 July, 1860, at Marmorpalais (Marble Palace), near Potsdam, Germany. She died on 14 March, 1917, at Clarence House, London, and was buried in the Royal Mausoleum, Frogmore, Windsor.

Issue of marriage:

(i) *Margaret Victoria Augusta Charlotte Norah*

She was born on 15 January, 1882, at Bagshot Park, Surrey. She married (Oscar Frederick William Olaf) Gustavus Adolphus VI, King of Sweden (1882–1973), on 15 June, 1905, at St George's Chapel, Windsor, and had issue:

1 Gustavus Adolphus Oscar Frederick Arthur Edmund

(1906–1947); he married Sybilla Calma Marie Alice Bathildis Feodora of Saxe-Coburg (1908–1972), and had issue.

2 Sigvard Oscar Frederick, Duke of Upland (b.1907); he married firstly Erika Maria Regina Rosalie Patzeck; they were later divorced. He married secondly Sonia Helen Robbert (b.1909), and had issue.

3 Ingrid Victoria Sophia Louise Margaret (b.1910); she married Frederick IX, King of Denmark, and had issue.

4 Bertil Gustavus Oscar Charles Eugene, Duke of Holland (b.1912).

5 Charles John Arthur, Duke of Dalecarlia (b.1916); he married Ellen Christine Margaret Wijkmark (b.1910).

6 Unnamed daughter (d. young).

Margaret died on 1 May, 1920, at Stockholm, Sweden.

(ii) *Arthur Frederick Patrick Albert*

He was born on 13 January, 1883, at Windsor Castle. He was made a Knight of the Garter on 15 July, 1902. He died on 12 September, 1938, at Belgrave Square, London.

Arthur married, on 15 October, 1913, at the Chapel Royal, St James's Palace:

Alexandra Victoria Alberta Edwina Louise

She was the daughter of Alexander William George Duff, Duke of Fife, by Louise, daughter of Edward VII, and she was born on 17 May, 1891, at East Sheen Lodge, Surrey. She succeeded her father as Duchess of Fife in her own right in 1912. She died on 26 February, 1959, at her house in Avenue Road, London, and was cremated at Golders Green Crematorium, London.

Issue of marriage:

(a) *Alastair Arthur*

He was born on 9 August, 1914, in Mount Street, London, and was styled Earl of MacDuff from birth. He succeeded his grandfather Arthur as Duke of Connaught and Strathearn and Earl of Sussex on 16 January, 1942. He died on 26 April, 1943, at Government House, Ottawa, Canada, and was buried in Mar Lodge Chapel, Braemar, Aberdeenshire.

(iii) *Victoria Patricia Helen Elizabeth*

She was born on 17 March, 1886, at Buckingham Palace. She

married Sir Alexander Robert Maule Ramsay (1881–1972) on 27 February, 1919, at Westminster Abbey (this was the first royal wedding to take place in the Abbey since Tudor times). She renounced her title of Princess, and assumed the style Lady Patricia Ramsay upon marriage. She had issue:

1 Alexander Arthur Alfonso David Maule (*b*.1919); he married Marjorie Flora (*b*.1930), daughter of Alexander Arthur Fraser, 19 Earl of Saltoun, and had issue.

Lady Patricia died on 12 January, 1974.

8 *Leopold George Duncan Albert*

He was born on 7 April, 1853, at Buckingham Palace. He was made a Knight of the Garter on 24 May, 1869, and created Duke of Albany, Earl of Clarence and Baron Arklow on 14 May, 1881. A haemophiliac, he died after an accident on 28 March, 1884, at the Villa Nevada, Cannes, France, and was buried in St George's Chapel, Windsor.

Leopold married, on 27 April, 1882, at St George's Chapel, Windsor:

Hélène Frederica Augusta

She was the daughter of George Victor, Prince of Waldeck-Pyrmont, by Helena Wilhelmina Henrietta Pauline Marianne, daughter of George William Augustus Henry, Duke of Nassau-Weilburg, and she was born on 17 February, 1861, at Arolsen, Waldeck, Germany. She died on 1 September, 1922, at Hinterris in the Austrian Tyrol, and was buried in Austria.

Issue of marriage:

(i) *Alice Mary Victoria Augusta Pauline*

She was born on 25 February, 1883, at Windsor Castle. She married Alexander of Teck, Earl of Athlone (1874–1957) (great-grandson of George III and brother of Queen Mary, wife of George V), on 10 February, 1904, at St George's Chapel, Windsor, and had issue:

1 May Helen Emma (*b*.1906); she married Colonel Sir Henry Abel Smith (*b*.1900), and had issue.

2 Rupert Alexander George Augustus, Viscount Trematon (1907–killed in a car accident, 1928).

3 Maurice Francis George (*b*.&*d*.1910).

In 1917, Alexander of Teck adopted the surname Cambridge,

which has since been used by his family. Princess Alice died on 3 January, 1981, at Kensington Palace, London, and was buried at Frogmore, Windsor.

(ii) *(Leopold) Charles Edward George Albert*

Known as Charles, he was born on 19 July, 1884, at Claremont House, Esher, Surrey, his father's posthumous son. He therefore succeeded at birth as Duke of Albany, Earl of Clarence and Baron Arklow. He succeeded his uncle Alfred as Duke of Saxe-Coburg-Gotha on 30 July, 1900. He was made a Knight of the Garter on 15 July, 1902. He supported Kaiser William II during the First World War, and was consequently struck off the register of the Knights of the Garter in 1915. He abdicated as Duke of Saxe-Coburg-Gotha on 14 November, 1918, and his English titles were formally removed by order of King George V in Council on 28 March, 1919. He died on 6 March, 1954, at Coburg, Germany.

Charles married, on 11 October, 1905, at Glücksburg Castle, Holstein, Germany:

Victoria Adelaide Helena Louise Marie Frederica

She was the daughter of Frederick Ferdinand George Christian Charles William, Duke of Schleswig-Holstein-Sonderburg-Glücksburg, by Victoria Frederica Augusta Marie Caroline Matilda, daughter of Frederick Christian Augustus, Duke of Schleswig-Holstein-Sonderburg-Glücksburg. She was born on 31 December, 1885, at Grünholz, Holstein, Germany. She died on 3 or 5 October, 1970, either at Coburg, Germany, or at Greinburg, Austria.

Issue of marriage:

(a) John Leopold William Albert Ferdinand Victor (1906–1972); he married firstly Feodora Mary Alma Margaret (*b.*1907), daughter of Baron Bernard von der Horst, and had issue; they were divorced in 1962. He married secondly Maria Theresa Elizabeth (1908–72), daughter of Max Reinde.

(b) Sybilla Calma Mary Alice Bathildis Feodora (1908–1972); she married Prince Gustavus Adolphus of Sweden (1906– killed 1947), and had issue.

(c) Dietmar Hubert Frederick William Philip (1909–1943).

314

(d) Caroline Matilda Louisa Eleanor Augusta Beatrice (*b*.1912); she married firstly Frederick Wolfgang, Count of Castell-Rudenhausen (1906–1940), and had issue; they were divorced in 1938. She married secondly Max Schnirring (1896–1944), and had issue, and thirdly Jim Andree (*b*.1912); they were divorced in 1949.

(e) Frederick Josias Charles Edward Ernest Cyril Harold (*b*.1918); he married firstly Victoria Louisa Frederica Caroline Matilda (*b*.1921), daughter of Hans, Count of Solmsbaruth, and had issue; they were divorced in 1946. He married secondly Denise Henrietta (*b*.1923), daughter of Gaston Robert de Muralt, and had issue; they were divorced in 1964. He married thirdly Katherine (*b*.1940), daughter of Dietrich Charles Bremme.

9 *Beatrice Mary Victoria Feodore*

She was born on 14 April, 1857, at Buckingham Palace. She married Prince Henry Maurice of Battenberg (1858–1896) on 23 July, 1885, at Whippingham Church, Isle of Wight, and had issue:

1 Alexander Albert, Marquess of Carisbrooke (1886–1960); he married Irene Frances Adza (1890–1956), daughter of William Denison, 3rd Earl of Londesbrough, and had issue.

2 Victoria Eugénie Julia Ena (who took the additional names Maria Christina upon entering the Roman Catholic Faith) (1887–1969); she married Alfonso XIII, King of Spain (1886–1941), and had issue.

3 Leopold Arthur Louis (1889–1922).

4 Maurice Victor Donald (1891–killed at the Battle of Mons, 1914).

Beatrice died on 26 October, 1944, at Brantridge Park, Balcombe, Sussex, and was buried in St George's Chapel, Windsor. Her remains were later removed to St Mildred's Church, Whippingham, Isle of Wight.

QUEEN VICTORIA

She died on 22 January, 1901, at Osborne House, Isle of Wight, and was buried in the Royal Mausoleum, Frogmore, Windsor.

She was succeeded by her son Albert, who styled himself Edward VII.

CHAPTER NINE

The House of Saxe-Coburg-Gotha becomes the House of Windsor

The Hanoverian line officially ended with the death of Queen Victoria. Her son, Edward VII, was the first sovereign of the short-lived royal House of Saxe-Coburg-Gotha, as the son of the Prince Consort. At the turn of the 20th century, the British royal family was enjoying its greatest pinnacle of prestige, with the British Empire – which had vastly expanded during the reign of Victoria – covering much of the globe. The Monarchy now had imperial status, and Victoria herself embodied all its highest ideals.

This state of affairs could not last. The 20th century has seen the most sweeping changes in our history, as well as two world wars. The great Empire did not long survive the Second World War, and became the British Commonwealth of Nations, although many have since become independent.

It was one of the supreme ironies of history that the monarchy which led Britain and the Empire through two wars against Germany should itself be of German origin, and its members closely inter-married with high-ranking supporters of Kaiser William II or Adolf Hitler. Queen Victoria herself spoke English with a strong German accent, and German at home with Albert. The royal family of Hanover and that of Saxe-Coburg-Gotha were British by birth, closely related to the British royal house. Yet so strong was the monarchy's identification with its people, and so anti-German was the popular feeling of its subjects, that in 1917 King George V decided to expunge all German names and titles from his House and family. Thus the House of Saxe-Coburg-Gotha became the House of Windsor; their Serene Highnesses the Prince and Princess of Teck became transformed by the surname Cambridge; and Battenberg – the name of one of the

316

most illustrious families of 19th- and 20th-century Europe – became Mountbatten.

Thirty years later, Mountbatten and Windsor were to become linked by marriage, when the present Queen married Lieutenant Philip Mountbatten, formerly Prince Philip of Greece. Since Elizabeth II's accession, it has become clear that, while the Queen's House and family are still known as Windsor, her children are surnamed Mountbatten-Windsor. George V decreed also that the title Prince or Princess might be borne, not only by the sons and daughters of the monarch, but also by the children of sons of the sovereign. Great-grandchildren in the male line are styled Lord (name) or Lady (name) Windsor. Primogeniture, as practised by the Plantagenets centuries ago, is still used to determine the order of succession to the throne.

Of course, the monarchy has adapted to change, and also to an age in which media intrusion has – rather dangerously, on occasions – sometimes reduced it to the level of a soap opera. This is perhaps the greatest threat it has faced since 1936, when Edward VIII abdicated for love, to marry a twice-divorced woman. That event shook the throne, and it was only the dedication and devotion to duty of King George VI and the late Queen Mother that restored its prestige. Her Majesty Queen Elizabeth II has maintained that tradition; as a sovereign reigning in an age that has seen great changes in the moral and social climate, she continues to embody all the domestic, and now some-times unfashionable, virtues that made Queen Victoria so successful a monarch; yet, unlike Victoria in her later years, Elizabeth II is a very visible monarch, seen to be performing her duties with sincerity and dedication, in full glare of the media. She is a constitutional monarch *par excellence,* whose long experience in politics and public life has earned her the respect of political leaders worldwide.

For all the rumours, it is unthinkable that the Queen will abdicate. The memory of Edward VIII is too fresh in the public mind. The succession is assured well into the 21st century, and we may confidently hope that the traditions of a thousand years of British monarchy will continue long into the future.

Edward VII

FATHER: *Albert, Prince Consort* (◊ page 305, under *Queen Victoria*).
MOTHER: *Queen Victoria* (◊ page 305).
SIBLINGS: (◊ page 306, under *Queen Victoria*).

EDWARD VII
Baptised Albert Edward, he was born on 9 November, 1841, at
Buckingham Palace, and was Duke of Cornwall and Rothesay, Earl of
Carrick, Lord of the Isles and Baron Renfrew from birth. He was
created Prince of Wales and Earl of Chester on 8 December, 1841, and
Earl of Dublin on 17 January, 1850. He was made a Knight of the
Garter on 9 November, 1858. In 1863, he renounced his courtesy title,
Duke of Saxe-Coburg-Gotha, inherited from his father. He was made
a Knight of the Thistle of 24 May, 1867. He succeeded his mother as
King of Great Britain and Emperor of India on 22 January, 1901, and
was crowned on 9 August, 1902, at Westminster Abbey.

Edward VII married, on 10 March, 1863, at St George's Chapel,
Windsor:

Alexandra Caroline Marie Charlotte Louise Julie
She was the daughter of Christian IX, King of Denmark, by Louise
Wilhelmina Frederica Caroline Augusta Julie, daughter of William X,
Landgrave of Hesse-Cassel, and she was born on 1 December, 1844, at
the Amalienborg or 'Gule' (Yellow) Palace, Copenhagen, Denmark.
She was made a Lady of the Garter in 1901. She was crowned Queen
on 9 August, 1902, at Westminster Abbey. She died on 20 November,
1925, at Sandringham House, Norfolk, and was buried in St George's
Chapel, Windsor.

Issue of marriage:

1 *Albert Victor Christian Edward*
He was born on 8 January, 1864, at Frogmore House, Windsor. He
was made a Knight of the Garter on 3 September, 1883, and was
created Duke of Clarence and Avondale and Earl of Athlone on 24

May, 1890. He died on 14 January, 1892, at Sandringham House, Norfolk, of pneumonia, and was buried in St George's Chapel, Windsor.

The Duke of Clarence is said to have married one Annie Crook of Cleveland Street, London (*d.*1920), during the 1880s, and is said to have had issue:

1 Alice Margaret Crook; she is said to have had a liaison with the painter Walter Sickert, and to have had a son, Joseph Sickert, who is the source of this information, which should, however, be treated with extreme caution.

Historically, the Duke of Clarence was betrothed to Mary of Teck, who later married George V.

2 *George V* (◊ page 320).

3 *Louise Victoria Alexandra Dagmar*

She was born on 20 February, 1867, at Marlborough House, London. She married Alexander William George Duff, Marquess of MacDuff, afterwards 1st Duke of Fife (1849–1912), on 27 July, 1889, in the Private Chapel, Buckingham Palace, and had issue:

1 Alastair (stillborn 1890).

2 Alexandra, Duchess of Fife (1891–1959); she married Prince Arthur of Connaught, grandson of Queen Victoria, and had issue.

3 Maud Alexandra Victoria Georgina Bertha (1893–1945); she married Charles Alexander Carnegie, 11th Earl of Southesk (*b.*1893), and had issue.

Louise was designated Princess Royal on 9 November, 1905. She died on 4 January, 1931, at her house in Portman Square, London, and was buried in St George's Chapel, Windsor. Her remains were later removed to the Private Chapel, Mar Lodge Mausoleum, Braemar, Aberdeenshire.

4 *Victoria Alexandra Olga Mary*

She was born on 6 July, 1868, at Marlborough House, London. She died on 3 December, 1935, at Coppins, Iver, Bucks., and was buried at Frogmore, Windsor.

5 *Maud Charlotte Mary Victoria*

She was born on 26 November, 1869, at Marlborough House, London. She married Prince Christian Frederick Charles George Waldemar Axel of Denmark, afterwards Haakon VII, King of

Norway (1872–1957), on 22 July, 1896, at the Private Chapel, Buckingham Palace, and had issue:

1 Olav V (Alexander Edward Christian Frederick), King of Norway (*b.*1903); he married Martha Sophia Louisa Dagmar Thyra (1901–1954), daughter of Carl, Prince of Sweden and Duke of Västergötland, and had issue.

Queen Maud died on 20 November, 1938, in London.

6 *Alexander John Charles Albert*

He was born on 6 April, 1871, at Sandringham House, Norfolk, and died there the following day. He was buried in Sandringham Church, Norfolk.

EDWARD VII

He died on 6 May, 1910, at Buckingham Palace, and was buried in St George's Chapel, Windsor.

He was succeeded by his son George.

George V

FATHER: *Edward VII* (◊ page 318).
MOTHER: *Alexandra of Denmark* (◊ page 318, under *Edward VII*).
SIBLINGS: (◊ page 318, under *Edward VII*).

GEORGE V

Baptised George Frederick Ernest Albert, he was born on 3 June, 1865, at Marlborough House, London. He was made a Knight of the Garter on 4 April, 1884, and was created Duke of York, Earl of Inverness and Baron Killarney on 24 May, 1892. He became Duke of Cornwall and Rothesay when his father succeeded to the throne on 22 January, 1901, and was created Prince of Wales and Earl of Chester on 9 November, 1901. He succeeded his father as King of Great Britain and Emperor of India on 6 May, 1910, and was crowned on 22 June, 1911, at Westminster Abbey. He was crowned Emperor of India on 11 December, 1911, at New Delhi, India. In 1917, George V changed the name of his House from Saxe-Coburg-Gotha to Windsor, which it remains today.

George V married, on 6 July, 1893, at the Chapel Royal, St James's Palace:

(Victoria) Mary Augusta Louise Olga Pauline Claudia Agnes

Known as Mary (or May within her family), she was the daughter of Francis Paul Charles Louis Alexander, Duke of Teck, by Princess Mary Adelaide of Cambridge, a granddaughter of George III. She was born on 26 May, 1867, at Kensington Palace, London, and was first betrothed to her future husband's elder brother, the Duke of Clarence, before his death. She was made a Lady of the Garter in 1910. She was crowned on 22 June, 1911, at Westminster Abbey; she was also crowned Empress of India on 11 December, 1911, at New Delhi, India. She died on 24 March, 1953, at Marlborough House, London, and was buried in St George's Chapel, Windsor.

Issue of marriage:

1 *Edward VIII* (◊ page 326).
2 *George VI* (◊ page 327).
3 *(Victoria Alexandra Alice) Mary*

Known as Mary, she was born on 25 April, 1897, at Sandringham, Norfolk. She married Henry George Charles Lascelles, 6th Earl of Harewood (1882–1947), on 28 February, 1922, at Westminster Abbey, and had issue:

1 George Henry Hubert, 7th Earl of Harewood (*b.*1923); he married firstly Maria Donata Nanette Pauline Gustava Erwina Wilhelmina (known as Marion) (*b.*1926), daughter of Erwin Stein, and had issue; they divorced in 1967 (Marion later married the Liberal M.P. Jeremy Thorpe). He married secondly Patricia Elizabeth (*b.*1926), daughter of Charles Tuckwell, by whom he has issue.

2 Gerald David (*b.*1924); he married firstly Angela (*b.*1919), daughter of Charles Stanley Dowding, and had issue; they were divorced in 1978. He married secondly Elizabeth Colvin, née Collingwood (*b.*1924), by whom he has issue.

Mary was designated Princess Royal on 1 January, 1932. She died on 28 March, 1965, at Harewood House, Leeds, Yorkshire, and was buried at Harewood.

4 Henry William Frederick Albert

He was born on 31 March, 1900, at York Cottage, Sandringham, Norfolk. He was made a Knight of the Garter in 1921, and was created Duke of Gloucester, Earl of Ulster and Baron Culloden on 31 March, 1928. He died on 10 June, 1974, at Barnwell Manor, Northants., and was buried in St George's Chapel, Windsor.

Henry married, on 6 November, 1935, at the Private Chapel, Buckingham Palace:

Alice Christabel

She is the daughter of John Charles Montagu-Douglas-Scott, 7th Duke of Buccleuch and 10th Duke of Queensberry, by Margaret Alice, daughter of George Cecil Orlando Bridgeman, 4th Earl of Bradford, and she was born on 25 December, 1901, in London. Since her husband's death, she has been styled H.R.H. Princess Alice, Duchess of Gloucester.

Issue of marriage:

(i) Miscarriage, late in 1937.

(ii) Miscarriage, Autumn 1938.

(iii) *William Henry Andrew Frederick*

He was born on 18 December, 1941, at Barnet, Herts. He never married. He was killed on 28 August, 1972, in an air crash at Halfpenny Green, Wolverhampton, Staffs., and was buried at Frogmore, Windsor.

(iv) *Richard Alexander Walter George*

He was born on 26 August, 1944, at Barnwell Manor, Peterborough, Northants. He succeeded his father as Duke of Gloucester, Earl of Ulster and Baron Culloden on 10 June, 1974.

Richard married, on 8 July, 1972, at the Parish Church of St Andrew, Barnwell, Northants.:

Birgitte Eva

She is the daughter of Asgar Preben Wissing Henrikson by Vivian, daughter of Waldemar Oswald van Deurs of Copenhagen, Denmark, and she was born on 20 June, 1946, at Odense, Isle of Funen, Denmark. Prior to her marriage, she used her mother's maiden surname 'van Deurs'.

Issue of marriage:

(a) *Miscarriage*
This occurred in 1973.

(b) *Alexander Patrick Gregers Richard*
He was born on 24 October, 1974, at St Mary's Hospital, Paddington, London, and has been styled Earl of Ulster from birth.

(c) *Davina Alice Elizabeth Benedikte*
She was born on 19 November, 1977, at St Mary's Hospital, Paddington, London, and is styled Lady Davina Windsor.

(d) *Rose Victoria Birgitte Louise*
She was born on 1 March, 1980, at St Mary's Hospital, Paddington, London, and is styled Lady Rose Windsor.

5 *George Edward Alexander Edmund*

He was born on 20 December, 1902, at Sandringham, Norfolk. He was made a Knight of the Garter in 1923, and was created Duke of Kent, Earl of St Andrews and Baron Downpatrick on 10 or 12 October, 1934. He was killed on 25 August, 1942, when his R.A.F. plane crashed into a hillside at Borgue or Morven, near Caithness, Scotland, whilst he was on active service during the Second World War. He was buried in St George's Chapel, Windsor, but his remains were later removed to the Kent Mausoleum, Frogmore, Windsor.

George married, on 29 November, 1934, at Westminster Abbey, and again – by Greek Orthodox rites – on the same day at the Private Chapel, Buckingham Palace:

Marina
She was the daughter of Prince Nicholas of Greece and Denmark by Helen Vladimirovna, Grand Duchess of Russia, and she was born on 30 November or 13 December, 1906, at Athens, Greece. She died on 27 August, 1968, at Kensington Palace, London, of a brain tumour, and was buried in the Kent Mausoleum, Frogmore, Windsor.

Issue of marriage:

(i) *Edward George Nicholas Paul Patrick*
He was born on 9 October, 1935, at 3, Belgrave Square, London. He succeeded his father as Duke of Kent, Earl of St Andrews and Baron Downpatrick on 25 August, 1942.

Edward married, on 8 June, 1961, at York Minster:

Katharine Lucy Mary

She is the daughter of Sir William Arthrington Worsley, Bt., of Hovingham Hall, Yorkshire, by Joyce Morgan, daughter of Sir John Fowler Brunner, Bt., and she was born on 22 February, 1933, at Hovingham Hall, Yorkshire.

Issue of marriage:

(a) *George Philip Nicholas.* Born on 26 June, 1962, at Coppins, Iver, Bucks., and has been styled Earl of St Andrews from birth. Married on 9 January, 1988, at Leith Register Office, Edinburgh: *Sylvana Palma.* She is the daughter of Max Tomaselli and Josiane Demers, and was born on 28 May, 1957, at Placentia, Newfoundland, Canada, and has issue: 1 Edward, Baron Downpatrick; born on 2 December, 1988. 2 Marina Charlotte; born on 30 September, 1992. 3 Amelia, born on 24 August, 1995.

(b) *Helen Marina Lucy.* Born on 28 April, 1964, at Coppins, Iver, Bucks., and is styled Lady Helen Taylor. Married in 1992 at St George's Chapel, Windsor, Timothy Taylor and has issue: 1 Columbus (*b.*1994). 2 Cassius (*b.*1996).

(c) *Nicholas Charles Edward Jonathan.* Born on 25 July, 1970, at University College Hospital, London, and is styled Lord Nicholas Windsor.

(d) *Stillborn child.* Born on 5 October, 1977, at the King Edward VII Hospital for Officers, Marylebone, London.

(ii) *Alexandra Helen Elizabeth Olga Christabel*

She was born on 25 December, 1936, at 3, Belgrave Square, London. She married Sir Angus James Bruce Ogilvy (*b.*1928) on 24 April, 1963, at Westminster Abbey, and has issue: 1 James Robert Bruce (*b.*1964); married to Julia (*b.*1965), daughter of Charles Rawlinson, and has issue. 2 Marina Victoria Alexandra (*b.*1966); married to Paul Mowatt (*b.*1962), and has issue; divorced 1997.

(iii) *Michael George Charles Franklin*

He was born on 4 July, 1942, at Coppins, Iver, Bucks.

Michael married, on 30 June, 1978, at a civil ceremony at the Rathaus, Vienna, Austria (and in so doing renounced his place in the succession, as his bride is a Roman Catholic):

Marie Christine Anne Agnes Hedwig Ida

She is the daughter of Baron Gunther Hubertus von Reibnitz by Marianne, Countess Szapary, and she was born on 15 January, 1945, at Karlsbad, Bohemia (now Czechoslovakia). She married firstly Thomas Troubridge (*b.*1939) on 14 September, 1971, at Chelsea Old Church, London, but this marriage was formally annulled by the Roman Catholic Church in May, 1978, on undisclosed grounds.

Issue of marriage:

(a) *Frederick Michael George David Louis*

He was born on 6 April, 1979, at St Mary's Hospital, Paddington, London, and is known as Lord Frederick Windsor.

(b) *Gabriella Marina Alexandra Ophelia*

She was born on 23 April, 1981, at St Mary's Hospital, Paddington, London, and is known as Lady Gabriella Windsor.

6 *John Charles Francis*

He was born on 12 July, 1905, at York Cottage, Sandringham, Norfolk. An epileptic who was kept away from the public eye, he died on 18 January, 1919, at Wood Farm, Wolferton, Norfolk, and was buried in Sandringham Church, Norfolk.

GEORGE V

He died on 20 January, 1936, at Sandringham House, Norfolk, and was buried in St George's Chapel, Windsor.

He was succeeded by his son Edward.

Edward VIII

FATHER: *George V* (◊ page 320)
MOTHER: *Mary of Teck* (◊ page 321, under *George V*).
SIBLINGS: (◊ page 321, under *George V*).

EDWARD VIII

Baptised Edward Albert Christian George Andrew Patrick David, he was born on 23 June, 1894, at White Lodge, Richmond, Surrey. He became Duke of Cornwall and Rothesay, Earl of Carrick, Lord of the Isles and Baron Renfrew upon his father's accession to the throne on 6 May, 1910. He was made a Knight of the Garter on 23 June, 1910, and was created Prince of Wales and Earl of Chester on the same day, being invested as such on 13 July, 1911, at Caernarvon Castle, Wales. He was made a Knight of the Bath in January, 1936. He succeeded his father as King of Great Britain and Emperor of India on 20 January, 1936. He was never crowned. He abdicated on 11 December, 1936, because he wished to marry a twice-divorced woman, the American Mrs Simpson (◊ below), and because this could not be consistent with his position as Head of the Church of England, an institution which does not recognise divorce. Edward was created Duke of Windsor on 8 March, 1937, having been so designated since 12 December, 1936. He spent the rest of his life in exile in France, apart from occasional visits to England and America, and a wartime spell as Governor of the Bahamas.

Edward VIII married, after his Abdication, on 3 June, 1937, at
  Château de Candé, Maine-et-Loire, France:
Bessiewallis
  Known as Wallis, she was the daughter of Teackle Wallis Warfield by Alice M. Montague, and she was born on 19 June, 1896, at Square Cottage, the Monterey Inn, Blue Ridge Summit, Pennsylvania, U.S.A. She married firstly Earl Winfield Spencer (1888–1950) on 8 November, 1916, at the Christ Protestant Episcopal Church,

Baltimore, Maryland, U.S.A.; they were divorced on 10 December, 1927. She married secondly Ernest Aldrich Simpson of New York (*d.*1958) on 21 July, 1928, at Chelsea Register Office, London; they were divorced on 27 October, 1936. She resumed her maiden name of Warfield on 7 May, 1937, by Deed Poll. Her marriage to the Duke of Windsor has been seen by some as morganatic (i.e. in contravention of the Royal Marriages Act 1772), but this was not so; neither did the fact that she was deprived of the style Her Royal Highness by George VI's Letters Patent of March, 1937, have any basis in law. She died on 24 April, 1986, at her house in the Bois de Boulogne, Paris, and was buried at Frogmore, Windsor. There was no issue of any of her marriages.

EDWARD VIII

He died on 28 May, 1972, at his house in the Bois de Boulogne, Paris, of cancer, and was buried at Frogmore, Windsor.

He was succeeded, after his Abdication in 1936, by his brother Albert, who assumed the style George VI.

George VI

FATHER: *George V* (◊ page 320).
MOTHER: *Mary of Teck* (◊ page 321, under *George V*).
SIBLINGS: (◊ page 321, under *George V*).

GEORGE VI

Baptised Albert Frederick Arthur George, he was born on 14 December, 1895, at York Cottage, Sandringham, Norfolk. He was made a Knight of the Garter in 1916, and was created Duke of York, Earl of Inverness and Baron Killarney on 4 June, 1920. He succeeded his brother Edward VIII as King of Great Britain and Emperor of India on 11 December, 1936, and was crowned on 12 May, 1937, at Westminster Abbey. He relinquished the title Emperor of India on 22

June, 1947, when India was granted independence.

George VI married, on 26 April, 1923, at Westminster Abbey:

Elizabeth Angela Marguerite

She was the daughter of Sir Claude George Bowes-Lyon, 14th Earl of Strathmore and Kinghorne, by Nina Cecilia, daughter of the Rev. Charles William Frederick Cavendish-Bentinck, and she was born on 4 August, 1900, either at Belgrave Mansions, Grosvenor Gardens, London, or in a London ambulance on the way to a London maternity home (the available evidence suggests that the Queen Mother herself believed she was born in an ambulance). She was made a Lady of the Garter in 1936. She was crowned Queen Consort and Empress of India on 12 May, 1937, in Westminster Abbey. On the death of the King on 6 February, 1952, she assumed the style of H.M. Queen Elizabeth the Queen Mother. She died on 30 March, 2002, at Royal Lodge, Windsor, and is buried in St George's Chapel, Windsor.

Issue of marriage:

1 *Elizabeth II* (↻ page 329).

2 *Margaret Rose*

She was born on 21 August, 1930, at Glamis Castle, Angus, Scotland. She married Antony Charles Robert Armstrong-Jones, 1st Earl of Snowdon (*b.*1930), on 6 May, 1960, at Westminster Abbey, and had issue:

1 David Albert Charles, Viscount Linley (*b.*1961); married to the Hon. Serena Alleyne (*b.*1970), daughter of Charles Henry Leicester Stanhope, Viscount Petersham, and has issue.

2 Sarah Frances Elizabeth (*b.*1964); married to Daniel Chatto (*b.*1957), and has issue.

Princess Margaret and Lord Snowdon were divorced in May, 1978, having lived apart since March, 1976.

Princess Margaret died on 9 February, 2002, at the King Edward VII Hospital, London. She was cremated at Slough Crematorium, and her ashes interred in St. George's Chapel, Windsor.

GEORGE VI

He died on 6 February, 1952, at Sandringham House, Norfolk, of cancer, and was buried in the King George VI Memorial Chapel, St George's Chapel, Windsor.

He was succeeded by his daughter Elizabeth.

Elizabeth II

By the Grace of God, of the United Kingdom of Great Britain and Northern Ireland, and of Her other Realms and Territories, Queen, Head of the Commonwealth, Defender of the Faith.

FATHER: *George VI* (◊ page 327).
MOTHER: *Elizabeth Bowes-Lyon* (◊ page 328, under *George VI*).
SIBLINGS: (◊ page 328, under *George VI*).

ELIZABETH II

Baptised Elizabeth Alexandra Mary, she was born on 21 April, 1926, at 17, Bruton Street, London. She succeeded her father as Queen of Great Britain on 6 February, 1952, and was crowned on 2 June, 1953, at Westminster Abbey.

Elizabeth II married, on 20 November, 1947, at Westminster Abbey:
Philip

He is the son of Prince Andrew of Greece and Denmark (of the House of Schleswig-Holstein-Sonderburg-Glücksburg) by Victoria Alice Elizabeth Julia Marie, daughter of Louis, Prince of Battenberg, Marquess of Milford-Haven, and he was born on 10 June, 1921, at Villa Mon Repos, Isle of Corfu, Greece. On 28 February, 1947, he renounced his Greek nationality and became a British subject, at the same time adopting the surname Mountbatten. He was made a Knight of the Garter in 1947, and was created Duke of Edinburgh, Earl of Merioneth and Baron Greenwich on 19 November, 1947. He was made a Knight of the Thistle in 1952. On 27 February, 1957, he was granted the style of H.R.H. The Prince Philip, with precedence over all other male members of the Royal Family.

Issue of marriage:

1 ***Charles Philip Arthur George***
He was born on 14 November, 1948, at Buckingham Palace. He

became Duke of Cornwall and Rothesay, Earl of Carrick, Lord of the Isles and Baron Renfrew upon his mother's accession to the throne on 6 February, 1952. He was created Earl of Chester and Prince of Wales on 26 July, 1958, being invested as such on 1 July, 1969, at Caernarvon Castle, Wales. He was made a Knight of the Garter in 1968, and a Knight of the Bath in 1976.

Prince Charles married, on 29 July, 1981, at St Paul's Cathedral, London:

Diana Frances

She was the daughter of Edward John, 8th Earl Spencer, by the Hon. Frances Ruth Burke, daughter of Edmund Maurice Roche, 4th Baron Fermoy, and she was born on 1 July, 1961, at Park House, Sandringham, Norfolk. The Prince and Princess of Wales were divorced on 28 August, 1996. Diana was killed in a car crash on 31 August, 1997, in Paris, and is buried on the island called the Oval at Althorp House, Northants.

Issue of marriage:

(i) *William Arthur Philip Louis.* Born on 21 June, 1982, at St Mary's Hospital, Paddington, London, and is styled Prince William of Wales.

(ii) *Henry Charles Albert David.* Known as Harry; born on 15 September, 1984, at St Mary's Hospital, Paddington, and is styled Prince Henry of Wales.

2 *Anne Elizabeth Alice Louise*

She was born on 15 August, 1950, at Clarence House, London. She married Captain Mark Anthony Peter Phillips (*b.*1948) on 14 November, 1973, at Westminster Abbey, and has issue:

1 Peter Mark Andrew (*b.*1977).

2 Zara Anne Elizabeth (*b.*1981).

Princess Anne was designated Princess Royal on 1 June, 1987. She was divorced in 1992 and married secondly Commander Timothy Laurence (*b.*1955) in December, 1992, at Crathie Church, Scotland.

3 *Andrew Albert Christian Edward*

He was born on 19 February, 1960, at Buckingham Palace. He was created Duke of York, Earl of Inverness and Baron Killalee on 23 July, 1986.

Prince Andrew married, on 23 July, 1986, at Westminster Abbey:

Sarah Margaret

She is the daughter of Major Ronald Ivor Ferguson by Susan Mary, daughter of Fitzherbert Wright of Corbisdale Farm, Ardgay, Co. Ross, and she was born on 15 October, 1959, at 27, Welbeck Street, London, W.1.

Issue of marriage:

(i) *Beatrice Elizabeth Mary.* Born on 8 August, 1988, at the Portland Hospital, Great Portland Street, London, W.1.

(ii) *Eugenie Victoria Helena.* Born on 23 March, 1990, at the Portland Hospital.

The Duke and Duchess of York were divorced on 30 May, 1996.

4 *Edward Antony Richard Louis*

He was born on 10 March, 1964, at Buckingham Palace, and was created Earl of Wessex on 19 June, 1999. Prince Edward married, on 19 June, 1999, at St George's Chapel, Windsor:

Sophie Helen

She is the daughter of Christopher Bournes Rhys-Jones by Mary O'Sullivan, and she was born on 20 January, 1965, at Oxford.

Issue of marriage:

(i) Miscarriage, December 2001.

Select Bibliography

The works consulted during the 22 years it has taken me to research this book are too numerous to mention. What follows is a list of the most important sources. Books marked * are especially recommended for researching royal genealogy. Every effort has been made to trace a publisher for each book listed; unfortunately, this was not possible in every case.

Adam of Usk: *Chronicon* (ed. E. M. Thompson, 1876).

Adamson, D. & Dewar, P. B.: *The House of Nell Gwynn* (Kimber, 1974).

Akrigg, G. P. V.: *Jacobean Pageant, or the Court of King James I* (Hamish Hamilton, 1962).

Albert, M. A.: *The Divorce* (Harrap, 1965).

Alderman, C. L.: *Blood Red the Roses: The Wars of the Roses* (Bailey and Swinfen, 1973).

Alexander, Marc: *The Outrageous Queens* (1977).

H.R.H. Princess Alice, Countess of Athlone: *For My Grandchildren* (Evans, 1966).

Altschul, M.: *A Baronial Family in Mediaeval England: The Clares, 1217–1314* (Johns Hopkins, 1965).

Ancient Charters, Royal and Private, prior to A.D. 1200 (ed. J. H. Round, Pipe Roll Society, 1888).

Andrews, A: *The Royal Whore* (Hutchinson, 1971).

The Anglo-Saxon Chronicle (ed. G. N. Garmonsway, Dent, 1954).

Anominalle Chronicle (ed. V. H. Galbraith, 1967).

Appleby, J. T.: *England without Richard* (Bell, 1965).

Appleby, J. T.: *Henry II, the Vanquished King* (Bell, 1962).

Appleby, J. T.: *The Troubled Reign of King Stephen* (Bell, 1969).

Archaeologia (102 vols., Society of Antiquaries of London, 1773–1969).

Argy, J. & Riches, W.: *Britain's Royal Brides* (Sphere Books, 1977).

Armitage-Smith, S.: *John of Gaunt* (Constable, 1904).

Ashdown, D. M.: *Ladies in Waiting* (Arthur Barker, 1976).

Ashdown, D. M.: *Princess of Wales* (John Murray, 1979).

Ashdown, D. M.: *Queen Victoria's Mother* (Robert Hale, 1974).

Ashley, M.: *Charles II, the Man and the Statesman* (Weidenfeld and Nicolson, 1971).

Ashley, M.: *The Glorious Revolution of 1688* (Hodder and Stoughton, 1966).

Ashley, M.: *James II* (Dent, 1977).

Ashley, M.: *King John* (Weidenfeld and Nicolson, 1972).

Ashley, M.: *The Stuarts in Love* (Hodder and Stoughton, 1963).

Ashley, M.: *William I* (Weidenfeld and Nicolson, 1973).

Ashton, R.: *James I by his Contemporaries* (Hutchinson, 1969).

Asser, Bishop: *Life of King Alfred* (ed. W. M. Stevenson, Oxford University Press, 1904).

Ayling, S.: *George the Third* (Collins, 1972).

Bacon, Francis: *The Life of Henry VII* (1622; ed. J. R. Lumby, Cambridge University Press, 1902).

Bagley, J. J.: *Henry VIII* (Batsford, 1962).

Bagley, J. J.: *Margaret of Anjou, Queen of England* (Herbert Jenkins, 1948).

Baker, Geoffrey le: *Chronicon* (ed. E. M. Thompson, Oxford University Press, 1889).

Baker, Richard: *A Chronicle of the Kings of England from the Time of the Romans' Government unto the Death of King James* (1643).

Baker, T.: *The Normans* (Cassell, 1966).

Barber, R.: *Henry Plantagenet: A Biography of Henry II of England* (Boydell Press, 1972).

Barlow, F.: *Edward the Confessor* (Eyre and Spottiswoode, 1970).*

Barlow, F.: *The Feudal Kingdom of England* (Eyre and Spottiswoode, 1961).

Barlow, F.: *William I and the Norman Conquest* (Eyre and Spottiswoode, 1965).

Battiscombe, G.: *Queen Alexandra* (Constable, 1969).

Baxter, S. B.: *William III* (Longman, 1966).

Bayley, J.: *History and Antiquities of the Tower of London* (Jennings and Chaplin, 1830).

Beamish, T.: *Battle Royal* (Muller, 1965).

Beaverbrook, Lord: *The Abdication of King Edward VIII* (Hamish Hamilton, 1966).

Beckingsale, B. W.: *Elizabeth I* (Batsford, 1963).

Bennett, D.: *King without a Crown* (Heinemann, 1977).

Bennett, D.: *Vicky* (Collins and Harvill, 1971).

Berry, P.: *By Royal Appointment* (Femina, 1970).

Bevan, B.: *Charles the Second's French Mistress* (Robert Hale, 1972).

Bevan, B.: *I was James the Second's Queen* (Robert Hale, 1963).

Bevan, B.: *King James III of England* (Robert Hale, 1962).

Bevan, B.: *Nell Gwyn* (Robert Hale, 1969).

Bingham, C.: *Edward II* (Weidenfeld and Nicolson, 1973).

Bingham, C.: *James V, King of Scots* (Collins, 1971).

Bingham, C.: *The Kings and Queens of Scotland* (Weidenfeld and Nicolson, 1976). *

Bingham, C.: *The Stewart Kingdom of Scotland* (Weidenfeld and Nicolson, 1974).

Black, J. B.: *The Reign of Elizabeth* (Oxford University Press, 1959).

Blackman, John: *Collectarium Mansuetudinum et Bonorium Morum Regis Henrici VI* (ed. M. R. James, 1919).

Bloom, U.: *The House of Kent* (Robert Hale, 1969).

Bloom, Ursula: *Princesses in Love* (Robert Hale, 1973).

Bone, Q.: *Henrietta Maria, Queen of the Cavaliers* (Owen, 1973).

The Book of Burials of True Noble Persons (MS. in the Royal College of Arms).

Borrow, G. W. S.: *Robert the Bruce and the Community of the Realm of Scotland* (Eyre and Spottiswoode, 1965).

Bowle, J.: *Charles the First* (Weidenfeld and Nicolson, 1975).

Bowle, J.: *Henry VIII* (Allen and Unwin, 1964).

Brooke, C.: *The Saxon and Norman Kings* (Batsford, 1963).

Brooke, J.: *King George III* (Constable, 1972).

Brooke-Little, J. P.: *Boutell's Heraldry* (Frederick Warne, 1973).

Bruce, M. L.: *Anne Boleyn* (Collins, 1972).

Bruce, M. L.: *The Making of Henry VIII* (Collins, 1977).

The Brut, or The Chronicles of England (ed. F. Brie, Early English Texts

Society, 1906, 1908).

Bryant, A.: *The Age of Chivalry* (Collins, 1963).

Brysson-Morrison, N.: *The Private Life of Henry VIII* (Robert Hale, 1964).

Burke's Guide to the Royal Family (Burke's Peerage, 1973).*

Burke's Peerage (various editions).*

Butler, I.: *Rule of Three* (Hodder and Stoughton, 1967).

Byrne, M. St. Clair: *The Letters of King Henry VIII* (Cassell, 1936).

Calendar of Charter Rolls preserved in the Public Record Office (6 vols., H.M.S.O., 1903).

Calendar of Documents preserved in France, illustrative of the History of Great Britain and Ireland, Vol. 1, 918–1206 (ed. J. H. Round, 1899).

Calendar of entries in the Papal Registers relating to Great Britain and Ireland: Papal Letters (ed. W. H. Bliss, 1893).

Calendar of Letters, Despatches and State Papers relating to Negotiations between England and Spain (ed. O. A. Bergenroth, 13 vols., H.M.S.O., 1862–1954).

Calendar of Letters and Papers, Foreign and Domestic, of the Reign of Henry VIII (ed. J. S. Brewer, J. Gairdner, and R. H. Brodie, 21 vols., H.M.S.O., 1862–1932).

Calendar of Patent Rolls preserved in the Public Record Office (H.M.S.O., 1906).

Calendar of State Papers: Milan (ed. A. B. Hinds, H.M.S.O., 1913).

Calendar of State Papers: Venice (ed. R. Brown and A. B. Hinds, 38 vols., Longman, 1864–1937).

Capgrave, John: *The Book of the Illustrious Henries* (ed. F. C. Hingston, Longman, Brown, Green, 1858).

Carpenter, E. (ed.): *A House of Kings: The History of Westminster Abbey* (Baker, 1966).

Cassavetti, E.: *The Lion and the Lilies: The Stuarts and France* (MacDonald and Jane's, 1977).

Cathcart, H.: *Anne and the Princesses Royal* (W. H. Allen, 1973).

Cathcart, H.: *The Duchess of Kent* (W. H. Allen, 1971).

Cathcart, H.: *Her Majesty* (W. H. Allen, 1962).

Chandos Herald: *Life of the Black Prince* (ed. M. K. Pope and E. C. Lodge, Clarendon Press, 1910).

Chapman, H. W.: *Anne Boleyn* (Jonathan Cape, 1974).

Chapman, H. W.: *Caroline Matilda, Queen of Denmark* (Jonathan

Cape, 1971).

Chapman, H. W.: *Lady Jane Grey* (Jonathan Cape, 1962).

Chapman, H. W.: *The Last Tudor King* (Jonathan Cape, 1958).

Chapman, H. W.: *Mary II, Queen of England* (Jonathan Cape, 1953).

Chapman, H. W.: *Privileged Persons* (Jonathan Cape, 1966).

Chapman, H. W.: *Queen Anne's Son* (Jonathan Cape, 1954).

Chapman, H. W.: *The Sisters of Henry VIII* (Jonathan Cape, 1969).

Chapman, H. W.: *The Tragedy of Charles II* (Jonathan Cape, 1964).

Chapman, H. W.: *Two Tudor Portraits* (Jonathan Cape, 1960).

Cheetham, A.: *Richard III* (Weidenfeld and Nicolson, 1972).

Chevenix-Trench, C.: *The Royal Malady* (Longmans, 1964).

Chrimes, S. B.: *Henry VII* (Eyre Methuen, 1972).

Chrimes, S. B.: *Lancastrians, Yorkists, and Henry VII* (Macmillan, 1964).

A Chronicle of England during the reigns of the Tudors (ed. W. Douglas-Hamilton, 2 vols., Camden Society, 1875).

Chronicle of the Grey Friars of London (ed. J. Nichols, Camden Society, 1852).

Chronicle of London, 1089–1483 (ed. H. Nicholas, Society of Antiquaries of London, 1827).

Chronicles and Memorials of the Reign of Richard I (ed. W. Stubbs, 2 vols., Rolls Series, H.M.S.O., 1864–5).

Chronicles of the Reigns of Edward I and Edward II (ed. W. Stubbs, Rolls Series, H.M.S.O., 1882).

Chronicles of the Reigns of Stephen, Henry II and Richard I (ed. R. Howlett, Rolls Series, H.M.S.O., 1885).

Chronicles of the White Rose (ed. J. O. Halliwell, Camden Society, 1835).

Chronicum Monasterii de Abingdon (ed. J. Stevenson, Rolls Series, H.M.S.O., 1858).

Chronique de la Traison et Mort de Richard II (ed. B. Williams, English Historical Society, 1846).

Chroniques des Comtes d'Anjou (ed. L. Halphen and R. Poupardin, 1913).

Clarke, J.: *George III* (Weidenfeld and Nicolson, 1972).

Clear, C.: *Royal Children* (Arthur Barker, 1984).

Clive, M.: *This Sun of York. A Biography of Edward IV* (Macmillan, 1973).

Cobbett's Complete Collection of State Trials (1809; Routledge and Kegan Paul, 1972).

Cole, H.: *The Black Prince* (Granada, 1976).

Cole, H.: *The Wars of the Roses* (Hart-Davis MacGibbon, 1973).

A Collection of the Wills of the Kings and Queens of England from William the Conqueror to Henry VII (ed. J. Nichols, 1780).

Commines, Philippe de: *Mémoires* (ed. M. Jones, Penguin, 1972).

The Complete Peerage of England, Scotland, Ireland, Great Britain and the United Kingdom (ed. G. H. White, 13 vols., St. Catherine's Press, 1910–59).*

Costain, T. B.: *Three Edwards* (Doubleday, 1958).

Cowan, I. B.: *The Enigma of Mary Stuart* (Gollancz, 1971).

Cowan, M.: *The Six Wives of Henry VIII* (Frewin, 1968).

Creston, D.: *The Youthful Queen Victoria* (Macmillan, 1952).

Creton, Jean: *Histoire de Roy d'Angleterre, Richard* (ed. J. A. C. Buchon, Collection des Chroniques Françaises, Paris, 1826).

Cronne, H. A.: *The Reign of Stephen, 1135–1154: Anarchy in England* (Weidenfeld and Nicolson, 1970).

Cullen, T.: *The Empress Brown* (The Bodley Head, 1969).

Dart, John: *The History and Antiquities of the Abbey Church of Westminster* (2 vols., 1723).

Davis, H. W. C.: *England under the Normans and Angevins, 1066–1272* (Methuen, 1905).

Davis, R. H. C.: *King Stephen* (Longmans, 1967).

Delderfield, E. R.: *Kings and Queens of England and Great Britain* (Raleigh Press, 1966). *

Denholm-Young, N.: *Richard of Cornwall* (Blackwell, 1947).

Dewhurst, J.: *Royal Confinements* (Weidenfeld and Nicolson, 1980).

Dictionary of National Biography (ed. L. Stephen and S. Lee, 63 vols., Oxford University Press, 1885–1900).

Donaldson, F.: *Edward VIII* (Weidenfeld and Nicolson, 1974).

Donaldson, G.: *Mary, Queen of Scots* (English Universities Press, 1974).

Donaldson, G.: *Scottish Kings* (Batsford, 1967).

Douglas, D. C.: *William the Conqueror* (Eyre and Spottiswoode, 1964). *

Duff, D.: *Albert and Victoria* (Muller, 1977).

Duff, D.: *Edward of Kent* (Muller, 1938).

Duff, D.: *Hessian Tapestry* (Muller, 1967).

Duff, D.: *The Shy Princess* (Muller, 1958).

Duggan, A.: *Devil's Brood: The Angevin Family* (Faber and Faber, 1957).

Durant, H.: *Sorrowful Captives: The Tudor Earls of Devon* (Griffin Press, 1960).

Dutton, R.: *English Court Life from Henry VII to George II* (Batsford, 1963).

Eadmer: *Historia Novorum* and *Vita Sancti Anselmi* (ed. M. Rule, Longman, 1884).

Earle, P.: *Henry V* (Weidenfeld and Nicolson, 1972).

Earle, P.: *James II* (Weidenfeld and Nicolson, 1972).

Edwards, Anne: *Matriarch: Queen Mary and the House of Windsor* (Hodder and Stoughton, 1984).

Elmham, Thomas: *Gesta Henrici Quinti* (ed. B. Williams, English Historical Society, 1850).

Elsberry, T.: *Marie of Roumania* (Cassell, 1973).

Elsna, H.: *Catherine of Braganza* (Robert Hale, 1967).

Elton, G. R.: *England under the Tudors* (Methuen, 1955).

Emerson, B.: *The Black Prince* (Weidenfeld and Nicolson, 1976).

An English Chronicle of the Reigns of Richard II, Henry IV, Henry V and Henry VI (ed. J. S. Davies, 1856).

Epton, N.: *Victoria and her Daughters* (Weidenfeld and Nicolson, 1971).

Erickson, C.: *Anne Boleyn* (Dent, 1984).

Erickson, C.: *Bloody Mary* (Dent, 1978).

Erickson, C.: *Great Harry: A Life of King Henry VIII* (Dent, 1980).

Erlanger, P.: *Margaret of Anjou, Queen of England* (Elek Books, 1970).

Fabyan, Robert: *The Concordance of Histories: The New Chronicles of England and France* (ed. H. Ellis, Rivington, 1811).

Falkus, C.: *Charles II* (Weidenfeld and Nicolson, 1972).

Farjeon, E. and H.: *Kings and Queens* (Dent, 1953, 1983).

The Fifteenth Century Chronicles (ed. J. Gairdner, 1880).

The First English Life of Henry V (ed. C. L. Kingsford, Clarendon Press, Oxford, 1911).

Florence of Worcester: *Chronicon ex Chronicis* (ed. B. Thorpe, English Historical Society, 1848–9).

Fothergill, B.: *Mrs. Jordan* (Faber and Faber, 1965).

Fowler, K. A.: *The King's Lieutenant: Henry of Grosmont, First Duke of Lancaster, 1300–1361* (Elek Books, 1969).

Fraser, A.: *The Life and Times of King James* (Weidenfeld and Nicolson, 1974).

Fraser, A. (ed.): *The Lives of the Kings and Queens of England* (Futura, 1977).

Fraser, A.: *Mary, Queen of Scots* (Weidenfeld and Nicolson, 1969).

Freeman-Grenville, G. S. P.: *The Queen's Lineage* (Rex Collings, 1977).*

Friedmann, P.: *Anne Boleyn* (2 vols., Macmillan, 1884).

Froissart, John: *Chronicles of England, France and Spain* (ed. J. Jolliffe, Harvill Press, 1967).

Fryer, M. B., Bousfield, A. and Toffoli, G.: *Lives of the Princesses of Wales* (Dundurn Press, 1983).

Fulford, R.: *From Hanover to Windsor* (Batsford, 1960).

Fulford, R.: *Royal Dukes* (Duckworth, 1933).

Fulford, R.: *The Trial of Queen Caroline* (Batsford, 1968).

Gaimar, Geoffrey: *L'Estoire des Engles* (ed. T. Hardy and C. T. Martin, Rolls Series, H.M.S.O., 1888–9).

Geoffrey of Monmouth: *History of the Kings of Britain* (ed. S. Evans and C. W. Dunn, Dent, 1963).

Gervase of Canterbury: *Historical Works* (ed. W. Stubbs, Rolls Series, H.M.S.O., 1879–80).

Gillen, M.: *The Prince and his Lady* (Sidgwick and Jackson, 1970).

Gillen, M.: *Royal Duke* (Sidgwick and Jackson, 1976).

Gillingham, J.: *Richard the Lion Heart* (Weidenfeld and Nicolson, 1973).

Given-Hilson, C. and Curteis, A.: *The Royal Bastards of Mediaeval England* (Routledge and Kegan Paul, 1984). *

Gorst-Williams, J.: *Elizabeth, the Winter Queen* (Abelard, 1977).

Grafton, Richard: *Continuation of Hardyng's Chronicles* (ed. Sir H. Nicholas, Society of Antiquaries of London, 1809).

The Great Chronicle of London (ed. A. H. Thomas and I. D. Thornley, Alan Sutton, 1983).

Great Dynasties (Various authors; Windward, New York, 1976, 1979).

Green, D.: *Queen Anne* (Collins, 1970).

Green, M. A. E.: *The Lives of the Princesses of England* (6 vols., London, 1849–55).*

Green, V. H. H.: *The Later Plantagenets* (Edward Arnold, 1955).*

Grinnell-Milne, D.: *The Killing of William Rufus* (David and Charles, 1968).

Hackett, F.: *Henry the Eighth* (1929; Chivers edition 1973).

Hall, Edward: *The Triumphant Reign of King Henry the Eighth* (ed. C. Whibley, 2 vols., T. C. and E. C. Jack, 1904).

Hall, Edward: *The Union of the Two Noble and Illustrious Families of Lancaster and York* (ed. H. Ellis, Rivington, 1809).

Hamilton, E.: *Henrietta Maria* (Coward, McGann and Geoghegan, 1976).

Hamilton, E.: *William's Mary* (Coward, McGann and Geoghegan, 1972).

Hamilton, R.: *Now I Remember: A Holiday History of England* (Pan, 1964).

Handbook of British Chronology (ed. F. M. Powicke and E. B. Fryde, Royal Historical Society, 1961).*

Harrison, M.: *Clarence* (W. H. Allen, 1972).

Harvey, J.: *The Plantagenets* (Batsford, 1948).

Hassall, W. O.: *Who's Who in History, Vol. 1, 55 B.C. to 1485* (Blackwell, 1960).

Haswell, J.: *The Ardent Queen* (Peter Davies, 1976).

Hatton, R.: *George I, Elector and King* (Thames and Hudson, 1978).

Hedley, O.: *Queen Charlotte* (John Murray, 1975).

Henry of Huntingdon: *Historia Anglorum* (ed. T. Arnold, Rolls Series, H.M.S.O., 1879).

Hibbert, C.: *Charles I* (Weidenfeld and Nicolson, 1968).

Hibbert, C.: *The Court at Windsor* (Longmans, 1964).

Hibbert, C.: *Edward VII* (1976; Penguin edition, 1982).

Hibbert, C.: *George IV, Regent and King* (Longmans, 1975).

Hichens, P.: *The Royal Baby Book* (Octopus Books, 1984).

Higden, Ranulph: *Polychronicon* (ed. C. Babington and J. R. Lumby, Rolls Series, H.M.S.O., 1865–6).

Histoire des Ducs de Normandie et des Rois d'Angleterre (ed. Francisque-Michel, Société de l'Histoire de France, Paris, 1840).

Histoire de Guillaume le Maréchale (ed. P. Meyer, Société de l'Histoire de France, Paris, 1891–1901).

Historiae Croylandensis Continuato (ed. W. Fulman, 1684; trans. T. Riley, Bohn's Library, no date).

Historiae Vitae et Regni Ricardi Secundi (ed. T. Hearne, 1729).

History of the Arrival of Edward IV in England and the Final Recovery of his Kingdoms from Henry VI, A.D. MCCCCLXXI (ed. J. Bruce, 1838).

Hoey, B.: *H.R.H. The Princess Anne: A Biography* (Country Life, 1984).

Holden, A.: *Charles, Prince of Wales* (Weidenfeld and Nicolson, 1979).

Holinshed, Raphael: *Chronicles of England, Scotland and Ireland* (ed. H. Ellis, 6 vols., Dent, 1927).

Holme, T.: *Prinny's Daughter: A Biography of Princess Charlotte of Wales* (Hamilton, 1976).

Holt, J. C.: *King John* (Cambridge University Press, 1963).

Hopkirk, M.: *Queen Adelaide* (John Murray, 1946).

Hough, R.: *Louis and Victoria: The First Mountbattens* (Hutchinson, 1974).

Howard, P.: *The Royal Palaces* (Hamilton, 1970).

Hume, M. A. S.: *The Wives of Henry VIII* (Eveleigh Nash, 1905).

Hutchison, H. F.: *Edward II, the Pliant King* (Eyre and Spottiswoode, 1971).

Hutchison, H. F.: *Henry V* (Eyre and Spottiswoode, 1967).

Hutchison, H. F.: *The Hollow Crown: A Life of Richard II* (Eyre and Spottiswoode, 1961).

Incertie Scriptoris Chronicon Angliae de Regnis Henrici IV, Henrici V et Henrici VI (ed. J. A. Giles, 1848).

Inglis, B.: *Abdication* (Hodder and Stoughton, 1966).

Ingulph's Chronicle of the Abbey of Croyland (ed. H. T. Riley, 1854; this contains the Third Continuation of the Chronicle, of which the original no longer exists).

Iremonger, L.: *Love and the Princess* (Faber, 1958).

Itinerarium et Peregrinorum et Gesta Regis Ricardi (ed. W. Stubbs, Rolls Series, H.M.S.O., 1864).

Jacob, E. F.: *The Fifteenth Century, 1399–1485* (Oxford University Press, 1961).

Jean le Beau: *Chronique de Richard II* (ed. J. A. C. Buchon, 1826).

Jenkins, E.: *Elizabeth the Great* (Gollancz, 1958).

Jenkins, E.: *The Princes in the Tower* (Hamish Hamilton, 1978).

Jenner, H.: *Royal Wives* (1967).*

Jocelin of Brakelond: *Chronicle* (ed. G. Rokewoode, Camden Society, 1840).

Joelson, A.: *Heirs to the Throne* (Heinemann, 1966).

Johnson, P.: *Edward III* (Weidenfeld and Nicolson, 1973).

Jolliffe, J. E. A.: *Angevin Kingship* (Adam and Charles Black, 1955).

Jones, F.: *The Princes and Principality of Wales* (University of Wales, Cardiff, 1969).

Jordan, R.: *Sophia Dorothea* (Constable, 1971).

Jordan, W. K.: *Edward VI: The Young King* (Allen and Unwin, 1968).

Jordan, W. K.: *Edward VI: The Threshold of Power* (Allen and Unwin, 1970).

Judd, D.: *The House of Windsor* (MacDonald and Jane's, 1973).

Junor, P.: *Diana, Princess of Wales* (Sidgwick and Jackson, 1983).

Kay, F. G.: *Lady of the Sun: The Life and Times of Alice Perrers* (Muller, 1966).

Keepe, Henry: *Monumenta Westmonasteriensia* (1683).

Kelly, A.: *Eleanor of Aquitaine and the Four Kings* (Harvard University Press, 1952).

Kendall, P. M.: *Richard III* (Allen and Unwin, 1955).

Kendall, P. M.: *Warwick the Kingmaker* (Allen and Unwin, 1957).

Kenyon, F. P.: *The Stuarts: A Study in English Kingship* (Collins, 1958).

Kirby, J. L.: *Henry IV of England* (Constable, 1970).

Knighton, Henry: *Chronica* (ed. J. R. Lumby, 2 vols., Rolls Series, H.M.S.O., 1889–95).

Kroll, M.: *Sophia, Electress of Hanover: A Personal Portrait* (Gollancz, 1973).

Labargé, M. W.: *Henry V: The Cautious Conqueror* (Secker and Warburg, 1975).

Labargé, M. W.: *Simon de Montfort* (Eyre and Spottiswoode, 1962).

Lacey, R.: *Henry VIII* (Weidenfeld and Nicolson, 1972).

Lacey, R.: *Majesty: Elizabeth II and the House of Windsor* (Hutchinson, 1977).

Laird, D.: *Queen Elizabeth the Queen Mother* (Hodder and Stoughton, 1966).

Lancaster, O.: *Our Sovereigns* (1937).

Lander, J. R.: *The Wars of the Roses* (Secker and Warburg, 1965).

Lane, H. M.: *The Royal Daughters of England* (2 vols., Constable, 1910). *

Lane, P.: *Princess Michael of Kent* (Robert Hale, 1985).

Langdon-Davies (ed.): *Richard III and the Princes in the Tower* (Jackdaw Series, 1965).

Larson, L. M.: *Canute the Great and the Rise of Danish Imperialism* (1912).

Leary, F.: *The Golden Longing* (John Murray, 1959).

Leland, John: *Collectanea* (ed. T. Hearne, 6 vols., 1774; Chetham Society).

Lenz-Harvey, N.: *Elizabeth of York, Tudor Queen* (Arthur Barker, 1973).

Letters and Papers illustrative of the Reigns of Richard III and Henry VII (ed. J. Gairdner, 2 vols., Rolls Series, H.M.S.O., 1861, 1863).

Letters and Papers of the Reign of Henry VIII (ed. J. S. Brewer, J. Gairdner and R. H. Brodie, 21 vols., H.M.S.O., 1862–1932).

Lindsay, P.: *King Henry V* (Howard Baker, 1934).

Lindsay, P.: *Kings of Merry England* (Howard Baker, 1936).

Lindsay, P.: *The Secret of Henry VIII* (Howard Baker, 1953).

Linklater, E.: *The Royal House of Scotland* (Macmillan, 1970).

Lloyd, A.: *King John* (David and Charles, 1973).

Lloyd, A.: *The Year of the Conqueror* (Longmans, 1966).

Lockyer, R.: *Henry VII* (Longmans, 1968; revised edition 1983).

Lofts, N.: *Anne Boleyn* (Orbis, 1979).

Lofts, N.: *Queens of Britain* (Hodder and Stoughton, 1977).

Longford, E.: *Elizabeth II* (Weidenfeld and Nicolson, 1982).

Longford, E.: *The Royal House of Windsor* (Weidenfeld and Nicolson, 1974).

Longford, E.: *Victoria R. I.* (Weidenfeld and Nicolson, 1964).

Louda, J. and MacLagan, M.: *Lines of Succession: Heraldry of the Royal Families of Europe* (Orbis, 1981).*

Luke, M. M.: *Catherine the Queen* (Muller, 1967).

Luke, M. M.: *A Crown for Elizabeth* (Muller, 1971).

Macalpine, I. and Hunter, R.: *George III and the Mad Business* (Allen Lane, 1969).

MacGibbon, D.: *Elizabeth Woodville, 1437–1492* (1938).

Mackie, J. D.: *The Earlier Tudors, 1485–1558* (Oxford University Press, 1952).

Magnus, P.: *King Edward VII* (John Murray, 1964).

Mancini, Dominic: *The Usurpation of Richard III* (ed. C. A. J. Armstrong, Oxford University Press, 1936).

Map, Walter: *De Nugis Curialum* (ed. T. Wright, Camden Society, 1850).

Marlow, J.: *George I* (Weidenfeld and Nicolson, 1974).

Marlow, J. and Mackay, E.: *Kings and Queens of Britain* (1977).

Marples, M.: *Poor Fred and the Butcher* (Michael Joseph, 1970).

Marples, M.: *Six Royal Sisters: The Daughters of George III* (Michael Joseph, 1969).

Marples, M.: *Wicked Uncles in Love* (Michael Joseph, 1972).

Marshall, D.: *The Life and Times of Victoria* (Weidenfeld and Nicolson, 1972).

Marshall, R. K.: *Mary of Guise* (Collins, 1977).

Martiensson, A.: *Queen Katherine Parr* (Secker and Warburg, 1973).

Martin, R. G.: *The Woman He Loved* (W. H. Allen, 1974).

Materials for a History of the Reign of Henry VII (ed. W. Campbell, 2 vols., Rolls Series, H.M.S.O., 1873–7).

Mathew, D.: *The Courtiers of Henry VIII* (Eyre and Spottiswoode, 1970).

Mathew, D.: *King James I* (Eyre and Spottiswoode, 1967).

Mathew, D.: *Lady Jane Grey: The Setting of the Reign* (Eyre Methuen, 1972).

Matthew, D. J. A.: *The Norman Conquest* (Batsford, 1966).

Mattingley, G.: *Catherine of Aragon* (Jonathan Cape, 1942).

Maynard-Smith, D.: *Henry VIII and the Reformation* (Henry VIII, 1962).

McElwee, W.: *The Wisest Fool in Christendom* (Faber, 1958).

McKisack, M.: *The Fourteenth Century, 1307–1399* (Oxford University Press, 1959).

The Metrical Chronicle of Robert of Gloucester (ed. W. A. Wright, 1887).

Middlemas, K.: *Edward VII* (Weidenfeld and Nicolson, 1972).

Middlemas, K.: *George VI* (Weidenfeld and Nicolson, 1974).

Miller, J.: *William and Mary* (Weidenfeld and Nicolson, 1974).

Miller, P.: *James* (Allen and Unwin, 1971).

Molinet, Jean: *Chroniques des Ducs de Bougogne, 1476–1506* (ed. J. A. Buchon, Paris, 1827–8).

The Monarchy in Britain (Central Office of Information, 1977).

Montague-Smith, P.: *The Country Life Book of the Royal Silver Jubilee* (Country Life, 1977).

Montague-Smith, P.: *The Royal Line of Succession* (Pitkin, 1967).*

Montgomery-Massingberd, H.: *Burke's Guide to the British Monarchy* (Burke's Peerage, 1977).

More, Sir Thomas: *History of King Richard III* (ed. R. S. Sylvester, Yale University Press, 1965).

Morris, C.: *The Tudors* (Batsford, 1966).

Morrow, A.: *The Queen* (Granada, 1983).

Morrow, A.: *The Queen Mother* (Granada, 1984).

Mumby, F. A.: *The Youth of Henry VIII* (Constable, 1913).

Murimeth, Adam: *Continuato Chronicarum* (ed. E. M. Thompson, Rolls Series, H.M.S.O., 1889).

Neale, J. E.: *Queen Elizabeth I* (Jonathan Cape, 1934).

Neilson, M.: *Matilda of Scotland* (in *The Lady*, November, 1968).

Nicholson, R.: *Edward III and the Scots, 1327–35* (Oxford University Press, 1965).

Nicolson, H.: *George V: His Life and Reign* (Constable, 1952).

Noel, G.: *Princess Alice: Queen Victoria's Forgotten Daughter* (Constable, 1974).

Oman, C.: *Elizabeth of Bohemia* (Hodder and Stoughton, 1938, 1964).

Oman, C.: *Henrietta Maria* (Hodder and Stoughton, 1936).

Oman, C.: *Mary of Modena* (Hodder and Stoughton, 1962).

Ordericus Vitalis: *Historia Ecclesiastica* (ed. A. le Prèvost, 5 vols., Société de l'Histoire de France, Paris, 1838–55).

Pain, N.: *Empress Matilda: Uncrowned Queen of England* (Weidenfeld and Nicolson, 1978).

Palmer, A.: *George IV* (Weidenfeld and Nicolson, 1972).

Palmer, A.: *Kings and Queens of England* (Peerage, 1976).

Paris, Matthew: *Chronica Majora* (ed. H. R. Luard, 7 vols., Rolls Series, H.M.S.O., 1872–3).

Paris, Matthew: *Flores Historiarum* (ed. H. R. Luard, 3 vols., Rolls Series, H.M.S.O., 1890).

Paris, Matthew: *Historia Anglorum* (ed. F. H. Madden, 3 vols., Rolls Series, H.M.S.O., 1866–9).

Parmiter, G. de C.: *The King's Great Matter* (Longmans, 1967).

Paul, J. E.: *Catherine of Aragon and her Friends* (Burns and Oates, 1966).

Pearson, H.: *Charles II: His Life and Likeness* (Heinemann, 1960).

Peers, C.: *Berkhamstead Castle* (H.M.S.O., 1948).

Pepys, Samuel: *Diary* (ed. W. Matthews, vols. 1–7, Bell, 1970–72).

Pernoud, R.: *Blanche of Castile* (Collins, 1975).

Pernoud, R.: *Eleanor of Aquitaine* (Collins, 1967).

Petrie, C.: *The Stuarts* (Eyre and Spottiswoode, 1958).

Picard, B. L.: *The Tower and the Traitors* (Batsford, 1961).

Picknett, L.: *Royal Romance* (Marshall Cavendish, 1980).

Pierre de Langtoft: *Chronicle* (ed. W. A. Wright, 2 vols., Rolls Series, H.M.S.O., 1846–8).

Pine, L. G.: *Heirs of the Conqueror* (Herbert Jenkins, 1965).

Pine, L. G.: *Princes of Wales* (Herbert Jenkins, 1959).

Platts, B.: *A History of Greenwich* (David and Charles, 1973).

Plowden, A.: *The Young Elizabeth* (Macmillan, 1971).

Plumb, J. H.: *The First Four Georges* (Batsford, 1956).

Pollard, A. F.: *Henry VIII* (Longmans, 1902).

Poole, A. L.: *From Domesday Book to Magna Carta, 1087–1216* (Oxford University Press, 1951).

Pope-Hennessy, J.: *Queen Mary* (Allen and Unwin, 1959).

Porter, M.: *Overture to Victoria* (1961).

Powicke, F. M.: *King Henry III and the Lord Edward* (2 vols., Oxford University Press, 1947).

Powicke, F. M.: *The Thirteenth Century, 1216–1307* (Oxford University Press, 1962).

Prebble, J.: *The Lion in the North* (Penguin, 1973).

Prescott, H. F. M.: *Mary Tudor* (Constable, 1940).

Priestley, J. B.: *The Prince of Pleasure and his Regency, 1811–20* (Heinemann, 1969).

Ralph of Coggeshall: *Chronica Anglicanum* (ed. J. Stevenson, 1875).

Ralph de Diceto: *Imagines Historiarum* (ed. W. Stubbs, Rolls Series, H.M.S.O., 1876).

Ramsay, J. H.: *Lancaster and York* (2 vols., Clarendon Press, Oxford, 1892).*

Recueil d'Annales Angevines et Vendômoises (ed. L. Halphen, 1903).

Redman, Alvin: *The House of Hanover* (Alvin Redman, 1960).

The Reign of Henry VII from Contemporary Sources (ed. A. F. Pollard, 3 vols., Longmans, 1913–14).

Richardson, J.: *The Disastrous Marriage* (Jonathan Cape, 1960).

Richardson, J.: *George IV: A Portrait* (Sidgwick and Jackson, 1966).

Richardson, J.: *Victoria and Albert* (Dent, 1977).

Richardson, W. C.: *Mary Tudor, the White Queen* (Peter Owen, 1970).

Ridley, J.: *Mary Tudor* (Weidenfeld and Nicolson, 1973).

Rishanger, William: *Chronica* (ed. H. T. Riley, Rolls Series, H.M.S.O., 1865).

Rival, P.: *The Six Wives of Henry VIII* (Heinemann, 1937).

Robb, N.: *William of Orange* (2 vols., Heinemann, 1966).

Roche, T. W. E.: *The King of Almayne* (John Murray, 1966).

Roger of Hovedon: *Chronica* (ed. W. Stubbs, 4 vols., Rolls Series, H.M.S.O., 1868–71).

Roger of Hoveden: *Gesta Henrici Secundi and Gesta Ricardi* (ed. W. Stubbs, Rolls Series, H.M.S.O., 1867).

Roger of Wendover: *Flores Historiarum* (ed. H. O. Coxe, English Historical Society, 1841–4).

Ross, C.: *Edward IV* (Eyre Methuen, 1974).

Roulstone, M.: *The Royal House of Tudor* (Balfour, 1974).

Round, J. H.: *The Early Life of Anne Boleyn* (1886).

Rous, John: *Historia rerum Angliae* (ed. T. Hearne, 1716).

Routh, C. R. N.: *Who's Who in History, Vol. 2, 1485–1603* (Blackwell, 1964).

Rowse, A. L.: *Bosworth Field and the Wars of the Roses* (Macmillan, 1966).

Rowse, A. L.: *The Tower of London in the History of the Nation* (Weidenfeld and Nicolson, 1972).

Rowse, A. L.: *Windsor Castle in the History of the Nation* (Weidenfeld and Nicolson, 1974).

Russell of Liverpool, Lord: *Caroline, the Unhappy Queen* (Robert Hale, 1967).

Rymer, Thomas: *Foedora* (ed. T. Hardy, Records Commission, 1816–69).

Salzman, L. F.: *Edward I* (Constable, 1968).

Sandford, Francis: *A Genealogical History of the Kings and Queens of England and Monarchs of Great Britain, 1066–1677* (1677), continued by Samuel Stebbings (1707; Newcombe, 1707).*

Saunders, B.: *Henry the Eighth* (Alvin Redman, 1963).

Scarisbrick, J.: *Henry VIII* (Constable, 1968).

Scofield, C. L.: *The Life and Reign of Edward IV* (2 vols., Frank Cass, 1923, 1967).

The Scots Peerage (9 vols., 1904–14).

Scott-Moncrieff, M. C.: *Kings and Queens of England* (Blandford Press, 1966).

Sergeant, P.: *The Life of Anne Boleyn* (Hutchinson, 1923).

Seton, A.: *Katherine* (Hodder and Stoughton, 1954).

Seward, D.: *Prince of the Renaissance* (Constable, 1973).

Seymour, W.: *Ordeal by Ambition: An English Family in the Shadow of the Tudors* (Sidgwick and Jackson, 1972).

Sitwell, E.: *Fanfare for Elizabeth* (Macmillan, 1946).

Sitwell, E.: *The Queens and the Hive* (Macmillan, 1962).

Slocombe, G.: *Sons of the Conqueror* (Hutchinson, 1960).

Smith, L. B.: *The Elizabethan Epic* (Jonathan Cape, 1966).

Smith, L. B.: *Henry VIII, the Mask of Royalty* (Jonathan Cape, 1971).

Smith, L. B.: *A Tudor Tragedy: The Life and Times of Catherine Howard* (Jonathan Cape, 1961).

Softly, B.: *The Queens of England* (David and Charles, 1976).

St. Aubyn, G.: *The Royal George* (Constable, 1963).

Steele, A.: *Richard II* (Cambridge University Press, 1941).

Stenton, F. M.: *Anglo-Saxon England* (Oxford University Press, 1943, 1971).

Stones, E. L. G.: *Edward I and the Throne of Scotland* (Oxford University Press, 1978).

Storey, R. L.: *The End of the House of Lancaster* (Barrie and Rockliff, 1966).

Stow, John: *The Survey of London* (1598; Dent, 1956).

Strickland, A.: *Lives of the Queens of England* (8 vols., Henry Colburn, 1851; reprinted by Portway, 1973). *

Strong, R.: *The House of Tudor* (H.M.S.O., 1967).

Tauté, A., Brooke-Little, J. and Pottinger, D.: *Kings and Queens of Great Britain: A Genealogical Chart Showing their Descent, Relationships and Coats of Arms* (Elm Tree Books, 1970, revised edition 1986). *

Thomas, D.: *The Royal Baby Album* (Arlington, 1984).

Thompson, C. J. S.: *The Witchery of Jane Shore* (Grayson, 1933).

Thomson, G. M.: *The Crime of Mary Stuart* (Hutchinson, 1967).

Thornton, M.: *Royal Feud: The Queen Mother and the Duchess of Windsor* (Michael Joseph, 1985).

Thornton-Cook, E.: *Kings in the Making: The Princes of Wales* (1931).

Titus Livius Forojuliensis: *Vita Henrici Quinti* (ed. T. Hearne, 1716).

The Tower of London: Official Guide (H.M.S.O., 1966).

Trease, G.: *Seven Queens of England* (Heinemann, 1953).

Turner, F. C.: *James II* (Eyre and Spottiswoode, 1948).

Turton, G. E.: *The Dragon's Breed* (1969).

Turton, W. H.: *The Plantagenet Ancestry of Elizabeth of York* (1928). *

Van Der Zee, H. and B.: *William and Mary* (Macmillan, 1973).

Vergil, Polydore: *Anglica Historia* (ed. D. Hay, Camden Series, 1950).

Vita Edwardi Secundi (ed. N. Denholm-Young, Nelson, 1957).

Wakeford, G.: *The Princesses Royal* (Robert Hale, 1973).*

Wakeford, G.: *Three Consort Queens* (Robert Hale, 1971).

Waldman, M.: *The Lady Mary* (Collins, 1972).

Walsingham, Thomas: *Annales Ricardi Secundi* (ed. H. T. Riley, Rolls Series, H.M.S.O., 1866).

Walsingham, Thomas: *Chronicon Angliae* (ed. E. M. Thompson, Rolls Series, H.M.S.O., 1874).

Walsingham, Thomas: *Gesta Abbatum Monasterii St. Albani* (ed. H. T. Riley, 3 vols., Rolls Series, H.M.S.O., 1867–9).

Walsingham, Thomas: *Historiae Anglicana* (ed. H. T. Riley, 2 vols., Rolls Series, H.M.S.O., 1863–4).

Walter of Guisborough: *Chronica* (ed. H. C. Hamilton, 2 vols., English Historical Society, 1848–9).

Warkworth, John: *A Chronicle of the First Thirteen Years of the Reign of Edward IV* (ed. J. O. Halliwell, Camden Society, 1839).

Warren, W. L.: *Henry II* (Eyre Methuen, 1977).

Warren, W. L.: *King John* (Eyre and Spottiswoode, 1962).

Warwick, C.: *Princess Margaret* (Magna, 1985).

Watson, D. R.: *Charles I* (Weidenfeld and Nicolson, 1972).

Wedgewood, C. V.: *The King's Peace, 1637–41* (Collins, *1955*).

Wedgewood, C. V.: *The King's War, 1641–47* (Collins, 1958).

Wedgewood, C. V.: *The Trial of Charles I* (Collins, 1964).

Weever, John: *Ancient Funeral Monuments within the United Monarchy of Great Britain, Ireland, and the Islands adjacent, their Founders, and what Eminent Persons have been in the Same Interred* (Thomas Harper, 1631).

Wentworth-Day, J.: *Princess Marina, Duchess of Kent* (Robert Hale, 1969).

Westminster Abbey: Official Guide (Jarrold, Norwich, 1966).

Wheeler-Bennett, J.: *The Life and Reign of George VI* (Macmillan, 1958).

Wilkins, J. H.: *Caroline the Illustrious* (Longmans Green, 1904).

Wilkinson, B.: *The Later Middle Ages in England* (Longmans, 1977).

William of Jumièges: *Gesta Normannorum Ducum* (ed. J. Marx, Société de l'Histoire de Normandie, 1914).

William of Malmesbury: *Chronicle of the Kings of England* (ed. J. A. Giles, 1866).

William of Malmesbury: *Historia Regum and Historia Novella* (ed. W. Stubbs, Rolls Series, H.M.S.O., 1887–9).

William of Newburgh: *Historia rerum Anglicarum* (ed. R. Howlett, 1884–5).

William of Poitiers: *Gesta Willelmi Ducis Normannorum et Regis Anglorum* (incorporated in *The Bayeux Tapestry and the Norman Invasion* ed. by L. Thorpe, Folio Society, 1973).

William of Worcester: *Annales rerum Anglicarum* (included in *Letters and Papers illustrative of the War with France,* ed. J. Stevenson, Rolls Series, H.M.S.O., 1864).

Williams, E. C.: *Anne of Denmark* (Longmans, 1970).

Williams, E. C.: *My Lord of Bedford* (Longmans, 1963).

Williams, N.: *Elizabeth I* (Weidenfeld and Nicolson, 1972).

Williams, N.: *Elizabeth I, Queen of England* (Weidenfeld and Nicolson, 1967).

Williams, N.: *Henry VII* (Weidenfeld and Nicolson, 1972).

Williams, N.: *Henry VIII and his Court* (Weidenfeld and Nicolson, 1971).

Williamson, H. R.: *The Butt of Malmsey* (Michael Joseph, 1967).

Williamson, H. R.: *The Marriage made in Blood* (Michael Joseph, 1968).

Williamson, H. R.: *A Matter of Martyrdom* (Michael Joseph, 1969).

Woodham-Smith, C.: *Queen Victoria: Her Life and Times, Vol. 1* (Hamish Hamilton, 1972).

Woodward, G. W. O.: *King Richard III* (Pitkin, 1972).

Ziegler, P.: *William IV* (Collins, 1971).

Special thanks are due to Anne Tauté for generously lending me some very rare books so that many gaps in the information included in *Britain's Royal Families* could be filled just prior to going to press.

Index

www.vintage-books.co.uk